THE SCIENTIFIC EVOLUTION OF PSYCHOLOGY

THE SCIENTIFIC EVOLUTION OF PSYCHOLOGY

Volume I

J. R. KANTOR

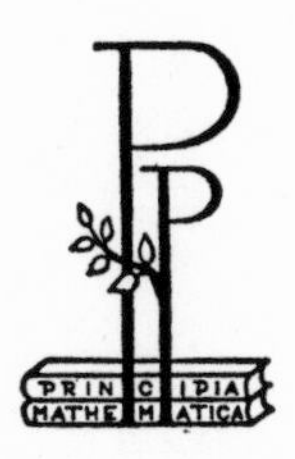

THE PRINCIPIA PRESS, INC.

Chicago, Illinois *1963* *Granville, Ohio*

THE PRINCIPIA PRESS, INC.

5743 S. Kimbark Avenue
Chicago 37, Ill.

Denison University
Granville, Ohio

This book is dedicated

to

the workers of all periods and of all nations who have labored to evolve a scientific psychology

CONTENTS

Section One

Problems, Procedures, Perspectives: General Orientation

Section Two

The Historico-Cultural Origins of Psychological Science

Section Three

The Hellenic Systemization of Psychology

Section Four

The Extinction of Systematic Psychology

Section Seven

Spirit Institutionalized

Section Eight

Arab Transformation and Transmission of Science

Section Nine

The Scholastic Transformation of Aristotle's Psychology

LIST OF FIGURES

LIST OF TABLES

LIST OF PLATES

LIST OF PLATES

PREFACE

THE GOAL I have set myself in this book is to trace the evolution of psychology as a science. I undertake a critical examination of the way scholars in the psychological tradition described and interpreted the interbehavior of organisms with stimulus objects. When I speak of the psychological tradition I strongly emphasize the fact that the science of psychology has not enjoyed a continuous naturalistic development. As is well known, the evolution of psychology includes periods in which scholars not only limited their studies to human interbehavior and neglected the behavior of other organisms, but, in addition, failed to describe and interpret that interbehavior as natural events. Instead, they thought of it as at least partially extranatural. Such theological and metaphysical periods must, however, be taken strictly into account because they articulate with and influence the naturalistic stages of psychological tradition. In fact, these scientific dark spots continue to influence the current course of psychological history.

Now, I must add that, although our primary interest is in the development of psychology, we cannot overlook the fact that this science has originated and evolved as a component star of a scientific constellation. Accordingly, I treat psychology as it grew and changed with the varying circumstances of the scientific culture of Western Europe. Furthermore, since obviously scientific culture itself exists only as a part of general culture or civilization, I also take account of this cultural matrix, which shapes all the sciences and in turn is shaped by them.

I have already implied that the scientific study of psychological evolution involves the same procedures which scientists use in studying any other class of events. I am assuming that the investigation of the successive interactions of psychologists with a particular type of stimulus-response interbehavior is a similar enterprise to that of studying any other type of interactions. For historical reasons, however, the psychological historian, perhaps more than other investigators, finds it expedient to throw into relief the assumptions that are basic to his work in order to improve his skill in handling the events of his science and, as far as possible, avoid enthrallment by conventional beliefs about those events. On the whole modern historians of psychology have been immured in a dualistic culture and thus have imposed a spiritistic patina upon psychological behavior. For example, when Ebbinghaus attempts to explain why psychology stood still from the fourth century B.C. to the eighteenth or nineteenth century A.D., he offers as his first reason that it was because of the intrinsic difficulty of studying the processes of the soul *(Seelenleben)*.[1] Obviously Ebbinghaus was basing psychology and its history on theological or philosophical foundations.

I depart radically from this tradition of psychological history. For me it is impossible to treat the evolution of psychology as a "record of beliefs about the soul and of the growth of the human mind in and through the development of those beliefs."[2] In sharp contrast to this, I am interested in the development of the observations, the investigative practices, and the theories concerned with the actual interbehavior of organisms with stimulus objects under specific conditions.

Although I draw a sharp distinction between 1) theories and practices in psychology and 2) the psychological tradition which includes so many departures from scientific study, I find it necessary to include among the contents of this book the ubiquitous doctrines of the soul and other transcendental things or processes. Thus I point out the striking contrast between what has improperly been thought to be psychology and what psychology is as an authentic natural science. Psychological history shows us that the traditional doctrines about *soul, mind,* and *consciousness* have consisted of nothing more than cultural beliefs imposed upon psychological events. For example, activities of knowing or awareness have been interpreted as transcendent psychic processes instead of ways that individuals interact with stimulus objects. A second exceedingly important reason for studying beliefs about the soul is to demonstrate how cultural attitudes churned up by the maelstrom of human events have affected and continue to influence psychological theory and practice even through the most intensive quantitative and experimental periods. Psychological history makes plain that all such constructions as *inner sense, immediate experience, apperception, sensation, consciousness,* and *introspection* concern various modifications of soul substance and process, and the putative methods for dealing with such nonobservable entities.

Students of psychological history today have a great advantage over their predecessors in freeing themselves from the fetters of dualistic culture. The march of scientific events has provided a wealth of data

[1] Ebbinghaus, "Psychologie," p. 135 in Hinneberg, ed., *Die Kultur der Gegenwart,* Part I, Section 6: *Systematische Philosophie.*

[2] Brett, *A History of Psychology,* Vol. I, p. x.

to make plain that authentic psychology could never be concerned with transcendent mental states. Only social and political circumstances have dictated that traditional psychology should be set apart as a *Geisteswissenschaft* from the natural sciences *(Naturwissenschaften)* which occupy themselves primarily with the accurate manipulation and measurement of things and events. The transformation of psychological events into mystical entities and processes at best represents a victory of practical needs over the actual investigation of nature. When scholars turned away from the study of the behavior of organisms to speculate about psychic principles they were directly influenced by the social circumstances of their time. Through such influences the behavior of organisms has become overlaid with properties which were simply invented on the basis, not of the observation and analysis of events, but because of human suffering and the need for personal salvation. To escape the traditional assumptions one has only to observe what psychologists have always done instead of what they believed and said that they were doing. I suggest that the postulates which I adopt in this work exemplify the inevitable corrigibility of science, in other words the progressive approximation of constructions to the traits of events studied.

As the Table of Contents indicates, I have organized the material of this book directly on the basis of the unique career of psychology. It is a striking fact of psychological history that in its earliest stages psychology fully met the criteria of a natural science, then diverged radically from them for almost twenty-five centuries, and has only recently taken some steps to reachieve this status. It is the detailed circumstances of these dramatic shifts in viewpoint that constitute the interesting and moving aspects of psychological history. Because of the enormous quantity of material, I, of course, make no attempt to present in chronological order all that has happened in the psychological domain. Nor do I try to show the contribution of each individual writer who is represented in the annals of psychology. Instead I simply emphasize the significant general movements that mark the evolution of psychology, including the cultural circumstances that have molded psychology into both scientific and nonscientific forms.

With the target of a naturalistic treatment of psychological development clearly in view, where should we begin the narrative? Ebbinghaus declared: "Die Psychologie hat eine lange Vergangenheit, doch nur eine kurze Geschichte"[3] and thought its authentic history centered in the nineteenth century. In doing this he exhibited a definite prejudice in favor of the experimental stage of psychological evolution even though that stage was based upon transcendental doctrines of mind. Though Ebbinghaus appreciated the astonishing ability of Aristotle to construct a psychological edifice which vied advantageously with any other science of the time, he is completely oblivious of the fact that the *De Anima* of the fourth century B.C., though elementary, was a well organized and completely naturalistic treatise. Overlooked, too, was the fact that the experimental psychology of the nineteenth century represented only a belated aspiration to return to the original naturalistic starting point. When the achievement of the Greeks is disregarded, the Behavioristic psychologists might well argue that psychology as a science did not develop until the twentieth century, since only then was a serious attempt made to separate psychology from the ideas imposed on it by the Neoplatonists, the Church Fathers, and the Mystics of the Dark Ages. In this book I take the position that the scientific values derived from studying the history of psychology can only be obtained by surveying the entire formal development of the psychological tradition. Only by considering the entire evolution of psychology can we fully understand its character and attain the orientation we need for the proper cultivation of the science.

The last sentence answers the question why we should study the history of psychology altogether. The answer goes beyond the frequently heard humanistic and educational arguments that increasing attention must be paid to the history of science because the facts of science are as interesting and as significant as political, military, and social events. Surely there is merit in these arguments, but we must go further. I want to emphasize that the history of science is potentially important for scientific investigation. This importance varies, of course, for the different sciences. For psychology the need to understand history is very great because it facilitates the appreciation of the proper subject-matter of the science. Historical study demonstrates that psychological work consists exclusively of the development of techniques and theories for the investigation of human and nonhuman interbehavior. Accordingly, the history of psychology can help to free the psychologist from phenomenological states or psychic experience, and thus is clearly not

[3] *Op. cit.*

merely a contemplative study. On the contrary, it is a method or tool for increasing the sophistication the psychologist requires to advance his science. In a significant sense the history of psychology is an aspect of psychological science itself.

Because science invariably operates with abstractive constructions it is always possible for a smaller or larger gap to exist between such constructions and the original events that are studied. I submit that psychological history can help to close the wide gap that now exists between scientific constructions (descriptions and explanations) and original psychological events. Whenever such a gap exists, what is considered to be a science may only consist of a mass of historically developed viewpoints. The history of psychology makes plain why writers on psychological topics presumed that the Greeks were concerned with soul or mind instead of with actual interbehavior of organisms with objects of various sorts, including other organisms. The peak of this divergence between actual things studied and propositions arbitrarily constructed was reached in the nineteenth century when it was thought that what was being quantified and experimented upon were transcendent states or processes of "consciousness," or "experiences" which were regarded as somehow related to the body and especially the brain.

Of historical writing it is wisely said that it is an exercise in selection. By limiting ourselves to the scientific evolution of psychology our exposition risks a number of illegitimate restrictions. In particular, it appears to overstress the influence of Western European culture with its powerful assimilation of technological complexities. I hope, however, that this appearance of provincialism does not efface the realization that much of the essence of scientific thinking has its roots in the Far East, especially India and China. When I mention the contribution of Eastern cultures, for example, Egyptian, Syrian, Mesopotamian, and Persian, it should be assumed that the interrelation of these cultures with those of India and China has had not only commercial and political repercussions, but intellectual ones also.

Throughout this work I have endeavored by generous quotation to allow scholars to speak for themselves. In some instances the translations quoted have been modified, and I hope improved, for the better appreciation of what the original writers had discussed. The Bibliography indicates readily available translations of sources important for the development of the psychological tradition, as well as a variety of pertinent modern works. Birth and death dates of writers mentioned, insofar as available to me, are indicated in the text and in the Name Index. Any discrepancy between the two may be attributed to the disagreement of authorities.

In conclusion, I want to acknowledge my appreciation to all those who have helped to make this book, first to the many students who have participated in the discussions of historical problems in my classes and then to the faithful assistants who have typed and retyped the manuscript, and checked materials in libraries. Also, I want to thank all those who have kindly provided photographs for the plates. They are identified on page XV in the List of Plates. I must express my gratitude to Dean J. W. Ashton and the Graduate School of Indiana University for providing a part-time assistant while work was in progress and likewise to the National Science Foundation for a small grant to defray part of the expenses of visiting some psychological centers in Europe. My friends Greer and Sue Allen were extremely kind in helping with the design of the book. My greatest indebtedness, however, is to Helene J. Kantor, who has most expertly edited and improved the entire manuscript and made the drawings for the illustrations.

September 1962 J. R. K.

SECTION ONE

PROBLEMS, PROCEDURES, PERSPECTIVES: GENERAL ORIENTATION

CHAPTER 1

HISTORY OF PSYCHOLOGY: PROBLEMS, PERSPECTIVES, PRESUPPOSITIONS

CRUCIAL PROBLEMS OF SCIENTIFIC HISTORY

IN THE Preface we have already suggested that the historical study of science in general or any particular branch of it is essentially a scientific enterprise. Certainly we must eschew the belief that scientific history is simply a panoramic display of the successive reactions of scholars to actual or putative facts.

Now if historical study is to be an effective tool we must be well oriented with respect to its potentialities. Accordingly, we must examine carefully the problems facing the historian of science, the effects of cultural environment upon his data, and the presuppositions that influence his investigations and results. Our first section (Chs. 1, 2, 3), therefore, is devoted to the consideration of issues which throw light on the historical enterprise both in general science and in the particular domain of psychology.

GENERAL PROBLEMS. To illustrate some of the problems of scientific history take the widely held belief that all history is a humanistic subject and thus the antithesis of science. History is purported to deal with particulars, whereas science is concerned with general principles. How can history, then, play a significant role in a scientific domain? But, overlooking these questions, it is asked how accurate history can be when it is concerned with events which may have existed in the past but exist no longer. More specific problems concern the interrelations of the sciences. What are the relations between psychology and physics, for example, or psychology and mathematics? Is psychology in any sense an independent science or is it a branch of biology? Then arises the devastating question as to whether psychology is a science at all. Is it not a branch of philosophy and thus beyond the bounds of observation and experiment? These are only a few of the challenging questions facing the student of psychological history.

THE PERSPECTIVES OF HISTORY. Among the many problems of historical orientation and perspective we may cite the following. What are the influences of particular time periods and general human conditions upon the theories and practices of scientists? It is an accepted belief that scientists are greatly influenced in their selection of problems and in the way they work at them by the cultural conditions which surround them. Can frail Clio be depended upon to provide reliable evidence concerning this type of influence? Would not historical evidence introduce an extremely arbitrary and relativistic factor into the situation? How effective can history be in providing a firm base for judgments concerning past events or criteria for analyzing continuities and discontinuities in the march of scientific development?

PRESUPPOSITIONS. It has become a commonplace that all scientific work entails a thorough appreciation of the assumptions which are central to many aspects of such work and which influence its prosecution in essential ways. It is not only mathematics that is a postulational enterprise; this is the case also with the more definite content and experimental disciplines. Among the content and experimental sciences probably the scientific study of the evolution of psychology demands a greater concentration upon interest and presupposition because there is no unanimity among psychologists as to the nature of the events they investigate.

PSYCHOLOGICAL HISTORY AS SCIENTIFIC METHOD

Science consists of the past and current interbehavior of persons with things and events whose traits (structures, relations, actions) they are interested in knowing and controlling, plus the products of such activities (investigations) in the form of descriptions, theories, and laws.[1]

Now it is inevitable that such complicated and difficult work should require varying kinds of tools and techniques. It is no simple matter to isolate the particular things and events that constitute one's proper subject matter, to analyze and resynthesize them, to exercise effective control over data, and finally to draw proper conclusions about the nature and operation of original events in the light of the investigative procedures.

One of the outstanding tasks of the scientist is to make as certain as possible that the assumptions which govern his investigations and the conclusions he reaches are centered on the events he is studying and are not adversely affected by cultural influences. This is the problem of suitable matching of guiding principles with events investigated.

[1] See section below "The Traits of Science," p. 17.

It is precisely the historical method that can be helpful in this connection because this method consists of the critical study of the evolution of the assumptions or postulates, the investigative techniques, and the findings of science. Though students of psychology[2] have most strongly emphasized the value of the historical or genetic method for their work this does not imply that comparable benefits do not accrue to workers in most scientific branches.[3]

The potentialities of the historical method stem from the fact that scientific work is an evolution from the everyday activities of individuals as they adjust themselves to their life conditions. We may venture even further and point out that the events transpiring on the scientific level are continuous with and are evolutions of the events antedating scientific situations.[4] We assume that scientific activities or interactions occur on a series of levels, the lowest of which only comes into the scientific domain after scientists discover the interactions occurring there and formulate ways and means of dealing expertly with these events.

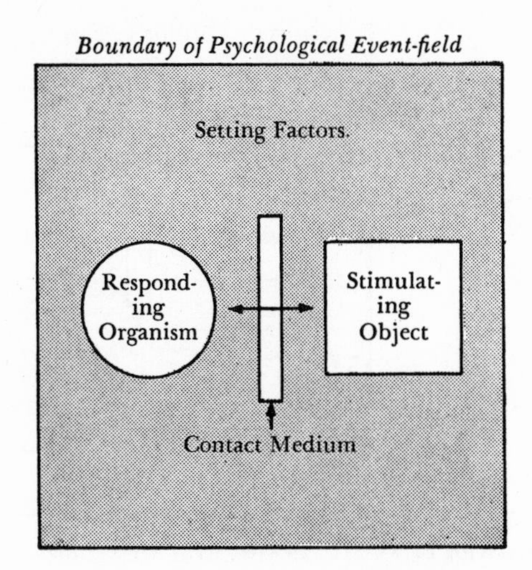

FIG. 1. DIAGRAM OF A PSYCHOLOGICAL EVENT FIELD

LEVEL OF ORIGINAL PSYCHOLOGICAL EVENT FIELDS (PRESCIENTIFIC LEVEL). The first or lowest level of interactional events is exemplified by the gravitational, radiational, magnetical, and electrical events of the physicist's domain; by the evolution, growth, and adjustment of

[2] See, for example, Dunlap, "The Historical Method in Psychology."

[3] See p. 4 above.

[4] See Kantor, *The Logic of Modern Science;* also *Interbehavioral Psychology,* 2nd ed.

organisms as the biologist observes them; and by the stimulus-response interactions studied by psychologists. When these original types of events, which are always complex event fields, become known to individuals (scientists) their investigation can begin. Striking examples of such original event fields are: the various radiations, some of which form the bases of new branches of science—radioactivity discovered by Becquerel (1896); x-rays discovered by Röntgen (1896); cosmic rays discovered by Wilson and others (1900); and extra-terrestrial electromagnetic radio interferences discovered by Jansky (1932). In the following and succeeding diagrams we restrict ourselves to psychological situations and therefore use the terms "responding organism" and "stimulating objects" for the primary components of the event field.

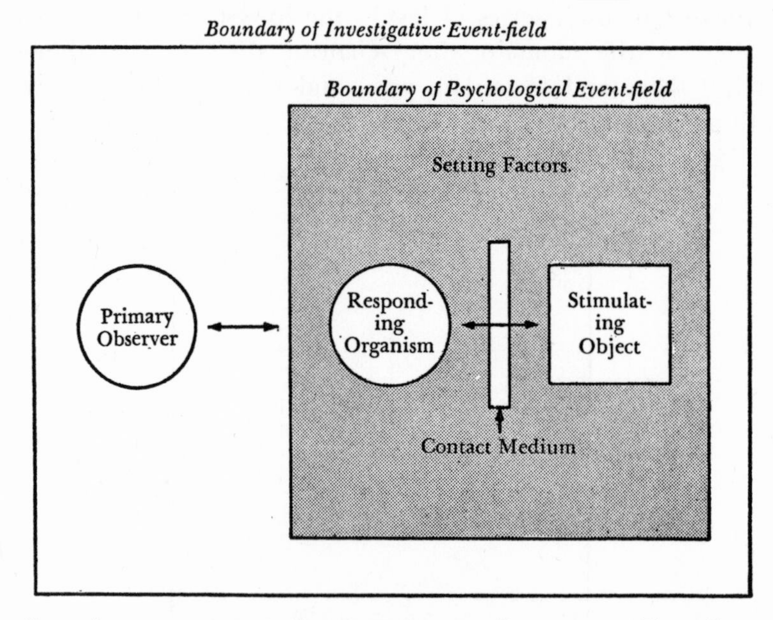

FIG. 2. INTERBEHAVIOR OF AN INVESTIGATOR WITH A PSYCHOLOGICAL EVENT FIELD

LEVEL OF PSYCHOLOGICAL INVESTIGATION (PRIMARY SCIENTIFIC LEVEL). In the psychological domain the events on the second level consist of interactions of psychologists with psychological interbehaviors such as those called perceiving, learning, danger avoiding, and numerous others. Such situations are frequently contrived by the psychologist when he experimentally manipulates the adjustments of organisms.

LEVEL OF HISTORICAL STUDY (SECONDARY SCIENTIFIC LEVEL). The third or historical level consists of the interactions of the historian-observer with the investigative behavior of scientists. Notice that the stimulating object now includes the original psychological observer.

HISTORICO-CRITICAL LEVEL (TERTIARY SCIENTIFIC LEVEL). On the fourth or uppermost level the stimulus object becomes complicated enough

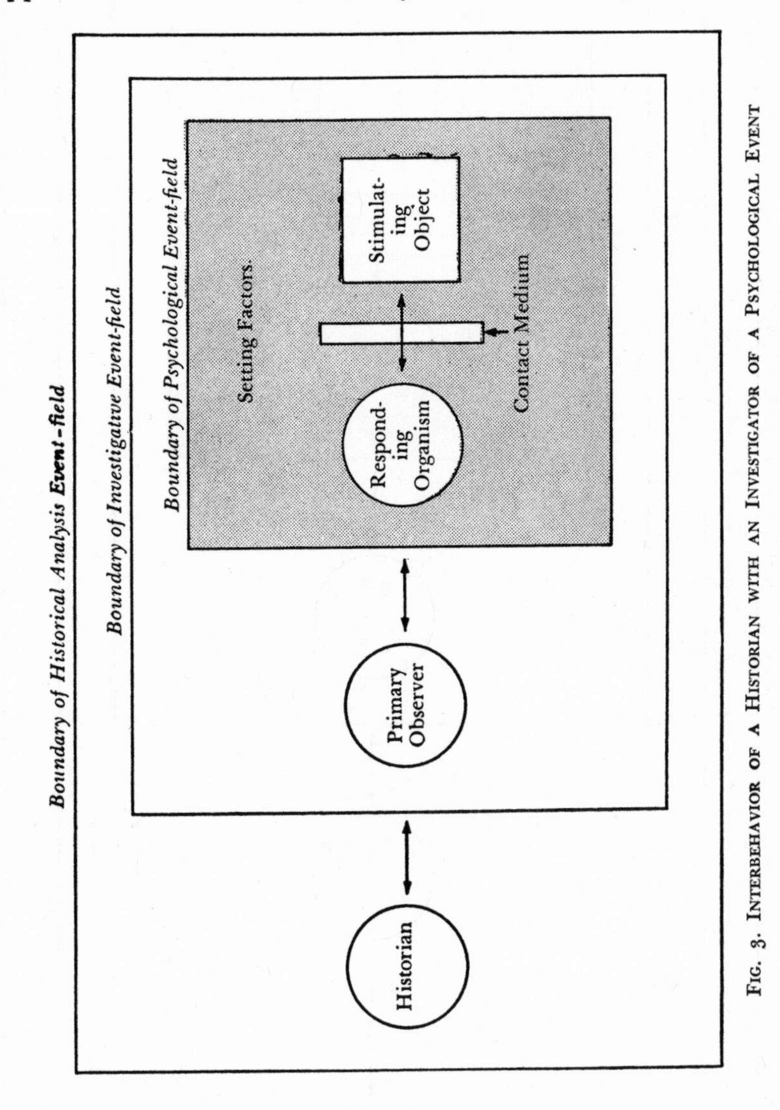

FIG. 3. INTERBEHAVIOR OF A HISTORIAN WITH AN INVESTIGATOR OF A PSYCHOLOGICAL EVENT

to include the historian and his interbehavior with the interactions of the primary observer and the original psychological field. We may assume that the responses of the historical critic are equally complicated.

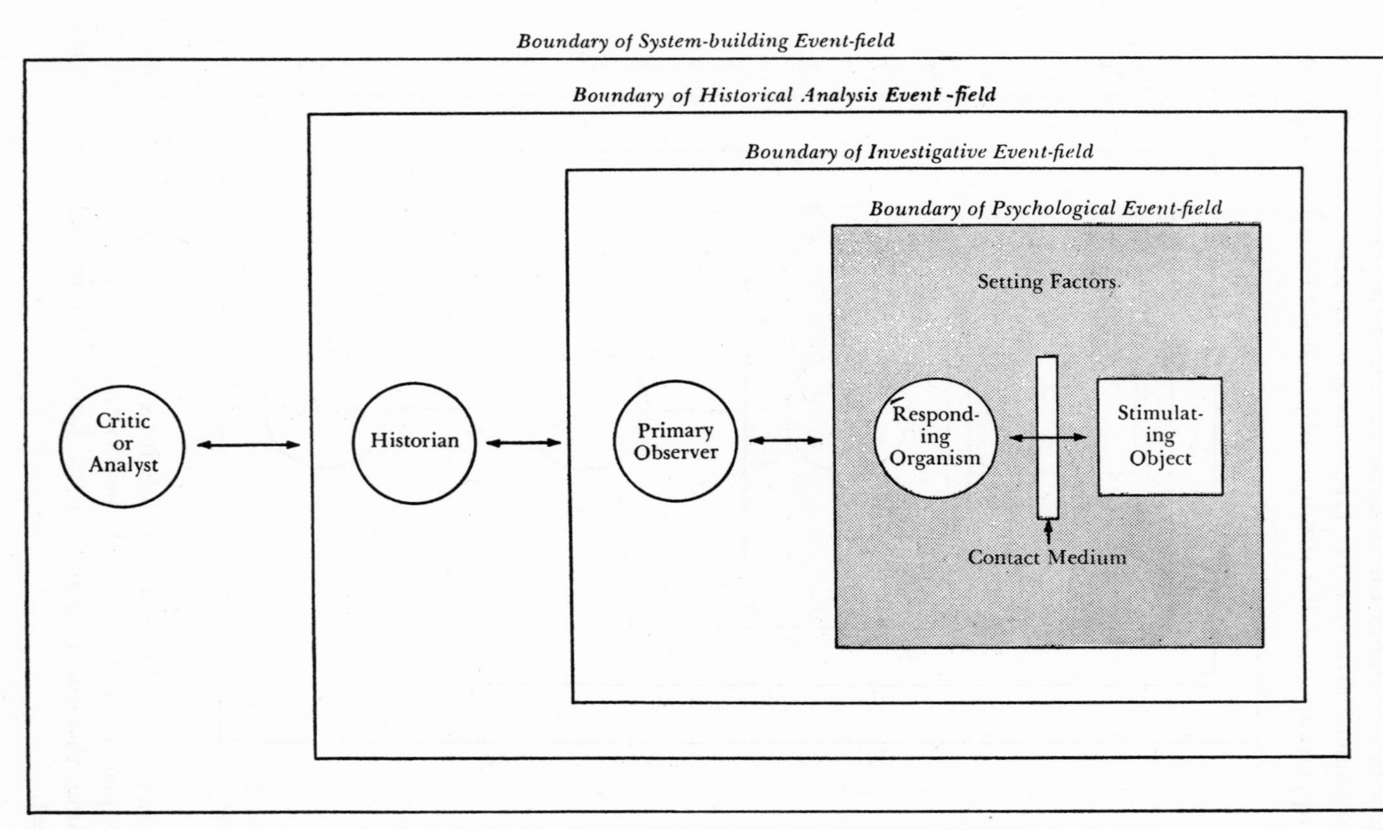

Fig. 4. Interbehavior of a Critic with a Reaction of a Historian

processes, and reactions. In the field of psychology the correspondences to the discovery of Pluto, of radioactivity, of energy quanta, or of numerous subatomic "particles" and their interactions are usually only greater or lesser variations of interbehaviors of fairly well known organisms with their simple or complex stimulus objects in new situations. Progress in psychology, it is said, consists mostly of postulational and interpretational changes comparable to such theories in physics as relativity and quantum mechanics. What the proponents of this view overlook are (a) the great importance of the specific details of actions and changes of action on the part of even the most familiar objects and (b) the fact that new interpretations are called for by observations of new features of events and by modifications in events by changes in their component factors. Granting that we have achieved valid generalizations or laws concerning the behavior of organisms in given situations, we still have ample scope for new laws describing the influence upon such behavior of various mutilations of the organisms or changes in other participating field factors.

There is little doubt that, partially because of the alleged difference between psychological and other sorts of events, psychology has been presumed to deal with psychical, that is, transpatial entities; accordingly, it has had leveled at it the imputation that it is not a science. But this is only a consequence of the fact that cultural conditions affecting scientists have always been potent factors in describing events. It is common knowledge that the term "psychology" has blanketed not only authentic events but also matters pertaining to theology, to folk wisdom, and to various phases of practical life. While it is established that psychological events are just as tangible and observable as the events dealt with by astronomers, physicists, chemists, and biologists, the psychological domain has historically been tightly controlled by nonscientists.

For example, if we look as far back as the Patristic era we find that the primary interest has been in man and his destiny. Accordingly, psychological events have not been treated as activities of organisms but have been transformed into entities expressing the social aspirations of people in troubled times. Such created entities as souls and their powers and faculties were made to supplant actual interbehavior completely. Following the theologians and building upon their constructions, moralists, economists, and students of politics have continued the tradition that the essence of human nature is some sort of transcendent principle.

We must conclude, therefore, that the historian of scientific psychology must not only keep close to authentic psychological events but must also be on guard against cultural traditions which influence him to substitute for the evolution of knowledge about psychological interactions various improper constructions about such interactions. We must add, too, that he must equally avoid shifting the base of his studies from authentic psychological events to the development of opinions and knowledge concerning other things and events, for example, biological happenings (neural or glandular events) or physical events (light and air energies) closely related to psychological events.[6]

THE PERSPECTIVES OF PSYCHOLOGICAL HISTORY

Because science is a cultural institution, even historians of science inevitably run into problems concerning the temporal and cultural backgrounds of scientific work. The more one is oriented toward such perspectives the better one understands what events scientists have worked with and the kind of theories they have formulated about them. Awareness of cultural perspectives helps greatly to forefend us against such improprieties, as, for example, treating Greek psychology as though it grew out of nineteenth-century soil. Similarly it is most inept to overlook that the behavioristic psychology of the twentieth century could only have arisen in a civilization very different from that which generated Berkeleyan spiritism.

The simplest scientific perspectives consist of two levels of cultural conditions. The first and more general is made up of a great complex of circumstances which may be briefly categorized as the political, social, industrial, and military conditions of a particular social or ethnic group. The second consists of the more specialized and more definitely structured intellectual institutions of a particular community or stratum of society. Variations in such intellectual and philosophical atmospheres have given rise to many scientific polarities; for example, the leaning toward continuity in Continental mathematics and light theory as against corpuscularity in Britain; the empirical trend of British scientists as compared with Continental rationalism; and the differences between the unified soul theorists of Southern Europe as compared with the atomistic views of the North.

When we keep before us the facts of Greek civilization as they existed in the fifth and fourth centuries B.C. we must judge it to be the height of folly to interpret Platonic psychology as spiritually trans-

[6] See section below entitled "The Historical Interrelation of Psychology and the other Sciences," 18*ff*.

cendent. Such an interpretation does not conform at all with Plato's cultural background or with the climate of philosophical opinion prevailing in his day.[7] Even though the spiritistic transcendentalism of the Church Fathers was created by the transformation of Platonic dualism, there is hardly anything in common between Plato's separation of the rationalistic constructions of mathematical formulae from the descriptions of crude observation, and the post-Greek differentiation of the transpatial world of faith from the spatio-temporal things of everyday events.

The importance of perspective orientation is strikingly illuminated by the consideration of the influence of cultural trends upon scientific work. Intellectual schools and specific traditional doctrines influence the choice of problems, the kind of organisms worked with, and the type of generalizations made. An example is the contemporary fact that it is primarily in the United States and in the Soviet Union that reflexology, objective psychology, and behavioristic ways of thinking loom large.

If the investigation and interpretation of current events are influenced by cultural perspectives, how much more so is this the case with the treatment of events on the historical level. Histories of science and especially of psychology are powerfully influenced by the general culture and philosophical perspectives of their authors. Because ours is predominantly a dualistic culture we find historians universally interpreting Platonic and Aristotelian psychology as though they were produced by St. Augustine and St. Thomas, whose cultures were very different from those of the Greeks though similar to ours. It must appear obvious that documents from different periods and cultures require careful analysis in order to discover what doctrines they actually contain.

An interesting example: while reviewing a historical work of Ribot, McCosh declares that although Ribot may not have set a sufficiently high value on the observations of consciousness, he has throughout carefully separated psychology, which is a science of observation, external and internal, from all metaphysical speculation.[8] Ribot himself declares that Fechnerian psychophysics as the science of the reciprocal relations of body and spirit is not only the glory of the author but satisfies the criteria of experimental science.

> Fechner's object is to inaugurate a positive era in this kind of research, or more exactly to build up a science resting upon experiment, calculation, and

[7] See Ch. 7.
[8] "Preface" to T. Ribot, *German Psychology of Today: The Empirical School.*

measure. In principle it places the new science outside of all metaphysical hypothesis.[9]

What changes in attitude the perspectives of time have brought about! Could the psychologist acquainted with twentieth-century behaviorism regard "reciprocal relations of body and spirit" as science and not metaphysics? The naturalistic psychologist holds that the only glory that accrues to Fechner is clearly earned only by his demonstration that psychology is essentially concerned with responses to stimulus objects arranged and controlled by the experimenter.

An effective way of pointing up the advantage of being aware of the perspectival backgrounds of historical events is to observe that such awareness allows us to take account of both the continuities and discontinuities which characterize the march of events. Once the psychological tradition got started in the culture of Western Europe it has continued with sometimes greater and sometimes smaller variations. Variations in both doctrine and practice can be illuminated by analyzing the cultural circumstances under which they arise.

At this point it is well to be reminded what an enormous role is played in scientific history by linguistic institutions in both distinguishing and confusing continuities and discontinuities. The continuity in psychology and other sciences is excellently illustrated by the fact that our scientific vocabularies are based on the Greek and Latin languages. Our term "psychology," for example, is ultimately derived from the Greek word "psyche." But today this term has a dualistic connotation, and writers who disregard the differences in cultural perspectives attribute to the Greeks the same mentalistic referent. So, to Aristotle are attributed such doctrines as the existence of a unitary soul or mind which is free from determination and which is originally a blank tablet. Obviously the use of the term "soul" as a translation of "psyche" results in a flagrant displacement of observations and opinions so that ancient doctrines are completely misinterpreted.

Although it is clear that a knowledge of cultural perspective is valuable in psychological history to avoid displacement of doctrines, to prevent errors based on language habits, and to obviate the insinuation of popular ideas into technical descriptions, these are all, in a way, negative virtues. The more positive value of perspectival study is the understanding it provides of events because they are viewed against the actual human scene which they reflect.

[9] *Ibid.*, p. 136.

THE PRESUPPOSITIONS OF PSYCHOLOGICAL HISTORY

We have already asserted that science is an interbehavioral enterprise not only continuous with other human behavior, even that of everyday living, but also with inorganic interbehaviors. What distinguishes scientific interbehavior from other kinds is mainly expertness of performance. This expertness consists primarily of two aspects. First and foremost, there is a sensitivity to events previously encountered so that adjustments are facilitated. And next, but not far separated from the former, is the interest in one's reflective attitudes toward things. In scientific practice reflective attitudes result in setting up deliberate and definite formulations (hypotheses and theories) as guides to the investigative and interpretative interbehavior with events. Scientific formulations we call definite assumptions, hypotheses, or postulates which grow out of ordinary presuppositions. Probably the most characteristic aspect of scientific enterprises is that they are postulational. Geometry became scientific when Gauss, Lobachevsky, Bolyai, and Riemann made plain its postulational character and this is true of the other branches of mathematics also.

Now we ask, what are the basic presuppositions or postulates of psychological history taken as a science? We have already made evident a number of those we adopt. But there are two types of presuppositions which we regard as especially important. These concern: (a) the kind of philosophy, or logic of science which is basic to psychological history; and (b) the nature of science.

THE NATURE OF PHILOSOPHY. Just as no scientific investigation can proceed without hypotheses or presuppositions, so no study of psychological history can be critically undertaken without considering the underlying logical or philosophical presuppositions. While attempting to elucidate the presuppositions of modern psychology a recent writer declares:

> However real and objective and physical an event may appear to be, philosophy can produce convincing and embarrassing arguments to the effect that things are not what they seem. The rat running in the maze may look like an independent physical object. The red on the color mixer may be regarded as dependent mental substance. . . . The belief in the real independent existence of the rat is a leap of animal faith. The belief in the subjectivity of red is equally insecure.[10]

As the quotation indicates, the author accepts without question the dualistic institutions and thinking that have prevailed in Western

[10] Pratt, *The Logic of Modern Psychology*, p. 12.

Europe for more than twenty centuries. The philosophy he speaks of is clearly nothing more than an intellectual formula developed in the theological stage of our culture, a formula which has hardly anything to do with the concrete facts of human living or the serious investigation of any event. Here is a splendid illustration of a world sicklied o'er with the pale cast of medieval thought.

The persistence of this kind of philosophy demonstrates the great value placed upon institutional theories as compared with actual events. Historically this type of philosophy constitutes a point on a vicious circle. It consists of a dualism set up in slow stages by the patristic scholars who attempted to establish a new world view to replace the naturalism of the pagan thinkers. After becoming established as a cultural institution it penetrated all branches of Western thought including psychology, where it resulted in the division of man into soul and matter or into mind and body. Hence philosophers derive aid and comfort for their spiritistic views from the science of psychology, while as we have seen, psychologists support their mentalistic views on the basis of well established philosophical traditions.

Small wonder it is that in our age, when so great a conquest has been made of natural things, thinkers should attempt to conceal their adherence to the traditional spiritism. Thus have arisen the great movements of positivism and linguistic philosophy. But nothing of all this has changed the mentalistic traditions. Scientists of all departments, especially physicists, have demonstrated the great hold which the traditional philosophies have had upon them. Thus in the great era of "uncertainty," "organismic nature," and the "identity of knowing and the known," certainly little progress has been made toward a philosophy which accords with man's actual place in nature, with the work scientists actually do, and with the results currently obtained. Yet such a philosophy can free the scientists completely from the misleading and disserviceable traditions which have so long prevailed.

How then shall we envisage philosophy and its relation to science? The answer can be facilitated by first clearing away erroneous traditional notions. Philosophy is not uncontrolled speculative construction about gods, transcendent cosmic things, or mystic powers of thinkers. Philosophical activity is behavior of persons continuous with all other behavior. On the positive side philosophy is orientational behavior exactly like the investigational behavior of science. In fact, philosophy is theoretical science and is bound by the same rules of interbehaving with events. The difference between the two is merely one of focus and concentration. By comparison with localized scientific research, philosophical investigation is not limited to a circumscribed analysis, measurement, or interpretation of a particular event or class of events. The scope of philosophy is somewhat broader. In its critical phase it questions the contradiction of conclusions obtained by one type of investigation or field of research by workers in another. For example, it checks the assumption that whereas in one domain transcendent principles are excluded, they are permitted in another. A further example is the condemnation by theoretical science or philosophy of the use within any single domain of a double standard, which insists upon strict contact with events at the point of research, but allows mystic notions in interpreting the results reached.

On the whole, scientific activities are closer to the technological points of the interbehavioral continuum than are philosophical activities. The theoretical scientist or philosopher can take into account wider ranges of information, for example, those not subject to immediate experimental test. He can also coordinate events from such widely varying domains as experimental physics, nature study as in ecological biology, and even the human behavior of an ethical or esthetic type.

THE TRAITS OF SCIENCE. The history of psychology, including the relationships between original events and their reconstruction in records, parallels, of course, the particular histories of the other sciences. Accordingly, it may be advisable to structure our assumptions concerning the nature of science.

Generally speaking, the scientific enterprise consists of the building of constructs (descriptions, interpretations) about events on the basis of contacts with them. Through procedures of analysis and manipulative observation, laws are formulated concerning the composition of event complexes and the interrelations of the factors composing them. The accompanying diagram illustrates the essential factors in scientific

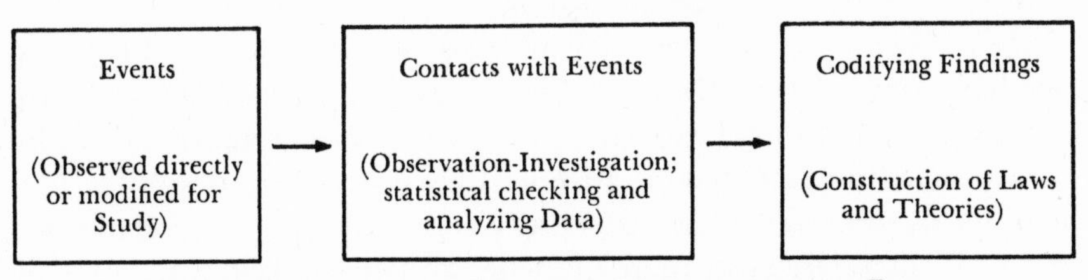

FIG. 5. THE DERIVATION OF LAWS FROM INTERBEHAVIOR WITH EVENTS

situations. Primary emphasis must be placed on the events which give rise to scientific problems and which control the solution of these problems. But just as important are all the procedures and techniques necessary for ascertaining the nature of the events and their relationship to other events. And finally there is the construction of descriptive and explanatory propositions concerning the events and what has been discovered about them. The latter propositions constitute laws and theorems.

Our diagram is obviously greatly simplified and idealizes the scientific enterprise. We have omitted all sorts of extraneous influences which affect primarily the scientific worker and his legitimate difficulties in determining whether the event he is presumed to investigate is in fact an authentic one. Nevertheless, the diagram does suggest the essential criteria for separating genuine from spurious scientific situations.

Consider the psychological domain. Although all psychological study obviously begins with definite interactions of organisms with stimulus objects, the data are frequently taken to be something else altogether; for example, faculties and powers within the organism. In such cases elaborate psychological doctrines are constructed without observation or investigation of the original events. In the history of psychology we find periods when writers moved by an interest in the destiny of man boldly indulged in grand pronouncements concerning his partially fragile and dissoluble characteristics on one side and his partial immortality on the other.

THE HISTORICAL INTERRELATION OF PSYCHOLOGY AND THE OTHER SCIENCES

It must be counted as a distinct merit of scientific history that it displays and condemns the numerous fallacies concerning the interrelation of psychology and the other sciences. Two of these historical fallacies stand out sharply. On the one hand, psychology has been denied membership in the fraternity of sciences and, on the other, psychology envisaged as the discipline concerned with psychic states has been made the dominant and universal discipline.

While discussing the crucial problems of psychological history we may have overstressed the difference between psychology and other sciences. This legitimate expository exaggeration is certainly misleading if it conceals the fact that in all essentials psychology is similar to all the other sciences as well as historically and culturally interrelated with them. All the sciences in their branches and specializations evolve as a unified constellation. They all arise out of a common matrix of events —a gigantic cultural complex—which includes the investigative interest and operations of scientists. Each of the sciences or branches sets up particular investigative processes depending upon its particular choice of subject matter. Variation in subject matter, too, will influence the time and rate of development of the individual sciences, thus imprinting special marks upon their histories.

The historical interrelation of the sciences plainly shows that psychology is an autonomous science which selects a set of particular events for its study. These events are not reducible to any other type or class. It is assumed, then, that all constructs must respect this autonomy. When psychology is not presumed to deal with intangible extraspatial entities or processes, reductions and substitutions are not at all necessary.

Since all events consist of fields of interacting factors, we can differentiate psychological science from other sciences by specifying that it investigate the interbehavior of organisms in various stages of evolution with objects, events, and relations with which they are inevitably and constantly in contact. Naturally these events cover a wide range of happenings, some simple and some complex. Psychologists differentiate between these events by means of such familiar names as reflexes, conditionings, learnings, perceivings, feelings, reasonings, and so on. These comparatively simple types of activities in all types of interrelations and combinations contribute to the development of such institutional products as law, group customs, social habits, scientific institutions, art, social organization, mythology, and religion. When such institutional products are developed they serve as stimuli, occasions, and backgrounds for all forms of complex interbehavior.

Once we have clearly distinguished the specialized events of psychology, we have to emphasize their close connection with the aspects of events which pertain to the other sciences. To begin with, stimulus objects may be physical, chemical, biological, or anthropological. Accordingly, psychologists must have some knowledge concerning the neighboring and cooperating sciences. Furthermore, since psychological behavior is only performed by biological organisms, psychological events include among their component activities an immense number of biological happenings. Biological events inevitably participate in many ways in psychological events. Unfortunately, this close relationship has led to serious confusions throughout psychological history, the most notorious being the historical body-mind dogma.

However, granted that psychology is an autonomous science, it can hardly be the basis and foundation of all the others. The history of psychology disclaims completely the standard and traditional attitude that makes psychology indifferent to the fact that chemistry, physics, and biology produce the knowledge concerning the character of objects which stimulate organisms in their interactions. It is this attitude which keeps perennially alive the presupposition that the qualities of things exist in the mind or in mental phenomena and are projected into the objects. The more likely view of the coordination of all the sciences makes it possible to accord due value to the contribution of all sorts of field factors to the sum total of the interactional processes which in their aggregate constitute psychological as well as other types of events.

An important item in the interrelationship of the sciences is that, despite the particular differences in the subject matter and modes of study, all the sciences are similarly affected by their common cultural matrix. When psychology suffers from dualistic and transcendental ways of thinking, the same disease affects physics, though in a different way. When Descartes condemned psychology to concern itself with extensionless entities his physics showed the same kind of scars. When physiologists assume that the action of the brain parallels the occurrence of mental states, the biology they espouse is extremely remote from the organic events they presume to understand. Similarly, when physicists assume that the primary data of their science as of all others consists not of independent events but of mental states constituting their own inner consciousness, they hark back to the teachings of the Church Fathers just as do psychologists who concern themselves with sensations and other psychic states.

THE SCIENTIFIC CAREER OF PSYCHOLOGY

By comparison with most sciences psychology has had a unique scientific career. If we grant that an expert interest in a certain class of events irrespective of how they are interpreted constitutes a science, then psychology has been continously cultivated longer than most sciences. The radical interpretive shiftings with respect to psychological events are in themselves evidences of a long career. Psychology is distinguished from the other sciences by beginning as a definitely objective discipline, then departing radically from that status, and finally struggling toward an objective position again.

Possibly because psychological events are so close to the scientific workers themselves, this discipline has been more sensitive than other sciences to the surrounding cultural institutions. Thus has arisen the general bifurcation between psychological tradition and psychological science, with the consequence that during the career of psychology events have most frequently been treated in terms of cultural conditions rather then on the basis of how they actually occur. And so, although unlike most of the other sciences, whose cultivation well nigh ceased for a long series of centuries, the psychological tradition testifies to a continuity of interest in psychological events, these have not been continuously treated as natural events. The psychological tradition reveals a cyclic process which can be symbolized by the following three periods.

THE GREEK OBJECTIVE PERIOD. In this earliest period of technical psychology we already find a simple but thoroughly naturalistic treatment of psychological events along biological lines. The Aristotelian corpus of psychological treatises constitutes a well-organized set of descriptions of psychological behavior. But as the history of psychology shows, this early naturalistic era did not last longer than a few centuries.

THE PATRISTIC AND MEDIEVAL PERIOD. Throughout this period the ideal of investigating any kind of events was set aside in favor of such other interests as man's salvation, his place in a theistic cosmos, and his rights and duties with respect to God and state. Since the theological and church civilization placed man and his habitation at the center of the universe, his essential behavior was envisaged as of a spiritual order. By means of verbal and symbolic formulations man, in part at least, was removed far from his actual place in a spatio-temporal world and made into a being who, because he was endowed with a soul, was in part akin to God and the angels. Psychological thinking lost the sense of scientific investigation and became preoccupied with christological doctrines. It was this aspect of faith and opinion which has permeated the entire development of psychology even to our own day.

THE SCIENTIFIC RENAISSANCE. With the active reemergence of scientific institutions as part of the great cultural complex which embraced the secular and technological civilizations of Western Europe, psychological events again became treated as objects of investigation. This treatment, at least from the seventeenth century forward consisted of the attempt by scholars to *naturalize the soul*. As we shall see, the gradual evolution of scientific culture has dictated that attempts should be made to bring the transpatial substance and process of the soul under the rule of number and measure (Herbart), of experimentation (Fechner), of physical and biological correspondence (Hartley), or by other means to overcome the uncrossable chasm between the "spiritual" and the "natural."

Because of the tortuous career of psychology, the student of its history faces the challenge of distinguishing between genuine psychological data and the folklore, the extrascientific impositions upon events, and the biased interpretations placed upon the authentic facts of the science. Only by keeping distinct the various phases can the scientific evolution of the discipline be recorded. A primary task of the historian, then, is to keep clear in the various periods the presuppositions or postulates as compared with the actual observations, particularly when the former deviate markedly from the latter.

THE STRUCTURING OF PSYCHOLOGICAL HISTORY

Historians must inevitably follow the chronological course of events. Origins, evolutions, and current interrelations are of the essence of whatever they study. Scientific events and the reactions to them, whether observational or interpretational, obviously also follow trends and patterns with occasional repetitions and retrogressions. Aside from chronological considerations, the historian of science may exercise a choice as to how he unfolds his narrative. He may follow a biographical plan and stress the contributions of persons who are presumed to play important roles in the evolution of the science. Again the historian may follow a geographical pattern emphasizing developments as they take place in particular countries. The geographical plan favors the inclusion of the mutual influences of scientific and other phases of culture, although the interrelations become enormously complex. Scientific historians may also give a particular pattern to their exposition by featuring the investigations and interpretations of particular classes of events. In the history of psychology, for example, one might emphasize the presentation of psychophysical or learning experiments, or the evolution of various theories concerning discrimination, feeling, or some other type of action.

Whatever primary plan a scientific historian adopts he is bound to include the alternative plans also. Though the primary aim of this book is to trace out the evolution of the scientific aspects of psychology by a chronological coverage of psychological development, the Table of Contents shows that the biographical, geographical, and topical modes of treating psychological history have likewise left their mark on the final product.

CHAPTER 2

THE HISTORY OF SCIENCE AND THE SCIENCE OF HISTORY

THE VALUE OF HISTORY AS SCIENTIFIC METHOD

RECENT DECADES have witnessed a tremendously increased interest in the history of science. In addition to a growing output of books, articles, and bibliographies on the subject, there are new journals, new university institutes and departments devoted to the pursuit of this subject. It would be gratifying if we could account for this vigorous intellectual development on the basis of an increased realization that scientific history is a valid and useful method of science. But this is not the case, and we have already had to distinguish between an interest in the history of science on the ground of its humanistic value and its function in scientific research. Moreover, there is the widely held belief that history itself cannot be scientific and therefore cannot be a tool of science. Before proceeding to the story of psychological evolution we must examine briefly the questions whether history can be scientific and what is its potential value for the advancement of science.

Many scientists, and especially physicists, deny any value to the historical study of their science because they regard themselves as having broken completely with the past. Although granting continuity between atomic physics and the speculations of Leucippus and Democritus, there is still, they believe, an uncrossable chasm which separates current problems and their investigation from Greek atomism. Current investigations appear remote from a period that knew not electrons, protons, mesons, pions, neutrons, neutrinos and other *particles,* nor the cyclotrons, bevatrons, cloud chambers, and other apparatus used to study them.

This rejection of history is apparently based upon the doubtful view that history is a universal all-embracing continuum and not a composition of segments of happenings of shorter or longer duration and of restricted scope. Those who adopt the specific and limited view of history may argue that what is of importance to physicists and other scientists is precisely the series of events concerned in the establishment of the new knowledge of atomic structure and atomic behavior along with the record of how these events have been investigated.

It must be granted, of course, that not every scientific research requires a historical tool for its prosecution. Nor is the history of science of equal value for all scientific departments. Still this does not cancel the view that the history of science is for the most part a cumulative report of the past interbehavior of workers dealing with the same class of events that stimulates the efforts of current researchers. From this standpoint it is indispensable to be soundly oriented with respect to similar enterprises.

When we consult the opinions of scientific workers we find that many of them are convinced of the importance of history for their studies. Watson says,

It is widely recognized by leading physicists that the training of young physicists in our universities should not be limited to modern knowledge but that senior students should be brought to interest themselves in the history of their subject—of the men and the development of ideas.[1]

Pertinent here, too, are the comments of Abetti, "I think that one cannot know astronomy really well without knowing its history,"[2] and Dingle, "In cosmological studies, then, a knowledge of the history and philosophy of science is not a superfluity; it is a necessity."[3] And when we turn to medical writers, we find as we should expect, a definite insistence upon the importance of history for their subject. Sigerist says

. . . medical history is not only history but medicine as well, part of the theory of medicine. If general history is an instrument of life in general, then medical history is an instrument of medical life. The picture a physician has of the past of his profession exerts a distinct influence on his thinking and therefore on his actions as well.[4]

Ackerknecht declares in a similar vein,

A man can be a competent doctor without a knowledge of medical history. But an acquaintance with medical history can make him a better doctor. It is no accident that so many of the great doctors of the last hundred years, whether the name be Osler, Halsted, Welch, Cushing, Andral, Virchow, Wunderlich, Claude Bernard, Charcot, Pasteur, Behring, or Sauerbruch, have had a profound interest in medical history and have often made valuable contributions to the field.[5]

Of very striking interest here is the view of Schrödinger[6] who asserts

[1] *On Understanding Physics,* p. x.
[2] *History of Astronomy,* Preface.
[3] "Science and Modern Cosmology," *Science,* 1954, p. 513.
[4] *History of Medicine,* p. 32.
[5] *A Short History of Medicine,* p. xvii.
[6] *Nature and the Greeks,* p. 16 *f.*

that it is of the greatest importance for scientists to study the history of Greek science in order to avoid the mistake the Greeks made. That mistake, Schrödinger thinks, is the adoption by the Greeks of the postulate that the scientist stands over against nature, which is his object of study. Schrödinger adopts the popular modern view that in the process of scientific study the scientist creates his data. This view implies that the scientist is not merely a spectator but a part of the events studied. I submit that this opinion reflects the exact opposite of the correct relations that exist between scientists and the events they study. Schrödinger, Bohr, Eddington, and the other scientists who adopt this postulate are surely confusing events and the constructs created with respect to them.

For the psychologist, history is perhaps more important than for any other scientist. In the first place, his subject matter is through and through historical and shaped by immediate surrounding conditions. Furthermore, in no other science are descriptions and interpretations of events studied so influenced by the varying cultural settings of the times and places in which they are formulated. Historical study is most useful in separating the characteristics of events from the culturally influenced interpretations imposed upon them.

Historical studies in science, it must be pointed out, are important both in the investigation of large scale problems touching general assumptions or specific postulates and in the analysis of individual researches. In both cases scientific history provides the scientist with a serviceable intellectual perspective which facilitates an understanding of problems, as well as supplies a source of available suggestions for solving them. In the case of specific researches historical orientation avoids much waste of time and materials when the investigator profits from knowing the work and techniques of others instead of resorting to the trial and error of entirely new efforts.[7]

The history of science probably is of the greatest significance for theory and interpretation. This follows from the fact that there is a continuity and contemporaneity of events that carry through long stretches of time. It is impossible to break the connection which exists between planetary wandering and modern astronomy, between the alchemical *fusion, reduction, calcination, distillation,* or *sublimation* and modern chemistry. The accumulation of discoveries constitutes a single line extending far back into the first acquaintance with similar

[7] Hence the importance of investigative bibliographies, reports of work in progress, symposia on investigation techniques and results, etc.

events. It is not essential for our purpose to argue for the invariable interconnection of all things with all others. It is only necessary to be able to take account of continuous developments in certain sciences or the interrelations of factors in current particular problems. The history of science as a record of contacts with events maintains its continuity through the continuity of these specific events.

The history of a science is, however, not exclusively a tool of investigation. It is at the same time a torch which illuminates not only the everyday work of science but science as an institution. It is an interesting speculation that perhaps an intimate understanding of scientific history might prevent atomic physicists from luxuriating in such vagaries as principles of uncertainty, impotency, and indeterminacy, since it may be readily ascertained that they are historically derived from nonscientific sources, namely spiritistic philosophy. Of all the sciences, probably psychology can profit most from an appreciation of its origin and evolution. Although psychology has reached a relatively high peak of technical development, its *basic constructs* are still rooted in traditional ways of thinking.

CAN HISTORY BE SCIENTIFIC?

If history is to be considered as a method or tool of science it must be itself consonant with science. But can history be scientific? So prominent is construction in history, so dependent is it upon substitute evidence instead of direct inspection, that the question arises whether there can be a science of history. The problem is easily understood. What looms large is not only the current absence of the events that the historian is interested in but also their nonexistence. At best there is a remoteness of events, a remoteness which has often induced writers to deny any possibility of precise information. Yet we must consider whether history deals only with what is past and isolated from the present, or whether there is a continuity of events which makes what is past definitely continuous with currently observable events.

All events are historical. Current happenings are evolved from previously occurring events and maintain a definite continuity with them. It is not improper to say that whenever events are considered in temporal perspective, they are always parts or phases of other events. For this reason we may always hope to discover events which are themselves authentic and vouched for, and can thus serve as usable evidence to provide a basis for sound judgment concerning the character and interrelations of past events.

Although obviously the historian of science, like the historian of other human events, must rely primarily upon documents in the form of treatises and commentaries, these evidences embody reactions to independently occurring events. In some instances, of course, treatises and other writings themselves clearly constitute the original events, as in the case of disputed authorship. In all cases we must exclude the assumption that knowledge of past events may be identified with the original events. The task of the historian is to discover by every available means what actually happened. There are strict limits to what he can do to control history as events. History is no autistic constructional process.

Whether or not history can be scientific depends upon one's postulation concerning historical study, the nature of science and its variations, the general nature of knowledge and of scientific laws.[8] It is evident that those who reject history as scientific and regard it as "fable agreed upon" do so on an absolutistic criterion. From history they would demand some sort of ultimacy whereas this is in no wise a characteristic of science, which is probabilistic and postulational. Again, history is often denied scientific status because it is not in subject matter or method entirely like physics or chemistry. But this is to overlook that serious historical study is, exactly like physics, an enterprise of investigating some class of events, and that it is only the detailed differences in events that give rise to different types of sciences. All types of events yield laws which must conform to the original events. While all events are unique in quality, or collocation of variants and temporal framework, it is precisely the task of the worker to search for useful generalizations of occurrence. After all that is the essence of a scientific law.

From what we have already said, it is plain that valid hypotheses for historical study in science would make knowledge simply the work of observing and recording the behavior of a scientist as he interacts with scientific stimulus objects. The fact that historical study and narrative is the work of persons does not imply the presence of any "creation" of the events that goes beyond the acts of description and documented reconstruction. The circumstance that documents and other evidence require interpretation in no manner implies that historical study must inevitably be subjective and the product of "mental" creation. The

[8] The following works offer suggestions concerning the possible scientific character of history: Cohen, *The Meaning of Human History;* Goldenweiser, *History, Psychology and Culture;* Miller, *History and Science;* Mandelbaum, *The Problem of Historical Knowledge;* Teggart, *The Theory and Processes of History;* Carr, *What is History?*

procedures of selection, interpretation, and organization in historical study, no more than in any scientific situation, change the fact that the historian is obliged to understand and report on a series of actual occurrences.

It is impossible to retreat from the realization that all the creative processes of individuals, howsoever great their initiative, must finally be brought down to operations upon events. Not only the ideals but also the practices of historians fit into a matrix of occurrences which are immune to the creative manipulations of historians. We must respect the distinction between events and constructs.

HISTORY AS EVENTS AND AS CONSTRUCTS

Because the term "history" is used to refer to both historical narration and the events narrated, the actual events and the constructional descriptions are frequently confused. And yet it is most important that they be precisely distinguished. The events of history consist of the actual things and activities which participate in a given set of changes and transformations. On the inorganic level such changes can be illustrated by the transformation of hydrogen into helium and other elements. In the case of civil history, events consist of the precise movements and actions performed by persons with respect to other persons and things under specific conditions. History as events consists, then, of the specific and intimate processes making up nature in all its aspects. We should stress here all the minutiae constituting spatiotemporal existence or reality.

By contrast, history as construct consists of the isolations, fixations, and manipulative transformations of the original events. There has been an injection of the action of the observer or manipulator into the original event situations. The most typical constructs consist of the icons or analogical things set up by observers to represent or to refer to original events. Constructs of history are, therefore, secondary, tertiary, or even more remote from the events which are the original starting points. Whoever respects the distinction just made cannot persist in the belief that history is unrelated to science. For valid history is a precise record of actual happenings. Its constructional aspects are capable of control by the original events. Scientific history in particular may be faithful to the events of which it is a record and a reminder.

To a certain extent the history of psychology is an exception among the histories of science. Unfortunately there has long prevailed an intermixture of event and construct, so that the demarcation lines which are so clear in some scientific situations have become blurred in the case of psychology. The result has been a perpetuation of folklore, of verbal traditions. The importance of historical studies lies precisely in their potentiality for eliminating these faults.

NATURAL HISTORY, CIVIL HISTORY, AND THE HISTORY OF SCIENCE

Up to this point we have generalized history as primarily the study of past events without differentiating between its different phases. This we must now do so that we can draw the proper implications from our results.

NATURAL HISTORY. By natural history we understand the evolution of things and events on the basis of various unique conditions. Some of these may be directly observed while others must be inferred from available evidences. Since all things and events are evolutional, the known developments are samples acquired by various means at our disposal. It is to be noted, too, that in the final analysis all civil history and the history of science, which in some ways is a part of civil history, are selected out of the great continuum of natural history. We can go further and say that science itself is derived from the events of natural history.

CIVIL HISTORY. Probably most of the problems and difficulties with respect to history stem from this type of study. Not only are the events complex and remote but also they are thoroughly interwined with the cultural prejudices of the document makers as well as of the students of history. Since social and political events are in question, Christian writers appear hampered by the divergencies of their culture from those of pagan or other nonchristian people. The fact that events are differently viewed and understood plays a large part in historical writing.

HISTORY OF SCIENCE. The history of science is, on the whole, free from some of the greatest difficulties that beset social and political history. Whereas the original civil events have for the most part completely vanished, the events dealt with by the historian of science remain in whole or part. The historian of astronomy has before him the same planets and stars that confronted Aristarchus, Ptolemy, Copernicus, and Newton. The historian of medicine or of biology is in immediate contact with the same classes of plants and animals and their adjustments and maladjustments as were the original observers or discoverers. The psychological historian is in contact with many of the identical classes of infrahuman and human behavior as the earliest historian or contemporary investigator. What are gone in fact and are not to be directly known are the individual activities, the responses, the attitudes of the astronomers, biologists, and psychologists.[9]

THE PROBLEM OF SCIENTIFIC ORIGINS

When did psychology begin? Or physics, or chemistry? Or any historical institution? The answer always implies the selection of some particular point on a continuum. Whatever point we choose as the beginning for events will itself have antecedents. Because origins usually are not only complex but also hazy, any attempt to determine beginnings involves some arbitrary procedures. But this circumstance simply brings scientific history into the field of science itself, where hypothesis and probability are inevitable guides to operation and achievement.

The determination of scientific origins is greatly facilitated by the fact that origins are always at one end of a developmental curve. There is no history unless the point of origin is continuous with a noticeable further development. It is this continuity which supplies the basis for tracing out the points of origin. New directions in science mainly consist of modifications of older theories and operations. Scientists regard Einsteinian physics both as a continuation of Newtonian physics and as a replacement for it. It is of interest to psychologists that when Aristotle became the first formulator of a psychological system he at the same time became the first historian of psychology.

The determination of origins is not only aided by the fact of continuity in human events; there are also the matrix circumstances which always throw considerable light upon the technical scientific events whose origins we seek to ascertain. Take for example the "miracle of Greece." Is it true that Aristotle or the Greeks originated all the sciences? Or did the miracle consist of a concentration of effort and achievement made possible by numerous social, political, military, and especially technological advances? What seems required here is a control of the tendency to make discontinuities out of prominent focal points. It is precisely the task of the historian to search for and discover the factors which fill in the gaps between already known points on a continuum.

[9] Included among the lost items are the false moves and failures of investigators which are ignored in reporting work or deliberately suppressed, as well as the unrecoverable protocols of past enterprises.

INTERPRETATION AND EVALUATION IN SCIENTIFIC HISTORY

The historian of science must inevitably assume that the current effectiveness and achievement of a particular science or of the institution of science in general have evolved by slow or rapid evolutionary processes. His task is set for him to isolate and describe the specific details of this evolution. But this is not all. There is in addition the task of evaluating the events dealt with. The interpretive and evaluative reactions of the historian must follow the paradigm of the original investigator.

Interpretation and evaluation thus represent the more spontaneous behavior of the historian. However, there is no measure of arbitrariness implied here. Always there is the continuity of scientific evolution to control the interpretations. And this precludes the acceptance of doctrines as merely reactions or products of reactions localizable at particular places at given times. There is the test of how close the reactions of workers at any point in the scientific evolution in question adhere to the criterion of keeping close to the events that are the subject matter of their science. In the original scientific situations all the operations, results, and laws must be evaluated in relation to the original events. On the historical level the same criteria are decisive.

Criteria arising from the fact that the history of science is itself a scientific enterprise control the scope of any historical treatment of a particular science. The specific events of the continuity may not be treated as isolated occasions. Since history is continuous the historian of science may not concern himself merely with arbitrarily chosen episodes. His aim should rather be the description of the evolutionary process insofar as he is able to obtain reliable evidence concerning the component details of past happenings.

CHAPTER 3

SCIENCE AS A CULTURAL INSTITUTION

SCIENTIFIC INSTITUTIONS AND THEIR CULTURAL MATRICES

TO ROUND OUT our general orientation to scientific history we should consider the institutional nature and origin of science. It is a basic assumption of the critical historian of science that all the scientific enterprises constitute specialized institutions set in their particular cultural matrices. Each science is thus envisaged as a definite establishment of interests, operations, and achievements with respect to a particular class of events. The soil or cultural matrix in which each particular institution germinates and grows consists of the specific societal circumstances which provide the conditions of origin and development. Only certain cultural conditions and not others favor the interest in science at all or in specific viewpoints and doctrines. The study of such cultural processes supplies the only legitimate referent for the term "cultural causation."

When we study the cultural matrices of the sciences we add greatly to our understanding of much that happens in the particular sciences. For example, if one asks why atomism is derived from Ionia and why Newton's corpuscular theory could dominate physics for several centuries, one may find an answer by considering the particular set of cultural circumstances amid which the theory originated and to which it was adapted. Probably psychology, wherever it flourishes, shows even more than the other sciences its deep rooting in its cultural background. The relations of scientific institutions and their cultural backgrounds can be equally well observed whether we focus on the general evolution of science, the development of the individual sciences, or the origin and evolution of specific theories, methods, or applications.

The existence of general science institutions depends upon the status of a particular community living at a particular place with various relationships to other groups. Among the factors favorable for the development of science may be mentioned a comparatively sizable and well organized population. Again it is clear that the life circumstances of the group, the ease or difficulty of maintaining its members, may favor or hinder the development of knowledge, research, and speculation.

The inception of the special sciences is favored by cultural circumstances which allow for a measure of specialization within the general scientific situation. The special sciences clearly represent concentrations of encounters with certain kinds of events stimulated by particular science needs, and the deliberate and accidental availability of tools and techniques of investigation. The operation of particular cultural factors is well illustrated by the question of a recent writer[1] who asks why there is so much interest in fuel cells in America and in Germany but not in England, where they were originally developed and where they are more needed than elsewhere. His own answer suggests unique social conditions, such as government sponsorship of military research and far-sighted private enterprise.

The influence of cultural matrices upon the development of particular doctrines, types of investigation, and modes of interpretation is made obvious by the concrete facts of scientific development. History indicates the origin of corpuscular (Newton) and atomic (Dalton) theories to be in England, evolution theory in England (Darwin, Wallace), physiology and organic chemistry in Germany. Certain communities and their cultural circumstances become selectively favorable for particular scientific developments in different periods. Thus physiology and blood circulation can be associated with Padua and London in the seventeenth century, while German centers become prominent for the development of biology in the nineteenth century.

When we turn to the scene of psychological science we find that England is fertile ground for atomic mind theories whereas the Continent provides more favorable soil for unified mind notions. Again, experimental psychology definitely begins in Germany (Weber, Fechner, Wundt), while in France abnormal or medical psychology flourishes. Within Germany, too, we have a differentiation between the northern acceptance of experimentation in psychology whereas southern districts are less favorable. In more recent days we observe a widely variable receptivity for psychoanalytic doctrines in certain countries while on the whole behaviorism and reflexology flourish in the United States and the Soviet Union but not elsewhere. All these variations suggest specific interrelations of doctrines and methods with particular social, economic, and political circumstances. Nor can we overlook the fact that the establishment of specific scientific disciplines and doctrines provides cultural matrices favorable or unfavorable to later doctrines and methods of work.

[1] F. T. Bacon, "Fuel Cells: Will they soon become a major Source of Electrical Energy," *Nature,* 1960, **186,** 589-592.

THE SCIENTIFIC SIGNIFICANCE OF CULTURAL ORIGINS

Our brief review of the interrelations of scientific institutions and their cultural matrices has suggested how important such interrelations are for the establishment of the sciences. Now we want to point to the deep and abiding influence of cultural origins upon the character and further development of scientific work. It is well known how constructs developed under particular and sometimes limited contacts with events take on the character of accepted presuppositions and established principles and axioms. The antidote to this preference for instituted constructs as against the claims of observed events is to trace back the institutions of science to their origins in the actual circumstances of everyday behavior. This procedure helps in the analysis of crucial problems and in the evaluation of the degree of success with which they have been solved.

The study of scientific origins reveals the operations of investigators; for example, whether they make their first observations and propose their first descriptions because of a free curiosity about events or through the stimulation of practical needs. Of especial importance is the question whether the subsequent developments are primarily influenced by the events confronted by the investigator or by notions derived from some other sources than the interest in concrete happenings. How far has physics developed from technology and how much has it in turn contributed to technological developments? Has chemistry evolved exclusively from the alchemical search for an elixir of life or a philosopher's stone, or also from problems arising out of such practical pursuits as tanning, mining, brewing, and the like.

Generally speaking, cultural origins supply us with the actual conditions which exist at the birth and evolution of the sciences. In the simplest stages we get information about operations or practices while on the more complex levels we learn about the assumptions, that is the hypotheses and the postulates which guide the scientists in their work. Of most importance, probably, is the light cultural origins shed on specific doctrines or ways of thinking. Consider a few examples from the psychological domain. There is hardly a doubt that all the complicated current lore concerning end-organs, and especially receptors, as mediators of mental states has arisen from such humble beginnings as the specification of what parts of organisms are primarily concerned with observed actions. When psychology originated, the simple observation was made that the eye was central to seeing, that the mouth was concerned with tasting and speaking, the ear with hearing, the nose with smelling, and so on. In Plato's poetry the head is the master of the body because in it "all the ruling senses are by nature set."[2] As psychology developed, such simple localizations became transformed into sophisticated structure-function ideas about the connection of anatomical parts with mental faculties and powers.

THEORIES CONCERNING THE GENERAL CULTURAL ORIGIN OF SCIENCE

That science is a phase of culture and has had a definite cultural origin must be admitted by all students of scientific history. But they do not agree upon the details of scientific origins. Usually students of culture adopt presuppositions which bypass the concrete details rooted in the naturalistic character of scientific activities and in the objective postulates covering the nature of men who engender scientific enterprises and institutions.

SCIENCE EVOLVES FROM MAGIC. A striking and famous formulation of this hypothesis is that of Frazer.[3] It is built on two pillars. One is the evolutionism of the nineteenth century which Frazer has focalized as the cultural succession of magic, religion, science. In a sense this hypothesis is behavioral in nature. It proposes to account for the varying and successive ways in which human actions developed from remotest primitivity to the heights of civilization. When primitive man resorts to magical practices he relies on his own strength and powers to adjust himself to a hard and hostile environment. But when this fails he advances to the religious stage in which he throws himself humbly upon the mercies of invisible, powerful beings. Evolution, however, is taken to be an onward and upward process so the inevitable third stage, that of science, is reached.

What is objectionable in the hypothesis is first its utter simplicity and abstractness. Magic, religion, and science are all taken as simple and discrete entities. When we treat these as institutions we find the concrete and complex behaviors involved quite distinctive and yet very similar in various particulars. Certainly they are not spread out on a unilinear scale of development so that one begins only after another ends. Scientific ways of acting, though to be sure in an incipient and simple way, are not to be denied to so-called primitives. Nor, of course, are so-called evolved peoples to be granted the boon of not behaving

[2] *Laws,* 943a.
[3] *The Golden Bough,* Vol. XI: *Balder the Beautiful,* pp. 304 *ff. et passim.*

magically or superstitiously. For Frazer, however, behavior is only an outer manifestation of internal mental processes. So his hypothesis stands on a psychical second pillar. Frazer assimilates the associationistic psychology of his day. Accordingly, he regards magical processes as false analyses of the similarity and contiguity aspects of the association of ideas. For example, the magical harming of an enemy can be accomplished by making a doll resembling him; when some actual thing belonging to him such as hair or some article of wearing apparel is made the basis of magical action, it is the law of contiguity that is falsified. Clearly such an analogical hypothesis could only appear plausible to one who shares the same climate of opinion as Frazer, who formulated it.

SCIENCE EVOLVES FROM SOCIAL BEHAVIOR. A contrasting hypothesis takes its departure not only from a more naturalistic psychology, but also from a more analytic attitude concerning man and his societies. The central feature of this hypothesis is that science has gradually evolved through actual contacts with objects, conditions, and the consequences of interacting with them. Vigorously eliminated are all arbitrarily constructed powers and principles such as social and mental forces presumed to determine the evolution of science.

The social evolution hypothesis demands the rejection of the fallacious view that primitive man acted on the basis of transcendent principles of any variety. It is a false accusation that primitive man peopled his world with transpatial entities and powers. It is equally false that he did not live in a natural world and carry on his activities as adjustments to the actual animals, plants, and inorganic objects and conditions he encountered.

It is doubtless the properly condemned theory of unilinear evolution that is responsible for the notion that aboriginal people were absolutely different and inferior from later so-called civilized men. Fortunately even if this kind of thinking, so well represented by Lévy-Brühl[4] and other philosophers, has not entirely run its course, it does meet with strong opposition.[5] So powerful has been the projective technique of imposing spiritistic characteristics upon aboriginal people that highly evolved and sophisticated modes of thinking have been attributed to them, though with a complete absence of evidence. Here is a striking example of a fairly complete replacement of actual events by a copious set of unfounded contructs.

[4] *Primitive Mentality.*
[5] See Radin, *The World of Primitive Man.*

INCEPTION AND DEVELOPMENT OF SPECIAL SCIENCES

Like the general scientific enterprise, the individual disciplines have arisen as specialized interests in particular types of events. Mathematics, astronomy, physics, biology, and psychology as well as the *social sciences* have become instituted through multifarious contacts with particular classes of events. The historical origin of the sciences is suggested by the term *history,* which originally referred to investigation. For example, Aristotle's *Historia Animalium* signifies a direction of scientific interest toward the events we now classify as zoology.

Scientific history records that psychology is an early scientific institution. The organized study of psychological events was established as long ago as the Greeks, although the name psychology is a late derivation dating back only to the sixteenth century. Klemm asserts that Melanchthon used the name psychology for some academic lectures, while R. Göckel in 1590 made it the collective title for the works of various authors.[6] It was probably Wolff who really established the term by using it in the titles of his two volumes, *Psychologia Rationalis,* dated 1732, and *Psychologia Empirica,* dated 1734. His master Leibniz still used the term "pneumatology."

There is no difficulty at all in specifying what the events are that belong to psychology as a scientific specialty alongside the other sciences. Simply stated, they consist of the actions of organisms performing various types of responses to particular objects, including other organisms. Though psychologists historically have tended to stress the actions of the organisms, it is plain that they have had to connect such actions with the so-called stimulating objects as well as with the organisms. This fact will be thoroughly demonstrated in our treatment of the earliest organized documents, namely, the Aristotelian writings (Chap. 9). It is the office of psychological history to study the way in which students of psychological events have described and interpreted them. As we shall see such descriptions and interpretations will mirror the cultural conditions of individual persons and periods throughout the development of the science.

Science is frequently defined in terms of its final formalized products as a system of propositions and equations embodying the laws concerning events. Nevertheless, this is an improper procedure. It is grossly misleading to overstress the end product to the neglect of the many complex operations which eventuate in those laws. To bypass all that happens when laws are developed makes possible the

[6] *History of Psychology,* p. 147.

confounding of events with law propositions and even with the language expressing these propositions. Such a confusion of constructs with original events obscures the fact that scientific laws are always functions of particular assumptions, apparatus, and operations. Yet we know that scientific knowledge is subject to constant correction which makes plain that all constructs are only selective samples from several probabilities.

The overstressing of the products, the formulae, gives rise to an undesirable rationalism. Room is thus made for trading in abstractions and for a disregard of the specific events that provide the basis and the opportunities for scientific work and make possible the application of the laws. The neglect of the sources of scientific laws leads in its turn to a false view of science and permits misinterpretation of its subject matter and hence of the proper procedures for studying it. Contrariwise, to keep alert to the actual evolution of particular sciences enables scientific workers to avoid, in part at least, the pitfalls mentioned. In the case of psychology, for example, we will not be misled into thinking that it is concerned with intangible and unobservable processes rather than with interbehaviors of organisms and stimulus objects.

We insist, then, upon the study of a science as a stage reached in a comparatively long evolution. As a type of interbehavior with specific kinds of events, even the most complex stages of science, in which the investigative operations and the products attained are both enormously complicated, not only look forward to greater and more effective complexity but also backward to the simpler stages from which they have developed. Scientific systems are all rooted in earlier presystemic periods which antedate organized research and the accumulation of theories. In the unsystemized stages the prescientific behavior has to do with practical adjustments to everyday life conditions. The food and shelter requirements of human animals provides an effective source for the development of instituted wisdom, scientific habits, and knowledge systems. In effect all the sciences including the most elaborate and abstruse have their sources in institutional beliefs, technology, social organization, commerce, and art.[7]

The following brief inspection of the nascent or protoscientific stages of some current sciences indicates some of the things and events which stimulated and maintained investigative interest.

[7] The view that the sciences originate in the living conditions of particular cultural groups is not to be confused with the Marxian doctrine of universal economic determination.

Protomathematics

Without pretending that we can actually arrange in order the various stages or intervals that mark the evolution of any science, we may still regard the protoscience of mathematics to be concerned with the processes of ordering, counting, weighing and measuring, as they have arisen in social evolution. It is unnecessary to assume any such questionable faculty as a number sense in infrahuman and human organisms as mathematical historians sometimes propose. It is sufficient to take into account the obvious interbehavior with relations of various sorts as occasioned by the increasing complexities of life conditions.

As specific examples of protomathematical situations and adjustments we may include: (a) the activities of the rope stretchers in the evolution of geometry; (b) the innumerable processes of matching, tallying, counting, calculating, and the recording of numbers, amounts and rates; (c) the invention and discovery of notation and instruments for handling groups, collections, and relations; and (d) the occasions for and the development of increasingly abstract procedures to replace concrete adjustments to place and time relations. We are assuming here a definite, though irregular continuity between all the various concrete protomathematical behavior of persons and complex developments of the geometric, algebraic, and analytic branches of the mathematical sciences.

Protomedicine

Nowhere in the entire domain of human behavior and civilization does the continuity of practice and knowledge stand out so starkly as in the field of health, sickness, and the processes of overcoming such maladjustments. Though we can know comparatively little of the actual development of the behavior of primitive man with respect to his own ills and those of his family and neighbors, still there are so many outstanding facts known about human organisms, their environments, and their maladjustments that we may feel entirely confident concerning the medical aspect of the protosciences. Even about many details we are fortunate to have available such a monumental work as Sigerist's *History of Medicine* to guide us toward data and sources which illustrate the evolution of paleopathology and paleotherapy into authentic medical science.

As indicators of some of the things and events which have played a part in the prescientific evolution of medicine consider what is known about the most primitive surgeons who trephined the skull for the purpose of relieving or curing patients. Even if Broca were partially correct in ascribing other than medical motives to such operations, it is hardly likely that the therapeutic intention was entirely absent from such activities. With respect to the curative and lethal effects of various vegetative substances we have a great store of authentic information. It does not matter that the primitives who used curare or other poisonous substances for their purposes knew almost nothing as compared with a chemist about the chemical nature of what they handled so well. To dissociate the prechemical and chemical periods and not to allow one to be in any sense the precursor of the other is to believe it possible to break the continuity of cultural development and to deny the existence and the effectiveness of the evolutional process. Certainly we cannot overlook the debt which the modern physician owes to the preliterate practitioners for handing on to him such substances as opium, cocoa, cinchona, ephedrine, caffeine, cascara sagrada, chaulmoogra, digitalis, ipecacuanha, podophyllum, pyrethrum, squill, and many others.[8]

Protosociology

It is hardly necessary to mention particular sources of origin for any of the social sciences inasmuch as there can be no hiatus between the processes of sheer living and the elementary behavior of reflecting about it. It is just as unnecessary to try and locate the particular point of origin of reflective behavior in the human animal. We need only indicate that all the complicated sciences of politics, economics, anthropology, and historiography are surely derived by a long and devious process from the earliest observations of social organization, interpersonal relations, and the need for and achievement of adaptations to the organic and inorganic surroundings.

What the character of the earliest forms of social science were we can easily infer from our earliest documents. For one thing there was probably an insalubrious admixture of the moral and the descriptive. Early social science was doubtless replete with social exhortation, the decrying of improper interpersonal relations in one's own group, and the justification of the favorable strata by those who occupied them. Furthermore, after the differentiation of the individual social sciences we find much curiosity exercised in comparisons and interpretations of varying social systems with the institutions of particular writers serving as criteria.

[8] Sigerist, *History of Medicine,* Vol. I. pp. 203-04. McKenzie, *The Infancy of Medicine,* Chap. 2.

Protocosmology

The evolutional origins of physics, chemistry, and astronomy can be more or less authentically traced back by a series of zigzag stages to the nonspecialized observations and speculations of aboriginal men. It is inconceivable that men even as early as the Cro-Magnon stage did not perform fairly elaborate reactions to the striking objects and conditions in their environment, such as the stars and planets, the conditions of the atmosphere, the floods of rivers and dryness of the land, and thunder and lightning, as well as the effects of all these on their own living conditions. And so it appears inevitable that an accumulation of many interactions and their results should develop toward increasingly effective formulations concerning the recurrence of all varieties of inorganic events. Such in general is the origin and evolution of all the astronomical, physical, and chemical sciences.

Enforcing the evolutional notion of the inorganic sciences is the enormous quantity of available records for the interconnection of man's daily activities and his development of technologies of every variety with the eventual appearance of a culminating scientific stage. There seems to be no good reason for assuming a break in the continuity of simple and complex interactions of men with the things and events of their environment. What prehistoric man discovered about fire, stone, and their relative properties are nuclei of our sciences. What early men knew about copper, iron, silver, sulphur, and other elements is incorporated in our chemistry.

In the way of our accepting the continuity and evolution of primitive knowledge toward modern science stand some preconceptions concerning the nature of our early ancestors. When we muster large quantities of facts depicting the reactions of successions of people to surrounding things and events we should be deterred from imposing exclusively magical characteristics upon man in his early development. It is undeniable that men have always intermixed superfluous rituals with their more relevant practices, but we must distinguish rituals, however unnecessary and redundant, from sophisticated theories about nonnatural and spiritistic entities and powers.

Protobiology

Many of the same events which have given rise to protomedicine have played their part in the development of the earliest stages of biological science. To these may be added facts connected with the way primitive men interacted with animals and plants of all sorts. If we think of human development as passing through a food gathering stage and a hunting stage there opens a broad vista of activities centering around the search for and acquaintance with the location of desirable food objects. We must infer the development of considerable knowledge about plants and their noxious and valuable properties. One of the earliest evidences of the development of anatomical knowledge is taken to be the Pindal cave drawing depicting a mammoth with the location of its heart. It is inferred that aboriginal man knew enough about animals to appreciate the most vulnerable spot.

With the development of agriculture and animal domestication the knowledge of biological events must have increased at a very rapid pace. An understanding of the nature and behavior of animals is definitely a prerequisite for a successful preoccupation with them. It is well known how early in human history man was concerned with problems of increase and kinds of offspring of both human and nonhuman organisms. It is fair to say that genetics, though formulated and named by Bateson, is a very early branch of biological lore.

Protopsychology

Because the events belonging to the psychological domain are intimately interrelated with those of physics, chemistry, medicine and biology, the development of psychology has included some of the steps which have led to the evolution of the other sciences. The events that belong to the special psychological domain were of course available to aboriginal men from the earliest periods of human evolution. Accordingly, our present knowledge of the behavior of organisms is continuous with that of the earliest builders of our common culture. It is no idle speculation that the dietary needs of early man made it necessary for him to develop a great deal of knowledge concerning the behavioral traits of the animals he hunted. The same thing is true when primitive people had to prevent other animals from attacking them and their families. Anthropological literature is replete with illustrations of the ingenuity early men employed to take advantage of the habits of animals. Linton describes a trap based on a knowledge of the persistence of guinea fowl in pecking on hard substances until they became disabled and easily taken.[9]

The advent of animal domestication marks a high point in the evolution of protopsychology.[10] Whatever may have been the motives or the procedures for this very important aspect of cultural evolution, the net

[9] *The Tree of Culture,* p. 83 *f.*

[10] See Zeuner, "Domestication of Animals" in Singer, Holmyard, and Hall, eds., *A History of Technology,* Vol. I, pp. 327-352.

result for the increase in biological and psychological knowledge was gigantic. It is an inevitable inference that the domestication of animals forced upon the domesticators the necessity and opportunity to evolve close and precise observations. It is evident, however, that even before opportunities existed for observations on other species of animals through domestication, primitive man was perforce greatly stimulated by the behavior of individuals of his own kind, including himself. There are a great many occasions for the observation of the behavior of infants, children, and adults in personal interrelations, and in the way individuals themselves deal with things and animals during the evolution of tool making and using in all the manifold situations of daily life.

We have intended to make clear that as a cultural institution the science of psychology may be regarded as firmly founded on the constantly available behavioral events. That such reactions could be the basis for the most precise observations and manipulations it is not hard to believe. It is an unfortunate, though understandable fact that students of primitive behavior have imposed interpretive notions upon it which they derived from cultural conventions. Accordingly, writers on primitive behavior have alleged that primitive man had miraculously looked upon his world with the dualistic eyes of Western European culture and hence peopled it with ghosts and many other transcendent entities. We are referring, of course, to the nineteenth century notions of animism and animatism.

The typical way that anthropological and psychological writers treat the reactions of primitive people to the events they encounter is to impose upon them characteristics derived from the sophisticated culture of the outside observer. Accordingly, anthropologists and psychologists interpret the reactions of primitive observers as dominated by ideas of transcendent powers generally referred to as souls. Probably the best example of this imposition of soul and the supernatural upon primitive people is Tylor's theory, which has dominated the thinking of anthropologists and psychologists for almost a century. This theory holds that primitive men speculated upon the difference between living and dead individuals, and on the nature of the human shapes which appear in dreams, and thus developed ideas about the animation of all objects in nature. As Crawley points out,[11] this dream theory was partially anticipated by Hobbes in the seventeenth century.[12] But if

[11] *The Idea of the Soul,* p. 5.
[12] Cf. *Leviathan,* Chs. 2 and 12.

the interpreters of primitive peoples impose dualistic views upon them, such attributions still take on specialized forms. A brief glance at some of these mistaken notions, which clearly are incongruous with the underlying facts, may help us to understand the evolution of the psychological tradition.

HISTORICAL MISCONSTRUCTIONS CONCERNING ABORIGINAL PEOPLES

PRIMITIVES AS UNEVOLVED AND INFERIOR. A tremendous obstacle in the way of understanding primitive people and their place in psychological evolution is to envisage them not as merely different from current populations but as made in an altogether unique mold. Anthropologists and ethnologists have traditionally been misled into believing that primitive peoples were situated on lower rungs of the evolutional ladder. They believed that human beings have evolved both mentally and physically in a sequential and linear manner so that there actually are or have been savages, barbarians, and civilized groups of peoples. Primitive peoples are treated as masses of identical units, are said not to react to things in natural ways and are in consequence ignorant, unobserving, superstitious, and lacking in intelligence. Some of the evidence adduced to support such erroneous attitudes are that primitive peoples cannot distinguish between animate and inanimate objects, do not know the role of the male in reproduction, cannot count beyond three or five, lack the power to generalize, and in other ways behave as unevolved creatures.[13]

The list of proponents of this view makes an impressive roster. But there are many prominent writers ranged on the other side. A most commendable naturalistic view characterizes the work of Payne,[14] Crawley,[15] Thomas,[16] and Radin.[17]

PRIMITIVES AS MYSTICAL. One of the most distinctive views concerning the impassable gap between primitive and sophisticated people is that the former lack logical minds. It is alleged that they look upon the world in a mystical and prelogical way.[18] They have no appreciation of the causal principle, the law of contradiction, and so on. It is interesting that a number of acute writers have attacked the prelogical view, but in the interest of the notion of psychic unity. This notion accords

[13] Cf. Thomas, *Primitive Behavior,* Ch. 18.
[14] *History of the New World Called America.*
[15] *Op. cit.*
[16] *Op. cit.*
[17] *Primitive Man as Philosopher,* and *The World of Primitive Man.*
[18] Lévy-Brühl, *How Natives Think* and *Primitive Mentality.*

all peoples an equal share in the common mentality of mankind. There is no intimation that both kinds of "mentality" are pure creations of spiritistic theory.

PRIMITIVES AS SPIRITISTIC. The most palpable imposition upon primitive peoples is to endow them with highly sophisticated ideas of two worlds, a psychic or spiritual one and a material one. Even those anthropologists who do not believe that a chasm exists between primitive and modern men endow primitives with ideas of the psychic such as are formulated and accepted by the prevalent European culture. Primitives are regarded as participating in the transcendental notion of soul. For example, when Crawley in his excellent study of the idea of the soul criticizes Tylor's theory of the soul, he merely disagrees with Tylor's view that primitives derive their ideas from the observation of dreams. Among his arguments is the notion that dreams are abnormal. Crawley wants to account for the origin of the idea of the soul among primitive people by the more pervasive and substantial "fact" of the existence of the mental itself. And so he traces back the idea of the soul and the supernatural to the operations of memory as over against direct perception. He declares that the spiritual world is the mental world under another name.[19]

What is lacking in this interpretation is any differentiation between events and constructs. Crawley complains that such a view as Tylor's suffers from the fact that it was formulated before the development of experimental psychology. Actually, his own view suffers from the fact that it antedates the development of an objective or behavioral view of psychology. Nothing is easier than to take account of the actual descriptions of primitive behavior—customs, rites, and reported beliefs—without imposing upon the originals the results of mentalistic ways of thinking.

The remarkable power of current mentalistic institutions is shown by the fact that critical students of primitive people are aware of the palpable and material character of the "soul" ideas as discovered among primitive people. For example, Payne in the book mentioned asserts,

> The conception of a spirit as a being composed, not of flesh and blood, but of some ethereal matter, is not fully established until the age of civilization, and has no fixed or recognized place, although it sometimes intrudes, in the ideas of savage or barbarous man. In these stages man for the most part remains a materialist. These imaginary beings are considered to be equally substantial with man himself. Thus in Australia the evil spirits,

[19] *Op. cit.*, p. 193.

when conquered, are killed, cooked, and eaten: in Western Africa, the spirit who wanders through the forest, catching and killing travellers, is himself met and resisted by a body of men, who wound him with spears, and sometimes kill him, in which case his body must be burnt, even to the smallest bone.[20]

Frazer, too, declares that the savage thinks of life or soul

as a concrete material thing of a definite bulk, capable of being seen and handled, kept in a box or jar, and liable to be bruised, fractured, or smashed to pieces.[21]

Finally Crawley says,

we may note that not until civilization has made some progress does the soul acquire an immaterial substantiality.[22]

From all this our conclusion must be that primitive notions of psychological behavior can only be interpreted as definite responses, verbal creations, developed in the framework of the culture of their time. It is impossible to believe otherwise than that primitives respond to things that happen on the basis of such cultural factors as (a) ignorance—the lack of instituted lore and genuine information, and (b) the kind of linguistic forms—myths, proverbs, folk tales, and so on current at the time.

TECHNIQUES OF FALLACIOUS CONSTRUCTION

Because all constructive activities consist of immediate adjustments to things and events or mediate adaptations to alleged events, fallacious constructions are simply behaviors of a purely linguistic sort or a more complex type of action—judgments, decisions, interpretations—involving linguistic components. These activities depart in some manner from the criterion that adjustments should correspond to events. On the scientific level fallacious constructions fail to provide more or less faithful, direct or indirect descriptions of the characteristics of things and events. How faithfully one can adhere to the criterion mentioned depends, of course, upon many situational factors, for example, availability of events for observation, availability of apparatus when necessary, the ability to avoid undue selection of properties, and the chance to counteract the influence of scientific traditions. For illustrative purposes we are indicating four of the techniques for constructing fallacious propositions about things and events.

[20] *Op. cit.*, Vol. I, p. 391.
[21] *The Golden Bough*, Vol. XI, *Balder the Beautiful*, p. 95.
[22] *Op. cit.*, p. 57.

MYTHOPOEIC SUBSTITUTION. When events are insufficiently known, when there is lacking an accumulation of records of the contacts with things and events, descriptions and explanations are created or supplied by supplementing with folklore elements. There is much inferential behavior exhibited in such theorizing procedures. Properties may be imposed upon things and events but these may be regarded as either naturalistic or not naturalistic, depending upon the cultural background of the myth maker. In the psychological domain the classic illustration is the substitution of soul, inner power, or the determination of visible behavior by irrational elements, for the interbehavior of organisms with things and events under specific surrounding circumstances.

INVALID HYPOTHESIZING. Though scientists are obviously concerned with raw data, they may describe such things and events by constructs that clearly do not fit them. Take, for example, the student of the nervous system who forgets that he is observing one of the numerous biological systems and endows it with psychic properties. He sets up the contrast between brain and body and makes the former into a seat of consciousness. Attributions are based upon hasty or inept analogies. Heat is regarded as a substance, for example, caloric or phlogiston. Interpretations may be based upon the accidents of observation and the fact that only certain kinds of operations can be performed upon some data. This technique of fallacious construction may be compounded of improper observation, biased belief, and faulty judgment or comparison.

CULTURAL IMPOSITION. In this type of description and interpretation the data are heavily outweighed by deliberate or nondeliberate cultural impositions. Culturally accepted properties of things mask those revealed by meticulous investigation. Primitive people are assumed to be motivated by the same conditions which obtain in the culture of the investigator's period. They are not envisaged as organisms adapting themselves to their actual environments by the natural means at their disposal but as operating with beliefs, ideas, and other institutions that could only have been developed at a much more complex and sophisticated level. Aboriginal people are presumed to distinguish between the natural and the supernatural and to know and speak about extrapolations beyond the spatiotemporal limits available to them.

AUTISTIC CONSTRUCTION. This is the process of dealing with things and events in almost complete departure from them. There is arbitrary creation of properties and relations in disregard of and sometimes open contempt for what is actually going on. The outstanding feature of this technique is the sort of linguistic manipuation which justifies perfectly Spencer's conception of metaphysics as a disease of language.[23]

ORIENTATIONAL SUMMARY

The results of our rather lengthy search for a proper orientation for our historical studies may be summed up as an adoption of interbehavioral principles. With respect to psychological science, the central presupposition is that, like all sciences, it is a concrete enterprise evolved to ascertain the nature of such interactions of organisms with stimulus objects as are popularly labeled sensing, thinking, feeling, reasoning, and so on. A further assumption is that all scientific work is continuous with earlier interactions of organisms, such as biological contacts with things and events and with more primitive physicochemical interbehavior of things.

Such continuity, on the one hand, makes possible a free development of science on the basis of accumulated contacts of persons with things and events. Scientific institutionalization carries with it a number of advantages for those who wish to know about things and events but also some hazards. The advantages lie in the increased opportunities for sustaining contacts with things by the establishment of standards, operational tools, and procedures, as well as concentrated efforts. The disadvantages center in the competition set up between authentic contacts with events and the social assumptions which lead to interpretation underived from contact with events. The history of psychology records the disservice of such assumptions as *man is a rational being, man is an irrational being, man is a dual or triple entity—mind and body or mind-body-spirit.*

As to history itself: On the interbehavioral basis historical work is of the same order as any kind of contact with things or events. The missing factors have to be ferreted out just as is the case when analyzing any current event, even of the simplest sort. The instruments and operations are in principle like those of any investigation. No intuitive or mystic powers are assumed in the one case any more then in the other. With this general orientation we are prepared to study the career of psychology. Let us consider first the origins of this scientific discipline.

[23] Cf. *Principles of Psychology,* Vol. II, p. 502.

SECTION TWO

THE HISTORICAL AND CULTURAL ORIGINS OF PSYCHOLOGICAL SCIENCE

CHAPTER 4

THE ORIGIN AND GROWTH OF PSYCHOLOGY

WHEN DOES THE HISTORY OF PSYCHOLOGY BEGIN?

BECAUSE THE SCIENCES represent uninterrupted evolutions from simpler forms of folk wisdom, it is impossible to pinpoint some definite date for the organization or founding of any particular science. Obviously no scientific system can appear fully formed at a particular historical moment. To specify when any scientific discipline originated is an arbitrary procedure which employs freely chosen criteria. Probably the most acceptable criterion is to discover when an attempt is first made to formulate and systemize propositions about a particular class of events and about the opinions and theories constructed concerning them.

On the whole, the earliest scientific propositions serve to identify the characteristics of a particular type of events and to distinguish them from other classes of events. We may call this the *definitional* or *classificatory* stage of scientific origins. Another stage is characterized by the collection of data and their analysis and comparison, and, in general, by the building up of a stockpile of information and record of contacts with such events. This we may call the *manipulative* or *operational* stage. A distinctive and relatively final stage of development arises when the system of assumptions or postulates which have been derived from the investigations are clarified. When this stage of formality is reached the science takes on a considerable measure of sophistication and stability. This stage of thorough scientific documentation may be called the *systematic* or *postulational* period of scientific evolution.

An effective example of stabilizing a science is afforded us by Euclid's scientific compilation called *The Elements.* Although the geometry of this period (3rd century B.C.) is simple and the document defective, *The Elements* does sum up the essential features of the subject matter and the study processes involved. It is evident, of course, that the elements and procedures were not as sharply distinct, one from another, as the treatise indicates. There is not in it the precise succession of

Definitions, Postulates, and Theorems or Propositions that Euclid suggests. In fact, the treatise is a system of mutually interacting factors which takes on the fixity and symmetry of organization only in the exposition. Nevertheless, *The Elements* exemplifies admirably the unmistakable point when a specific science of geometry was established.

For the science of psychology we have similar documents, so we can safely date the establishment of that discipline in a Greek environment as early as the fifth and fourth centuries B.C. Obviously, the types of documents which give witness to the establishment of the different sciences vary, but we can certainly accept part of Plato's *Phaedo* as such a document. It may be assumed that Socrates formulates the basic assumptions of psychological science when he sets forth his anti-physiological views and asserts that psychology or the interpretation of human behavior must be made in what we may call a motivational form.

It is impossible to overstress the fact that whatever formal statements or propositions are incorporated in the founding documents of the sciences, the assumptions and observational records have all emerged from simpler notions developed in a long succession of periods during which individuals have been in contact with behavioral events. As effective evidence of the continuity of technical formulations concerning psychological events with the earlier, informal but adequate observations, we may cite the many references to psychological events in our most ancient literatures. These references are not limited to simple ostensive statements but appear to be even more than elementary descriptions; in fact, they serve as explanations or interpretations. Outstanding among these descriptions are the many references to parts of the organism where the cognitive and affective actions were thought to have a local habitation or instrumental base. For example, there are many biblical passages specifying the close association of understanding, thinking,[1] sorrow, and rejoicing with the heart, compassion with the bowels in the sense of the viscera;[2] yearning with the liver; thought and intentions with the heart and kidneys.[3] We need only consider such statements as references to elementary observations of the conditions and changes in the organism when it performs the actions mentioned.

In the Homeric poems and in many other classical works we find similar associations made between psychological actions and particular parts of the organism. As one must expect, Homer mentions the heart

[1] "For as he thinketh in his heart so is he," *Proverbs* 23, 7.

[2] *I John* 3, 17.

[3] "I am he which searcheth the reins and hearts," *Revelation* 2, 23.

and diaphragm or lungs[4] as centers for affective behavior. In other writings the liver and other viscera play leading roles. As we shall see, this attempt to connect complex actions with special organs continues into the era of Aristotle's highly technical period of psychological description. It was Aristotle who set the fashion of connecting seeing with the eye as the organ, hearing with the ear as the organ, and so on. This fashion has continued throughout the development of psychology. It is poetically expressed in Shakespeare's

> Tell me where is fancy bred,
> Or in the heart or in the head.[5]

CRITERIA SUGGESTED FOR PSYCHOLOGICAL ORIGINS

When we mentioned that students of psychology rely upon arbitrary criteria to date the origin of psychology as a science we did not intend to imply that such criteria lack either relevance or value. On the contrary, an examination of some of these criteria yields considerable information about the course of psychological history.

Subject Matter Criterion. Aristotle, the first historian of psychology, declares that psychology was instituted as the study of that which originates movement and as that which senses or discriminates.[6] The former criterion he connects with Leucippus, Democritus, the Pythagoreans, and especially with Anaxagoras. Though the notions of movement-initiation were to a great extent cosmological, the version offered by Anaxagoras could be linked with organic behavior. The cognitive or discriminative criterion Aristotle connected with a long list of writers beginning with Empedocles. As Aristotle remarks, some writers adopt one of these criteria while others adopt both.[7]

The Formal Treatise Criterion. A well-recommended criterion is that a science becomes established not merely when the subject matter is effectively differentiated, but when it becomes organized. A further development of this criterion indicates that the organization of a discipline should specify the conditions and methods of study. On the basis of this enlarged criterion it is held that the admirable treatises of Aristotle warrant his designation as the founder of the science of psychology. Those who do not accept this criterion may point out that a science includes in addition to the accepted and established materials also the evolution of the study. As to the claim that Aristotle was the founder

[4] See Onians, *The Origins of European Thought,* Part I.
[5] *The Merchant of Venice,* iii, 2.
[6] *De Anima* 403^{b} 25.
[7] *Ibid.,* 404^{b} 27.

of scientific psychology, it is strongly supported by the fact that he makes psychology a definite branch of biological science.

The Experimental Criterion. Since the development of experimental psychology in the nineteenth century, a strong sentiment has grown to the effect that experimental methods must be stressed in psychology as a warrant of its scientific character. Accordingly, psychologists have insisted that only the experimental period of Weber, Fechner, and Wundt is the authentic starting point of psychological science. Obviously, this criterion stresses methods and manipulations with blatant disregard of the subject matter to which the methods are presumed to apply. In consequence it is assumed that one can experiment upon subject matter which is in principle different from the things and events manipulated by all other experimental scientists. Critics of experimentation as an exclusive and arbitrary criterion point out that on the one hand it induces psychologists to neglect important types of data and that on the other experimentalists even of our day build their psychological systems upon constructs—for example, sensations, ideas, brain centers—that are no different from those developed by metaphysicians and theologians of medieval times and even earlier.

The Behavioristic Criterion. Behavioristic, that is anti-mentalistic psychologists, insist that scientific psychology began only when the behavior of nonhuman organisms became the subject matter of psychology. On this basis it was not the classic mentalistic-introspectionistic experiments but animal studies which made psychology into a science. It is easy to recognize the valuable points in this suggestion, but no less easy to see that it narrows the field to a very small part of the whole and also leaves the way open for those interested in complex human behavior to perpetuate the mentalistic doctrines of previous historical periods.

The Continuity-Corrigibility Criterion. We have already mentioned that the criterion adopted in this book is that the science of psychology originated when an interest in the psychological type of interbehavior became instituted. This means that we must look for a certain date when some satisfying (valid) principles were formally set down. Our criterion presupposes that psychological science reveals a continuity similar to that found in all the sciences, a continuity in which elementary and casual attitudes and judgments became more complex propositional systems as students became more familiar with the events of their specialty. Implied here is the view that science is an enterprise displaying the constant correction and improvement of specific constructs and the total system.

To a certain extent the five criteria concerning psychological origins themselves illustrate the continuity and corrigibility principle. More effectively, perhaps, they illustrate that views about science, no less than scientific propositions, arise out of a cultural background existing at the time and place the views are formulated.

HISTORY OF PSYCHOLOGY: INTELLECTIVE-TECHNOLOGICAL COMPLEXES

If we grant that psychology, like all sciences, was evolved as a specialized institution within the framework of Western European culture, we have implicitly adopted a view concerning all sorts of particular relationships. At every stage of evolution psychology must be considered in its mutual interconnections with other intellectual institutions of the time. Also, at every stage of evolution we must be alive to the interrelation of psychology with the current technological circumstances. It is such technological conditions which influence the development of precise observation and apparatus for experimentation. It is not to be thought, however, that any science or other item of culture becomes so isolated and autonomous as to operate exclusively upon or to influence other more passive components. On the contrary, all the factors of a scientific situation constitute mutually interacting features of a large cultural complex.

The continuities and interrelations of scientific situations and their connections with social and political circumstances are based, of course, on the general continuity of cultural and noncultural events. As culture becomes more complex and specializations of cultural components become increasingly refined, their interrelations become more rather than less marked. For example, because events are complex as well as continuous, the various specialized studies remain closely related. Psychological events are at the same time biological events and, when the stimulus objects are taken into account along with the activities of organisms, they are likewise physiochemical events.

A consequence of special importance follows from the interrelations of all the factors in a cultural complex. This is the community of both valid and invalid scientific principles. For example, scientific progress may be participated in by all or most of the sciences of a given period and by the same token they may all share in a common regression. When psychologists concern themselves with sensations or other psychic processes, physicists and other scientists cling to the same invalid doctrines. The continuity of culture makes it inevitable that a dualistic separation of substances into psychic and material should affect physics as well as psychology.

Nothing that we have said overlooks the fact that at times particular sciences may become independent and even dominant. In our own culture it is often the physicochemical sciences that achieve the dominant position. Psychology, on the other hand, has historically lacked recognition and even stability and coherence. Moreover, there have been historical periods when psychology was almost completely dissolved in a theologico-philosophical solvent.

STAGES IN PSYCHOLOGICAL EVOLUTION

Standing at the present point of psychology's most advanced and complex development, we may easily look backward and discern numerous successive stages of growth and expansion which have emerged after that dim period when psychology originated. Despite the inversions and transformations which psychology has experienced, the steps in its evolution are clearly visible. We select three such stages to illustrate the entire series.

Prescientific Stage. At this period in the dim past there occurred the naive and simple observations which gradually grew into a permanent interest in the interbehavior of human and infrahuman organisms with their surrounding stimuli. It is no strain to imagine that the necessities of daily living forced upon aboriginal man the dull or keen appreciation that it was important to understand the reactions of individuals to other persons, nonhuman organisms, and things. It is a safe speculation that at this stage was established a simple interest in what eventually became a science of psychology.

Protoscientific Stage. The nascent scientific stage of psychology begins roughly with the invention of writing in various parts of the world. The protoscientific stage of psychology is characterized by the appearance of records, not only of what activities have been observed but also of the opinions and beliefs as to how these events occurred. What became embodied in the records of epic and lyric poetry were to a great extent reports of what happened to observers under various conditions of interpersonal encounters. These reports may be characterized as self-inspective.

It is in the later phases of this protoscientific stage that we find the relatively more abstract description of what happened to the observer while performing acts of shame, rejoicing, thinking, suffering, and the like. As these reports became relatively technical, psychology attained the many descriptions of the localization of behavior in those organs that are prominent when psychological actions are performed.[8] Because of the stability and permanence of the institution marking the brain as somehow a central feature of psychological performances, we must point to the great chorus of writers, both ancient and modern, who have lauded Alcmaeon for sponsoring this view.[9]

Authentic Scientific Stage. The Greeks were the first, so far as we can tell, to establish an authentic psychological science. It is one of the remarkable features of psychological history that as early as the fourth century B.C. a definite and systematic treatise should be created. There is no doubt that the Aristotelian corpus constitutes a formal system which is the culmination of previous observations and reflections concerning psychological events. The psychological works of Aristotle, though they may be only lecture notes prepared by Aristotle or his students, are systematic descriptions of a number of basic and important psychological events. In structure the Aristotelian corpus actually consists of a series of monographs covering the history, basic problems, and many data of psychology. When we study the details of the Aristotelian system in Chapter 9 we shall find that many of its propositions fall readily into the framework, first, of biology and, beyond that, of physics.

Although we regard the psychological corpus of Aristotle as the documentary origin of an authentic psychological science, it represents, of course, the end product of much scientific work. As we know, the complex enterprise of science consists probably for the most part of elaborate interbehavior of workers—that is, observers, manipulators, calculators, and law constructors with certain types of events. In their best form, scientific treatises consist of the records and products of such scientific workers as we have mentioned. From the standpoint of the history of a science the existence of treatises such as those in the Aristotelian corpus is the best available evidence concerning the work of investigators and the results they have achieved in their time.

In the next two chapters we trace the roots of Greek psychological science in the surface soil of Greek scientific institutions and in the deeper layers of general Hellenic civilization.

[8] See above pp. 52-53.

[9] See, for example, Farrington, *Greek Science,* Vol. I, p. 51; Ackerknecht, *A Short History of Medicine,* p. 48; and Sarton, *A History of Science,* Vol. I. pp. 333, 355, 357.

SECTION THREE

THE HELLENIC SYSTEMIZATION OF PSYCHOLOGY

CHAPTER 5

THE CULTURAL BACKGROUND OF HELLENIC PSYCHOLOGY

THE GREEK ESTABLISHMENT OF PSYCHOLOGICAL SCIENCE

A FAIRLY COMPREHENSIVE system of psychology came into being in Athens as the work of Aristotle in the fourth century B.C. But the Aristotelian system was not merely comprehensive, providing a treatment of many important psychological events; it was in the best sense of the term scientific. As we know, the initiation of a specialized science presupposes the existence of a favorable intellectual matrix which, in turn, is rooted in a suitable cultural substratum. What then are the characteristics of Hellenic civilization that proved to be the source of this remarkable achievement? We hope that this question does not suggest the operation of some magical cause or determining conditions. The wise course here is to seek a set of cultural circumstances which parallel the traits of the psychological system mentioned. Since Aristotle developed a naturalistic and objective description of the psychological events that he treated, we may legitimately inquire into the facts of Hellenic social, economic, and political life which correspond to the characteristics of Greek psychological thinking. In other words, we may ask what are the primary characteristics of Greek cultural institutions?

Obviously there is a selective process involved here, one that we hope reflects the Hellenic social conditions that really existed. We may well admit that so complex a thing as Hellenic society comprises numerous traits, not all of which are congruous, while each is more or less fluid, as cultural traits always are. The reader will note, too, that the following selected characteristics are not always entirely independent of the others and sometimes are actually aspects of a common trait. Furthermore, while our theme concerns Hellenic social characteristics, the descriptions will sometimes be especially or even exclusively applicable to Athenian society.

GREEK ATOMIC SOCIETY. Hellenic civilization is characterized by an extreme atomism. The Greeks were divided and subdivided into small units. These were called *poleis,* a term usually translated as city states. But, as Kitto points out, "the normal *polis* was not much like a city, and was very much more than a state."[1] In numbers a *polis* might contain about five thousand inhabitants including women and children, as well as slaves. Plato believed that a *polis* of this size was the ideal group. The Athenian *polis* with which we shall be especially concerned had a population of somewhat more than twenty thousand citizens. We may estimate the total population of the Athenian *polis* as comparable to that of a modern city of around a hundred thousand inhabitants.

The atomic organization of Hellenic culture carried with it a number of corresponding traits favorable for the development of science. In the first place, there was no complete overshadowing of individuals by their own social system. Again, the size of the community gave scope to individuality, competition, and aggressiveness of the small groups. The field was open wide for persons to observe differences, make comparisons, and, in general, profit by the great opportunity that acquaintance with different cultures affords for the development of originality and initiative. Corresponding to the opportunities for trade and other international relations were those for individuals to borrow intellectual institutions. So Thales, Herodotus, and many others brought the germs of the sciences from neighboring states and even from distant cultures—from Egypt and Mesopotamia.

DISTINCTIVENESS OF THE POLIS. A characteristic of the Greek *polis* important for intellectual evolution is its unique nature and organization. Small political units like city states could cultivate an ideal of *autarkia* or self-containment. Whatever form the structure of the state took on that pattern could be extensively modified. The Greek *polis* was thus extremely individualistic. Within a small area there could exist a number of *poleis,*[2] each with its own social and intellectual character and its own unique institutions. These traits represented the ideal or pattern which suited the participant members of the group and which they cherished. Consider the differences between the Spartans, Thebans, and Athenians or between any other two of the many Greek political units. The former prided itself on ideals of personal hygiene and perfection while the latter cherished its art and wisdom. Isocrates declares,

Our city has so far surpassed the rest of mankind in wisdom and its expression that her pupils have become the teachers of the world; and she has

[1] *The Greeks,* p. 64.

[2] It is said that the island of Crete harbored as many as fifty independent city states (see Kitto, *op. cit.,* p. 65).

brought it about that the name "Hellenes" no longer denotes a race but a kind of intellect, and men are called "Hellenes" rather because they share Athenian culture than because of community of blood.[3]

Isocrates here gives expression to his ingrained belief that

> . . . if all the athletes should acquire twice the strength which they now possess, the rest of the world would be no better off: but let a single man attain to wisdom, and all the men will reap the benefit who are willing to share his insight.[4]

There is no doubt that the trait of uniqueness and distinctiveness found in so many forms among Greek schools of thought and art is an extension of the attitude of self-differentiation and self-election which is symbolized by the contrast between Hellenes and Barbarians. Even if the term "barbarian" was not meant to be derisory, it all the more emphasizes the fact of differences between peoples.

PARTICIPATIVE ASPECTS OF THE POLIS. For the development of scientific habits of thinking which are based on self-reliance and independence we may look to the participative trait of the Greek *polis.* Every city state expects the complete participation of each citizen in the regulation and maintenance of the group. Each citizen is a ruler and judge. Each person is responsible for the well-being of the individuals of the community and the commonwealth, as well as of the whole social and political unit. Inasmuch as there were no professional administrators, there were no specialized judges or lawyers. Each individual citizen was presumed to be interested in the affairs of state and to exercise his functions of government, defense, and the administration of justice. Socrates addresses his own defense against the charges made by Anytus, Meletus, and others, to the men of Athens although he was more than seventy years of age and appearing for the first time before a court of law.[5]

The participative aspect of the city state has far-reaching consequences for the citizens. It provides the basis not only for political and civic freedom, but also favors the development of self-confidence and in turn the formation of numerous personal traits advantageous for the development of the arts and sciences. The general lack of standardization among the city states themselves is mirrored in the relations of the persons participating in the individual states. Citizens not only are presumed to develop in their own individual ways but are responsible for

[3] *Panegyricus,* p. 51.
[4] *Ibid.,* p. 2.
[5] Plato, *Apology* 17.

satisfying their own criteria of action and excellence and for arriving at the peak of their powers.

A distinctive characteristic of the participative state and, in particular, that of Athens was the ebullient vitality[6] which showed itself in curious and aggressive behavior. The Greeks were curious about many things: the facts of science and of political life; the things and events of the environment; and the underlying determining conditions. The entire history of the Greek states is witness to the indefatigable efforts of the population to expand their territories and spheres of influence. This aggressiveness is shown by the many explorations, the planting of colonies, the increase of trade, and the enlargement of Hellas to include *Magna Graecia* and other distant lands. The aggressiveness and boldness of the Hellenes extended to the acquisition of knowledge and wisdom. And so they were tolerant of and even receptive to knowledge wherever it was to be found. Wisdom the Greeks numbered among their favored primary virtues along with justice, temperance, and courage.

EUTOPIAN ASPECT OF GREEK SOCIETY. An outstanding characteristic of the city state as embedded in long tradition and in political theory is its ideality. In great part the state is not merely an instrument for harmoniously living together, but a means for achieving something substantive in the way of excellence. Aristotle sums up the eutopian nature of the state in his assertion that it comes into existence in order to satisfy the bare needs of life but its continuation is for the sake of the *good* life. To be sure, the purpose of living together or of joining several villages to form a community is to obtain effectively the necessities of existence, but this is not enough. The greater needs lie in the striving of people to enhance their existence, to live better, and to increase continually the gap between human and other animals.

Greek society is notoriously a leisure society, that is one not limited to economic pursuits and labor for its own sake. Political life includes public recitals of Homer, attendance at tragic and comic dramatic performances, and the games and processions that graced the daily living of Greek communities.[7] As if to emphasize the advantages of leisure for achieving social excellence there arises the problem of slavery. There is no question that esthetic enjoyment and self-cultivation was made possible by a system of social organization which included a specialization into freemen and slaves. Those interested in the moral problem which Greek slavery forces to the surface divide themselves into condemning

[6] See Bowra, *The Greek Experience,* p. 74.
[7] See Kitto, *op. cit.,* p. 74.

judges who know no extenuation and the exculpating defenders of a practice which yielded such notable compensation.

That the idealism of the Greek state did yield precious fruit is clearly attested by the records of history. Even writers, who display little sympathy for the naturalistic Greek pagans have to admit that at least for a time their society

> . . . did inspire magnificent achievements in the fields of art, poetry, science, and philosophy, as well as in the fields of politics and war. Under this man-made dispensation, Greek men learned to portray nature realistically, to think rationally, to express their thoughts lucidly, and to govern themselves democratically.[8]

The idealistic character of the Greek state coupled with the others we have mentioned not only allows for the good life but also aids in advancing it. A secure and contented citizenry will be moved to exert considerable artistic, moral, and intellectual efforts toward developing the potentialities of man. That the Greeks reached a lofty goal in the scientific field is an incontrovertible finding of history.

STABILITY OF GREEK SOCIETY. Despite the constant strife and shift of political power among the Greek city states, carried even to the point of mutual destruction, they persistently maintained within themselves a stable place for the individual citizens. What was a supreme fact in peaceful times was not effaced in times of trouble. Contributing to this character of the Greek political unit is the fact that it was at all times securely esconced in nature. There was no Hercules who could sunder it from its safe attachment to earth as he had Antaeus. Rooted as the Greeks were in the concrete facts of human events, they did not and could not think of themselves as subsisting in temporary misery while awaiting glory in some future state. This flavor of stability is well expressed in Pericles' praise of those ancestors who helped to establish the Greek states.

> They dwelt in the country without break in the succession from generation to generation, and handed it down free to the present time by their valour. And if our more remote ancestors deserve praise, much more do our own fathers, who added to their inheritance the empire which we now possess, and spared no pains to be able to leave their acquisitions to us to the present generation. Lastly, there are few parts of our dominions that have not been augmented by those of us here, who are still more or less in the vigour of life; while the mother country has been furnished by us with everything that can enable her to depend on her own resources whether for war or for peace.[9]

[8] Toynbee, "The Ancient Mediterranean View of Man," *Man's Right to Knowledge* (J. B. Brebner, ed.), p. 7.

[9] Thucydides, *History of the Peloponnesian War* ii, 6, 37.

The potentialities residing in Greek society for the development of the sciences, including psychology, appear clearly indicated. That there were such potentialities is demonstrated by the actual sciences the Greeks produced. For psychology, specifically, the evidence lies, of course, in the development of the Aristotelian treatises and their forerunners. But what is perhaps of even greater importance, since a psychological science was bound to develop, is the availability of cultural materials among the Greeks for the fashioning of a particular kind of psychology, a kind that we must characterize as objective and naturalistic. Because the points we have made are so well supported by the universally known Funeral Oration of Pericles we present part of it here as a symbol of the kind of psychology we should expect to arise out of this particular type of civilization.

Before Pericles begins his panegyric of the fallen he relates the road by which Athens reached her exalted position, the form of government which made her great, and the national habits which led to her success. He says,

Our constitution does not copy the laws of neighbouring states; we are rather a pattern to others than imitators ourselves. Its administration favours the many instead of the few; this is why it is called a democracy. If we look to the laws, they afford equal justice to all in their private differences; if to social standing, advancement in public life falls to reputation for capacity, class considerations not being allowed to interfere with merit; nor again does poverty bar the way, if a man is able to serve the state, he is not hindered by the obscurity of his condition. The freedom which we enjoy in our government extends also to our ordinary life. There, far from exercising a jealous surveillance over each other, we do not feel called upon to be angry with our neighbour for doing what he likes, or even to indulge in those injurious looks which cannot fail to be offensive, although they inflict no positive penalty. But all this ease in our private relations does not make us lawless as citizens. Against this fear is our chief safeguard, teaching us to obey the magistrates and the laws, particularly such as regard the protection of the injured, whether they are actually on the statute book, or belong to that code which, although unwritten, yet cannot be broken without acknowledged disgrace.

Further, we provide plenty of means for the mind to refresh itself from business. We celebrate games and sacrifices all the year round, and the elegance of our private establishments forms a daily source of pleasure and helps to banish the spleen; while the magnitude of our city draws the produce of the world into our harbour, so that to the Athenian the fruits of other countries are as familiar a luxury as those of his own.

If we turn to our military policy, there also we differ from our antagonists. We throw open our city to the world, and never by alien acts exclude foreigners from any opportunity of learning or observing, although the eyes of an enemy may occasionally profit by our liberality; trusting less in system and policy than to the native spirit of our citizens; while in education, where our rivals from their very cradles by a painful discipline seek after manliness, at Athens we live exactly as we please, and yet are just as ready to encounter every legitimate danger. In proof of this it may be noticed that the Lacedaemonians do not invade our country alone, but bring with them all their confederates; while we Athenians advance unsupported into the territory of a neighbour, and fighting upon a foreign soil usually vanquish with ease men who are defending their homes. Our united force was never yet encountered by any enemy, because we have at once to attend to our marine and to despatch our citizens by land upon a hundred different services; so that, wherever they engage with some such fraction of our strength, a success against a detachment is magnified into a victory over the nation, and a defeat into a reverse suffered at the hands of our entire people. And yet if with habits not of labour but of ease, and courage not of art but of nature, we are still willing to encounter danger, we have the double advantage of escaping the experience of hardships in anticipation and of facing them in the hour of need as fearlessly as those who are never free from them.

Nor are these the only points in which our city is worthy of admiration. We cultivate refinement without extravagance and knowledge without effeminancy; wealth we employ more for use than for show, and place the real disgrace of poverty not in owning to the fact but in declining the struggle against it. Our public men have, besides politics, their private affairs to attend to, and our ordinary citizens, though occupied with the pursuits of industry, are still fair judges of public matters; for, unlike any other nation, regarding him who takes no part in these duties not as unambitious but as useless, we Athenians are able to judge at all events if we cannot originate, and instead of looking on discussion as a stumbling-block in the way of action, we think it an indispensable preliminary to any wise action at all. Again, in our enterprises we present the singular spectacle of daring and deliberation, each carried to its highest point, and both united in the same persons; although usually decision is the fruit of ignorance, hesitation of reflexion. But the palm of courage will surely be adjudged most justly to those, who best know the difference between hardship and pleasure and yet are never tempted to shrink from danger. In generosity we are equally singular, acquiring our friends by conferring not by receiving favours. Yet, of course, the doer of the favour is the firmer friend of the two, in order by continued kindness to keep the recipient in his debt; while the debtor feels less keenly from the very consciousness that the return he makes will be a payment, not a free gift. And it is only the Athenians who, fearless of consequences, confer their benefits not from calculations of expediency, but in the confidence of liberality.

In short, I say that as a city we are the school of Hellas; while I doubt if the world can produce a man who where he has only himself to depend upon, is equal to so many emergencies, and graced by so happy a versatility as the Athenian. And that this is no mere boast thrown out for the occasion, but plain matter of fact, the power of the state acquired by these habits proves. For Athens alone of her contemporaries is found when tested to be greater than her reputation, and alone gives no occasion to her assailants to blush at the antagonist by whom they have been worsted, or to her subjects to question her title by merit to rule. Rather, the admiration of the present and succeeding ages will be ours, since we have not left our power without witness, but have shown it by mighty proofs; and far from needing a Homer for our panegyrist, or other of his craft whose verses might charm for the moment only for the impression which they gave to melt at the touch of fact, we have forced every sea and land to be the highway of our daring, and everywhere, whether for evil or for good have left imperishable monuments behind us. Such is the Athens for which these men, in the assertion of their resolve not to lose her, nobly fought and died; and well may every one of their survivors be ready to suffer in her cause.[10]

GREEK SCIENCE: MIRACLE OR EVOLUTION?

It is impossible to minimize the glorious achievements of the Greeks in the development of their unsurpassable arts and sciences. But by the same token it is folly to believe that the Greeks were miracle workers. Even the fact that we are partially their direct cultural descendants can blind us to the obvious origin and evolution of the particular objects and technics we most admire in their civilization. Accordingly, we are obliged to take into account all the cultural tributaries that have flowed into the great stream of Greek achievement in psychology and the other sciences.

In recent years there has been a laudable effort on the part of scholars to correct the mistake of regarding the Greek accomplishments as ungenerated, as novelties suddenly arising by spontaneous creation. Many evidences are now accumulating that an authentic evolution in all phases of Greek culture has occurred. The influence upon the Greeks of what happened in Babylonia, Egypt, and other neighboring and more distant civilizations is becoming known with increasing precision. Historians of science feel obliged to begin their books with chapters on Egyptian, Mesopotamian, and other civilizations that developed before Greece.[11] The pre- and proto-sciences evolved in the Near Eastern civilizations have found their way into the sciences the Greeks synthesized and brought to a remarkable point of completion.

Great credit for bringing about the newer attitude concerning scientific evolution belongs to archeological research. When the historian of science becomes familiar with original materials concerning the scientific work of the Babylonians, Egyptians, and other precursors of the Greeks, he cannot avoid seeing Greek science in its proper perspective.

[10] *Ibid.*, ii, 6, 37-41.
[11] For example, Sarton, *A History of Science.*

It becomes clear to him that the Greeks owe a great debt to their forerunners just as the successors of the Greeks, in their turn, are obligated to the Greeks. Scholars still differ as to the magnitude of this debt which the Greeks owed to their Babylonian and Egyptian predecessors; some think it was very small[12] while others think it was very great.[13] It may be safe to say that the greater the familiarity with recent sources the greater the estimate of the scientific influence exerted upon the Greeks by their intellectual ancestors.[14]

How much specifically did the Greeks derive from older cultures for their psychological evolution? The answer is, probably less than in the case of physics or mathematics. Nevertheless, archeologists have provided telling evidence of scientific practices and theories which the Babylonians and Egyptians developed before the Greeks. From such sources as the medical papyri, especially the Papyrus Edwin Smith and the Papyrus Ebers, we learn a great deal about the status of science in Egypt. Similarly the discovery and accumulation of clay tablets by archeologists in Mesopotamia disclose a rich source of scientific achievements which could feed the psychological stream.

[12] For example, Reymond, *History of the Sciences in Greco-Roman Antiquity.*
[13] See Dunbabin, *The Greeks and their Eastern Neighbors.*
[14] See Neugebauer, *The Exact Sciences in Antiquity.*

CHAPTER 6

THE SCIENTIFIC MATRIX OF HELLENIC PSYCHOLOGY

THE SCIENCE of any country or period is inevitably rooted in a specific culture complex localized in a given time and place, as we have said in Chapter 3. The existence or nonexistence of any science, whether it is deductive or inductive, speculative or experimental, depends directly on the underlying culture. A similar dependence likewise influences the cultivation of a particular specialty of science, whether medicine, physics, astronomy, or ethics. That the traits of a scientific discipline depend upon the general civilization of a community simply emphasizes the fact that the intellectual and scientific items of a culture constitute a specialized level of that culture and so are more or less homogeneous with it.

Now we must differentiate between the scientific and nonscientific elements of a culture and the variant ways in which they influence a scientific discipline or doctrine. The nonscientific aspects of culture in the form of the economic, political, and social conditions of a society are less specific than the intellectual and scientific aspects and generally influence the special sciences in a more effective way. This is perhaps true because scientific doctrines and investigations are more definitely the products of individual effort and often bear the names of particular persons. They become most like other cultural items when they are embodied in documents and hence become palpable and as easily manipulated as the other objects belonging to the culture.

In a genuine sense, then, any particular science has moorings in two levels of underlying cultural conditions. Any special science thus constitutes a third level of cultural things and events. This relationship is suggested in the accompanying diagram (Fig. 6).

Since we are interested in the assumptions and postulates of Greek psychology we must examine the characteristics of its scientific matrix. Because Greek science is objective and naturalistic the psychology of the Greeks will likewise be free from the transcendent factors with which the later periods of psychological history become infected.

For convenience in examining such an important and specialized cultural complex as Greek science we divide our exposition into two parts, the one dealing with general cosmology or metascience and the other giving samples of the more specialized disciplines.

HELLENIC COSMOLOGY OR METASCIENCE

In the Greek dawn of science cosmology was an unspecialized discipline. To a great extent it consisted of a most unsophisticated set of astronomical opinions integrated with a number of basic assumptions

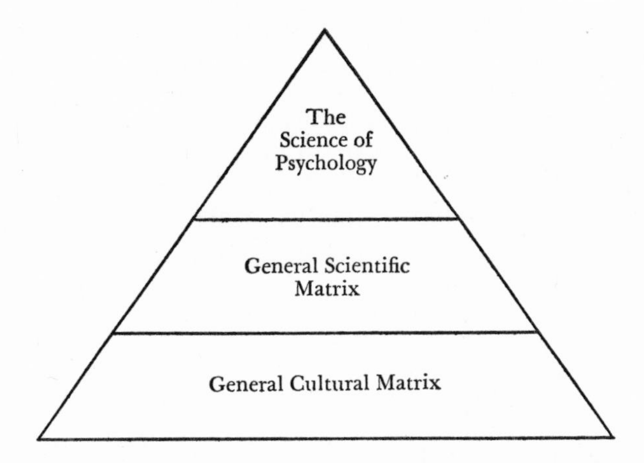

Fig. 6. The Two Matrix Levels of the Science of Psychology

concerning the limited sort of universe which the ancients knew. In the following paragraphs we select for consideration some of the most outstanding postulates of Greek metascience.

The Realistic Attitude of the Greeks. The Greeks are essentially realistic. They are prone to assume that their constructs, whether abstractive or extrapolative, have an independent existence just as is the case with the events that they describe, sum up, and account for. In other words, they reify the reference to or description of a thing to make it stand beside the original object or one of its properties. For example, causation, effect or consequence, whiteness, and destructibility are set up as things. This view bespeaks an improper admixture of constructs and events, but the Greeks attempted to justify their procedure because they believed that events include the idea, pattern, or formula upon which they are ordered and modeled. The best illustration of the realistic thinking of this period is Plato's theory of the independent existence of forms (ideas) in which things participate according to the measure of their existence or reality. Certainly the Greeks never thought of transcending the boundaries of elementary space and time.

It is often asserted that Greek cosmology is riddled with teleology. On a commonsense level this is not to be denied. But it is highly undesirable, to say the least, to interpret these expressions as implying some transcendent entity which foresees or foreordains some result or outcome. It is certainly not Greek to think that causes of things or events lie not in what precedes them, but in what lies ahead of them—some purpose or end. The commonsense attitudes of the Greeks dictate rather that controlling forces or purposes are nothing more than uses or processes. This point is made entirely clear by Aristotle, who is almost universally condemned as an arch teleologist. He writes,

> As every instrument and every bodily member subserves some partial end, that is to say, some special action, so the whole body must be destined to minister to some plenary sphere of action. Thus the saw is made for sawing, for sawing is a function, and not sawing for the saw.[1]

He is equally clear concerning the ends subserved by the whole organism.

> Instances of what I mean by functions and affections are Reproduction, Growth, Copulation, Walking, Sleep, Locomotion, and other similar vital actions.[2]

We may take another example, from the social domain; according to Aristotle the purpose of a political unit is to provide the services essential for a group of participants.

The Greek Cosmos: Concrete and Bounded. Even when the Greeks were dealing with the widest and most inclusive principles concerning their cosmic environment, they still bounded their universe severely. Basically, they did not get far from commonsense or matter-of-fact situations. Actually their world was extremely limited and did not extend beyond the surface visibility and tactibility of everyday objects and processes.

Absolutistic-Finalistic Attitudes. Characteristic of Greek intellectual life is the great inclination toward ultimacy and finality. Hence the great role played in Hellenic thought by the completed definition and, still more, the syllogism. Not only does Greek absolutism imply a certainty, but also an unmovable boundary surrounding any event or situation. The certain and endless proposition is strictly deductive. Also the Greeks loved dichotomy. To reduce situations to ultimate opposites or

[1] *De Partibus Animalium* 645[b], 14.
[2] *Ibid.*, 646[a], 34.

differences was a highly desirable goal. To impale things on a polarity of yes—no, either—or, all—none, appeared a method without any vagueness or looseness.

Universality and Perfectibility. Whatever principles, definitions, or species could be attained by a Greek thinker were of no satisfaction to him unless they became completely comprehensive. Conclusions must be all-embracing. Nothing could be left out. This intellectual trait of total inclusiveness fits well with a limited and bounded universe.

Closely coupled with universality is the Greek love of excellence and perfection. To a great extent what the Greek thought of as perfect was anything complete, rounded out, entirely symmetrical, and without obtruding corners or protuberances. Perfection goes with completeness, compactness, and essential fittingness.

Durability. As a final Greek intellectual institution we select that of durability or lastingness, unbroken continuity. Much in the universe is immortal, without beginning or end. It is as though the attitude here is governed by the words used, since one of the best examples of immortal things is the circle. Plainly the terms "beginning" and "end" have several meanings or usages. Arrangements, organizations, systems display this durational character, as, for example, the organ-function association is immortal. That is, the conjunctions of acts and actors are permanent.

GREEK SCIENCE: THE SPECIALIZED DISCIPLINES

Hellenic Mathematics

That the Greeks labored mightily to organize and systemize mathematics and achieved splendid results is now an accepted notion of mathematical history. It is also well established that the primary characteristics of Greek mathematics are its static character, its deductive absoluteness and finality, and its concreteness. A further trait dependent on those already enumerated is its finitude. Greater than their abhorrence of a vacuum was the Greeks' aversion to the infinite.

Greek mathematics is deductive. This means that any mathematical system is a finalistic and closed one. Its demonstration is complete, rigid, and ultimate. From the deductive system of definitions, axioms, and theorems nothing is omitted and everything is placed in the closest and firmest articulation.

The assiduous cultivation of geometry by the Greeks is sometimes attributed to the fact that they could not tolerate the irrationalities of numbers.[3] Whether or not one accepts this hardly more than partial

[3] Bernal, *Science in History*, p. 129.

truth, the zealous pursuit of geometry bespeaks the static character of Greek mathematics as well as its containment within the framework of things. What the Greeks were interested in were fixed and rigid forms, figures that stayed in place and were readily manageable.

The Pythagoreans are universally regarded as prominent, if not initiating formulators of the propositions "numbers rule the world" and "of all things number is the essence." What these meant to the Greeks was that numbers, that is relations, were localized and bound to things. Number and relation abstracted from all things were for them utterly vague notions. What was significant for them was the quantitative and measurative properties of things. Mathematics was no remote and idle trifling; its subject matter was the essential and the reasonable features of actual things.

The utter anti-transcendence of Greek mathematics is excellently illustrated by its abhorrence of the mathematical infinite, which is so much at home in the thinking of the Middle Ages and modern times. With respect to the Greek treatment of a straight line as a definitely limited segment rather than an unending extension in both directions, Whitehead says,

> The Greeks never seem to have found any use for this conception which is now fundamental in all modern geometrical thought. Euclid always contemplates a straight line as drawn between two definite points, and is very careful to mention when it is to be produced beyond this segment. He never thinks of the line as an entity given once for all and as a whole. This careful definition and limitation, so as to exclude an infinity not immediately apparent to the senses, was characteristic of the Greeks in all their many activities.[4]

Clearly the definition of a straight line from minus infinity to plus infinity was meaningless to the Greeks.

Infinitesimals, too, the Greeks regarded with great suspicion and hence they could not adopt the view that curves are polygons with an "infinity" of sides.[5] As Heath so well points out, Archimedes imposed static and limited properties upon the "method of exhaustion." Instead of admitting that he has compressed the equal-sided polygonal figures inscribed in and circumscribing a circle so that all three coincide, he adopts the indirect method of *reductio ad absurdum.* The whole matter is clearly set forth in Chapter 7 of Heath's "Introduction" to *The Works of Archimedes,* from which we quote at length.

[4] *Introduction to Mathematics,* p. 119.
[5] Cf. Jourdain, *The Nature of Mathematics,* p. 50.

. . . Greek geometers shrank from the use of such expressions as infinitely great and infinitely small and substituted the idea of things *greater* or *less than any assigned magnitude.* Thus, as Hankel says, they never said that a circle *is* a polygon with an infinite number of infinitely small sides; they always stood still before the abyss of the infinite and never ventured to overstep the bounds of clear conceptions. They never spoke of an infinitely close approximation or a limiting value of the sum of a series extending to an infinite number of terms. Yet they must have arrived practically at such a conception, e.g., in the case of the proposition that circles are to one another as the squares on their diameters, they must have been in the first instance led to infer the truth of the proposition by the idea that the circle could be regarded as the limit of an inscribed regular polygon with an indefinitely increased number of correspondingly small sides. They did not, however, rest satisfied with such an inference; they strove after an irrefragable proof, and this, from the nature of the case, could only be an indirect one. Accordingly we always find, in proofs by the method of exhaustion, a demonstration that an impossibility is involved by any other assumption than that which the proposition maintains. Moreover this stringent verification, by means of a double *reductio ad absurdum,* is repeated in every individual instance of the method of exhaustion; there is no attempt to establish, in lieu of this part of the proof, any general propositions which could be simply quoted in any particular case.

The above general characteristics of the Greek method of exhaustion are equally present in the extensions of the method found in Archimedes. To illustrate this, it will be convenient, before passing to the cases where he performs genuine *integrations,* to mention his geometrical proof of the property that the area of a parabolic segment is four-thirds of the triangle with the same base and vertex. Here Archimedes *exhausts* the parabola by continually drawing, in each segment left over, a triangle with the same base and vertex as the segment. If A be the area of the triangle so inscibed in the original segment, the process gives a series of areas

$$A, \tfrac{1}{4}A, (\tfrac{1}{4})^2A, \ldots$$

and the area of the segment is really the sum of the infinite series

$$A\,\{1 + \tfrac{1}{4} + (\tfrac{1}{4})^2 + (\tfrac{1}{4})^3 + \ldots\}.$$

But Archimedes does not express it in this way. He first proves that, if $A_1, A_2, \ldots A_n$ be any number of terms of such a series, so that $A_1 = 4A_2$, $A_2 = 4A_3, \ldots$, then

$$A_1 + A_2 + A_3 + \ldots + A_n + \tfrac{1}{3}A_n = \tfrac{4}{3}A_1,$$

or

$$A\,\{1 + \tfrac{1}{4} + (\tfrac{1}{4})^2 + \ldots + (\tfrac{1}{4})^{n-1} + \tfrac{1}{3}(\tfrac{1}{4})_n{}^{-1}\} = \tfrac{4}{3}A.$$

Having obtained this result, we should nowadays suppose n to increase indefinitely and should infer at once that $(\frac{1}{4})^{n-1}$ becomes indefinitely small, and that the limit of the sum on the left-hand side is the area of the parabolic segment, which must therefore be equal to $\frac{4}{3}$ A. Archimedes does not avow that he inferred the result in this way; he merely *states* that the area of the segment is equal to $\frac{4}{3}$ A, and then verifies it in the orthodox manner by proving that it cannot be either greater or less than $\frac{4}{3}$ A.

I pass now to the extensions by Archimedes of the method of exhaustion which are the immediate subject of this chapter. It will be noticed, as an essential feature of all of them, that Archimedes takes both an inscribed figure and a circumscribed figure in relation to the curve or surface of which he is investigating the area or the solid content, and then, as it were, *compresses* the two figures into one so that they coincide with one another and with the curvilinear figure to be measured; but again it must be understood that he does not describe his method in this way or say at any time that the given curve or surface is the limiting form of the circumscribed or inscribed figure.[6]

Hellenic Astronomy

If Hellenic mathematics is so closely based on simple and direct contacts with things and thus limited in its constructional scope, how much more so must this be the case with the more concrete sciences, including astronomy. As a matter of fact, Greek astronomy consists primarily of identifications, enumerations, patternings (constellations), recorded motions, and other simply observable features of astronomical things and events, and their interrelations. This is no dispraise of the Greeks, who wrought so marvellously in science, as in so many of the things which they undertook to do. Rather this is simply an appraisal of the situation at a period before our common culture had had the time to grow into the greater maturity of our current stage.

Without attempting to distinguish what the Greeks derived from their forerunners and what they achieved for themselves, we can discern a hierarchy of scientific developments, each level of which fits into a completely naturalistic scheme. At the bottom, of course, stands the recognition of about forty-eight constellations and enough knowledge to make it possible for the Greeks to attribute to Thales the prediction of the eclipse of 585 B.C.[7] At this time, too, the Greeks were well aware of the difference between fixed and wandering stars and knew the zodiac. Probably the peak of this level is the introduction of the gnomon by Anaximander and the use of the astrolabe and other instruments to facilitate observation.

A distinctive second level of Greek astronomical development centers around the problems of the constitution and behavior of the astronomical bodies. To the Pythagoreans and especially Philolaus (*ca.* 450 B.C.) are attributed various speculations concerning the nature of the sun,

[6] *The Works of Archimedes,* pp. cxlii-cxliv.

[7] *Herodotus* i, 74.

earth, and other astronomical bodies and the relative motions of each. Despite the invention by the Pythagoreans of the "central fire" and the *antichthon* or counter-earth, they accepted the views of Parmenides (*ca.* 470 B.C.) that the earth was a sphere. Of Heraclides of Pontus, a disciple of Plato, it is said that he regarded all the astronomical bodies as solid and round, each suspended in a universally pervading ether surrounded by an atmosphere.[8] Moreover, he held that the earth rotated about its own axis from west to east in about a one day period.[9] Aristarchus of Samos (*ca.* 310-230 B.C.), too, in the Alexandrian period stressed the diurnal rotation of the earth and is credited with setting up the earliest thorough-going heliocentric theory. Thus, Aristarchus erected an astronomical model different from the epicycle and deferent system of Apollonius of Perga (260-200 B.C.) and of the great Ptolemy of the *Almagest,* who lived in the second century A.D. Although the culture of Western Europe remained unreceptive to the heliocentric theory until modern times, the work of the heliocentric thinkers did not lose its validity despite the long prevalence and great acclaim of the theory that placed the earth in the center of the cosmos with the sun revolving around it.

The construction of mathematical and mensurational methods constitutes a third level or stage in Greek astronomical development. Eudoxus of Cnidus (409-356 B.C.) is credited with the first attempt to construct a mathematical model for planetary motion. Accepting the fairly common view of astronomers that planets move in circular orbits, he constructed a set of twenty-seven concentric spheres at the equator of which astronomical bodies were carried. These equators were presumed to revolve with uniform speed around the two poles of the spheres. For the fixed stars one sphere was enough to account for the daily revolution of the heavens. For the sun and moon three spheres each were necessary and for the five planets, Mercury, Venus, Mars, Jupiter, and Saturn four each were required.

Alongside the attempts of Callipus (370-300 B.C.) and Aristotle (384-322 B.C.) to improve the concentric circle model, there arose an era of mensuration and calculation during which knowledge was sought concerning the dimensions and locations of astronomical bodies. Callipus added six spheres to those of Eudoxus, while Aristotle increased the number by a further twenty-two to a total of fifty-five.[10] Aristotle also

[8] Abetti, *The History of Astronomy,* p. 35.
[9] See Dreyer, *A History of Astronomy from Thales to Kepler,* Ch. 6.
[10] *Ibid.,* p. 113.

attempted to transform the geometric model into a concrete astronomical description.

Actual astronomical measurements and calculations were, of course, preceded by random estimates and guesses. Anaximander believed the circle of the moon to be nineteen times as great as that of the earth and that of the sun twenty-eight times as great.[11] Plato asserted that the ratios of the distances of the planets from the earth are 1:2:3:4:8:9:27. It was Aristarchus of Samos who first devised a geometric method to calculate astronomical distances. He developed an ingenious triangle connecting the earth, moon, and sun in an endeavor to ascertain the ratio of distances between them. Two methods of determining the size of the earth were devised by Eratosthenes (*ca.* 273-195 B.C.) and by Posidonius of Apamea (*ca.* 135-51 B.C.). In both cases the rationale was to measure the distance between two points on the same meridian and to determine the corresponding arc for this distance.

Our brief coverage of outstanding items in the history of Greek astronomy reveals the comparatively simple and limited features involved in it. Even the most inept of the descriptions and interpretations, however, reveals no departure from basic observable data. The tidy static universe of Greek astronomy suggests a cosmos erected on simple observations.

Hellenic Physics

When we consider that some of the most prominent achievements of the Greeks lay in the field of mechanics and that the peaks of those achievements were the Archimedean hydrostatics and laws of the lever, we must conclude that the physiochemical sciences of the Greeks illustrate excellently their static and fixed scientific traits. In the lever law the factors exhibit a purely local system bounded by a rule of symmetry and simple proportion. In hydrostatics, however, there is a slight branching out toward a significant qualitative aspect of things, namely, density, which can be quantitatively treated on a two-dimensional continuum. What appears as most characteristic and important in Hellenic physics is the slight account taken of temporality. The Greeks emphasized the fixed and static factors of durability, finality, and completeness, and neglected variability in time.

It is not only Greek mechanics, however, that is static and close to surface observation. What little knowledge they acquired about light and sound they formulated in the timeless framework of simple geometry

[11] Sambursky, *The Physical World of the Greeks,* p. 76.

and in the propositions of elementary ratios. As to magnetic things and events, the Greeks stand at the very threshold of knowledge and have hardly crossed the line which leads from haphazard and insignificant observation to the definite building of constructs about things and events and the reactions performed with respect to them. Surely no student of Greek physics can accuse the Hellenic writers of including anything in their work that suggests belief in transcendent data or constructions.

Hellenic Biology

If it is true that the Greeks were more successful in biology than in the other special sciences, the reason may well be that which Aristotle gives in the *De Partibus Animalium.* By way of comparing the merits of intimate biological study with the study of the more remote objects of astronomy Aristotle says:

> Natural objects fall into two great classes, the immortal ones that are without beginning or end, and those that are subject to generation and decay. The former are worthy of honour, for they are divine, but they are less within the reach of our observation. All our speculations about them and our aspirations after knowledge of them can only in the rarest instances be confirmed by direct perception. But when we turn to the plants and animals that perish, we find ourselves better able to come to a knowledge of them, for we are inhabitants of the same earth. Anyone who is willing to take the necessary trouble can learn a great deal about all the species that exist. Both enquiries have their charm. In the case of the heavenly bodies we can achieve little owing to their being out of our reach, yet the veneration in which they are held imparts to our knowledge of them a degree of pleasure greater than appertains to any of the things that are within our reach, as a lover would rather catch a chance glimpse of his beloved than have a complete view of many other precious things. But terrestrial objects, owing to our better and fuller acquaintance with them, have the advantage from the scientific point of view. Indeed their nearness to us and their kinship with us may be said to counterbalance the claims of divine philosphy. And, as I have already expressed my views on the former subject, it remains for me to treat biology, omitting nothing so far as I can avoid it, however little or great be the honour in which it is held.[12]

It is not surprising that such effective systemizers as the Greeks should bring together tremendous masses of information concerning plants and animals. Obviously, in such a complex culture sources were not lacking from which to glean information. In the first place, food problems furnished a sharp incentive to study plant and animal organ-

[12] *De Partibus Animalium* 644^b–645^{a}8 (quoted from Farrington, *Greek Science,* Vol. I, p. 126 *f*).

isms. Not far behind were the incentives of health and illness which stimulated the investigation of the anatomy and physiology of the human organism. It is indisputable that Greek biology is richly furnished with knowledge of the structures and functions of organisms. Aristotle alone mentions five hundred different species, both terrestrial and marine.[13]

It creates no surprise that references to Greek biology center around the work of Aristotle. He treats problems belonging to almost every branch of the subject except for those based upon the microscope and the chemistry developed long after his time. Through his interest in form and function he displays a deep knowledge of certain kinds of anatomy and physiology. Ecology is well represented in his writings, while his interest in sex, reproduction, and heredity has led him to many valuable researches into genetics, embryology, and comparative botany and zoology. Historians of biology accord a large place to Herophilus and Erasistratus, who stand out as the great students of human biology, a subject which is not elaborately treated by Aristotle. To them are attributed a great many observations and discoveries in anatomy and physiology.[14]

In view of the brillant record of the Greeks in the biological domain it surely seems out of place for anyone to denigrate Greek science. For that record amply shows a commendable attack by the Greeks upon the problems of the nature of many things. It is not rare to find it said that

> Most of Aristotle's biological work reads like that of a modern naturalist, for his methods were closely similar to those of our own time.[15]

But how can such a statement square with the traditional conventions which belittle the great Stagirite? Of Aristotle it is said that he was a teleologist and responsible for the belief in Final Causes. It is evident that Aristotle is the victim of his adoption by St. Thomas and the Middle Ages. A critical reading of his emphasis on necessity, on fittingness, and on means and ends convinces us that what he is driving at is simply adjustment. Teleology in Aristotle signifies primitivity and simplicity but not transnaturalism. It is a sign of scientific immaturity to say that animals possess horns or fangs as a means to a protective end. Still this is not to imply that Aristotle believed in some supernatural power which prescribed the forms and functions of animals, thus providing them with the means first of attacking enemies and secondly of combating them.

[13] *Ross, Aristotle,* p. 112 *f.;* and Lones, *Aristotle's Researches in Natural Science,* p. 214 *f.*
[14] Nordenskiöld, *The History of Biology,* p. 51. See also Ch. 12 below.
[15] Singer, *A Short History of Science,* p. 44.

Plate I. Hippocrates, *see p. XV.*

All in all, it is difficult to escape the fact that Greek biology, however simple in places, conforms with the canons of scientific research and belongs to a system of naturalistic thinking.

In a curious passage Nordenskiöld criticizes Aristotle for his lack of appreciation of infinitude, which he regards as the dark side of Aristotle's great gift for form.

> He who saw in form the true content of existence could not imagine a world to be other than finite—spherical for the sphere is the most perfect form—and as he could not visualize an infinite world, he could not imagine infinite potentialities of knowledge; on the contrary, he expressly declared that his own system, complete as it was, would make it possible to solve all problems.[16]

Hellenic Medicine

On all sides it is firmly acknowledged that Hellenic medicine is practical and naturalistic. This is, of course, made possible by the general cultural characteristics of Hellenic civilization but also by the medical situation. Although the contributing factors to disease or maladjustment may be subtle and hidden, much of the medical situation is obvious and revealed. That is perhaps the reason that Greek medicine is so much concerned with the patient, the organism as a whole, rather than with diseased parts. Because Greek physicians in substance considered pathology as "experiments of nature,"[17] they had of necessity to take into consideration all aspects of the illness situation. This applies both to the etiology and therapeutics of disease.

Hellenic medicine, emerging at a date when specialization was still concealed in the womb of time, profited from the evolution of naturalistic views by the Greek cosmologists. With the advent of Hippocrates and the medical schools of Cos and Cnidus we have a medical specialization which has won and justly merited the enthusiastic acclaim of many competent scholars. Writing about some items of the Hippocratic Corpus[18] Jones asserts:

> The style of each work is grave and austere. There is no attempt at "window dressing." Language is used to express thought, not to adorn it. Not a word is thrown away. The first two treatises have a literary finish, yet there is no trace in them of sophistic rhetoric. Thought, and the expression of thought, are evenly balanced. Both are clear, dignified—even majestic.
>
> The matter is even more striking than the style. The spirit is truly

[16] *The History of Biology*, p. 38.

[17] A favorite phrase of Dr. Adolf Meyer; see *The Collected Papers*, especially Vols. III and IV, *passim.*

[18] The *Prognostics, Regimen in Acute Diseases*, and *Epidemics* i and iii.

scientific, in the modern and strictest sense of the word. There is no superstition, and, except perhaps in the doctrine of critical days, no philosophy. Instead, there is close, even minute, observations of symptoms and their sequences, acute remarks on remedies, and recording, without inference, of the atmospheric phenomena, which preceded or accompanied certain "epidemics." Especially noteworthy are the clinical histories, admirable for their inclusion of everything that is relevant and their exclusion of all that is not.[19]

Hellenic medicine strikingly illustrates the basic scientific procedures. Within the limits of their knowledge and means the Greek physicians treated their patients on the basis of what examination revealed. Indeed they are charged with a too-keen interest in conditions as they are without sufficient effort to overcome them. But even if such a charge could be sustained it would be only with respect to medical practice and not with respect to their attitude toward nature. There is no other conclusion than that, in an age lacking knowledge of bacteria and chemistry and without the use of microscopes, thermometers, stethoscopes, and many other pieces of apparatus now available, the Greeks still carried on their work in accordance with the data and techniques then within their grasp.

One of the most powerful arguments for the complete objectivity and naturalism of Greek medicine lies in the type of hypotheses they made, even though these are from the standpoint of more sophisticated and better equipped times mistakes. Howsoever crude and simple were the doctrines of the four humors and their harmony and disharmony in health and disease, these theories still were based upon the observation of organisms and their changes through variations of environing circumstances. Blood, phlegm, and yellow and black bile are obviously fluids observed during the physician's contacts with patients.

Innumerable writers on Greek medicine, especially on the Hippocratean period, extoll the Greek virtue of rejecting traditional and superstitious ideas about epilepsy. In the treatise *On the Sacred Disease* Hippocrates, or whoever the writer was, definitely rejects the idea that epilepsy or the falling sickness is to be accounted for by other than natural causes or conditions. Epilepsy is to be explained by the improper action of various organs channeling and regulating the various body fluids, especially blood and phlegm. A prominent part in epilepsy is played by the brain. When phlegm gets into the veins leading to the head and obstructs the passage of air to the brain, the result is an epileptic

[19] General Introduction to his translation of *Hippocrates,* Vol. I, p. xv.

fit. Fanciful as all this may be, it does not depart far from the organs and functions so inadequately known but persistently pursued.

Followers of the medical traditions set up in Hellenic times laud the Hippocrateans for holding to notions still favored. For example, when the ancient writer on the so-called sacred disease connects the brain so closely with psychological action this is taken to be the acme of correctness. Mistaken as this attitude is, the fact remains that the ancient writers are exhibiting a laudable naturalistic view. An examination of the text, *On the Sacred Disease,* indicates where reverence is due and where the simplest mythology is allowed to creep in. Thus, an ancient writer asserts:

> Men ought to know that from the brain, and from the brain only, arise our pleasures, joys, laughter and jests, as well as our sorrows, pains, griefs and tears. Through it, in particular, we think, see, hear, and distinguish the ugly from the beautiful, the bad from the good, the pleasant from the unpleasant, in some cases using custom as a test, in others perceiving them from their utility. It is the same thing which makes us mad or delirious, inspires us with dread and fear, whether by night or by day, brings sleeplessness, inopportune mistakes, aimless anxieties, absent-mindedness, and acts that are contrary to habit.[20]

In such a case we applaud the intention of the ancient physician to connect the behavior of man with special organs, for that is a naturalistic attitude. However, when the brain itself is made to bring about good and bad results by becoming abnormally hot, cold, moist, or dry the mythology becomes apparent. Similar inept statements are that madness comes from the moistness of the brain and intelligence from the brain being still.[21]

Probably nothing argues so eloquently for the naturalism and objectivity of Greek medicine as the emphasis on case histories which the Hippocrateans present with such fullness and faithfulness. In the treatise, *Of the Epidemics,* there are many excellent descriptions of the course and outcome of particular diseases.

It is entirely unnecessary to exaggerate the wisdom of the Greeks or to endow them with mysterious powers in order to evaluate and admire their close attachment to facts and their institution of a medical science which makes use of the tried canons of observation and interpretation.

Hellenic Theology

Before proceeding to examine what the Greeks thought about the

[20] *Hippocrates,* Vol. II, p. 175.
[21] *Ibid.*

gods, it is expedient to pause briefly to justify, if possible, the inclusion of theology among the scientific disciplines. Let us say at once that this problem would not arise if we did not project modern views upon the Greeks. If Hellenic religion and theology were treated as cultural items embedded in their own place and period, there would be no difficulty in studying the reactions of Hellenic thinkers with respect to their gods and the nature of divinity. In fact, since the theological thought of the Greeks was harmonious with their physical, biological, and astronomical sciences, a study of it helps us to appreciate the entire Greek scientific cultural complex as a matrix for their science of psychology. I give one example. If scholars could refrain from imposing Christian notions of godhood, soul, and immortality upon Greek thinking, they would free themselves from seeking (and not finding) in Aristotle evidence of his belief in immortality and transmigration.[22]

Here the question arises whether Hellenic civilization carried within it traits of a later age, such as the assumption that persons could cope with ineffables, invisibles, and other self-projected creations. There is no evidence that the Greeks imposed supernatural attributes either upon the gods themselves or upon their own views about them. Hellenic theology was natural theology and since Hellenic civilization embraced gods and theories about them, as well as other cultural things and events, it is justifiable for practical purposes to accept Greek theology as a primitive but informative type of social science.

Now we may ask what propositions the thinkers of the Hellenic culture constructed in the theological domain. How did they react toward important and naive products such as gods, religious heroes, and all the myriads of ritualistic and liturgical practices? Did they talk about things that were presumed to be not of the actual world or did they embellish, transform, and invent modifications of persons, animals, plants, growth, reproduction, and other things and happenings in order to make them more desirable, perfect, or powerful? Have the Greeks ever allowed themselves to forget that everything in the religious domain was wrought by humans and that no god could be accepted as the source and creator of all? The latter, of course, is the authentic Christian attitude so well stated by St. Augustine, who grouped all the prechristian gods together as at best not creators, but creatures.[23]

It is no wonder that St. Augustine, the grand creator of Christian dogma, cannot tolerate a classification, such as Varro's (116-27 B.C.) of

[22] See Guthrie, *The Greeks and Their Gods*, p. 369.
[23] *De Civitate Dei contra Paganos* vi, Ch. 1.

the gods into the mythical, the political, and the natural. Of course, St. Augustine fully recognizes the great variety of gods even as Varro depicts them, but he rejected them in favor of the abstracted, supernatural, omnipotent, spiritistic creator of the Christian theological tradition.

What makes it difficult for modern writers to accept the view that Hellenic theology was concerned with gods whose constructional characteristics were completely akin to those of other things met with or inferred, is the fact that modern Christian culture carries within it many items originally developed in Hellenic times but which have been totally transformed. This is true of theological constructs as well as words. It is said that Plato was the first to use the word "theology" and that he evidently was the creator of the idea.[24] But, though words and ideas such as theos, god, divine, immortal, and many others have their roots in Greek and other cultures, still the fruits that are grafted on them have been grown in an entirely different culture. How is it possible to associate the lifeless, unknowing, changeless, unmoved mover of Aristotle with the creative, personal, compassionate, and all-loving god of Christian tradition?

Hellenic theology can be well understood by observing the contrast between it and the later supernatural Christian doctrines. Greek gods were human or were derivations from human prototypes with greater or lesser exaggerations. While none of the specialized anthropological theories of those who trace the origin of the gods from social and political happenings in the life of a people can be taken as complete explanations, they do contribute factors toward an explanation. Murray presents an excellent statement of the contrast between the Hellenic and the later Christian viewpoint:

> Any one who turns from the great writers of classical Athens, say, Sophocles or Aristotle, to those of the Christian era must be conscious of a great difference in tone. There is a change in the whole relation of the writer to the world about him. The new quality is not specifically Christian: it is just as marked in the Gnostics and Mithras-worshippers as in the Gospels and the Apocalypse, in Julian and Plotinus as in Gregory and Jerome. It is hard to describe. It is a rise of asceticism, of mysticism, in a sense of pessimism; a loss of self-confidence, of hope in this life and of faith in normal human effort; a despair of patient inquiry, a cry for infallible revelation; an indifference to the welfare of the state, a conversion of the soul to God. It is an atmosphere in which the aim of the good man is not so much to live justly, to help the society to which he belongs and enjoy the esteem of his fellow creatures; but rather, by means of a burning faith, by contempt

[24] Jaeger, *The Theology of the Early Greek Philosophers,* p. 4.

for the world and its standards, by ecstasy, suffering, and martyrdom, to be granted pardon for his unspeakable unworthiness, his immeasurable sins. There is an intensifying of certain spiritual emotions; an increase of sensitiveness, a failure of nerve.[25]

Religion as the matrix of theology is obviously a complex feature of cultural life, and therefore it can only be treated abstractly and selectively. It is patently an oversimplification to characterize religion as concerned with a god or any sort of divinity. Religion may be, of course, ethical, political, and economic. It is highly interesting that recent writers who wish to deny that Greek religion is completely rational attempt to do so in terms of psychic principles derived from recent spiritistic viewpoints.[26] The irrational is equated with the supernatural which, of course, is an unwarranted imposition.

Hellenic History

The mere fact that Greek historians of the fifth century B.C. could raise problems concerning the critical attitude of historical writers, as Thucydides did in his *History of the Peloponnesian War,* indicates some of the prominent traits of Hellenic intellectual culture. The fact, too, that Thucydides writes so self-assuredly of his own merits as a historical narrator and as a depreciating critic of others, points in the same direction. For him no question exists whether history is or can be a science. Thucydides firmly believes that since a historian is charged with the description and explanation of the interrelations of nations, he can achieve the goal of truth by sifting evidence and critically examining whatever records may have survived from the past.

More positively stated, Thucydides' historical conclusions will not be disturbed,

either by the lays of a poet displaying the exaggeration of his craft, or by the compositions of the chroniclers that are attractive at truth's expense. . . .[27]

He goes on to say:

The absence of romance in my history will, I fear, detract somewhat from its interest; but if it be judged useful by those inquirers who desire an exact knowledge of the past as an aid to the interpretation of the future, which in the course of human things must resemble if it does not reflect it, I shall be content. In fine, I have written my work, not as an essay which is to win the applause of the moment, but as a possession for all time.[28]

[25] *Five Stages of Greek Religion,* p. 119.
[26] Cf. Dodds, *The Greeks and the Irrational.*
[27] *History of the Peloponnesian War* i, 1, 21.
[28] *Ibid.,* i, 1, 22.

Modern historians are divided as to the intrinsic merits of Thucydides, and even when they accord him a clear superiority over Herodotus some still find him falling short of the highest scientific ideals.[29] It is a great tribute paid to Hellenic culture of the fifth century that modern historians adopt the premise that the Greeks may be judged by the same canons as modern scientists. For example, Thucydides is criticized, together with all other ancient historians, for neglecting social and economic forces in historical explanations.[30]

Whether or not Thucydides was able to suppress all the mythology that he so keenly disapproved of, he still stands out as a model historian of any time for his appreciation of the scientific character of historical study. In a highly laudatory essay Cochrane places Thucydides upon an enormously elevated pedestal, asserting that not only had he grasped and applied the principles of scientific method, but also that these principles were as well established in general science as they possibly could be. Cochrane, in fact, believes that Thucydides knew Hippocrates and was imbued as much as he with the ideal of observing events and describing them without recourse to myth or legend. Referring to the interpretations or constructions which Thucydides developed in his work, Cochrane remarks that they:

> . . . represent the attempt of Thucydides to do for history what Hippocrates was at the same time trying to do for medicine—the attempt, that is, to establish such classifications or formulations (τὰ εἴδη) as would raise history from the level of mere chronicle, characteristic of the annalists (λογογράφοι), just as in medicine the same formulations were needed if medical science was to escape from the mere empiricism of the Cnidian school. Through the symptoms to arrive at a general description and thence to penetrate, if possible, to the true classification of the malady, this is the procedure which Hippocrates advocates and which he designates by the words *semeiology* and *prognosis*. But this was the very process which Thucydides sought to apply to history, which thus for him becomes the semeiology and prognosis of human life.[31]

With regard to Thucydides' descriptive details Cochrane says:

> The unforgettable picture of the plague at Athens, copied by Lucretius and imitated by Procopius in ancient, as it was by Gibbon in modern times, has always been accepted as one of the best illustrations of Thucydides' temperament, the keenness with which he observed concrete fact, the cold detachment with which he reported the symptoms of a malady to which he himself had fallen victim, the precise analytical power with which he portrayed the changes (μεταβολαί), not merely bodily but

[29] See Cochrane, *Thucydides and the Science of History,* Introduction.
[30] Shotwell, *The History of History,* p. 208 *f.*
[31] *Op. cit.,* p. 26.

also mental, of the disease. For the commentators generally the account of the plague has illustrated these characteristics. For us it does more; it constitutes the most intimate link between Thucydides and Hippocrates, and seems indeed to be the bridge between the two.[32]

We consider it established that the situation in history fits in with that in other departments of Greek intellectual culture. To sum up, we have an intellectual world accommodating both myths and scientific descriptions. What happened in history could be told by some admixture of both or by a resort to the description of events well enough known or aptly inferred from critical evidence. In either case the situation is not far removed from a naturalistic attitude toward the interrelations of persons and states, and states with states.

Hellenic Ethics

An interesting symptom of the homogeneity of Hellenic culture is the obvious conformity of Greek ethics to the ideals of order, system, completeness, measure, proportion, and finality. The essence of Hellenic morality is summed up by the motto at the shrine of Delphi, "Nothing in excess." A just and exact balance there must be between individual desire and the public good, and still more between the permission of convention and the dictates of nature.

Symbolic of Hellenic ethics is the figure of a balance in utter symmetry. The ideal of goodness is moderation, the highest form of propriety, which can only be disregarded by incurring severe penalties. *Hybris* is the condemnatory name for disrespect to the symmetry and balance of action. Plato has impressively indicated the penalty for injustice and other violations of order and measure in behavior, a penalty consisting not of escapable stripes or death but of an inescapable development of unfittingness or disharmony in the members of society.

> There are two patterns eternally set before them; the one divine and most happy, the other godless and most wretched: but they do not see them, or perceive that in their utter folly and infatuation they are growing like the one and unlike the other, by reason of their evil deeds; and the penalty is, that they lead a life answering to the pattern which they are growing like.[33]

Hellenic ethics is basically characterized by a distinct naturalism. Despite the definiteness and firmness of the Greek moral standards, they are bounded by human circumstances and are intended to promote the welfare of the individual and the city state. Up to this period there has not been set up any transcendent principle or sanctions to

[32] *Op. cit.* p. 27.
[33] *Theaetetus* 176.

govern the behavior of men. The aim of the moral life is to serve the needs of people living in a community, and so emerge the four cardinal virtues, courage, temperance, justice, and wisdom.

How deeply humanistic and social is the ethical world of the Greeks is made plain by the great emphasis on knowledge as a basis of morality. Rigid as rules or principles of conduct may be, they are localized within the domain of actual behavior. And so the moral situation is subject to examination that may lead to assent and conformity or dissent and rejection. To behave fittingly, that is morally, an exact knowledge of what is involved in the situation is required. There are no transcendent criteria or sources of external compulsion. Virtue is a learned trait because it is based on knowledge; otherwise no improvement of action could take place. Blind obedience is remote from the situation, which calls for insight and understanding.

Insight and knowledge as the basis of virtue and moral action not only eliminate absolute and transcendent elements and replace them by scientific analysis and situational investigations, but they also argue for a reasonable appreciation of motives and ideals. For it may be claimed that feelings and arbitrary desire are the guides to such moral conduct as is free from imposed necessity. Socrates and others who espouse the rule that virtue is knowledge reject the guidance of unanalyzed feelings as ineffective means to attain harmony between man and things or man and the social order.

Hellenic Esthetics

Hellenic art in both practice and theory stresses a perfectionism which attains its greatest expression in symmetry and proportion. The study of Greek art of the fifth and fourth centuries B.C. reveals the artist searching for the utmost significance of that which he creates and portrays. When the artist fashions a portrait or depicts some event he is not content to imitate the surface traits of things, but rather seeks to penetrate to their ultimate reality. By what technical means this is carried out depends on many detailed circumstances. But the product must approach the artist's appreciation of the ideal thing as closely as his capacities permit. Since beauty is the theme of art, it is as if the artist employs the human figure or whatever he paints or sculpts as a means of attaining to the *Summum Pulchrum*.

But however persistent the search of the Greek artist for ultimate reality, he kept well within the bounds of everyday life. His pursuit of ultimate and perennial values is embodied in the glorification of the human figure, in the games that are so effectively played, in the ceremonials and festivals of the communal life. And if he so often depicts the gods of his well-stocked pantheon, that is because they are part of the household and are only glorified persons with their unique strengths and frailties.

When seekng the primary characteristics of Greek art we find them represented by substantiality and immutability. The trait of substantiality is well exemplified by the many temples built foursquare and so adapted to their locations as to appear an integral part of their environment. Immutability is illustrated by the crystallization and perpetuation of significant activities and situations. The activities may be dancing, jumping, running, or any of the behavior involved in games or warfare. Situations like participation at symposia or the heroic feats by legendary characters are enshrined in colorful clay or lasting marble and bronze. Bowra's suggestion that Greek art was a means of "defeating time," of "keeping memories alive" or "sustaining glory after death" is apt.[34] This externalization of scene and act has, of course, been superbly signalized by Keats in his "Ode on a Grecian Urn."

The esthetic theory of the Greeks naturally stemmed from their general cultural characteristics and their reflections on their art products. Beauty is an independent and absolute quality which in some measure is found in things. When the artist seeks to attain to this exalted universal he may be obliged to combine the most beautiful details of several models.[35] It is the emphasis of the Greeks upon the independent and objective existence of absolute esthetic qualities which engenders the paradox of craftsmanship. To present the beauty of things may require the synthetic production of a beautiful whole from parts selected for their beauty.

Greek esthetics emphasizes three factors in an esthetic situation. First and foremost, there is beauty. The symmetry and proportion which constitute it may exist in objects or parts of objects. It may be imitated, it may be admired, but it is not an impalpable imposition upon things. The determination of its quantity and measure always presupposes its priority and authenticity. There are, in addition, the techniques by which an artist embodies it in his works. The operations involved are many and various. They center around the selection of material, whether marble, clay, bronze, paint, and so on, and the theme, whether a male or female figure, a ceremonial, a myth, and vary with the type and calibre of the artists involved. The creation of art is rooted in the

[34] *The Greek Experience,* p. 163.
[35] Xenophon *Memorabilia* iii, 10, 2.

cultural matrix. Production is seldom independent of appreciation or other forms of consumption. Beauty must be recognized and cherished. It must be culturally functional. Those who react to the works of art will influence the kinds of products and their fittingness in the total art situation. Here arise problems of decoration and adornment, social eulogy, and glorification, homiletic teaching or immediate entertainment, simple enrichment or cathartic benefit.

The comparatively practical and naturalistic character of Hellenic art and esthetics is well demonstrated by the constant emphasis on imitation by Greek estheticians. Consider the Platonic paradox of a superb mythologist and poet who would banish poets from his ideal state. The paradox hinges on the problem of imitation. Poets imitate, but what, is the question? Plato objects to the imitation and presentation of the wrong things. There is a use in poetry as well as a delight.[36] The poet must sing and eulogize what is good and proper in individual heroes and in states and, above all, strive to know the significant and essential in things and events. Plato, being an absolutist and abstractionist, would have poets and artists in general combine ultimate good and ultimate beauty.

As a writer of fairly specialized esthetic interest, Aristotle analyzes esthetic situations primarily from a behavioral standpoint. Esthetic objects he looks at from the angles of their productive action and of the appreciative response to them. Art objects detached from these two types of activity are of little significance.

On the side of production, Aristotle stresses two basic types of action. The first is imitation, which he regards as central in human behavior. The origin of poetry, as no doubt of all types of art, can be traced to the imitative propensities. Furthermore, there is the great delight in works of imitation; in this way the person learns, and learning is the greatest of pleasures.[37] The representation of objects, even those painful to see such as the lowest animals and dead bodies, affords delight because the beholder gathers the meaning of things when they are portrayed in art.

Supreme among art objects for Aristotle is tragedy which on the stage superbly imitates action. Tragedy portrays not persons but action and life, happiness and misery.[38] That is why the plot of tragedy is its most essential part, the very life of it. And the most fundamental kind of tragedy is that which arouses in the beholder pity and fear. As every-

[36] *Republic* 607[e].
[37] *De Poetica* 1448[b] 4-24.
[38] *Ibid.*, 1450[a] 16.

one knows, Aristotle considered the response of the persons reacting to tragic works to be so intense that they experienced a cathartic effect. The character of this catharsis has been the subject of innumerable speculative essays. But we need only follow Aristotle's general trend of thought. It is only to be expected that when the pitiful and horrible actions of the characters of a tragedy are presented the reaction of the beholder should be most significant, his learning of the most impressive sort, and the elimination of wrong or cloudy thinking the most complete. That Aristotle used a term current in the vocabulary of physicians merely illustrates the practical and naturalistic complexion of his way of thinking.

RECAPITULATION

Our brief summary of the character of Greek scientific culture was undertaken for the light it would cast on the nature of Hellenic psychology. Our first finding disclosed a series of traits homogeneous with those of general Greek civilization. Greek science we found to be concrete and bounded. Observation and descriptions were valued according to their correspondence with visible and palpable objects. Theories and hypotheses were cast in a mold of which the main ingredients were the availability of things and the ultimacy of pronouncement about them. Deduction and finality were the rewards of a diligent study of nature, and the end of knowledge was to achieve mastery of this limited and complicated domain. Greek scientists abhorred the transcendent, the tentative, and the uncertain. For this reason they involved themselves with dogmatic and teleological propositions which gained them the contempt of later scientists. Hellenic teleology was a reflection of their desire to complete the job and include in their descriptions statements of what things were for and how they worked, or in terms of modern mechanical models, they searched for the dynamics of things. Actions of specified kinds were the ends or purpose of things.

In accordance with the scientific traits just specified, we may expect the psychology created by the Greeks to include no factor beyond the activities of organisms. When we study Hellenic psychology as consonant with the other specific disciplines of the period, we find in it no room for any item that does not answer to the characteristics of essence, action, and end found in astronomical and terrestrial bodies, animal and plant organisms, or in the behavior of states or other human groups.

CHAPTER 7

SOCRATIC ANTHROPOLOGY

SOCRATES AS SOURCE AND LINK OF SCIENCE

IN THE CONTEXT of science Socrates plays a most paradoxical role. At every Athenian crossroad he proclaimed himself an ignoramus and a sterile midwife of ideas. By contrast with those who were falsely boasting how much they knew, Socrates declared that his reputed sagacity consisted only of knowing that he knew nothing.[1] Yet, according to the accepted facts of Greek history and the testimony of Aristotle, he was not only a transmitter of knowledge which became permanently institutionalized but also an innovator, an authentic source of scientific wisdom and method. On the psychological level Socrates was an extremely effective builder of scientific foundations.

There is really nothing strange about the Socratic paradox if we consider that Socrates lived at the dawn of our scientific culture. In the Athens of the fourth century B.C. it was possible for an informal, unremunerated teacher, one welcoming all who cared to learn, to draw effective blueprints for the construction of scientific institutions. If Socrates could not know many of the great number of events with which we concern ourselves today, he was able to discourse expertly on the manner in which we must approach the data our modern world has revealed. When we reflect upon how much our most recent scientists have been occupied with problems of terms and their meanings or referents, with general linguistic problems, and with theoretical speculations, we may count Socrates as a current scientist.

SOCRATIC ANTHROPOLOGY

Aside from his study of the processes by which knowledge is obtained and improved, Socrates was vitally interested in a specialized class of events. He was primarily interested in what we call the cultural or social sciences as against the physical and biological sciences.[2] What was of perennial and consuming interest for him is excellently described by Xenophon.

[1] Plato *Apology* 20-22.
[2] Plato *Protagoras*.

His own conversation was ever of human things. The problems he discussed were, what is godly, what is ungodly; what is beautiful, what is ugly; what is just, what is unjust; what is prudence, what is madness; what is courage, what is cowardice; what is a state, what is a statesman; what is government, and what is a governor;—these and others like them, of which the knowledge made a "gentleman" in his estimation, while ignorance should involve the reproach of "slavishness."[3]

Socrates may be regarded as one of the initiators of the science of anthropology. Under this rubric are subsumed studies of political behavior, ethics or the science of the good and happy life, economics as the proper organization of the living conditions of citizens and the state, and esthetics as the study of the beautiful, the perfect, and the ugly. Naturally, these aspects or departments of anthropological science are all of the most primitive sort. We should perhaps speak of them as protosciences. Nevertheless, we cannot exclude them from the scientific domain out of respect for the continuity and evolution of wisdom. What Socrates and others developed has become absorbed in the stream of Western European culture. For us the focus of interest is the impact Socratic anthropology made upon the development of psychology in the Greek world. Certainly Aristotle built upon the crude beginnings of psychology which germinated in Socratic anthropology. His psychology, however, was not limited to human behavior since Aristotle did not draw any sharp line between the various classes of animals.

SOCRATES BUILDS A MODEL FOR SCIENCE

If science is to evolve from everyday knowledge, it must reach stability and reliability. To achieve these goals it is highly desirable to construct a model for expert and valid knowledge. Moreover, rules must be available for separating what is trivial from what is important, and what is casual and temporary from what is definite and lasting. The rules of model-making must differentiate opinion or even mere assertion from representative and consequential statements. Custom and usage must be set aside in favor of the determination of what happens and the analysis and assessment of the results of inquiry.

Scientific model-making inevitably must center around language. Assertions and reports must be standardized and crystallized. Declarations and casual assertions must be evolved to the stage of propositions. As a child of a realistic culture Socrates undoubtedly exaggerated the efficacy of a model to achieve the ideal duration and exactitude of knowledge. The model he constructed, however, is not absolutely tied

[3] *Memorabilia* i, 1, 16.

to his notion of the ultimate essence of things. It may serve to differentiate things and events, to point out their traits or characteristics and their interrelations with other things.

The model Socrates constructed was, of course, not treated by him in any formal way. He would have resented the imputation to him of expertness to deal with such a problem. As the arch amateur he assumed that he was just talking about things and would not admit that he was reaching basic conclusions or attaining the essence of things. But Aristotle is witness to the fact that Socrates was seeking to syllogize, and the essence of things is the starting point of syllogisms.[4]

Though granting that Socrates only succeeded in beginning the construction of a scientific model, we can point out the two basic parts of it which he did complete or at least definitely set up.[5] The first is universal definition. This is a tool that helped to focus inquiries upon essentials and to facilitate the analysis and description of the subject matter dealt with. The other is inductive procedure, the attainment of a general proposition from an examination of particulars or samples.

THE SOCRATIC NOTION OF SOUL

How important Socrates' investigative model is may be estimated by the psychological historian when he applies it to the acute problem of the nature of soul, according to the Greeks in general and Socrates in particular. We contend that linguistic analysis shows how persistently modern ideas are read back into Greek doctrines. Simply put, since the term "soul" now signifies some supernatural thing or substance and since "soul" is a synonym of "psyche" and Socrates spoke of *psyche,* it is assumed that Socrates shared the modern belief in transpatial things.

Linguistic and situational analysis show that what Socrates meant by soul was similar to what is meant today when one speaks of a person as being the "soul of goodness" or "kindness." In other words, soul was for Socrates the name for certain essential and perhaps valuable traits. Indeed Burnet has argued strongly for such an interpretation.[6] He does so on the ground of the historical development of Hellenic ways of thinking and, more particularly, of the employment of the term "psyche" by the writers and teachers of the succeeding generations of Greek thinkers.

There is another fundamental consideration. It is obvious that the interpretations of the sayings and the thinking of historical personages

[4] *Metaphysica* 1078b 24.
[5] See Aristotle *Metaphysica* 1078b 30.
[6] "The Socratic Doctrine of the Soul," in *Essays and Addresses,* pp. 126-162.

is a function of the interpreter and the intellectual environment in which he lives. To us it seems quite remarkable that Burnet has reached his conclusions while himself immersed in our dualistic culture. For him there still exist the two worlds of things and mentalistic consciousness. But what if one frees himself from this prison of cultural beliefs? Then, at least, it becomes easier to evaluate the views of Socrates and to look upon them as the necessary result of living under particular political, economic, social, and interpersonal circumstances. On such a basis we can see clearly the nascent system of naturalistic psychology which Socrates formulated.

SOCRATES' NATURALISTIC PSYCHOLOGY

It would be unwise to overlook the comparatively primitive nature of Socratic psychology, which was inevitable since it developed so early in the history of the discipline. We should expect Socrates to speak metaphorically, to make use of figures of speech, and to adopt a poetic style of exposition. His was still an age when philosophers composed their weighty doctrines in literary style. But we have no difficulty in penetrating to his basic thought and observing his reflections concerning man and his conduct within the framework of the institutions of his time.

Let us turn to the *Phaedo,* which presents the most technical formulation of Socrates' cherished convictions. Struggling with the problem of the causes to be discerned in nature, he depicts his arrival at the crossroads of doubt and hesitation until he:

. . . heard someone reading, as he said, from a book of Anaxagoras, that mind was the disposer and cause of all, and I was delighted at this notion, which appeared quite admirable, and I said to myself: If mind is the disposer, mind will dispose all for the best, and put each particular in the best place; and I argued that if anyone desired to find out the cause of the generation or destruction or existence of anything, he must find out what state of being or doing or suffering was best for that thing, and therefore a man had only to consider what was best and most desirable both for the thing itself and for other things, and then he must necessarily also know the worse, since the same science comprehended both. Arguing in this way, I rejoiced to think that I had found in Anaxagoras a teacher of the causes of existence such as I desired, and I imagined that he would tell me first whether the earth is flat or round; and after telling me this, he would proceed to explain the cause and the necessity of this being so, starting from the greater good, and demonstrating that it is better for the earth to be such as it is; and if he said that the earth was in the centre, he would further explain that this position was the better, and I should be satisfied with the explanation given, and not want any other sort of cause. And I thought

Plate II. Socrates, see p. XV.

that I would then go on and ask him about the sun and moon and stars, and that he would explain to me their comparative swiftness, and their returnings and various states, active and passive, and in what way all of them were for the best. For I could not imagine that when he spoke of mind as the disposer of them, he would give any other account of their being as they are, except that this was best; and I thought that while explaining to me in detail the cause of each and the cause of all, he would also explain to me what was best for each and what was good for all. These hopes I would not have sold for a large sum of money, and I seized the books and started to read them as fast as I could in my eagerness to know the best and the worse.

How high were my hopes, and how quickly were they lost to me! As I proceeded, I found my philospher altogether forsaking mind and making no appeal to any other principle of order, but having recourse to air, and ether, and water, and many other eccentricities. I might compare him to a person who began by maintaining generally that mind is the cause of the actions of Socrates, but who, when he endeavoured to explain the causes of my several actions in detail, went on to show that I sit here because my body is made up of bones and muscles; and the bones, as he would say, are hard and have joints which divide them, and the muscles are elastic, and they cover the bones, which have also a covering or environment of flesh and skin which contains them; and as the bones swing in their sockets, through the contraction or relaxation of the muscles I am able to bend my limbs, and this is why I am sitting here in a curved posture—that is what he would say; and he would have a similar explanation of my talking to you, which he would attribute to sound, and air, and hearing, and he would assign ten thousand other causes of the same sort, forgetting to mention the true cause, which is, that the Athenians have thought it better to condemn me, and accordingly I have thought it better and more right to remain here and undergo my sentence; for I strongly suspect that these muscles and bones of mine would long ago have been in Megara or Boeotia, borne there by their own idea of what was best, if I did not think it more right and honourable to endure any penalty ordered by the state, instead of running away into exile. There is surely a strange confusion of causes and conditions in all this. It may be said, indeed, that without bones and muscles and the other parts of the body I cannot execute my purposes. But to say at the same time that I act from mind, and that I do as I do because of them and not from the choice of the best, is a very careless and idle mode of speaking. I wonder that they cannot distinguish the cause from the condition without which the cause would never be the cause; it is the latter, I think, which the many, feeling about in the dark, are always mistaking and misnaming 'cause.'[7]

The psychology which Socrates formulates here and rejects is nothing less than an anticipation of the physiological hypothesis of twentieth century behaviorism. Naturally, Socrates is ignorant of modern physiology and biology, and shows, along with a superficial though signifi-

[7] *Phaedo* 97b-99b.

cant appreciation of muscles, bones, ligaments, and other factors in a reaction, no inkling of the neural factors which twentieth century behaviorists feature. And yet his statements reveal a most striking appreciation of psychological issues. Furthermore, Socrates' rejection of the behavioristic view implies attitudes that are valid today. He insists that the main point has been left out. Most remarkable is Socrates' assertion that while the physiological factors he mentions participate in behavior and are essential for its occurrence, they do not cause or account for the behavior.

In terms of recent psychology Socrates demanded a motivational description, a description which includes relevant factors of human circumstances. Moral ideals, the proprieties of political circumstances, are what caused him to remain in Athens to undergo death, and not the equipment of muscles, ligaments, and bones. Much as modern psychology is out of sympathy with such moral and political factors of behavior, they belong to the age of Socrates as facilitating and inhibiting variables which influence behavior. The psychology of Socrates does not even hint at anything outside the range of objective and naturalistic facts. Dispositions, ideals, prejudices can all be included within the general domain of behavior precisely as we include potential and actual reactions among the behavior of chemical compounds.

CHAPTER 8

PLATONIC DIALECTICS AND PSYCHOLOGY

OF PLATO it may truly be said that he has been unduly tossed about on the waves of history. A realistic thinker solidly ensconced among natural events, he has been plunged into a sea of casual and mystical beliefs; an uncompromising searcher for truth, he has been charged with dabbling in mysteries. It must be granted, of course, that his writings do lend themselves to contrasting and sometimes bizarre interpretations; still, he should be viewed in the perspective of the actualities of his time and not be subjected to evaluational impositions based on other cultures. Plato was an Athenian of the late fifth and early fourth centuries B.C. and not a product of the post-Alexandrian Hellenism. Plato's dualism, for example, is severely contained in a comparatively simple spatio-temporal universe, and he was a stranger to the linguistic sophistication of his Judaeo-Christian successors who transformed his philosophy. Though a master myth-maker, Plato must not be confused with Philo, the allegorist, who could not distinguish between an expository aid on one side and a sign which reveals the ultimate, transcendental reality on the other, or with Plotinus, the Neo- that is, the inverted Platonist.

DETRANSLATION OF PLATONIC DOCTRINES

No one can doubt that Plato's writings have exerted a powerful influence upon all Western European thought since their publication; it is probably just as certain that they have been able to do so because Platonic doctrines have been modified and adapted to different social and intellectual circumstances. What is called for, then, if we want to assess the authentic Plato, is to scale off from his writings the various patinations with which later writers have covered his dialogues. We can only accept as authentic those Platonic doctrines the orientation of which is consonant with Greek culture of the fourth century B.C.

Specifically we must clear away the interpretation that Plato was concerned with transcendental entities. The entire set of Platonic constructions was placed in a definite spatio-temporal environment. The world beyond the heavens to which Plato relegated his Ideas he did not think of as outside space. Nor did his ascription of immortality to Ideas remove them from the confines of concrete spatio-temporal coordinates. Ideas or patterns were for him durational only in the sense that the seal outdates the impressions it makes. True too, Ideas were discovered by graded steps, but such gradations could not be carried beyond the natural processes of abstraction and practical enumeration. If Plato extrapolated far beyond the allowable bounds of observation and separated Ideas too far from concrete objects, as Aristotle believed, he still did not reach out to any supernatural. He was far too much attached to the ideal of actual existence and significant reality. We are not overlooking the characteristic method of Platonic exposition—the filling in of gaps in information by myths. Demiurges, creators, and fanciful processes fill the pages Plato has written. But is this more than a sign that the Greeks loved expository ornamentation as a feature of narrational perfection?

How scholars impose alien views upon Plato's writings and the need to set aside such impositions are excellently illustrated by the laudatory comments of a psychological historian upon Plato's scientific attitudes. Brett says of Plato:

> The work of science is to reconstruct the universe so that the eye of the mind may survey it as a whole and feel the beauty of its perfection. This was no vain imagining for Plato; it was a passion and a vision. It led him to wide study, anxious thought, and elaborate composition: only a consummate master of expression could so easily conceal the raw material of his discourses. In Plato we find the first conscious attempt to systematise the results of Greek speculation; no branch of learning was left out; every science contributed its doctrine or furnished an example of error; the universe was studied from every point of view as one might travel a wide country and talk to many men before constructing a final description of its character. The comprehensiveness of this survey is not yet fully grasped: new discoveries continually show that every page of Plato has its pointed references, and nowhere more than in the departmental sciences among which his psychology, in part at least, must be counted.[1]

But when Brett discusses Plato's psychology, he says that for Plato the soul is only in part the object of scientific knowledge; in part it is the object of metaphysical thought or religious feeling.[2] How does this fit in with the fact Brett mentions, namely, that Plato regards Hippocrates as one who reached true results by true methods? Clearly Plato is made the victim of the psychophysical presuppositions of his commentator even though the psychic had not yet been invented in

[1] *History of Psychology,* Vol. I, p. 65.
[2] *Ibid.,* p. 66.

Plato's day. An irreducible requirement for the understanding of Plato, as of all Greek thinkers, is to discard as far as possible traducing translations of what he said and to treat his handling of intellectual problems on the basis of conditions prevailing at his time. Admittedly, this may not be easy to do as it requires the releasing of one's attitudes from the tight control exerted by one's own cultural environment. Yet it must be done.

PLATO AND THE EVOLUTION OF SCIENTIFIC INSTITUTIONS

Without unduly magnifying the potentialities that existed in Plato's age for inaugurating and advancing the scientific enterprise, we may still recognize in Plato some authentic materials for creating scientific ways of thinking. Plainly stated, Plato laid a number of stones in the foundations of science. As primarily a mathematical thinker he did most, of course, for the formal aspects of scientific work. He did not contribute much concrete data except in what would now be called the social sciences. But he did accomplish a tremendous lot in the logic of science, in the systemization of scientific thinking. Only those who do not value the processes of generalization in science, or the problems concerned with the structuring of scientific work and its rules, can minimize the achievements of Plato in initiating dialectic procedures.

The excellence of the work of a historian may be judged by the extent to which he is able to control his evaluations influenced by the conditions prevailing in his time in order to make use of the criteria of the period he describes. It is certainly true that the categories and the models of scientific procedure which Plato helped to establish have become crystallized and have adversely affected the logic of science in our day; but this is rather the fault of the users of the system, not of its founders. The continuing search for fixities, for absolute invariances as over against the fluidity and the variabilities of events, testifies to the undue emphasis of constructional institutions which can occur once they have been established. However, the misuse of orders and systems in science detracts nothing from their value. Plato is not to be condemned for any later mishandling of the dialectic which was exceedingly valuable for his time.

THE MATHEMATICAL BASIS OF PLATONIC DIALECTICS

The tradition that the entrance to the Platonic academy carried the inscription, "Let not the nongeometrician enter here" symbolizes not only the general rationalism of Hellenic culture but also the specific absolutism and fixity of the Platonic dialectics. Essentially, what Plato sought to accomplish with his dialectics was to arrive at final reality, the firm and ultimate nature of things. Doubtless the source of his view is the Pythagorean dictum that the numerical aspect of things is the most fundamental and the most abiding.

Assuming, then, that the essence of things is the ultimate goal in science, as in the rational world in general, Plato formulated his dialectics as a method, or operational principle. It may be described as a procedure to carry one from the superficial material of things to the underlying forms. As primarily a mathematician, Plato would be attracted by the process of going from the dots and diagrams used to represent relations to the ultimate forms making up the relational realities. The lines and figures observed in things and practically represented by geometric drawings are only participants in the true forms that are neither visible nor tangible and cannot but be most inadequately represented by anything directly met with.

Dialectic is a process of thinking or reasoning which contrasts with observation or immediate contact. In terms of the commonsense psychology prevalent in his day Plato regards dialectics as the activity of pure thought uncontaminated by sensory activity.

THE PLATONIC DUALITY OF IDEAS AND EVENTS

From our present point of vantage we may see clearly that Plato's dialectics constitutes an overemphasis on constructs and an overevaluation of the processes of abstraction and definitional construction. However harmless and workable this overemphasis may prove to be in mathematics, it soon becomes obnoxious in the scientific fields concerned with concrete things and events. To carry too far the preference for patterns, formulae, and formality is to distort the knowledge process and the things known.

A unique paradox lies at the basis of the Platonic dialectics. The stress on construction and the resulting transfiguration of scientific labor and findings arose from the extreme realistic emphasis upon the ultimate nature of things. Though Platonic Ideas are palpable constructs they are presumed to be literally contained in things as their ultimate reality. Here is a harmful outcome of the formal realism of Hellenic thinking. First there is an unjustifiable overemphasis on things as over against either knowledge of them or, what is better, the system or organization of the reactions of knowing or evaluating things. The stress on things cannot perhaps be overdone if it entails an analysis and manipulation of individual things, which, however, was not much the practice in Plato's day. Actually, it is precisely the remote or rational handling of things that makes possible the excessive emphasis on them. In addition, of course, account must be taken of the cultural institutions of absoluteness and ultimacy that favored the search for hidden realities underlying the things actually encountered.

PLATO'S DOCTRINE OF IDEAS

Plato's doctrine of Ideas consists basically of a schema whereby things can be shown to be related to their patterns, models, or intrinsic formulae. The great analogy, of course, is the relation of manipulable numbers to their absolute prototypes, the relation of apparent figures to their real and incorruptible Ideas. Probably the best interpretation of the doctrine is that it has been designed to achieve stability of knowledge, on the one hand, and significance or validity, on the other. Plato assumes that below and beyond the superficial appearances of things there are abiding qualities and structures. While no one can produce a perfect circle or demonstrate a precise tangential point, it is these that are scientifically important. It is perfectly clear that Plato had very little actual appreciation of the role of construction in the manipulation and description of things and events, but after all we cannot overlook the fact that he lived in the days when scientific models were only beginning to be institutionalized.

The central point then in Plato's doctrine of Ideas is the process of participation or resemblance. The scientist observes and records the similarities of things and their relative approach to a standard. That standard is specifiable in a formula or most perfect instance. It is more or less culturally inevitable that Plato should describe his Ideas or prototypes in substantive terms as Forms existing in some inaccessible location—in the world beyond the heavens, but the incorporation of the Ideas and their function in the domain of a nascent science is beyond dispute.

GLEANINGS IN PLATONIC PSYCHOLOGY I: GENERAL ASPECTS

The Platonic *Dialogues* may be envisaged as the capstone of the presystemic period of psychology. We might, therefore, expect them to contain a considerable amount of material belonging to the psychological domain. Indeed we may glean from the profusion of Plato's writings on the social, moral, and political nature and conduct of man, a number of descriptions and theories concerning psychological behavior. The historian of psychology, therefore, must order these materials into a suitable perspective. From such an organization of informal opinions and doctrines we do not obtain, of course, a system of psychology but some important raw materials which demonstrate the essential nature of Hellenic thinking concerning psychological events. But beyond this we also discover those ingredients which were later incorporated into systematic psychology when it became instituted.

GENERAL NATURE OF PSYCHOLOGICAL PROCESSES. Psychological events enter into Plato's philosophical world primarily through the consideration of the ethical aspects of man's conduct. It is fashioned from the suggestions provided by both the Hellenic dynamic cosmologists and the anthropological views of Socrates. The psychological nature of man mirrors the actions and changes of the cosmos of which man is a part. In human as over against cosmic psychology the principles of action are associated mainly with social or moral values. Goodness, reasonableness, moderation, irascibility, and impetuosity are authentic examples of psychological events.

Of course, as a Greek writer of his day Plato follows the lead of other writers in substantizing his principles of action and even the actions themselves. Reasoning behavior becomes Reason or a manifestation of Reason. And thus the principles of action in all their instances and forms take on the fixity of a substantive *psyche* which later encouraged the translation of "psyche" as "unified soul." Furthermore, the substantizing of actions and principles of actions serves to connect them with the things and organisms performing actions. Thus arose the powerful tradition of localizing the psychic in particular parts of the organism.

OPPOSITION OF PSYCHIC AND BODILY ELEMENTS. There are two reasons for bringing to the front Plato's ideas concerning the existence and interrelation of psychic and bodily entities. The first is to exhibit Plato's poetic and mythic style of exposition, especially as it appears in his talk about the transmigration of souls. The second is that the consideration of the Platonic opposition of the psychic and the bodily reveals the commensense basis for his most abstruse tales and theories.

Consider first Plato's famous figure of the charioteer and his two different steeds.[3] This is certainly nothing more than an allegorical representation of various activities such as cravings or appetites, reasoning, and ideals. What Plato is pointing to, of course, are the variations in action based upon conventional criteria. While asessing

[3] *Phaedrus* 246, 248, 253.

the value of Plato's descriptions we must, on the one hand, admit the disparity between them and the behavior as observed; but, on the other, we must insist that nowhere does Plato make use of modern constructs which did not exist in his day. What Plato actually does is to systemize the thinking of his age in an informal and poetic manner, and on the basis of categories which have since been absorbed into the traditions of technical psychology.

METEMPSYSCHOSIS. In the *Meno*[4] Plato makes Socrates say he has heard that the soul of man is immortal, and at one time has an end called dying, and at another time is born again. The point to the fable is that a man ought to live always in perfect holiness as the souls purged by Persephone became noble kings and mighty men great in wisdom. This is part of the fanciful doctrine of reminiscence—that all inquiry and all learning is recollection. Similarly in the *Phaedo*[5] this sort of fable is elaborated in the cause of propriety and goodness, a motif which is repeated in the *Phaedrus*,[6] the *Republic*[7] and the *Laws*.[8] A slightly different motif is introduced into the *Timaeus* to make the transmigration serve to reflect the difference between men, women, and lower animals.

It is clear that these fanciful notions of immortality, persistence, and transmigration are characteristic Platonic myths designed to reinforce his moral exhortation. It is never to be forgotten that Plato was keenly aware of the procedure he was employing. Myths were tools deliberately used to attain certain results in argument. This is clear when Plato makes Socrates say in the *Phaedo:*

> A man of sense ought not to assert that the description which I have given of the soul and her mansions is exactly true. But I do say that, inasmuch as the soul is shown to be immortal, he may venture to think, not improperly or unworthily, that something of the kind is true. The venture is a glorious one, and he ought to comfort himself with words of power like these, which is the reason why I lengthen out the tale.[9]

In no sense does Plato depart from the Socratic notion of soul as the characteristics, the virtues, and the dignity of man. We must, however, note that wisdom and judgment are included among the so-called moral qualities. We must not be misled by the language used to think that Plato was able to attain to the highly sophisticated notions of transpatiality.

[4] 81.
[5] 70, 81.
[6] 248-9.
[7] 616.
[8] 903-4.
[9] 114.

THE SOUL-BODY PROBLEM. Since Plato understood by soul or psyche (a) the moral qualities of man, (b) activities, for example, thinking or contemplating, and (c) the behavioral sources of many types of action (for example, reasoning and assessing what is fit), it should appear futile to connect his views with modern ideas of mind and body. Modern ideas involve entities alien to Greek culture, especially the transnatural and transpatial mind which had not yet been invented in Plato's day.

However, refraining from the imposition of non-Hellenic ideas upon Plato's thinking does not prevent us from taking account of his references to acts which involve the body more than others. It may properly be said that for Plato ordinary sensing and feeling are gross acts of the organism, whereas the acts of pure thought or understanding are refined and subtle movements performed in the absence of the objects concerned, or when there are no objects separate from the acts. In keeping distinct the partial and inexpert descriptions of Plato from supernatural ways of thinking about them, it is helpful to remember that always Plato is talking about persons and their actions.

GLEANINGS IN PLATONIC PSYCHOLOGY II: SPECIFIC ACTIVITIES

When Plato discusses particular behavior such as discrimination, remembering, thinking, and dreaming, his exposition, however bizarre from our standpoint, stresses a naturalistic approach. It is apparent how lacking he is in information as to how such activities take place and also how different his descriptions are from those which presuppose transcendent factors. We bring together some illustrative materials from the *Timaeus,* the *Theaetetus,* and other dialogues under selected headings.

DISCRIMINATION. In general, discrimination is treated as an interaction of the organism with some quality or condition of things which produces an impact upon it.[10] The reaction of the organism is a motion which is diffused over the entire organism but can be primarily localized in special parts. In addition to discriminating the qualities of things, the transmitted motions may act to disturb the normal conditions of parts, thus resulting in unpleasantness and pain, or to restore the original conditions, thus producing pleasantness.

Taste. The organic reactions in taste consist of contractions and dilations as in other parts of the organism, but also in more roughness and smoothness localized in the veins of the tongue than in other affections. Bitter tastes are produced by earthy particles entering the small

[10] See *Theaetetus* 156.

veins, resulting in some degree of consumption of flesh, as by the action of potash or soda. Particles deficient in alkaline quality and producing moderately smooth and pleasant effects result in salty tastes. Sour and sweet tastes are produced when particles refined by putrefaction enter the narrow veins to cause these opposite effects. Sour or acid tastes result from bubbling agitation or more violent boiling or fermenting motions in the veins. But when the entering particles are congenial to the tongue and bring about a smoothing and settling effect in the veins there is a pleasant and agreeable sweetness.[11]

Smell. Olfactory events Plato regretfully treats in a more general manner as he can find no way of differentiating odors or even of applying particular names to them. Because the veins about the nose are too narrow to admit earth and water and too wide to retain fire and air, these elements are not smelled. What can be smelled are bodies that are damp, putrefying, liquefying, or evaporating, in brief bodies in an intermediate state when water is changing to air (mist) or air to water (vapor). In line with Plato's general reliance upon the doctrines of the medical writers, he regards some reactions to odors as irritating and disturbing to the whole cavity situated between the head and the navel. These are the painful odor responses. The opposite effects are produced by pleasant odors.[12]

Hearing. Hearing is quaintly described as the sensing of sound which is an impact passing through the ears and transmitted by way of the air, the brain, and the blood. The hearing reaction itself consists of the vibrations set up in the head by the impact which ends in the region of the liver. Acute sounds move swiftly, while grave sounds are more slowly transmitted. Regular sounds are equable and smooth while harsh sounds are the opposite. Loudness of sound depends upon the volume.[13]

Sight. The keenest of the senses[14] is described as an interacting process. Seeing occurs when the gentle light from the nonburning fire contained within the eye issues forth to meet the outside light. Objects then become visible and are seen. This interactional process Plato works out elaborately in intimate connection with color.[15] Particles coming from outer bodies to the eye may be larger, smaller, or equal to those they meet there. If the inner and outer particles are equal, the result is transparence and imperceptibility. When the external

[11] *Timaeus* 65-6.
[12] *Ibid.*, 66-7.
[13] *Ibid.*, 67.
[14] *Phaedrus* 250[d]; *Theaetetus* 156.
[15] *Timaeus* 67-8.

particles are larger they produce contraction in the eye, and when smaller dilation. White dilates the visual ray and black contracts it. The various hues are generated by a rather sharp and violent admixture of inner and outer fire along with a moisture produced by their meeting. For example, red—the color of blood—is produced by a mild, nonflashing or intermediate external fire meeting with the moisture of the eye. The following table shows the results of the admixture of various colors with brightness and burning conditions.

TABLE I. COLOR MIXTURES AND THEIR RESULTS ACCORDING TO PLATO

Mixture	*Result*
bright blue + red + white	auburn
red + black + white	purple
red + black + white + burning	umber
black + white	dun
auburn + dun	flame color
white + auburn	pale yellow
white + brightness + full black	dark blue
white + dark blue	bright blue
flame color + black	leek-green

Plato is aware of the great mystery attending the color mixing processes and concludes, that while there is no difficulty in observing how color mixtures are produced, according to probability rules it is not possible for men to perform the combining and resolving operations.

Touch. For Plato sensing or perceiving consists primarily of the four types enumerated. Touching he does not treat as an important special type of activity. He discusses touch only incidentally and mainly by enumerating a series of touch qualities, for example, thickness, thinness, softness, hardness,[16] and hot and cold.[17] To pass imperceptibly from a sensory or perceiving mechanism to the qualities of objects perceived or sensed is a common trait of Plato's exposition.

A summarizing glance at Plato's entire handling of sensory discrimination impresses us with the utter simplicity and constraint of his attempts at description. Even when we take into account the date at which Plato lived we cannot overlook his lack of knowledge concerning the activities he discusses and the absence of scientific analysis. Still, the very crudeness of his descriptions redounds to the glory of the writer and his time. There is nothing here but attempts, however feeble and halting, to discuss complex happenings in terms derived from a simple observation of events. The faultiness of Plato's constructions is

[16] *Republic* 523.
[17] *Timaeus* 67.

based upon mythopeic substitution and invalid hypothesizing rather than by more inferior techniques of fallacious construction.[18]

IMAGINATION. For Plato imagination is constructive behavior (image-making) which results in some form of product that varies according to intention on one hand, and the character of the things worked upon or reacted to on the other.[19] Because Plato locates his discussion in the context of examining the Sophists, criteria of truth or falsity and real or unreal are introduced. Imaginative behavior is then divided into two general kinds, image production which is fairly faithful to the original things and phantasy production which results only in an appearance or partial imitation.[20]

It is significant that Plato attacks the Sophist because his creative behavior departs from contacts with real or existing things and therefore tends toward ignorance and deceit. As is characteristic with Plato, his entire discussion of imagination stresses a proper commerce with actual things and avoids the phantastic which is laden with opinions instead of with sensible things, and whose unreality is aggravated by the adroit use of language.

At first glance it appears remarkable that Plato should treat imaginal behavior in connection with the production of works of art, for this is a noteworthy anticipation of an approach which has only been developing in our time. But when we reflect that in Plato's time there had not yet developed any sophisticated commerce with psychic powers and procedures, we should expect him to deal with imaginal processes as they occur in typical situations of everyday life.

REMEMBERING AND RECOLLECTING. Plato's descriptions of remembering are awkwardly confused with his ideas of knowledge and his beliefs concerning the character of known things. Still, it is possible to separate what he describes as actual memorial processes as they can be observed to occur from his arguments about absolute knowledge, which is not developed in personal experience.

Memorial processes are of two general sorts. The first is a kind of enregistration of some sensory action.[21] This is described as an imprinting similar to the impression of a figure on wax by means of a signet ring. Anything seen, heard or thought can thus be preserved.[22] The ineptitude of the description notwithstanding, Plato is simply indicat-

[18] See Ch. 3 above.
[19] *Sophist* 235-40, 265-7.
[20] *Ibid.*, 260.
[21] *Philebus* 34.
[22] *Theaetetus* 191 *ff.*

ing the crude fact that persons do know what they have heard or seen after the original contact with those things has passed. The second type of memorial process, recollection, is similarly described as a process of reacting to things when they are no longer present. In recollection a longer time interval is involved. From seeing the picture of a horse or a lyre one can recollect a man. Again from the picture of Simias one can recollect Cebes or even Simias himself.[23] Plato specifies that recollection operates on two principles, those of likeness and difference. When a person is unable in this way to react to one thing on the basis of another then there is forgetting.

Such simple recollection Plato contrasts with the more momentous process of reminiscence.[24] The latter is a notion that belongs to Platonic epistemology and was designed to account for the stability of knowledge. There is, however, a link between the two. The doctrine of reminiscence is an argument for purity and exaltedness of knowledge and is talked about in terms of pure mind or soul, as distinct from activities connected with sensory and bodily processes.

While Plato's descriptions lack the precision desired by the modern student of psychology he is not to be interpreted as departing from the commonsense notion that psychological processes or mind consist of anything but action or qualities of behavior. The purest and most abstruse dialectical processes simply create valuable constructs but do not transcend spatial and temporal bounds.

DESIRE. Although it is impossible for Plato not to embroil himself with all sorts of cosmic ideas and ultimate theories whenever he touches on some specific psychological topic, he still manages to present some concrete descriptions of desiring behavior. At various points in the *Dialogues* he discusses the operation of such action, its relation to reasoning behavior, the restraint and control of desire, as well as the moral implications of such behavior.

The nature of desire Plato discusses in the context of love. In the *Symposium*[25] he describes desire as the reaction performed when something of known and valued quality is lacking. Surely this description is directly derived from observed behavior, and no less so when the thing desired is the immortality of procreation as so vividly described in the dialogue mentioned.

SLEEP AND DREAMS. Plato's treatment of sleep is extremely interesting

[23] *Phaedo* 73.
[24] *Phaedrus* 275.
[25] 192, 200 *f.*

Plate III. Plato, see p. XV.

for the double reason that he stresses a psychological rather than a biological description, and at the same time keeps close to a description of behavior and its conditions. To this may be added also that Plato makes the activity and conditions of sleep a potent factor in the determination of dreams and other kinds of psychological behavior.

When describing sleep in general, Plato points out in his own inimitable way that it occurs when an individual is cut off from stimulation. In the *Timaeus*[26] Plato illustrates his point by considering what happens when night comes on and effaces the objects which take part in the seeing interaction. Thus, sleeping is a definite behavior condition which differs from the waking state. In sleep there is a relaxation and removal of the inhibitions that restrain unapproved and violent behavior. In sleep, Plato asserts, there peers out even in the most highly respectable person a lawless wild-beast nature.[27] Beyond this he treats sleeping behavior in connection with dreaming.[28]

Dreams Plato fancifully describes as an activity occurring when internal fire, held in by the closing of the eyes, causes internal motions. These motions engender the visions in dreams. It may be assumed that nonvisual dreams are engendered in similar fashion. In the *Theaetetus* Plato takes for granted the frequency and prevalence of dreaming and makes use of this point in arguing about the certainty of knowledge, in rather striking anticipation of Descartes' discussion of similar problems.

Despite a passage in the *Republic* in which Plato seems to fall into an exaggerated notion as to what dreams can accomplish in the way of discerning truths unknown in the waking condition, he usually handles sleep and dreams in a simple, matter-of-fact way. This may be because he follows the lead of the medical writers[29] though it might be equally well interpreted as simple reliance on everyday observations.

FEELING. Feelings are treated by Plato as affections of pleasure and pain, reactions that are factors of the social and moral life of man.[30] Distributed through the various dialogues are many simple, everyday formulations which, even when they border upon the phantastic from our standpoint, are fairly directly connected with concrete events.

The affections are either motion or related to motion. In the *Re-*

[26] 45.
[27] *Republic* 571-2.
[28] *Theaetetus* 158; *Republic* 571, 574.
[29] Brett, *History of Psychology*, Vol. I, p. 71.
[30] *Philebus* 49.

public[31] Plato asserts that pleasure and pain are motions of the psyche, while in the *Timaeus* this statement is elaborated to include the kinds of motion and the things moved:

> An impression produced in us contrary to nature and violent, if sudden, is painful; and, again, the sudden return to nature is pleasant; but a gentle and gradual return is imperceptible and *vice versa.* On the other hand the impression of sense which is easily produced is most readily felt, but is not accompanied by pleasure or pain; such, for example, are the affections of the sight, which as we said above, is a body naturally uniting with our body in the day-time (54); for cuttings and burnings and other affections which happen to the sight do not give pain, nor is there pleasure when the sight returns to its natural state; yet very clear and strong sensations arise for every affection of sight, whether the eye is passive or is deliberately turned upon an object. The reason is that no violence at all is involved in the separation and reunion of the visual ray. But bodies formed of larger particles yield to the agent only with a struggle; and then they impart their motions to the whole and cause pleasure and pain—pain when alienated from their natural conditions, and pleasure when restored to them. Things which experience gradual withdrawings and emptyings of their naure, and great and sudden replenishments, fail to perceive the emptying, but are sensible of the replenishment; and so they occasion no pain, but the greatest pleasure, to the mortal part of the soul, as is manifest in the case of perfumes. But things which are changed all of a sudden, and only gradually and with difficulty return to their own nature, have effects in every way opposite to the former, as is evident in the case of burnings and cuttings of the body.[32]

On the whole, pleasure and pain correspond to the harmonic or disharmonic conditions of the organism. Sometimes this is a matter of gross health and disease[33] and at other times these affections are connected with lacks and deprivations or replenishment and restoration,[34] and at still other times with intellectual achievement.[35] In the *Philebus,*[36] Plato discusses the affections in connection with thirst, freezing, anticipation, and other situations.

KNOWLEDGE AND OPINION. Plato's discussion of knowledge, opinion, conjecture, and understanding covers the continuous range from everyday cognitive behavior to the loftiest activities concerned with the immutable ideas attained by the purest dialectic. When he deals with the latter he, of course, indulges in statements which appear to belie

[31] 583.
[32] *Timaeus* 64-65.
[33] *Republic* 583.
[34] *Philebus* 31 and 42 *f.*
[35] *Republic* 585.
[36] 32.

the plain activities of knowing and conjecturing performed by persons when they are in either direct or indirect contact with things. For example, Plato puts into the mouth of Socrates bizarre statements of how the body hinders the acquisition of knowledge, and how readily the soul attains to knowledge when it is severed from the body, and the man is dead.[37] And yet keeping before us Plato's cultural background and the expository technique of the master mythologist, we can interpret his statements in a completely naturalistic way. On a naturalistic basis, it is easy to see how Plato propagates his view of the primacy of constructs, of definitions, and of deductive abstractions as against indefinite and variable discriminations of concrete events. As to knowledge reactions in which the body shares, as in seeing and hearing, they are intermixed with the reports of "inaccurate witnesses."[38] Accordingly, for a Greek perfectionist and rationalist it seemed proper to claim that it would be best to abandon the body altogether and move to pure absolute dialectic where absolute thought holds sway as an unimpeded activity concerned with absolute being.

It would be completely futile to look to a presystemic writer for an organized psychological discussion of knowing and understanding. Nevertheless, it is remarkable how much material the Platonic writings provide for a systematic exposition. Here are some examples.

Knowledge is differentiated from ignorance on the basis of relevance to things known.[39] Of course, Plato is prejudiced in favor of what he calls absolute knowledge. But, despite his abstruse mathematical approach, he still makes room for opinion as a middle type of action[40] between knowing and understanding, although it only gives halting, inexact, and even false information.[41] False opinion results from a close linking of thought with perception.[42] Knowledge is also distinguished from belief and faith.[43] Belief and faith are remotely, if at all, connected with things available for reaction and test, but consist more of such responses as conviction or persuasion. Since Plato places belief and faith in the context of rhetoric, it follows that they are reactions to words or language and not to actual things.

Conjecture is similarly separated from knowledge. It consists of contacts with things but without arithmetic, without the weighing and

[37] *Phaedo* 65-70.
[38] *Phaedo* 65^{b}.
[39] *Theaetetus* 188 *ff*.
[40] *Symposium* 202.
[41] *Theaetetus* 193 *f*; *Sophist* 240.
[42] *Theaetetus* 195.
[43] *Gorgias* 454.

measuring which belong to knowledge.[44] In making this distinction Plato comes closer to an operational criterion than he does in other cases, but nowhere can his behavioral treatment of all the cognitive actions be doubted.

Understanding activities Plato places higher among the cognitive activities than opinion, though they cannot be associated with the highest kinds of knowledge. The superiority of understanding lies in its contemplation of geometry and kindred mathematical subjects. In terms of knowledge Plato arranges a scale ascending from the lowest item, namely perception, which deals with shadows, through belief, faith, and conjecture, and beyond these through understanding to reason.[45]

THINKING AND REASONING. These processes for Plato basically belong to the domain of dialectics. Now, since the Platonic dialectics have to do with the attainment of the highest realm of thinking and living, that of the immutable and imperishable Ideas, one may be inclined to believe that for Plato thinking and reasoning were separated from human behavior. However, this is an impossible position to take in view of the nature of his entire system of thought. Despite all of Plato's exaggerations and extrapolations, he is only attempting to achieve stability and reliability of knowledge, both for its own value and for its later application to practical situations.

That Plato regarded thinking and reasoning as concrete activities is evidenced by his description of thinking as the soul holding conversation with herself.

> . . . the soul when thinking appears to me to be just talking—asking questions of herself and answering them, affirming and denying.[46]

As compared with thinking, which is closer to nonmathematical situations, reasoning follows the lead of mathematical abstraction and is the process of achieving the absolute and final goal—connection with the Ideas, the highest forms of reality.

THE ROLE OF PLATO IN THE HISTORY OF PSYCHOLOGY

Rashness of the deepest sort is required to call Plato a psychologist. And yet he stands out starkly as a preparer, an effective agent in bringing psychological events to that stage of expert interest and reasonable organization which makes possible the birth of a science. As our gleanings from the Platonic writings have shown, there is a wealth of

[44] *Philebus* 55.
[45] *Republic* 511.
[46] *Theaetetus* 190; see also *Sophist* 263 *f.*

psychological material in the moral and political studies which Plato made. Though Plato's labors were not directed toward the production of a system of scientific psychology, no one could delve so profoundly into human nature and human behavior without turning up data and theories of psychological import. In the history of psychology Plato effectively played the part of conveyor and supplier of building materials which then stood ready for structuring into a distinctive edifice.

This is not, however, the whole story. What Plato furnished to the learning of his time were psychological descriptions of an exemplary naturalistic sort. They lent themselves at once and without elaborate modification to organization into a discipline, if not a definite system. Plato, then, stands out as an important figure who helped greatly to change everyday observations of behavior into data for scientific purposes.

CHAPTER 9

ARISTOTLE: INSTITUTOR OF BIOPSYCHOLOGY

ARISTOTLE'S PLACE IN THE HISTORY OF PSYCHOLOGY

ARISTOTLE ATTAINED a commanding position in the general history of the humanistic and nonhumanistic sciences and in the histories of logic and the arts. The magnitude of his achievement is easily assessed. Consider that in none of the departments of European intellectual achievement is Aristotle ranked as a mere contributor to scholarly and scientific endeavor. On the contrary, in most of the fields in which he worked he stands as a founder of scientific institutions and an innovator. As late as 1787 the celebrated Kant could utter his famous remark that "since Aristotle it [logic] has not had to retrace a single step."[1] Indeed, not until the nineteenth century was Aristotle forced to relinquish his position as a logical institution along with Euclid, who until then occupied a similar position in the domain of geometry. The eminence of Aristotle in many special sciences, and notably in biology, is acknowledged on every hand. The same thing is true for the social sciences, and it is also commonly held that Aristotle dominates the world of art theory, especially the thinking about tragedy.[2] Here it must be noted that the reputation of Aristotle is quite independent of his institutional character, established since the thirteenth century, as the colossus of medieval philosophy.

Though Aristotle is eminent in so many sciences, he occupies an even more elevated position in the history of psychology. What makes him so outstanding in psychology is that in a genuine sense he continues to be a pacesetter for students of the subject today. It is indisputable that Aristotle was a naturalistic thinker in psychology despite all his crudities and downright ineptitudes. Not only did he set the pattern for psychological study, thus shaping psychological treatises from his time to our own, but he also provided a corpus of psychologi-

[1] *Critique of Pure Reason,* 2nd ed. (Müller trans.), p. 688.
[2] Lucas, *Tragedy in Relation to Aristotle's Poetics,* Ch. 1.

cal doctrine, if not a system, which is a scientific model worthy of our homage even after a lapse of several millennia. Whatever may have been the failings of Aristotle in physics when considered from the standpoint of our day, his approach and achievement in psychology must stimulate the admiration of those who strive to cultivate psychology as a natural science. Cultural circumstances have necessarily operated to transform some of the basic features of his writings, but it may not be questioned that the Aristotelian psychological corpus has had a continuous life from the fourth century B.C. until the present.

As a scientific product Aristotelian psychology constitutes a remarkable first step in establishing psychology among the scientific institutions. This is not to overlook the peculiarities and the absurdities to be found in Aristotle's psychological writings, as for example his correlation of each of the sensory organs with one of the four elements.[3] Aristotle asserts that the part of the eye concerned with vision consists of water, the sense organ of sound consists of air, and that of smell consists of fire, while the organ of touch proper consists of earth. Such trivialities themselves strongly point to the completely naturalistic character of Aristotle's psychology. Aristotle approached psychological events with the same attitude as he did the events of physics and biology. In fact, he used the same method when he studied perceiving, thinking, sensing, imagining, dreaming, and reasoning as he did when he occupied himself with the motions of inorganic bodies. As his works make abundantly clear, his psychology actually is a branch of biology. Psychological behavior he treats as the actions of animals and plants. Moreover, as specific events, biological activities belong to the general domain of physics, as do the general actions of inorganic things.

Obviously from the standpoint of current erudition Aristotle's psychology is tentative, immature, and grossly insufficient. Still, it is inescapable that his outlook and specific treatment of particular types of behavior are in the fullest and most authentic sense scientific. Not only is there no transnatural factor in his system, as would indeed be culturally impossible, but beyond this he treats every topic as a matter of definite observation. Psychological events for him are localizable on the event continuum as distinct from the abstractions which he derives from them and which belong to his metaphysics—that is, the speculative system erected on the basis of mathematical models. The propositions of his psychological and other treatises are definitely derived from concrete encounters with events.

[3] *De Sensu* 438^{b} 17 *ff*.

THE PROTOPROPOSITIONS OF ARISTOTLE'S PSYCHOLOGY

In entering upon a study of the psychological work of such a historian and logician as Aristotle it is highly desirable to set forth some of his basic ideas concerning science in general and the science of psychology in particular. His general scientific assumptions we formulate as the protopostulates of psychology, while his basic psychological assumptions are organized as metapropositions. As we have already indicated, these basic assumptions are deeply set in the matrix of Greek general culture and among the special institutions of science. As the following quotation indicates, Aristotle stood for a sharp separation between the work of science and that of dialectics.

> Lack of experience diminishes our power of taking a comprehensive view of the admitted facts. Hence those who dwell in intimate association with nature and its phenomena grow more and more able to formulate, as the foundations of their theories, principles such as to admit of a wide and coherent development: while those whom devotion to abstract discussions has rendered unobservant of the facts are too ready to dogmatize on the basis of a few observations. The rival treatments of the subject now before us will serve to illustrate how great is the differenec between a "scientific" and a "dialectical" method of inquiry. For, whereas, the Platonists argue that there must be atomic magnitudes "because otherwise 'The Triangle' will be more than one," Demokritos would appear to have been convinced by arguments appropriate to the subject, i.e. drawn from the science of nature.[4]

The Aristotelian philosophy of science is, of course, a specialization of general Greek philosophy, especially as it had culminated in the thinking of Socrates and Plato. It is no doubt best characterized as a major shift toward observation and concreteness. However simplicistic Aristotelian ideas may be from the standpoint of things and events, there is a constant effort to report accurately the events actually encountered. This is attested to even by Aristotle's acceptance of the four crude elements and his insistence upon ends or purposes. Once we free Aristotle's ideas from the spiritistic and general metaphysical interpretations imposed upon them by the scholastics, we can observe his constant endeavors to keep close to concrete events. The merits of Aristotle's logic and philosophy of science are faithfully reflected in the following six protopropositions.

Protoproposition 1. The Substance or Material of Things consists of Four Basic Elements or Components and their relative Conditions. From general Ionian tradition Aristotle had taken over and preserved

[4] *De Generatione et Corruptione* 316ᵃ 5 *ff.*

the simple view that all bodies are composed of fire, water, air, and earth. These components operate differently according to their conditions of hot, cold, moist, and dry. Nothing more concrete than these elements has ever been proposed. The acceptance of this basic protopostulate bespeaks Aristotle's definiteness and matter-of-factness with respect to his philosophy of science.

Protoproposition 2. There are Four Types of Causes basic to the Existence of Things or their Changes. In line with his simple and concrete approach to things, Aristotle analyzes things and events on the basis of the four causes: the Final, the Formal, the Efficient, and the Material aspects of things.

Final causes in their various aspects may best be described as the plans or purposes, specifications, and fittingness which are analyzable out of things and which serve to account for their existence, shape, or operation.

Formal causes concern the plan or shape of things; Aristotle insists that form is inseparable from matter—the shape of a vessel from its material, stone, metal, or wood. Often the formal cause is connected with the finality and perfectibility of things—their excellence for use, enjoyment, or desirability.

Efficient causes represent the work of bringing a bit of material to the shape or perfection of an object. In general they represent all the changes and transformations involved in an object's coming to be.

Material causes probably come closest to Aristotle's notion of the concreteness of things. In his various examples he mentions gold, silver, bronze, and stone as types of "that out of which a thing comes to be and which persists."[5] Though we may dwell upon the superficiality of the analysis or the immaturity of the scientific level which it reveals, nevertheless it must impress us as a fair attempt to deal with the immediate features of available objects and conditions.

Protoproposition 3. Events consist primarily of Changes from a particular State of Actuality through Potentiality to another State of Actuality. Interested in all concrete objects and events, Aristotle is impressed with the perennial shifts, changes, and transformations of things. Possibly there is an influence here of biological things in which origins, metamorphoses, growth, and deterioration stand out above all other traits. At any rate, the fact of potentiality brings the observer straight to the heart of actual things in all their variety and ways of acting. Though Aristotle in some places looks upon potentiality as a

[5] *Physica* 194[b] 24.

power to change things, in most instances he regards it merely as a state or stage of change. To offset the ineptness of making potentiality into a power he makes it identical with actuality.[6] On the whole, Aristotle insists that potentiality is secondary with respect to actuality. The latter is always prior to the former. The net result is that potentiality consists of the intimate details of variance when some actual thing changes its character or state.

Protoproposition 4. Changes and Developments of Things are limited at one End by Origin or Inception and at the Other by Attainment or Maturity. The first point stressed by this protoproposition is that things which develop, in contrast to those which do not, attain a culmination point. This point may be regarded as an end of a single, unique sort, or as a combination of such phases of fulfillment. Such ends may be described as use, purpose, function, or perfection. Furthermore, Aristotle places emphasis upon a fixed point of attainment. He assumed that there is a definite, observable form or pattern that is to be attained. No indefinite and unpredictable form or function is tolerated. While on the one hand this protoproposition sets forth a belief in fixity and finality of result attained by an indefinite means, on the other it forces to the front the belief in the practical and proximate characteristics of the ends of things. Purpose and perfection, as well as all other ends, have to do with immediate terrestrial processes and not with vague, cosmic, non-spatiotemporal principles. We may well take as examples of typical Aristotelian doctrine that the soul, essence, *entelechy,* or purpose of an axe is to cut, while sight or seeing is the purpose and perfection of the eye. Critics who interpret Aristotle as proposing a non-spatiotemporal purpose or utility simply translate his terms in a medieval and modern transcendental sense.

Protoproposition 5. Things and Events exist in numerous continuous and interrelated States. For a comparatively unsophisticated observer such as Aristotle a prime variation in things and their changes is that of corporeality or solidity, and incorporeality as exemplified by gaseous or liquid states. This distinction is basic to the differentiation of form from function, the substantive being from the actions it performs, and also divides off temporary aspects or states from the continuing and compact structures of objects.

Protoproposition 6. Things vary in Durability from the Perishable to the Unchangeable and Eternal. With characteristic naïveté Aristotle specifies the durability of things and events on a scale of change or

[6] *Metaphysica* 1045^b 29.

permanence. The heavens and astronomic bodies he regards as ungenerated and indestructible. He says,

Of things constituted by nature some are ungenerated, imperishable, and eternal, while others are subject to generation and decay. The former are excellent beyond compare and divine, but less accessible to knowledge.[7]

And again,

That the heaven as a whole neither came into being nor admits of destruction, as some assert, but is one and eternal, with no end or beginning of its total duration, containing and embracing in itself the infinity of time . . .[8]

What is of especial interest to us is the great contrast between Aristotle's own view about duration and immortality and the imposed interpretation stemming from post-Greek times. Whereas for Aristotle immortality signifies permanence because of certain concrete conditions, his views have been incorporated into an entirely different intellectual system. What Aristotle regards as permanent or divine has been misinterpreted to the advantage of medieval faith in personal powers. For Aristotle circular motion is immortal, so heaven, a divine body, possesses a motion which is circular.[9] Aristotle quotes Alcmaeon's belief in the immortality of soul, an immortality which

. . . belongs to it in virtue of its ceaseless movement; for all the "things divine," moon, sun, the planets, and the whole heavens, are in perpetual movement.[10]

Circularity of motion is primary and of a unique quality.

THE METAPROPOSITIONS OF ARISTOTLE'S PSYCHOLOGY

To appreciate better the Aristotelian system of psychology it is important to lay bare the metasystemic propositions which form its essential foundation. Generally speaking, the metasystemic phase of a scientific system consists of the basic propositions which specify and delineate the boundaries and significance of the system proper. For us, obviously, the significance of the present metapropositions lies in the attempt to separate Aristotle's own views from those impressed upon them by commentators writing under the influence of a later culture. The following metapropositions we take as adequately representing the foundations of Aristotle's psychology.

[7] *De Partibus Animalium* 644^b 21 *ff*.
[8] *De Caelo* 283^b 26.
[9] *De Caelo* 286^a 12.
[10] *De Anima* 405^a 30.

Metaproposition 1. Psychological Events are Phases of biological Events. Inasmuch as *psyche* (ψυχης) is in some sense the principle of animal and plant life,[11] psychology must be a special part of biology. It concerns the functions or acts of organisms as over against their structure or organization, and their development or evolution. The basic function is movement when organisms are considered in isolation, and discrimination or knowledge when they are considered in their normal and inevitable relations to their surroundings. Since actions may be considered as distinct from objects acting, Aristotle stresses the incorporeality of the functions or acts as compared with the morphological characteristics of organisms.

Metaproposition 2. Psyche constitutes the essential Characteristic of Organisms. Because the movements and discriminations of organisms constitute the uses, ends, or fulfillment of the lives of organisms, psychological events are the most characteristic biological events. Therefore, psychology, as the science of the detailed activities of organisms, is the central department of biology.

Metaproposition 3. Psychology is concerned with the Elucidation of the concrete Actions of Organisms as They maintain Themselves in their Environment and act to promote their Well-being. Organisms perform many varieties of behavior. They not only come to be, but grow and decay also. Moreover, they sense, think, pity, learn, get angry, remember, and so on. Psychology as a branch of biology treats these activities or functions of the organisms. Such acts are specialized behavior growing out of the more simple acts conditioned by the morphology and physiology of organisms. Though Aristotle thinks constantly in formal terms (form, matter, cause, and stress), and prefers generalized questions of existence and nature, he does describe psychological events as interactions with environing things and conditions.

Metaproposition 4. Psychology and Biology, as the Sciences of particular Organisms and their Activities, belong to the general Department of concrete Events, namely Physics or the Science of Nature. For Aristotle physics, as the study of concrete particulars, contrasts with mathematics, as the study of abstractions from natural things.[12] As we have seen, Aristotle distinguishes sharply between science and dialectics. The former is concerned essentially with particular things and events that are directly or indirectly observed, the latter with abstractive constructions.

[11] *De Anima* 402ᵃ 5, 412ᵇ *et passim.*

[12] See for example *De Caelo* 299ᵃ 15 *ff. et passim.*

ARISTOTLE'S SYSTEM OF PSYCHOLOGY: HISTORY AND BACKGROUND

Aristotle has been called the first historian of psychology. He deserves the title because his exposition of the opinions of his predecessors concerning the nature of psychological events covers the development of psychology up to his time. Aristotle's ideas about psychological events have thus been formulated with a full realization of what his forerunners had developed. Much he accepts from the past, though he is exceedingly selective and critical.

All students of psychology, Aristotle finds, agree upon the proposition that psychological events are characterized by (a) movement, (b) discrimination or knowledge, and (c) incorporeality. Aristotle agrees but, just as his predecessors disagree among themselves as to the basis for these traits, he has his own views, doubtless derived from his own observations made at a later, more sophisticated and specialized period of science. For this reason, Aristotle legitimately thinks that he is making a completely fresh start and is formulating a new, general determination of *psyche* or psychological events.

In consonance with the established Hellenic intellectual traditions, the three traits of psychological behavior are thoroughly tied up with the simple concrete elements—fire, water, air, and earth. Also, the views about them are integrated with problems of substance and accidents, that is, whether the soul principle is self-moving only or moves other things, and in general whether the soul is or is not an autonomous cosmic or physical principle. Aristotle's relatively advanced biological assumptions provide him with an effective set of criteria for testing the views of his predecessors. Though he is as thoroughly tied to simple concrete events as his forerunners, he is able to make finer distinctions than those who start with physical (mechanical) rather than biological premises. Let us see what Aristotle is able to accept from the scientific traditions concerning the three basic traits of soul, and what he rejects.

Movement. Aristotle rejects the view that soul is a principle and source of movement which is autonomous and separable from the things moved. His primary targets here are the atomists Leucippus and Democritus, who declare that the fine, spherical particles are the most mobile, so that both fire and mind consist of such particles.

Aristotle calls the roll of those who make soul consist of one element or more. Among the former he mentions Hippo, who made soul consist of water; Diogenes, air; Heracleitus and others, fire. In fact, each of the elements has found its partisan with the exception, perhaps, of earth, though that must be included too, since there are those who make soul consist of all elements.[13] To be mentioned here, too, is Critias, who held soul to be made of blood.

Aristotle himself strongly opposes the view of the soul's autonomous motion. It is impossible for him to think so simply. Motion is ascribable to soul in so far as it is a phase or feature of organisms. Otherwise one might accept the superstition of a soul entering or leaving an organism or transferring from one to another. From Aristotle's biological standpoint, the soul moves as does an organism in connection with sensible objects or, as we should say, in correspondence with stimulating objects.[14]

Discrimination or Knowledge. Aristotle takes a strong stand against the elementalistic notion of cognition or knowing. It is absurd to argue that like is known only by its like, as Empedocles and many others say. Aristotle spurns the statements of Empedocles:

> For 'tis by Earth we see Earth, by Water Water,
> By Ether Ether divine, by Fire destructive Fire,
> By Love Love, and Hate by cruel Hate.[15]

For Aristotle discrimination is a complex action of an organism in contact with a complex and independent object. The knowing act depends as much on the objects known or discriminated as upon the organism.

Incorporeality. Though Aristotle insists that *psyche* is a substance, that is a distinctive thing or process, this does not mean that it is an object.[16] Otherwise it would be corporeal or elementalistic. Nor is it a number or quantum as the mathematicians say. No more is it a spatial quantity, quale, or motion. Another rejected notion of incorporeal *psyche* is that it is a harmony or proportion. The incorporeality of soul stems from the fact that it is a function or action of a complex organism interrelated with actions of things acting along with it.

THE STRUCTURE OF THE PSYCHOLOGICAL CORPUS

Although there is a definite structure in the writings of Aristotle on psychological subjects, the organization of the materials is not quite as clear-cut as in a modern treatise. Scholars are agreed that what we have are lecture notes made by Aristotle or his students. Accordingly, the psychology of Aristotle has to be brought together from various writings. For the most part these materials are contained in three treatises, which have come down to us under the names of *De Anima, Parva Naturalia,* and *Historia Animalium.*

[13] *De Anima,* 404^b 30-405^b 30.
[14] See *De Anima* 406^b 10.
[15] Diels, *Die Fragmente der Vorsokratiker,* Vol. I, p. 351, Frag. 109.
[16] *De Anima* 414^a 15 *ff.*

Plate IV. Aristotle, see p. XV.

As it is necessary for us to reorganize the materials, we present first for comparison the tables of contents of the three treatises mentioned. In the case of the *Historia Animalium* the material which may be regarded as the first treatise on animal psychology is contained in the last two books, VIII and IX.

In our reorganization we plan to avoid the repetitions which we find in the *De Anima* and *Parva Naturalia* so that we will have only one heading for each topic. It is to be noted that the *Parva Naturalia* appears as a series of small treatises on particular subjects. The *De Anima,* on the other hand, has the structure of a modern treatise. For example, of the three books into which the material is divided the first may be regarded as introductory. Here Aristotle defines the subject of psychology and indicates the problems with which it is concerned. Next, he considers the opinions of his predecessors for the purpose of indicating what is acceptable in Greek thinking concerning psychological events, and what is to be rejected.

Book II covers some of the same types of material as Book I, though in this case Aristotle presents his own views about psychological events. The main part of the book, which may be entitled *The Nature of Psychological Events,* is devoted to the study of the simpler types of psychological behavior. This includes the general definitions of *psyche,* the description of the various types of psychological action, and then a series of discussions of various sensing and perceiving activities, for example, sight and its objects, hearing and its objects, and so on.

Book III consists mainly of the discussion of complex psychological behavior. Thus, there is a treatment of the common sense, thinking, imagining, and the nature of motivation and what stimulates such activity.

As the accompanying outline of the contents of the *Parva Naturalia* indicates, there is a repetition of the topics of the senses and memory, and after that Aristotle treats sleep, dreaming, and a number of topics which in current specialization belong to biology; however, since Aristotle is presenting what must be called a biopsychology, this inclusion is in no way objectionable.

THE NATURE OF PSYCHOLOGICAL EVENTS

DEFINITION OF PSYCHOLOGICAL EVENTS. There are three features of objective Greek thinking which influence Aristotle's specification of the essential character of psychological events. First, there is the formalistic or deductive style of logic or organization of propositions. This

Table II. The Aristotelian Psychological Corpus

A. *De Anima*

Book I (Introduction to Psychology)

Sec. 1. The aims and problems of psychology.
Sec. 2. Opinions of early thinkers about soul.
Sec. 3-5. Critical examination of soul theories.
Sec. 3. Movement not essence of soul.
Sec. 4. Soul not moved by non-local movement.
Soul not a self moving number.
Sec. 5. Soul not composed of elements.
Soul not present in all things.
Divisibility and indivisibility of soul.

Book II (The Simpler Acts)

Sec. 1. First definition of soul.
Sec. 2. Second definition of soul.
Sec. 3. The functions of the soul.
Sec. 4. The nutritive function.
Sec. 5. Sense-perception.
Sec. 6. The different kinds of sensible object.
Sec. 7. Sight and its object.
Sec. 8. Hearing and its object.
Sec. 9. Smell and its object.
Sec. 10. Taste and its object.
Sec. 11. Touch and its object.
Sec. 12. General characteristics of simple sensory action.

Book III (The Complex Acts)

Sec. 1-2. The number of the simple senses.
Sec. 2. Common sense.
Sec. 3. Thinking, perceiving, and imagining distinguished.
Sec. 4. Knowing and thinking.
Sec. 5. Actual and potential knowledge.
Sec. 6. Simple and complex thinking.
Sec. 7. Practical and contemplative thinking.
Sec. 8. Sensory basis of complex actions.
Sec. 9. Problems of movement.
Sec. 10. Appetite and the cause of movement.
Sec. 11. What originates movement in various animals.
Sec. 12. The relations and importance of the various soul functions.
Sec. 13. Touch and its importance for animals.

B. *Parva Naturalia*

De Sensu (On the Senses)
De Memoria et Reminiscentia (On Memory and Reminiscence)
De Somno et Vigilia (On Sleep and Waking)
De Somniis (On Dreaming)
De Divinatione per Somnum (On Divination by Dreams)
De Longitudine et Brevitate Vitae (On the Longness and Shortness of Life)
De Iuventute et Senectute (On Youth and Old Age)
De Vita et Morte (On Life and Death)
De Respiratione (On Respiration)

C. *Historia Animalium*

Book VIII Ecology, Habitology, Pathology
Book IX Characterology, Sex Differences

throws Aristotle's exposition into the formal procedure of specifying and classifying things instead of describing them as occurrences. Hence there is a gap between his expository references and the observations and opinions he actually holds.

Next, his exposition stresses substance or thing instead of occurrence or event. Although this stylistic institution does not occlude his basic views, it does remind us of the date of the first systematic psychological treatise. In the fourth century B.C. it is entirely appropriate to think or write in terms of the earliest analyses of the categories. Here, again, there is no question of what Aristotle treats or what views he holds, though it is readily seen how later commentators could find a basis in this structuralism for their transfiguration of Aristotelian theory.

And finally, Aristotelian writings are influenced by general systematic views. There is not and could not be at that time a strict separation between general philosophical and detailed scientific thinking. Accordingly, there is an aura of universality and finalism in Aristotle's exposition. Thus the definition of psychological events reveals clearly Aristotle's metaphysical concern with actuality and potentiality, form and matter, and the like.

Surely it is a distinctive merit of Aristotle that the three influences mentioned do not bind him too tightly. Actually, his definitions of *psyche* or soul are more concrete than his philosophy demands. Nor is he satisfied with one definition. Two of these we reproduce.

> . . . soul is the first grade of actuality of a natural body having life potentially in it.[17]

> . . . soul is an actuality or formulable essence of something that possesses a potentiality of being besouled.[18]

PROBLEMS CONCERNING PSYCHOLOGICAL EVENTS. Whenever Aristotle employs his technique of demonstrative exposition, he always parallels it with a discussion which emphasizes the concrete facts. This point is evident in the problems which he raises concerning psychological events.

Substance or Quality. We have already indicated Aristotle's substantive treatment of *psyche*. *Psyche* is not simply an accident, a quality, or quantity, that is a characteristic of something else. He does not deny that substances are sometimes most effectively known through their accidents, but in the case of *psyche* he wants to emphasize that it is an

[17] *De Anima* 412ᵃ 30.
[18] *Ibid.*, 414ᵃ 27.

independent feature of psychological events. It is, of course, as we have seen, the form, perfection, or culmination of such facts.

Potential or Actual. Psyche is decidedly a realized feature of psychological action. In fact, so far as biology is concerned, *psyche* is the very principle of actuality. Although psychological actions are potential in the sense that an organism that is not now speaking can speak or one that is not seeing can see, the essential feature of *psyche* is the actualization of behavior.

Divisibility. The problem of divisibility probably grows out of Aristotle's characterization of *psyche* as a substance. Still, he rejects forthwith any notion that there is divisibility. As we know, *psyche* for him is function or action and there simply is no point to the question of divisibility.

Homogeneity. If *psyche* is indivisible, it is still not something that is always and everywhere the same. Psychological actions or functions must be described as they are observed. Since there are so many differences in actions, so many different types of psychological behavior, the different instances will vary greatly one from another.

Psyche as Generic or Specific. As form, *psyche,* of course, is generic and different from other analyzable features of an organism or some other object. On the other hand, when the various types of psychological action are considered, as for example in the differentiation of perception from either thinking or remembering, *psyche* is specific. Moreover, when one considers the type of organism that performs the psychological act, then, of course, differences have to be stressed. In this connection Aristotle complains that up to his time those who have discussed and investigated soul seem to have confined themselves to the human organism. As a biologist concerned with the actual behavior of organisms, Aristotle does not even confine psychological study to human and non-human animals but includes plants also.

Relations of Psyche and Soma. The problem which Aristotle raises concerning the connection between the behavior and the morphology of the organism reflects most acutely his views concerning psychology. Assuming that action or soul is the form of the organism while the tissues and organs constitute the matter of the organism, Aristotle insists that it is impossible for the one to exist without the other. In consequence *psyche* and *soma* are simple results of logical analysis. All affections of the *psyche* are affections of the complex of *psyche* and *soma.*

> ... there seems to be no case [of affections of the soul] in which the soul can act or be acted upon without involving the body; e.g., anger, courage, ap-

petite, and sensitivity generally. Thinking seems the most probable exception; but if this too proves to be a form of imagination or to be impossible without imagination, it too requires a body as a condition of its existence.[19]

SPECIFIC PSYCHOLOGICAL ACTIVITIES

NUTRITIVE BEHAVIOR. As a thoroughgoing biopsychologist, Aristotle maintains a close continuity in his exposition of the functions as behavior of organisms. To him, as to modern psychologists, it does not seem at all strange to include metabolic activities in a psychological treatise. Indeed, from his standpoint, it would be highly illogical not to include among soul functions those which are responsible for keeping the organism alive in the first place.[20]

Nutritive behavior obviously consists of adjustments to food. Aristotle habitually analyzes psychological behavior into three factors: (a) what the organism does; (b) the morphological means or basis for the action, what enables the organism to do it; and (c) the objects concerned in the action. In the case of nutritive behavior, which Aristotle divides into (1) digestion and absorption of food, and (2) reproductive acts, the morphological and physiological means are obvious while the objects interacted with are foods of various sorts. Such objects correspond to perceptual or intelligible objects in the performance of discrimination or cognitive behavior.[21]

Because growth and decay are the primary and basic soul traits and give rise to other and more elaborate actions such as sensibility and motion, Aristotle constructs what may be called a ladder of living things. Plants stand on the bottom rung. They perform only nutritive action. Animals not only perform nutritive behavior, but sensitive or discriminative acts also. Living things that are sensitive must be orectic or appetitive too. Some animals, though not all, are able to change their location, so locomotor behavior stands on the next higher rung of the ladder, of which the highest is calculative thinking and reasoning. The last, of course, is the prerogative of the human animal.[22] The accompanying diagram (Fig. 7) represents the Aristotelian schema.

SENSORIAL AND PERCEPTUAL BEHAVIOR. As a naturalist or ecological biologist Aristotle discusses sensory and perceptual behavior from the point of view of the preservation and well being of organisms. Psycho-

[19] *De Anima* 403^a 5 *ff*.
[20] *See De Anima* 416^b 18.
[21] *De Anima* 415^a 15.
[22] *De Anima* 414^a, 414^b 1-20.

logical behavior is in this way studied as a natural extension of morphological and physiological investigations. Sensing and perceiving activities are performed when animals interact with food objects and shun noxious and destructive things. Sensory and perceptual activities are not, of course, limited to maintenance processes, but serve also as the basis of information about things for intelligent animals, so that they

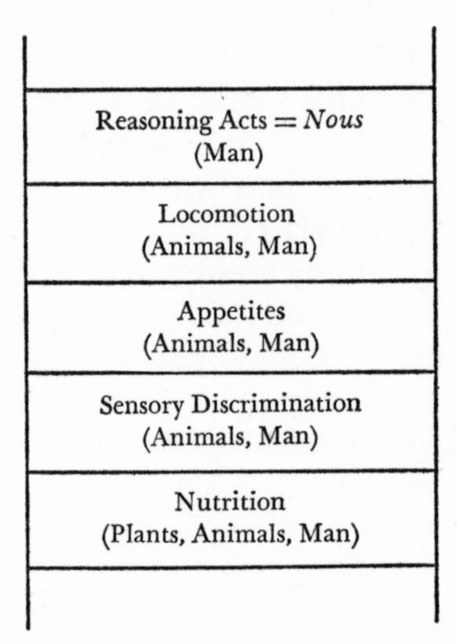

FIG. 7. ARISTOTLE'S HIERARCHY OF MORPHOLOGY AND BEHAVIOR

can attain practical and speculative orientation.[23]

A paramount problem for Aristotle, the biopsychologist, is to assign to each factor its proper place in sensing and perceiving situations. To begin with, there is the organism and, in fact, there may be a particular part of the organism, a sense organ, which plays a prominent part in the sensory situation. It is this emphasis on the organism and its parts which induces him to assert that there are five senses and no more.[24] Consequently he associates each sense with an organ; touch with flesh, sight with the eyes, hearing with the ears, smell with the nose, and taste with the tongue. It is clear, of course, that when Aristotle discusses sensing in the closest connection with end organs or parts of the organism, he is concerning himself with properties of objects, colors, odors, tastes, savors, and contact; but when he deals with the objects in which these qualities inhere, he must connect them with parts of the organism or with the entire organism. Outstanding here are the

[23] *De Sensu* 436^b 18, 437^a 1-3.
[24] *De Anima* 424^b 20.

interactions with the common sensibles, that is the dynamic or quantitative characteristics of things; for example, movement, rest, figure, magnitude, numbers, and unity. Common sensibles undoubtedly are reacted to by no special organ.[25] It is this variation in activity, focused now on one special part, now on several, or on the total organism, which basically distinguishes sensing from perceiving.

Next there are the stimulus objects, which exist prior to and independently of the reactions.[26] Sense objects for Aristotle consist of qualities or properties and also of objects, including organisms and persons. Generally speaking, sensing behavior consists of the discrimination of qualities, whereas in perceiving reactions objects are discriminated. The perceptive functions distinguish one person or thing from another, whereas the sensory functions localized in a particular sense-organ differentiate either the different qualities of objects, for example, the white and sweet qualities, or simply particular kinds of qualities, such as white and black, by sight, and sweet and bitter, by taste.[27]

Aristotle observes a third factor in sensing and perceiving situations, namely the media of sensing. For sight it is the translucent or transparent, for hearing air, for touch contact with flesh. Only taste has no medium as do the other senses.[28] The accompanying schema of the sensing and perceiving situation represents Aristotle's views (Fig. 8).

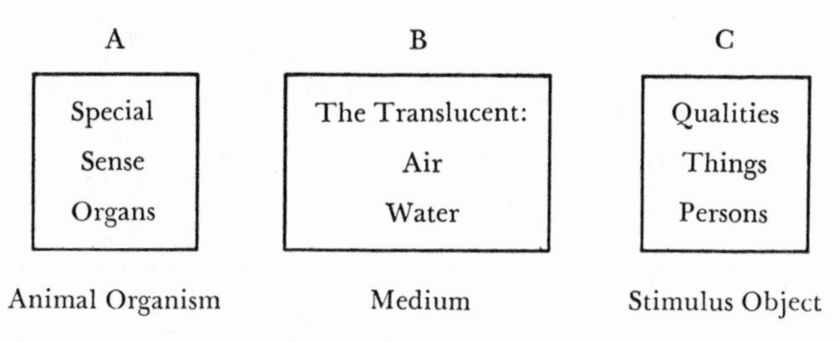

FIG. 8. THE ROLE OF THE MEDIUM IN SENSING AND PERCEIVING

In summing up the basic characteristics of all sensory behavior, Aristotle describes sensing as the power or function of the organism to receive the sensible form of things without the matter.

> This must be conceived of as taking place in the way in which a piece of wax takes on the impress of a signet-ring without the iron or gold; we say that what produces the impression is a signet of bronze or gold, but its particular metallic constitution makes no difference: in a similar way the

[25] *De Anima* 425ᵃ 27.
[26] *De Categoriae* 7ᵇ 35 and *Metaphysica* 1010ᵇ 35.
[27] *De Anima* 426ᵇ 7 *ff.*
[28] *De Anima* 422ᵃ 15.

sense is affected by what is coloured or flavoured or sounding, but it is indifferent what in each case the *substance* is; what alone matters is what *quality* it has, i.e. in what *ratio* its constituents are combined.[29]

It is no deviation from Aristotle's own descriptive intention to point out that sensory and perceptual doctrine specifies that organisms interact with stimulus objects through a medium. He expresses this by saying that smelling is an observing of the result produced by an odorous object first upon the air, which in turn stimulates the organism.[30]

The completely objective character of Aristotle's doctrine of perception becomes fully evident when seen in the light of an attempt by a prominent translator to impose a psychistic interpretation upon it. Smith remarks that the objective statements indicated above represent Aristotle's vain

> endeavours to bridge the gap between the two senses of 'perceiving,' (a) the physical affection of the sense-organ by the sensigenous object, and (b) the psychical activity or reaction which consists in becoming or being aware of its sensible quality.[31]

ELEMENTARY DISCRIMINATION BEHAVIOR. *Sight and its Object.* Seeing is a kind of action or motion with respect to a visible object. In general there are two sorts of visible objects, a) color and b) the transparent. The latter is not visible in itself but is seen by means of the color of other objects. The medium of sight is light[32] without which there is nothing to activate the sense organ by the movement set up in it by the visible object. Because of the creative-perception tradition so powerful in our day, it is especially significant to notice that Aristotle is firm in his insistence that there is an interaction between the organism and the object. Moreover, Aristotle insists upon distinguishing between savor or color and the act of sensing these qualities or any others.[33]

Color for Aristotle consists of a magnitude or ratio between white and black. Colors, then, constitute a series located at intermediate points between the extremes of lightness and darkness. Black and white may be juxtaposed in the ratio of 3 to 2, 3 to 4, or in the ratio of other numbers, even incommensurable ones.[34] In general colors represented by simple numerical ratios are the agreeable ones, as in the case of concordant sounds in music. This is the case with purple, crimson, and a few other colors. Aristotle suggests an alternative hypothesis to that of

[29] *De Anima* 424^a 17 *ff.*
[30] *De Anima* 424^b 15 *ff.*
[31] Ross, ed., *The Works of Aristotle,* Vol. III: *De Anima* 424^b 19, note 1.
[32] *De Anima* 418^b 1 *ff.; De Sensu* 438^b 3.
[33] *De Anima* 425^b, 25, 526^a 23; *De Categoriae* 7^b 35, 8^a 9 *f.; Metaphysica* 1010^b 31-1011^a 2.
[34] *De Sensu* 439^b 27.

the ratio of black and white in intermediate positions. Instead of mixing infinitesimally small amounts of black and white, he proposes that white and black surfaces of various extents be overlaid so the one is seen through the other as a medium. As in the former hypothesis, the variations in color would depend upon the ratio of the two contributing factors. Aristotle uses as an example the varying appearances of the sun, which in itself is white but takes on a crimson hue when seen through a fog or smoke cloud.[35]

Although all things are colored and thus are distinctly visible, there are some things that do not require light for visibility. This is true only for proper color. Fiery or shiny things like fungi, flesh, scales, eyes, and heads of fish may be seen in darkness.[36]

Hearing and its Object. Auditory interactions consist of contacts with sounding bodies through the intermediation of air which is set in motion by the sounding body.[37] Water, too, may serve as a medium for sound, which is thus brought into contact with the hearing organ.

Aristotle devotes much of his discussion to the object of hearing. Sound is generated by the impact of one body upon another. In general only smooth and solid objects can generate sounds which can impinge upon the organ of hearing. The essential feature of sound production is the impact of two solids upon each other and against the air, which is usually the medium of contact between the sounding body and the hearing individual.

The actual medium of sound propagation is the air, which operates as a continuous mass. At the point of contact with the hearing organism there is an impact with a smooth surface. Aristotle assumes that for hearing there must be a condition at the point of the medium's delivery of the motion similar to that at the receiving end.

Although Aristotle is necessarily vague about the organ of hearing, he does refer to the spiral construction of the cochlea. Primarily the hearing organ is an air-containing and confining chamber in which air is put into motion, thus bringing about a reverberation in the hearing organ as in a horn. This motion in the interior of the hearing organ is interfered with by an ingress of foreign material, such as water. When this happens the organism is deafened just as when the tympanic membrane is damaged or destroyed.[38]

Because of the connection between hearing, speech, and, in the end,

[35] *De Sensu* 440ᵃ 10.
[36] *De Anima* 419ᵃ 3 *ff*.
[37] *De Anima* 419ᵇ 4-421ᵃ 5.
[38] *De Anima* 419ᵇ 14.

rational discourse, Aristotle rates auditory behavior very high. It is through speech that hearing competes with vision. Although vision is the most highly developed sense[39] and such common sensibles as figure, magnitude, motion and number are not perceived by hearing but only by vision, hearing does have a great indirect advantage. Hearing, according to Aristotle contributes most to the growth of intelligence or wisdom.

Smelling and its Object. The interactions in this domain are not so easy for Aristotle to describe since he feels handicapped by the inferiority of the human to other animals in discriminating odors.

The objects of smelling are the odorous and the inodorous. The former are in general describable as sweet and bitter, though odor characteristics cover also pungency, astringency, acidity, and succulency. Aristotle admits that the classification and description of odors is greatly helped by drawing upon the flavor qualities of tastes, with which they are closely connected. Unlike other animals man smells only when he inhales.[40] Also, the organ must be dry as contrasted with tasting acts, for example, which require moisture. The medium for smelling is either air or water. For humans, of course, the medium is air, but Aristotle observes that water animals make directly for food from a distance if it has any scent.[41]

Tasting and its Object. Taste discrimination is a unique type of interaction with flavors as the objects. Unlike seeing, hearing, and smelling, there is no intervening medium between the organism or its taste organs and the objects tasted. Taste interactions are more like touch reactions with their direct impacts, though touch does have a solid medium.

In general, the objects of taste, the flavors, are of two sorts, the sweet and the bitter. Secondarily the sweet-tasting objects are succulent while the bitter ones are saline. Between the objects with the two main kinds of tastes are those classifiable as pungent, harsh, astringent, and acid. But it is not only the flavors that are objects of taste. Tasteless objects in the sense of slightly tasteful or bad tasting things are reacted to also.[42] Only liquids or what can be liquefied are tastable, and so the tongue as the organ of taste must not be dry though it must maintain its solid character and not be too moist.[43]

[39] *De Anima* 429ᵃ 3; also *De Sensu* 437ᵃ 4-15.
[40] *De Anima* 421ᵇ 14.
[41] *De Anima* 421ᵇ 12.
[42] *De Anima* 422ᵃ 30.
[43] *De Anima* 422ᵇ 5.

Touching and its Object. Although touching interactions involve direct and immediate contact with objects, they still include a medium, though not one that intervenes between two relatively distant objects. That medium is flesh. The actual touch organ is located within the flesh or muscle tissue. When contact is made with some touch object we are not affected successively by the medium but simultaneously with it.[44]

Touch objects are distinctive qualities of things such as hot, cold, dry, moist, hard, and soft. But there is for Aristotle an unresolved question as to whether the touch sense is one or several. As in other cases, the actual stimulus must be a ratio between the qualities. For example, an object that is equally hot or cold or hard and soft cannot be perceived. A quality located at the neutral point will not be discriminated.

Aside from the separate discussion of the organs involved and the kind of objects distinguished by each sense, Aristotle also proposes some essential features of each interaction. For example, the object must set up a minimal intensity of action or motion in the medium; otherwise the inertia of the sense organ will not respond. Secondly, the ratio of the qualities in objects must be different from the ratio of the same qualities in the reacting organ. If the hand is of the same ratio of hot and cold as the objects, there will be no discrimination. In the third place, there is a limit to the variation of the ratios. Too intense a difference would impair and destroy the discriminating organ and perhaps prove fatal to the organism.[45]

SIMPLE DISCRIMINATION AND COMPLEX IDENTIFICATION ACTIONS. According to Aristotle's analysis of the behavior of organisms, it is only possible to point to local organ action as at least the nucleus of simple discrimination acts. When the organism interacts with complex objects or abstract and non-surface properties of things such as movement, rest, unity, number, figure, and magnitude the acts are organismic, although Aristotle, with the structure-function bias of the biologist, says that they are perceived by all the senses or at least by more than one. For example, certain kinds of movement are perceptive by touch and by sight.[46]

When treating indirect or incidental perception, Aristotle perforce runs into the fact that his ideal of an activity as a function of specific structure breaks down. When an organism perceives that the white object before him is the "son of Diares," the white quality which can be connected specifically with an act of the eye is really incidental or

[44] *De Anima* 423^b 15.
[45] *De Anima* 424^a 14, 426^b 32, 429^a 29-429^b 3.
[46] *De Anima* 418^a 19.

auxiliary. The quality of being "the son of Diares" in no way affects a particular organ but is a function of the entire perceiving organism.[47] This problem arises also in more direct perception. Since it is only by sight that we distinguish colors and only by taste the various flavors then how are the different qualities of white and sweet sensed or perceived when they appear in either the same or different objects? It follows from this that the organism must operate as a unit.[48] Apparently there are great variations in the interrelationship between organisms and objects in different psychological situations. It is important at this point to summarize the various gradations.

Vegetative Behavior. Here the organism directly and effectively becomes one with the food objects with which it interacts. There is no point to differentiating various parts of the organism in this situation or to keeping the organism and object separate. The following diagram (Fig. 9) serves to indicate the relationship of organism and object.

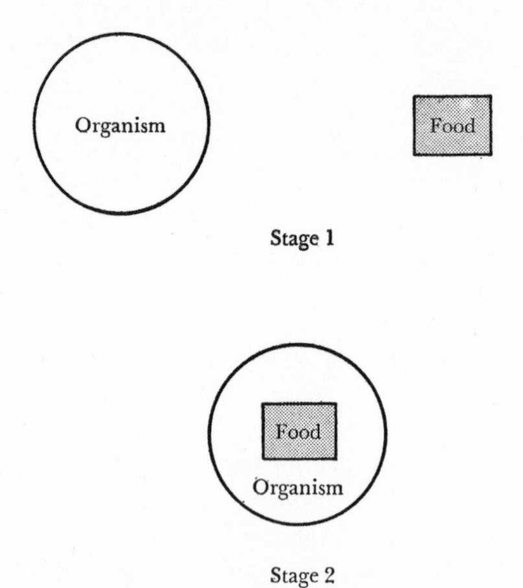

FIG. 9. THE RELATIONSHIP OF ORGANISM AND OBJECT IN VEGETATIVE BEHAVIOR

General and Special Sensory Behavior. Here there are two types of interrelationship. One is illustrated by touch reactions and in part by taste responses. Observe that in this situation the organism and object permanently remain distinct though they are in direct contact. This contact is sustained at any point of the organism since it is flesh, which

[47] *De Anima* 418ᵃ 20 *ff.*
[48] See *De Anima* 426ᵇ 17 *ff.*

is the undifferentiated medium, and the sense organs are localized somewhere below the external tissues of the organism (Fig. 10).

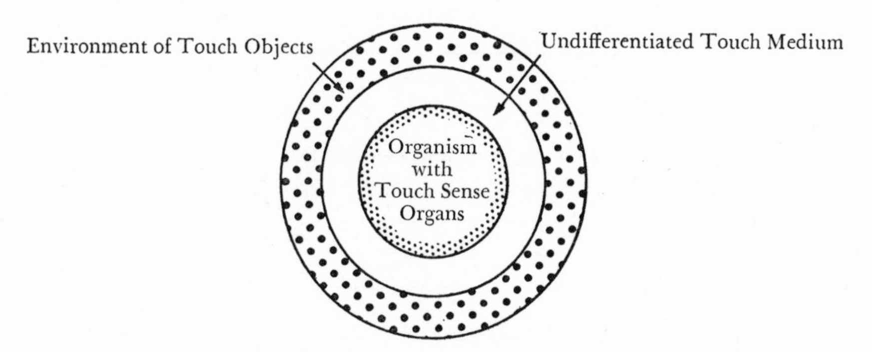

FIG. 10. GENERAL SENSORY INTERACTIONS

The second type of sensory organism-object interrelationship is illustrated by the sensory discriminations of vision, hearing, and smelling. In these cases the organism is in direct contact with the objects by a specialized medium and at a point of a specialized structure. The following diagram illustrates the situation (Fig. 11).

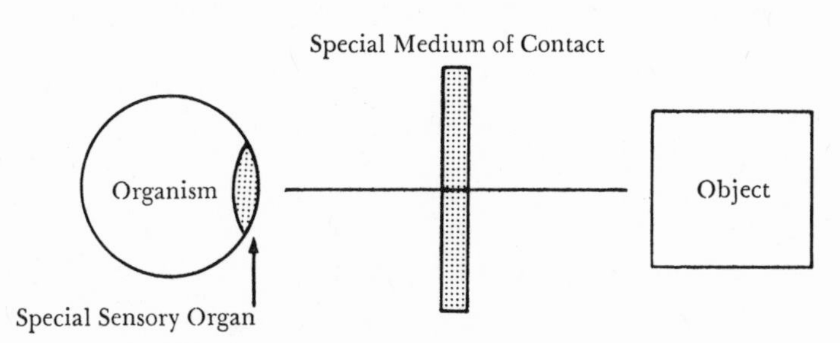

FIG. 11. INTERACTIONS BY MEANS OF SPECIAL SENSE ORGANS

Common Sense Interactions. In these situations we have to take into account the divergence between the description Aristotle favored, namely, that several specialized end organs would be in direct contact with objects, and the compromise he was forced to accept because of the observed events. Accordingly, we require two diagrams (Figs. 12, 13) to represent his views of the interrelationship with common sensibles. The first is simple enough, but the second involves two stages of action, one requiring special sense-organs, as represented in Figs. 11 and 12, and the other the operation of the entire organism (Fig. 13).

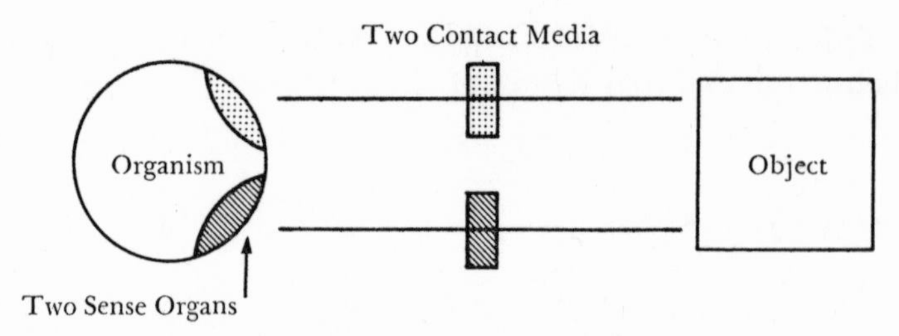

FIG. 12. CONTACT WITH OBJECTS THROUGH SEVERAL SENSE ORGANS

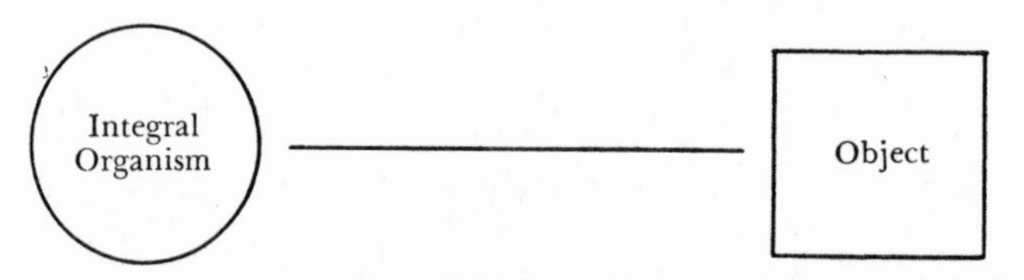

FIG. 13. INTERACTION OF THE UNIFIED ORGANISM WITH COMPLEX THINGS

Imagination or Phantasmic Interactions. Here we have a unique situation in which the object reacted to is entirely absent. Actually, this is only an extrapolation from the case of indirect contact in perceptual situations. In the imagination situation a completely different object must be in contact with the organism. Clearly, in this case there is no special organ or part of the organism operating to effect an interaction.

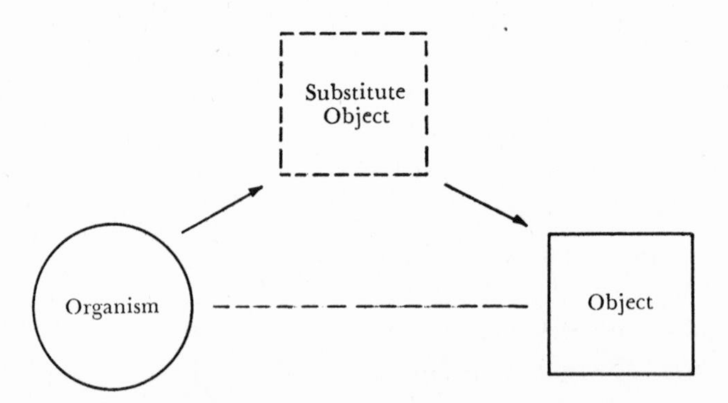

FIG. 14. INTERACTION WITH ABSENT OBJECTS THROUGH SUBSTITUTE STIMULI: "PHANTASMIC INTERACTIONS"

Thinking and Reasoning Interactions. It is extremely interesting that complex thinking and reasoning situations are similar to vegetative actions in that no special part of the organism is operating. Beyond this, however, thinking and reasoning show a closer connection between organism and object than is true in vegetative behavior. Not only are organism and object thoroughly assimilated to each other, but the very existence of the object depends upon the activity of the organism. Abstract objects are for the most part creations of the organism. As Aristotle says, in the case of objects which involve no matter but only form, that which thinks and that which is thought about are the same.[49]

> *Nous* when it is thinking the objects of mathematics, thinks as separate elements which do not exist separate. In every case *nous* which is actively thinking is the object which it thinks.[50]

In view of the great complexity and subtlety of thinking and reasoning action, it is very difficult to diagram the interrelationship between organism and object, but in Fig. 15 we try to suggest tentatively that some kind of construction and ejection of the objects is involved.

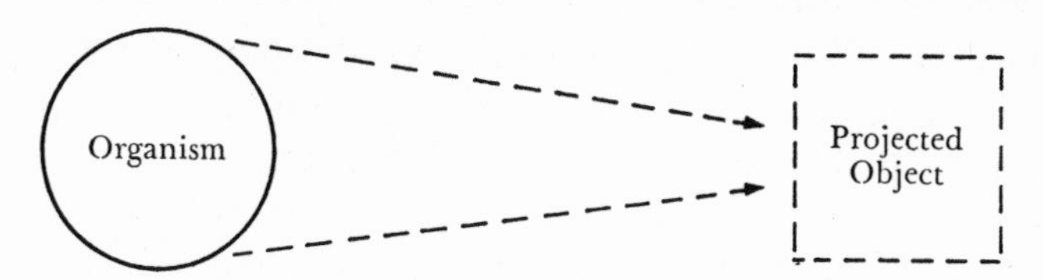

FIG. 15. THINKING AND REASONING INTERACTIONS

APPETITE AND MOTION. In consonance with his notion that psychological events are basically movements, Aristotle, of course, makes a great deal of the facts of motion and of the conditions of the organism's action. The activities of animals can be summed up as (a) discrimination, or thought and sense, and (b) the incitement of movement in space.[51] Now what influences movement is that psychological activity called appetite.[52] Aristotle varies this theme by asserting that it is the object of appetite which initiates movement. In general, however, it is the appetite which at once moves and is moved.[53]

Appetite functions are different both in definition and effectiveness from the nutritive, sensitive, and imaginative actions[54] though they

[49] *De Anima* 430ª 4.

[50] *De Anima* 431ᵇ 15 *ff*. Doubtless the same factors that move Aristotle to reduce thinking to its object induce him to declare that no bodily activity is connected with reasoning. Reasoning is at the opposite pole from walking, which cannot go on without feet; see *De Generatione Animalium* 736ᵇ 21 *ff*.

[51] *De Anima* 432ª 15.

[52] *De Anima* 433ª 18, 27, 28, 31; 433ᵇ 12.

[53] *De Anima* 433ᵇ 16.

[54] *De Anima* 432ᵇ 3.

operate in conjunction with them; for example all organisms performing sensing action also perform appetitive acts.[55] Again, when imagination originates movement it necessarily involves appetite;[56] in fact there is no appetite without imagination.[57] What Aristotle appears to separate sharply from appetite is deliberation.[58]

Although in the *De Anima* appetite is regarded as the primary basis of action, though aided by the other actions, Aristotle sometimes varies his exposition slightly but not his doctrine. In the *Magna Moralia*[59] the action-initiating functon is also attributed to impulse. Impulse, however, is given three forms; namely, appetite, passion, and wish. The *De Anima* has it that appetite is the genus of which desire, passion, and wish are species.[60] Desire is the appetite for what is present, while anger is the appetite for retaliation.[61]

Aristotle's discussion of appetition clearly corresponds to modern expositions of motivation. It is hardly necessary to add that he treats this topic, like all others, in an objective and naturalistic manner. The initiation of motion and its direction is a form of adaptation of an organism to the specific objects of its environment.

IMAGINATION (PHANTASIA) AND IMAGES. A special form of behavior in Aristotelian psychology is imagination or phantasia. Imagination is very close to sense behavior but at the same time leads very definitely toward the complex activities of thinking, calculating, and reasoning. Obviously, then, imagination is a complex and important sort of action and because of its necessary connection, though not identity with, sensing and perceiving action, it belongs in the continuum of actions closely interrelated with concrete stimulus objects.

That imagining is not sensing Aristotle demonstrates by the following criteria.[62] (a) Sensing is a potential or actual contact with objects as in being able to see or seeing. Imagining is activity not performed in the presence of actual things as in dreaming. (b) Even animals that perform sensing actions do not all perform imagination actions. Aristotle cites as nonimaginative animals the ant, the bee, and the grub. (c) Sensing actions are veridical, while imagination actions are usually false. (d) Only when we are in doubt about the identification of a perceived

[55] *De Anima* 414ᵇ 1.
[56] *De Anima* 433ᵃ 20.
[57] *De Anima* 433ᵇ 29.
[58] *De Anima* 434ᵃ 11.
[59] 1187ᵇ 38.
[60] 414ᵇ 1, 2.
[61] *De Anima* 403ᵃ 30.
[62] *De Anima* 428ᵃ 5 *ff*.

object do we say we imagine it. (e) Finally, visions appear to us even when the eyes are closed.

The outstanding characteristic of imaginative behavior is that it can be performed in the absence of the stimulus object. Since even in perception the sense organs receive the object's form without matter, it is possible for sensing and imagining to occur in the sense organs after the original objects are gone.[63] Though imagination is not sensing, obviously it is not only derived from sense but also operates closely within sensing situations. For example, it is the action of imagination which supplies the basis for reacting to the universal characteristics of common sensibles, and to the secondary or indirect qualities of things, as in perceiving the white object as the "son of Diares."[64] Again, Aristotle points out that the name phantasia (φαυτασια) has been formed from the word φαος, referring to light.[65]

Imagination behavior as a type of movement in Aristotle's sense is definitely and directly derived from sensing situations[66] but, of course, is very different. The active unit of imagination is the image. During dreaming and thinking images are operationally the representational acts for absent things and thinking. Aristotle refers to images as phantasms or residuary movements.[67] It is this activity in the absense of the original objects which makes dreaming, thinking, calculating, and deliberating possible. Images and imagination behavior derive their effectiveness from this relative freedom from the objects to which they are reactions and thus provide the organism with a measure of power and autonomy.[68]

Aristotle appears to be fully aware of the pervasiveness of imagination action. Imagination occurs in other than special imaginative situations, for example, an animal is not capable of appetite without imagination.[69] All animals perform imagination reactions although they may be only imperfect and indefinite acts.[70] Because some animals have only touch sensitivity, their imagination is limited and indefinite. Others perform more elaborate imagination acts, though they cannot go beyond sensorial imagination. On the whole, even if nonhuman animals are not restricted to the simplest forms of phantasmal action,

[63] *De Anima* 425^b 25.
[64] *De Anima* 418^a 20 *ff.*
[65] *De Anima* 429^a 3.
[66] *De Anima* 429^a 1.
[67] *De Somnis* 461^a 19.
[68] *De Anima* 427^b 17.
[69] *De Anima* 433^b 29.
[70] *De Anima* 434^a 1, 5.

they do not attain to the elaborate imagination connected with deliberation, calculation, and thinking.

REMEMBERING AND RECOLLECTING. Aristotle's treatment of memorial behavior represents a sharpening and systematizing of the commonsense observational descriptions formulated by his predecessors, especially Plato. While Plato admirably describes behavior with respect to absent objects, with a commendable emphasis upon the function of substitute objects to make the reactions possible, he does so on the basis of only everyday situations. His procedure is well illustrated in the following excerpt:

> . . . what is the feeling of lovers when they recognize a lyre, or a cloak, or anything else which the beloved has been in the habit of using. Do not they, from knowing the lyre, form in the mind's eye an image of the youth to whom the lyre belongs? And this is recollection. In like manner anyone who sees Simmias may often remember Cebes; and there are endless examples of the same things.
>
> Endless, indeed, replied Simmias.
>
> And is not this sort of thing a kind of recollection—though the word is most commonly applied to a process of recovering that which has been already forgotten through time and inattention?
>
> Very true, he said.
>
> Well; and may you not also from seeing the picture of a horse or a lyre recollect a man? and from the picture of Simmias, you may be led to recollect Cebes?
>
> True.
>
> Or you may also be led to the recollection of Simmias himself?
>
> Quite so.
>
> And in all these cases, the recollection may be derived from things either like or unlike?
>
> It may be.[71]

Aristotle, on the other hand, analyzes and brings to the surface the deeper-lying factors. For one thing, and a most important one, memory acts involve time in a unique way. In other words, remembering responses involve several points in time, or a time interval. The organism does not just react to immediate things which incidentally serve to connect it with things present upon former occasions, but primarily to the things in the former encounter. Aristotle stresses the pastness in the interval and since his time there has remained alive the belief that remembering has to do with the past as a characteristic of the action. It is possibly out of place to criticize Aristotle for overlooking the importance of all the points in the memorial time interval. Sufficient it is that he treats remembering as a naturalistic act.

[71] *Phaedo* 73[d] *ff.*

A second important factor in remembering is that it is an outgrowth of perceived action. As Aristotle puts it, remembering belongs to the primary activities of sense perception.[72] Remembering involves presentation in the sense of reacting in the presence of particular things, as well as a sort of re-presentation. Remembering, it follows, has to do with objects previously reacted to and also, and this is a very important point, the awareness of the time relation between the two. While remembering one must be saying to oneself, "I formerly heard (or otherwise perceived) this" or "I formerly had this thought.[73]

Recollection for Aristotle is a more directed and deliberate form of behavior than remembering, or at least a more definite phase of reacting to absent things. Aristotle is careful to separate recollection from the original activities with things present, which make possible the later reactions to absent things, and from the reactivation of memorial behavior. For him recollection is an active search into the past for some object or event. Primarily this search consists of activating a stimulus which by its connection or association with a chain of other objects as stimuli will lead to the recovery of the object sought. To illustrate this point Aristotle offers the rather trivial and amusing mnemonic series. In recovering autumn, the misty season, one may start from milk, proceed to white, from white to air or mist, and thence to damp or moist.[74] The easiest objects to recollect are mathematical problems, since they possess an orderly arrangement. The successive geometrical demonstrations are closely interlocked. All badly arranged subjects are recovered, if at all, with considerable difficulty.[75]

Recollection, then, involves considerable fortuity and probability. One may follow a well-chosen method of searching for the object to be recovered but the result may or may not be successful. Among the conditions Aristotle mentions as aids to recollection are similarity of things, their contrariety, their contiguity in general situations, and the frequency of contact with things to be recovered.

INTELLECTUAL BEHAVIOR. In Aristotle's behavior continuum the various subtle activities, such as knowing, thinking, opining, and many others, find their proper places along with the crudest vegetative actions. One need only take account of the variations in each class. It is pertinent here to point out that only in an objective and narrational way did Aristotle abstract "functions" and "processes" from the interactions of organisms with stimulus objects. Aristotle had none of the dif-

[72] *De Memoria et Reminiscentia* 450^a 14.
[73] *Ibid.*, 449^b 24.
[74] *Ibid.*, 452^a 15.
[75] *Ibid.*, 452^a 5.

ficulties of the modern writers who distinguish acts from thought, making the latter into pale wraiths either connected or unconnected with motions, manipulations, or other palpable contacts with things.

Aristotle expressly points out that it is improper to assume that there are acts of detached soul, such as pitying, learning, or thinking. What happens is that the man does these acts.[76] He goes on to point out that psychological activities like sensing, remembering, loving, hating, and thinking become impaired or disappear when the individual or his organs become defective through drunkenness or disease.[77] If the old man could acquire the right kind of eye he would see just as well as the young man.[78]

As to specific characteristics, thinking behavior is set off from perceiving on several grounds. For one thing perceiving is universal in the animal world, but thinking is confined to a small division of it.[79] Again, perceiving is so closely interrelated with its stimulus object that it is always or almost always a veridical type of action. Thinking behavior may be mistaken, misdirected, and even false. Furthermore, sensing and perceiving behavior are subject to fatigue and adaptation. After strong sensory stimulation there is an interference with seeing, hearing, and smelling. In the case of intellectual behavior, which is not so integrally connected with a particular organ, the more intense the interaction the more capable is the individual afterwards of responding to equally intelligible or less intelligible objects.[80]

More positively described, thinking acts are partially imaginal and partially judgmental. It is for these reasons that they are subject to error. On the other hand, it is the relative detachment from objects and their probabilistic character which makes such actions effective and serviceable in complex situations.

By comparison with sensory and perceptual action, thinking is more definitely knowledge of both a practical and a speculative form. It is not sheer awareness or sensitivity. As we have already indicated on p. 139 above, Aristotle considers that in knowledge there is so intimate a connection between the act and the object as to amount to an identity.[81]

Knowledge and intellectual behavior in general are described as both active and passive. Although the text is not complete and clear in its

[76] *De Anima* 408ᵇ 15.
[77] *De Anima* 408ᵇ 20 *f*.
[78] *De Anima* 408ᵇ 21.
[79] *De Anima* 427ᵇ 6.
[80] *De Anima* 429ᵃ 30-429ᵇ 1 *f*.
[81] *De Anima* 430ᵃ 4 and 430ᵃ 20.

exposition, it cannot be doubted that Aristotle is here differentiating between potential knowledge, in the sense of the mere presence of all the factors in a knowledge situation, and the actual performance of the knowledge act.

In the individual, potential knowledge is in time prior to actual knowledge, but in the universe as a whole it is not prior even in time.[82]

In this passage appears the contrast between two phases of an event. In the first or potential phase, we have the factors that may or may not, according to individual circumstances, be consummated as knowledge or learning. Take, for example, the school where the words are written on the blackboard and the teacher is ready to bring the child into contact with them and to stimulate interest in learning them. In addition, there is the active process of the child partaking in and effecting the learning process. Actual knowledge exists when the words to be learned are identical with the actual act of learning or reciting them.

For Aristotle the distinction between practical and speculative or contemplative knowledge simply sets off knowledge closely linked with performative and manipulative activities from knowledge limited to information. In many ways this is a simple differentiation of units of action, but it must be recalled that speculative and practical knowledge are both, as knowledge, set off from other kinds of actions. In addition, there are innumberable specific characteristics even aside from subtlety and refinement of operation. The situations calling for practical and contemplative behavior differ greatly in their details and in the opportunities and consequences they provide.

Students of the history of psychology, who should marvel at the relative completeness and effectiveness of Aristotle's *De Anima,* have been more impressed by the lacunae, and the fragmentary and, in part, incomprehensible, features of the lecture notes. We should like to consider one feature in the context of thinking and knowing. This is the reference made by Aristotle to the independence from the body of thinking activities and to the immortality of the soul as a psychological activity. The relevant passages include the statement that, whereas in sensing acts the bodily factors are prominent, in the intellectual actions mind is separable from body.[83] Again, Aristotle says,

When mind is set free from its present conditions it appears as just what it is and nothing more: this alone is immortal and eternal.[84]

[82] *De Anima* 430ª 20.
[83] *De Anima* 429ᵇ 4.
[84] *De Anima* 430ª 23.

Surely it is only the presence of the dualistic tradition that could suggest a mind-body interpretation here with transcendental spirit as the mind factor. How can all the conditions of culture and the basic biological postulates of Aristotle be set aside? But there is still an intrinsic problem to be taken care of. What could Aristotle mean by making knowledge or thinking independent of the organism and identical with the objects known or thought? This is not a difficult problem when we keep before us the realistic views of an Athenian thinker. Notice that the objects of knowledge and thought, even more than the common sensibles, are unrelated to any specific organ. Notice also that such objects are purely formal, or as we should say, they are intellectually constructed. They are so far abstracted and remote that they cannot be in direct contact with any particular organs or with the entire organism, as in the cases of visual or tactual objects. It is also entirely reasonable to regard an abstract formula or equation as identical with the process of constructing such abstractional products. In sum, although certain isolated passages in the *De Anima* can be made to read like post-Greek dualistic propositions, this is only by wrenching them forcibly out of their Greek objective context. Howsoever slightly developed may be Aristotle's knowledge and description of thinking and knowing activities, he did not treat them otherwise than as acts performed by persons in complex objective situations.

REASONING. After due allowance for vacillations, flexible classification, and other factors associated with pioneering efforts and the ambition to be complete as well as sound, we may assume that Aristotle thought of reasoning as essentially inference. In the words of the Aristotelian corpus,

> Reasoning is an argument in which, certain things being laid down, something other than these necessarily comes about through them. (a) It is a 'demonstration,' when the premises from which the reasoning starts are true and primary, or are such that our knowledge of them has originally come through premises which are primary and true: (b) reasoning, on the other hand, is 'dialectical' if it reasons from opinions that are generally accepted.[85]

Formally, the study of reasoning is treated more fully and more adequately in the logical rather than in the psychological treatises. For Aristotle, of course, this presents no problems, as he is far from such a distinction as private and mental for psychology, and public and propositional

[85] *Topica* 100ᵃ 25 *ff*.

for logic. In attempting to clarify the characteristics of reasoning it is well to be reminded that for Aristotle the syllogistic form of inference is the safest and the surest. By way of pinning down the kind of activity and the kind of situation in which syllogisms are employed Aristotle says,

> A syllogism is discourse in which, certain things being stated, something other than what is stated follows of necessity from their being so. I mean by the last phrase that they produce the consequence, and by this, that no further term is required from without in order to make the consequence necessary.[86]

Aristotle's discussion of reasoning in all its phases enforces the opinion that logic is concerned with activities performed by persons. But, on the basis of his doctrine of the identity of a series of relations or abstract objects with the acts of knowing or relating them, he gives at times unjustified vent to his notions of absoluteness and universality. He invokes the notion of necessity to an unwarranted extent.

WAKING, SLEEPING, AND DREAMING. Anyone attempting to formulate Aristotle's system of biopsychology must, as a matter of course, approve his juxtaposing of psychological and biological discussions. For Aristotle it is not anomalous to place in a single series problems of respiration, youth and old age, length of life, life and death, and so on. We are not, then, surprised at Aristotle's inclusion of waking, sleeping, and dreaming among psychological topics. The last, of course is a definite kind of psychological activity which occurs under the most variant of human circumstances. As to waking and sleeping, it would indeed be anomalous to object to a discussion of problems concerning the greater or lesser intensity of contacts with stimulus objects occurring during these states.

In general, waking and sleeping are contrary conditions of organisms which serve to maintain and preserve them. Waking is a period of intense action, while sleeping is a condition of reduced behavior or cessation of action tending toward rest and recovery. Sleep, therefore, serves to maintain the health and proper functioning of the organism.[87] Aristotle regards sleep as an inhibitive process which puts a limit to the partial or the total action of the organism, as well as to the relative intensity of such action.

Aristotle constructs a biological cause for sleep which he locates in the sanguineous and nutritional processes. Since sleeping is a process of minimum action, Aristotle attempts to account for it by ascertaining

[86] *Analytica Priora* 24^b 18 *ff*.

[87] *De Somno et Vigilia* 453^b 11-455^a 3.

what happens at the source of both sensing and motion. The process begins with the ingestion of food, which gives rise to an evaporation which enters the veins and there, undergoing changes, becomes blood, which makes its way to the heart. Because of the heat generated in the heart, the substance in the veins moves upward in the organism to the brain, where it is cooled and thus driven back in its course. Sleep is a kind of concentrated natural recoil of the hot matter as it is driven downwards toward the heart. This results in a weighing down of the primary sensory organs and a consequent drowsiness and cessation of motion and discrimination. In an evaluation of Aristotle's theory of sleep it may be said that the lack of information as to what is really going on is somewhat compensated for by the convention of the time according to which explanations were couched in the naturalistic terms of superficial observation. Psychologically speaking, sleep is primarily an inhibition of sensory action and any subsequent motion. Clearly, Aristotle is formulating his views of sleep and waking in terms of the behavior of organisms.

Dreaming for Aristotle consists primarily of a peculiar activity of sense presentation when the organism is not operating in contact with sense objects as in waking. As a basic description of dreaming Aristotle proposes a process of persisting sensory action after the stimulation by the object has been completed.

> . . . even when the external object of perception has departed, the impressions it has made persist, and are themselves objects of perception;[88]

Aristotle is definitely aware of the abnormal or illusory character of such perceiving and compares the illusions of dreams with the illusions of illness or strong affective conditions. The entire meagre treatment of dreams shows the double influence of insufficient biological knowledge and the attitude which limits complex human adjustments to the immediate activities of an organism. What are lacking are the many ecological details which would impart content to the specific kinds of dreams and the special situations under which they occur.

There is one important exception to Aristotle's limitation of dream factors. He does offer in his *De Divinatione per Somnum* an argument for the naturalistic character of dreams based upon the life conditions of the dreamer. When denying the prophetic character of dreams he brings forward arguments based on the exaggeration of stimuli and the

[88] *De Somnis* 460[b] 1.

modification of waking behavior because of preceding dreams. He accounts for prophesy mainly on the basis of coincidence. Also, when Aristotle explains the vividness of dreams about certain persons on the basis of the intimacy between the dreamer and the dreamed about, he is definitely taking account of the subtle dream action as part of a pattern of general behavior interrelated with particular persons and situations. Such discussions serve well to round out his thoroughly naturalistic system of psychology.

DE ANIMA: SUM AND PERSPECTIVE

Historians of science are no longer astounded at the miracle of Greek science—a truly remarkable achievement, which evolved so quickly and endured so briefly. It is now well recognized that the evolution of Greek science is much more a fact of rapid burgeoning than a miracle of spontaneous generation. Scientific historians are discovering a multitude of sources for the scientific materials which the Greeks brought together and focused as a basis for expansion and systemization. It is no belittling of the scientific merits of the Greeks to point out that they were highly efficient purveyors and organizers.

The biopsychology of Aristotle, however, still looms up as a miraculous exception—not, of course, because of any unique, sudden generation, but for its scope and value as a permanent scientific institution. Aristotle's *De Anima,* as the nucleus of Greek systematic psychology, is an outstanding achievement and product. Here is a well-developed and neatly integrated series of psychological descriptions and also, what is much more remarkable, a model that has endured to our own day. The pronouncement that all philosophies are either Platonist or Aristotelian may not be true, but in some sense, at least, all psychologists are Aristotelians. Moreover, it is not at all an exaggeration to say that, despite all the data amassed by psychologists down the centuries, we have not yet fully caught up with Aristotle. What makes Aristotle's psychology so remarkable is that it is a fairly comprehensive psychological corpus thoroughly grounded on naturalistic foundations. If modern psychologists have attained a scientific position, it has been only by a rigorous selection of events, the exclusive study of animal behavior to the neglect of human action, or by reducing human action to a biological component. Aristotle's biopsychology was intended to stress the total psychological event.

Properly to appreciate the peak attained by the *De Anima* we must envisage it in its original historical perspective. As an outgrowth of

Hellenic culture the study of *psyche* had to fall within the science of nature.[89] On a behavioral basis one takes into account both the formulable essence of a psychological event, its use or function, and the thing or material that performs this act or function. Aristotle's illustration is that the proper study of anger is not only formulable as the desire to return pain for pain but also as a boiling of the blood or the warm substance surrounding the heart.[90]

Viewed in the light of history, the *De Anima* firmly established a discipline concerned with the actions of animals, including man, and even plants, both by integrating a series of doctrines and by naming the study. Despite all the transformations and misinterpretations to which the *De Anima* became subject, the science of psychology has always been a study of Aristotelian *psyche*—the adjustmental or adaptational behavior of organisms.[91]

The history of psychology also reveals the many specific doctrinal anticipations to be found in the *De Anima*. The list is long, but the following are good representatives.

1) The developmental nature of psychological activity

2) The continuity of human and nonhuman organisms and their behavior

3) The interaction of stimulus objects and organisms

4) The doctrine of five senses

5) The connection of sensory action and local sense organs

6) The similarity, contrast, and contiguity principles of association

Not the least important features of the Aristotelian heritage are the occasions the *De Anima* provided for controversies concerning issues central to science, and especially to psychological science. We give two examples. Take, first, the teleological problem. As a biologist Aristotle stressed the use, purpose, and action of parts and their relation to each other as well as the general morphology of organisms. But modern writers, overlooking the context and the conditions in which Aristotle worked, misinterpreted him as imposing extra-organic and extra-environmental factors upon organisms and their actions.[92]

The second example concerns what modern biologists and psychologists unite in regarding as perverse ideas about the brain and its func-

[89] *De Anima* $403^{a \text{ and } b}$.

[90] *De Anima* 403^{a} 30.

[91] Shute attempts an unusually rare presentation of Aristotle's psychology in an objective way in his *The Psychology of Aristotle*.

[92] A recent notable exception is Randall, *Aristotle;* see pp. 124, 186 *f.*, 225 *f.*

tions. Instead of envisaging the brain as the central organ for all psychological processes, Aristotle makes it primarily a refrigerating and general heat-regulating organ. Here, again, modern writers overlook the naturalistic and biological premises upon which Aristotle builds his psychology. When it is recalled that Aristotle offers a sensible list of biological reasons for his views about the brain and the heart, and also that the modern views which make the brain the central psychological organ rest on a dogmatic basis, such criticisms of Aristotle lose their point.

SECTION FOUR

THE EXTINCTION OF SYSTEMATIC PSYCHOLOGY

CHAPTER 10

THE METAMORPHOSIS AND DECLINE OF SCIENTIFIC PSYCHOLOGY

GREEK SCIENTIFIC PSYCHOLOGY: TRANSIENCE AND PERMANENCE

THE GREEK VENTURE into scientific psychology, resplendent as it was, suffered an equally remarkable extinction. As soon as a naturalistic science of behavior had been instituted it became modified in various ways and quickly disappeared altogether. At first, psychological thinking lost its independent and systematic character. Psychology became subordinated to political and humanistic interests though it remained naturalistic until at least the first century B.C. After that date it lost its naturalistic character too. Many were the historical circumstances that influenced Greek psychology to veer away from the naturalistic line of cultural evolution upon which it had started so auspiciously. What happened to psychology, happened, of course, to all the sciences, but in a somewhat different way and at a somewhat later period. Indeed, the extinction of Aristotelian psychology almost immediately after it was systemized appears so striking precisely because other Greek science did not reach its highest peak until the Alexandrian period.

Clearly, there is something unique about psychology which makes it a special case in the history of science. Actually, Aristotelian psychology possesses a trait of permanence as well as one of transience. For example, whereas most of Greek science was not welcomed back into modern scientific civilization, Aristotelian psychology became a fixture of Western European culture. At least since the renaissance of science in the fifteenth and sixteenth centuries, the slogan "Science versus Aristotle" was developed as though science could only prosper by the eradication of everything Greek. However, this did not apply to psychology in its metamorphosed form. As we shall see, as late as the seventeenth century the representatives of modern psychology, Descartes, Hobbes, Locke, and Leibniz, basked in the moonlight of Aristotelian psychology as transformed by St. Thomas.

There is, then, something cometary about the *De Anima,* which shone so brightly, vanished so promptly, and then returned again, albeit with a completely new character and only after many centuries, to exert a momentous influence upon later ages. The paradox may be resolved in Aristotle's terms. What persisted was the form which Aristotle constructed, with some of its everyday matter. But the basic constructions, the fundamental descriptions and postulations, were lost until very recent days.

The paradoxical transience and yet permanence of scientific psychology and the difference in the career of psychology as compared with that of the other sciences can be partially explained by the shifting of the center of science from Athens to Alexandria. This shift was, of course, part of a general metamorphosis of Eastern Mediterranean civilization. That transformation resulted from the intermixture of intellectual, social, political, and economic conditions. The streaming of learning and intellectual pursuits into Alexandria, along with the great concentration at that strategic point of industrial and commercial occupations, provided a strong impetus for the development of a number of special sciences and humanities.[1] But psychology was not one of the sciences which flourished at Alexandria. It gave way first to a type of practical and ethical anthropology, and later to a form of spiritistic theology. The lag of psychology behind the other sciences may probably be accounted for by the fact that formal psychology is more sensitive than mathematics, physics, and astronomy to the basic cultural presuppositions of a community. Commerce and industry may demand and receive improvements in calculation, in measurement, in the appreciation of the strength of materials, and of the motions and changes in things. Psychological events, on the other hand, are so intimately related to the scientist that a lack of perspective may easily result. In the early and cruder scientific stages there is little awareness of the importance of assumptions and postulates. Also, in the intellectual atmosphere of Alexandria there developed little sympathy for an objective appreciation of psychological activities. Doctrines of inwardness and subjectivity prevailed. Psychological events melted away to the point of inaccessibility.

Obviously the cultivation of science waxes and wanes with the general development of civilization. In the two centuries following the establishment of Alexandria and the death of its founder there was an amazing upsurge of scientific development. Then a decline set in, with new social, political, and economic conditions. The grandeur of

[1] See Ch. 12.

Rome was developing, with the absorption and suppression of the glories of Greece. After the Roman conquest Greek culture, including Greek science, was avidly exploited, but its doom was sealed.

So far as psychology is concerned, we repeat that what Aristotle and his predecessors wrought continued to exist for an indefinite period beyond the recession of Greek science in the Western European world. But only the form and institution of psychology remained. Already in the Alexandrian period the objective-behavior content was being replaced by a nebulous transcendental filling. The scientific character of psychology was lost for more than a score of centuries. Only after a long history was the shell of psychology partially emptied of the spiritistic content with which the Dark and Middle Ages filled it. We shall soon consider this aspect of psychology's career in a discussion of the two cycles in psychological history.

THE HELLENISTIC DECLINE OF SCIENTIFIC PSYCHOLOGY

An easy way to sum up the cultural occasion for the decline of scientific psychology is to refer to the great transformation of Greek culture when it was expanded during the Hellenistic era. We will sketch briefly this stage of Western civilization, the one transitional between the objective Greek period and the subjective medieval one.

The accelerated intellectual systemization of the fourth century B.C. was a definite reflection of the unified and glorified Periclean Age. The rapid and solid work of unifying and formalizing the sciences paralleled similar conditions in the other facets of Hellenic civilization. While Plato and Aristotle were standardizing and solidifying the intellectual trends of their time, the travails of the Athenians in the fourth century B.C. were already manifesting their devastating cultural effects. The cultural conditions which made possible and supported the systematic thinking of Plato and Aristotle were to give way to the reduction of classical Hellenic culture and the upsurge of a new human condition which is well named Hellenism. The intellectual and scientific achievements of the Greeks are to be changed, diluted, and eventually transformed by the campaigns, conquests, and political manoeuvring of Alexander, and more especially his successors.

The fourth century was not only a time of great political upheaval and military peril but the beginning of the end for the proud city states of Greece. In 404 Athens in her extremity capitulated utterly to Sparta. The century became a period of concentrated strife, and the Greeks with their individualistic and autonomous local governments were ripe for conquest by the Macedonians and for subordination into a political system at least partially oriental in makeup. Here is a socio-political situation which, favorable as it may have been for the development and maintenance of a superior intellectual culture, also contained the seeds for that culture's rapid decline and disappearance. And this decline went on apace and increased its momentum so that each century and each decade were marked with a greater departure from the naturalistic position so strongly held by classical Greek culture. The early days of Hellenistic civilization were indeed promising, and there was a large share of fulfillment. The unifying activities of Philip the Second and Alexander brought a rich harvest. But the peace and harmony did not last long. The progressive and creative stage enjoyed a short life. The historian of the period paints a sad picture of the closing days of the pre-Christian era.

One war followed another, wars between the leading monarchies, regional wars, domestic wars within the monarchies and city-states, revolutions of the natives against the Greeks. And all the wars became more and more destructive, more and more cruel, more and more demoralizing. Not satisfied with destroying by their own hands what had been just created, the Hellenistic powers invited a new partner into their destructive game. The shadow of Rome appeared on the Western horizon, and Rome soon took an active part in the political life of the Hellenistic world, first as protector of Greek liberty against the monarchies, next as benevolent adviser in the internal affairs of the Hellenistic states, and finally as an exacting and ruthless master of the Greek cities and Hellenistic monarchies alike.

The climax was reached when, after a short outburst of active protest against the Roman rule in the times of Mithridates and Sulla, Rome showed her real face to the Orient and firmly established her selfish, ruthless, exacting, and exasperating purely colonial regime in the East, a regime aggravated by the role which the East involuntarily played in the great tragedy of the Roman civil wars.[2]

What is of special interest to us is the basic change in civilization, which is the background of intellectual and scientific interests. Briefly, the conditions were such as to discourage independent and unbiased search for objective scientific orientation and to turn thinkers completely toward mythology and superstition.

One of the phenomena of this Oriental *revanche* was the complete surrender of the Greek, indeed of the whole ancient world, to the great enemy of genuine Greek spirit—astrology.[3]

[2] Rostovtzeff, *The Mentality of the Hellenistic World and the After-Life,* p. 16.
[3] *Ibid.,* p. 18.

The social and economic circumstances that gave rise to this development of subjectivism, transcendentalism, and the verbal construction called spiritualism are well depicted by Rostovtzeff.

Their life was hard and gloomy, and became ever gloomier, their material hardships were great, the prices high, the incomes small and ever diminishing, the insecurity of their daily life tremendous. For example, no one was safe even for one day from being made a prisoner of war, or from being kidnapped by pirates and thus from becoming a slave perhaps to the end of his days. Their city, their beloved *polis,* was no longer able to give its people protection. Even the most glorious cities like Athens and Rhodes were deeply humiliated and demoralized. Nor did the proud kings prove to be more efficient: in truth they were broken reeds. No wonder that in such an atmosphere the despicable Graeculus of the Roman writers was born: demoralized, dishonest, a professional liar and flatterer, a selfish profiteer and exploiter. And no wonder that, under pressure of poverty and insecurity, each man hoping to attain at least a minimum amount of well-being for himself and his one or two children, the Greeks began to practice freely exposure of children and other related means to limit their families and entered the path of systematic race-suicide.[4]

The decline of Hellenic culture must not be thought of as a precipitous drop but rather as a devolution taking place through a period of three centuries. Partially, too, it is a decline that is inhibited somewhat by the grace of Roman stability and seeming permanence. Nevertheless, for those who are interested in the final outcome, there is no overlooking the complete reversal of a culture which turns from contact with and interest in the only world of things and events available to man toward another unseen world to come. How the change from Hellenic to Hellenistic times affected psychology we can clearly see in the two cycles which we point out in the next section.

THE TWO CYCLES IN PSYCHOLOGICAL HISTORY

The history of scientific psychology exhibits at least two clear and distinctive cycles. The first ends with the dissipation of interest in the systematic discipline which Aristotle built up. Because of its short duration one might consider Greek scientific psychology only an incident in psychological evolution. But, as we know, Aristotle built a solid and enduring institution which survived in some form beyond its first disappearance from the intellectual scene. It even survived its revival, transformed at the hands of St. Thomas, in the thirteenth century. Many of its doctrines have exerted a powerful influence on the later development of the discipline.

[4] *Ibid.,* p. 18 *f.*

The decline of systematic psychology corresponded with the dissipation of its supporting cultural basis in the home of its origin. Psychological learning becomes reduced to an archaic condition of casual wisdom and sporadic doctrine. But it must be made clear that the objective attitude toward psychological events continued. Psychological doctrines in the hands of the Cynics, Stoics, Epicureans, and Sceptics were turned in the direction of practical and moral action. Even though continuing to envisage naturalistically the behavior which they did treat, the schools dissipated the general systematic viewpoint formulated by Aristotle.

The beginning of the second cycle is marked by the complete reduction of the naturalistic viewpoint. Classic Greek culture becomes dissolved in the spiritistic solvent of the Greco-Roman civilization. The observation of organisms in action becomes replaced by verbal constructions without parallel in actual events. Freedom and even license of speech take the place of restraint by events. The utter extinction of the Greek achievement in psychology is marked by the complete preoccupation of psychological students with transcendent psychic processes. From this starting point begins the long process of building up a second cycle of systematic psychology. Systematic psychology reappeared in Western European culture, notably in the thirteenth century, but only in the form of textual revival. Significant for the historian is the transforming process by which the *De Anima* was made into a system consonant with Patristic and medieval ways of thinking. As the history of psychology informs us, the evolution of scientific psychology in the second cycle proceeds very differently from that in the first. In addition to the organizational task of bringing together attested knowledge into a system, the psychologist faces the arduous job of separating psychological data from the deep incrustations of psychic theory with which the events have been overlaid. So great is the task that the work has not yet been completed. In Figure 16 an attempt is made to suggest some of the high points in the two psychological cycles. Among other points, the figure is intended to show that on the Greek scene a scientific psychology evolved, that is a systematic naturalistic discipline, on a limited scale but always based on the accumulation of simple objective observations. After a gradual decline, systematic psychology became extinguished, though the tradition of studying psychological events continued. The second cycle includes in its early stages not only antiscientific doctrines but also positive assertions and beliefs concerning the partially transcendental and supernatural character of man. Not until the twentieth century has there developed a deliberate movement

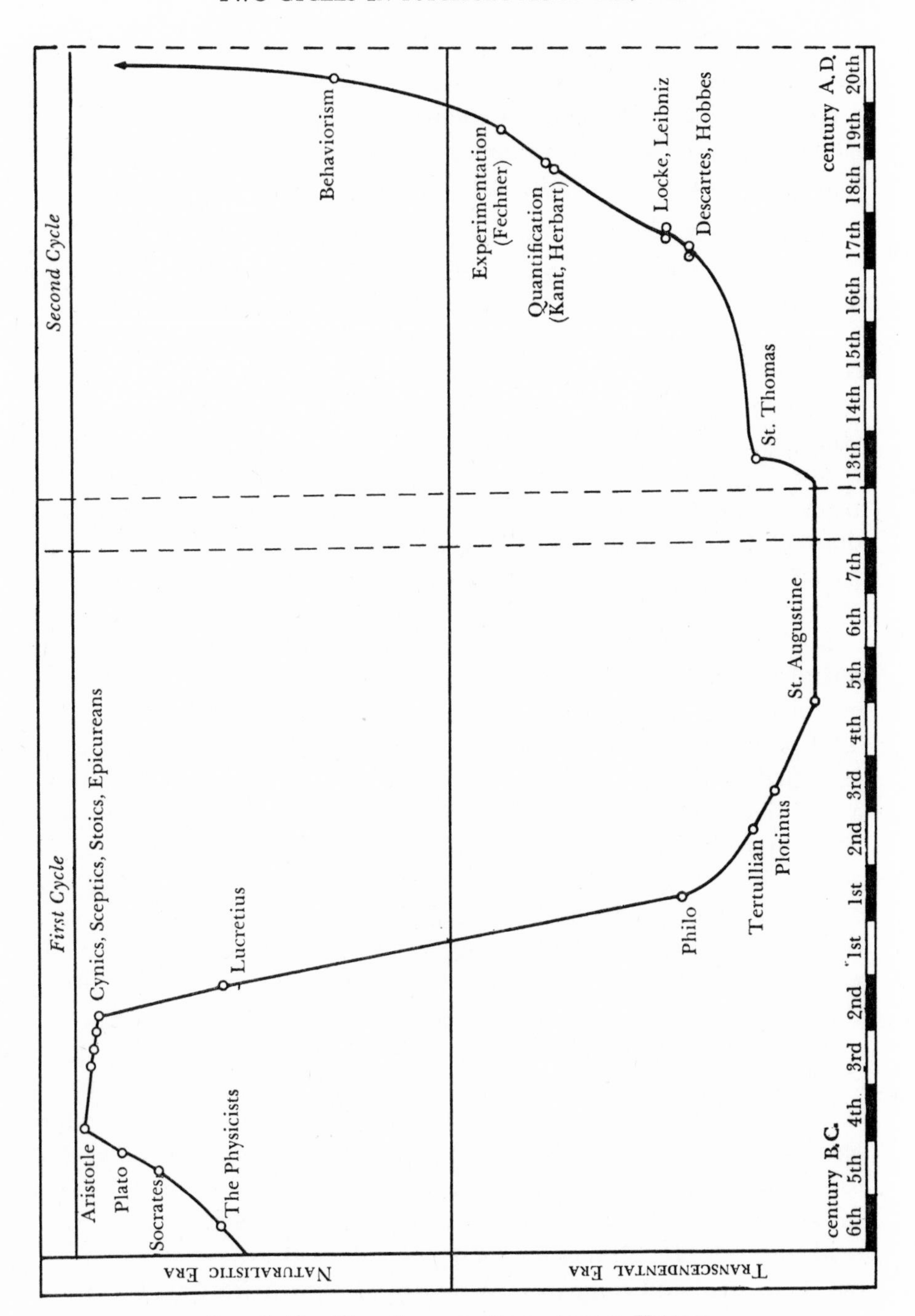

Fig. 16. The Two Cycles in Psychological History

to bring psychology back into the naturalistic realm occupied by the other sciences. It is interesting to note that the gradual build-up toward a modern scientific psychology includes the attempt to naturalize psychology by adopting observational, quantifying, and experimental techniques from the nonpsychological sciences.[5]

FORMAL SCIENCE AND CULTURAL CONTINUITY

The relative permanence of Aristotle's formulation of psychological science is a lesson in cultural continuity. The *De Anima* grew out of a complex of cultural institutions which included an interest in and cultivation of the sciences, among which psychology was a member. Accordingly, the disappearance of Aristotle's formal system did not obliterate the interest in psychological events. Obviously, the original events of any science are in no sense dissipated by the lack of formal treatises or even particular informal acts of observation and interpretation. Whenever events occur, the probability exists that they will be recorded, pondered over, and proclaimed, though with accents as different as the social life in which the events are noticed.

Intellectual products may continue to exist through various historical periods. This continuity is aided by various specific means, two of which stand out prominently. The first is social or cultural tradition. This process concerns most particularly the continuation of informal intellectual institutions, such as conventional interests in certain events and beliefs and attitudes about them. Such wisdom and knowledge are transmitted by the ordinary means of social behavior. Through casual and deliberate teachings the younger members of groups take over established ideas and opinions. Once established, the cultural institution of psychology goes on from age to age, and interest persists in soul, reason, sense, appetite, will, and feeling. Doctrines, as secondary institutions, will inevitably change with changes in the conditions of people.

The second process of cultural continuity operates by means of specific formulations such as treatises and other literary documents. No better examples can be required than the Aristotelian treatises which have played so significant a role in psychological tradition. What Aristotle initiated in constructing the *De Anima* was continued by Tertullian, Plotinus, St. Thomas, and many others, some of whom actually used the name *De Anima* for their psychological works.[6] If one singles out Tertullian and compares his *De Anima* with Aristotle's, it becomes

[5] See pp. 416-421 below.

[6] For example Theophrastus, Dicaearchus of Messina, Tertullian, and others.

crystal-clear how Aristotle's successors in the tradition maintained the doctrinal form while completely transforming the content. Aristotelian naturalism becomes Tertullian supernaturalism. This transformation represents cultural changes made necessary by the civilizational conditions current in the succeeding periods. Thus, the career of Aristotelian psychology displays the operation of both the processes of cultural continuity we have mentioned.

In our next chapter we will examine the first step in the decline of scientific psychology occasioned by the shift of psychological interest from general systematic doctrine to problems affecting primarily human behavior and human circumstances.

CHAPTER 11

HUMANISM DISPLACES SYSTEMATIC PSYCHOLOGY

FROM ATHENIAN SCIENCE TO IMPERIAL SOCIETY

As a first stage in the decline of systematic psychology we may count the great shift of interest from intrinsic psychological events to principles of political and moral behavior. In the beginning, this shift of interest bespoke no retreat from objective and naturalistic attitudes. Not the methods and procedures but rather the subject matter changed. In general the move toward humanistic studies implied a growing deviation from cosmical, physical, and biological science. The powerful disinclination to study mathematics, astronomy, physics, and biology corresponded to the corrosion and disappearance of the Greek city states. Stimulated by the loss of stable and traditional political and social institutions the thinkers of the fourth and third centuries became powerfully sensitive to the relations of men to the societies in which they lived. The need to find a solid basis for political adjustment turned thinkers back to Socratic principles, as expressed in the statement that "the men who dwell in the city are my teachers, and not the trees, or the country."[1]

In the place of the investigators of nature, the stage of Greek thought became preempted by social thinkers, by men whose problems concerned the ethical or humanistic domain. Such schools of thought as the Stoic, Sceptic, Epicurean, and Cynic all strove to achieve for man an independence of the world. Accordingly, they cultivated problems of personal freedom and how to maintain private dignity by a greater or lesser withdrawal from social affairs. The wisdom of the time did not reach out to the discovery of the properties of things, but was confined to achieving and maintaining imperturbability amidst the uncontrollable turmoil of social life.

In one sense, of course, psychological studies were powerfully intensified. To turn from the study of nonhuman things to the problems of man and his fundamental nature, and his relation to the social system in which he finds himself leads to the analysis of psychological

[1] Plato *Phaedrus* 230.

behavior. Especially among the Cynics and the Sceptics the liveliest debate arose concerning the basis and validity of judgment, when it should be exercised and when suspended. Among the Stoics and Epicureans the nature and value of happiness and problems of motivation became much prosecuted topics. But the basis for the interest in human action was pragmatic and personal, not scientific. More important still, the very idea of drawing a line between man and surrounding nature constituted a debilitating factor. This demarcation process is the beginning of an intellectual movement which ends in the mysticizing and denaturalizing of man and the creation of properties for him that are unmatched in *rerum natura.* From a doctrine of personal self-sufficiency there developed gradually a belief in the utter uniqueness of some of the characteristics of man: his dual composition from natural and mystical qualities, the complete privacy of the mystical properties, and their transcendence of the bounds of nature.

Among the outstanding general cultural changes that followed upon the decline of the Greek city states are the loss of self-assuredness and of the notion of Greek civilization as stable and permanent. The absolutism and the finalism of Greek thinking are badly shaken. Realism is giving way to cynicism and scepticism, while the universality engendered by the similarities and uniformities of events is being replaced by a subjective monism. The humanistic period is characterized by a unique sort of pseudosophistication in which arguments and puzzles take the place of investigation. On the whole, it may be said that the post-Aristotelian humanists are intellectual escapists rather than searchers into the nature of things.

INTELLECTUAL INDIVIDUALISM AND THE MULTIPLICATION OF SCHOOLS

There is a great analogy between the efficiency and success of Greek science, as exemplified by Aristotle, and the military and political exploits of his erstwhile pupil, Alexander. Unparalleled in scientific history is Aristole's conquest of the many scientific domains. Although he was primarily a biologist, he built a scientific empire which left hardly any domain untouched. His limitations based on his biological inclinations revealed themselves mainly in the lack of specialized treatises on mathematics. Otherwise, he dominated both the social and the physical sciences. He wrought better in some specialties than in others, but he made advances in such far-separated fields of events as physics and poetry, astronomy and ethics, metaphysics and physiology. Like Alexander, too, Aristotle consolidated his conquests and partially, at least, succeeded in building a vast systematic empire within the limits of his actual knowledge and postulational resources. Historians have emphasized the likeness between Aristotle and Alexander by relating the story that Alexander supplied materials from his conquered lands to aid his former tutor to build his intellectual empire.

Surely it is no chance coincidence that the Aristotelian intellectual system, like the empire of Alexander, crumbled even before it was completely established. Political and social history is replete with details concerning the interrelation of peoples and of cultures that were briefly linked and then assumed separate and autonomous existences. The Aristotelian intellectual system reflects the characteristics of an enlarged and reinforced city-state. Its purpose is the survey and analysis of things and events in so objective a way as to promote agreement concerning being and becoming, potentiality and actuality, and similar issues.

Post-Aristotelian science and philosophy is no longer Athenian, and while the wisdom and technology of the Greece dominated intellectually by Athens had always depended upon Egyptian and Asiatic contributions, a new complexion now marks the Greek world of learning. Vying with Athens are Rhodes, Pergamum, and other cities, while Athens is about to be completely supplanted by Alexandria.

When the empire of Alexander disintegrated, a series of new states was built upon its foundations. Individual generals set up their own political units of large proportions. The Seleucids took possession of Mesopotamia and the Ptolemies ruled Egypt, while Macedonia came into the hands of the Antigonids. Later the Attalids found room to establish a dynasty in Pergamum. It is unnecessary for us to follow the tangled skein of the campaigns and wars that followed Alexander's demise or to describe the numerous conflicts between the various rival Hellenistic dynasties. Rather it is our interest to point out the analogous divisions, disagreements, and individualisms that became manifest on the intellectual side of Greek culture. We must stress an individualism of thought which was based primarily on personal attitudes established as schools or ways of thinking and which led to a universalism without the fixed and solid foundations of scientific observation. We will illustrate this situation by a description of the four schools of thought already mentioned, which show a decided independence of outlook. In consonance with the character of the four systems, stress will be put on the social and human objects of reflection, and the great sensitivity of the various formulations to the social and political changes in the Mediterranean world will be noted. As we shall see, each of the new conditions in its own way turned the stream of reflection into a channel greatly deviating from the specific and exact sciences, though these remained close to the naturalistic main stream of Greek thinking.

THE CYNICAL REJECTION OF THE SOCIAL ORDER

Diogenes Laertius naively declares that all philosophers fall into one of two classes. In one group are the Dogmatists, who make assertions about things, believing they can be known; and in the other the Sceptics, who discount knowledge.[2] Dichotomies are frequently as trivial as they are over-simple. But in the case of these Greek philosophers who are excessively sensitive to social and cultural conditions, that is, the humanistic and ethical thinkers, it may be proper to say that either they accept and conform to the obvious social institutions, or they are unhappy about them. In the latter case they may reject the social order in whole or part and appeal to a conventionless form of life, or they may attempt to escape from intolerable circumstances by carpingly criticizing the established order. While doing so, they may muster reasons for questioning the judgment and operational competence of those who establish and support the prevailing conventions.

The Greek thinkers called the Cynics excellently exemplify an extreme dissatisfaction with things as they are, and of course, they found sufficient cause in the hapless fortunes of the Greek city-states, including that of the greatest, Athens. It is clear, too, that there were many Cynics and that they form a succession with marked differences in the details of their thinking. The term Cynic is a generic one and in the present context signifies primarily the propagation of intellectual concern with man's life conditions and not with the presumably more remote and abstract problems concerning the nature of things.

It is probably an error to think of the cynical episode in the third century as a school, since this is a time of great social mobility and fluidity. Accordingly, we need not ask who founded the school or movement or who were enrolled in it. The records of the time show in fact the close contacts and actual fusion of one school or movement with another. For purposes of general orientation, however, we may consider Antisthenes of Athens as a formulator of cynical doctrine. Scholars believe that Cynicism originated as a questioning and severely testing attitude toward accepted, but not examined, knowledge institu-

[2] *Lives of Eminent Philosophers* i, 16.

tions. Antisthenes stems from the Sophistic and Socratic era, and of him it is said that he intensified his sceptical and distrusting attitudes toward accepted knowledge and became an authentic Cynic. Historians generally describe the early sceptical attitude as primarily a distrust of sensory knowledge, and consequently it remained within the framework of scientific inquiry. This was changed during the period under discussion.

Diogenes of Sinope, who lived in Alexander's time, has long and faithfully symbolized the full-fledged Cynic. His period was especially conducive to the rejection of established institutions. He was an eye witness to the dissolution of Greek society and to the Macedonian domination. Commixture of social orders is not favorable to confidence in and cherishing of any particular established order. There is too much evidence for contrast, for expediency, for transition through interaction. Diogenes Laertius has collected numerous anecdotes to illustrate the Cynic's rejection of culture, patriotism, the virtues, and the judgments of the society in which he lives.[3] By sheer force of circumstances the Cynic became a cosmopolite, an adherent to the ideal of a universal cultural community. But Diogenes would have been no popular Greek philosopher, no dabbler in the broadest generalities, no seer beyond the common horizon, if he had not moved far beyond cultural bounds to what was then called nature. Many of Laertius' anecdotes are designed precisely to show that Cynics really intended to live the lives of dogs. It is not that human communities are faulty and not good enough; rather, they are intrinsically bad.

In adaptation to the unsatisfactory world around them, Hellenistic thinkers sought to achieve *autarckia,* that is the self-sufficiency, the freedom, and the independence of the individual; to achieve this it was essential to withdraw from society by curtailing interests and desires. Stobaeus has preserved some excellent expressions of the cynical abnegation of the time as formulated by Teles, which he derived from Bion of Borysthenes. They concern the necessities of living, citizenship, and personal and domestic relations.

> Food? The roads are full of herbs and the springs of water. Look, says Teles, at those old women singing in quavering voices as they munch a common barley-cake. . . . You don't need a kitchen of your own to fry your couple of sprats. The bronze founders will no doubt let you use their furnace.[4]
>
> Native country? What of substantial worth does the exile lose? I am excluded, you may say, from the governing body of citizens in a strange city.

[3] *Lives of Eminent Philosophers,* vi, 20 *ff.*

[4] Bevan, "Hellenistic Popular Philosophy," p. 85.

But how many people in your own country are excluded from the governing body—women, slaves—and do not make a grievance of it?[5]

The Cynics, and to a certain extent the Sceptics, were more extreme than the Stoics and Epicureans. They were destroyers and had no inclination to project a better society. Hence, they levelled the ground so thoroughly as to leave room for the construction of personal theories out of nonexistent materials. All the four Hellenistic schools contributed to the future ways of thinking which replaced the organized scientific conditions of fifth and fourth century B.C. Athens, but the Cynics contributed most.

THE CULTURAL INCITATION TO SCEPTICISM

The intensification of sceptical attitudes in the Hellenistic period of our civilization is a simple, but inevitable, counterpart of the breakdown of the Greek city-states and the advent of Alexander's conquests. The basic principles of Scepticism—the search for what is not available in the way of knowledge, and the suspension of judgment—are simply a phase of intellectual activity which is unavoidable in the face of resistant facts. What is important, then, is to notice the intensification of sceptical attitudes on the part of thinkers who observe their shrinking grasp of social and political events.

That scepticism, agnosticism, and the suspension of judgment (*epoché*) are not discoveries of Pyrrho (*ca.* 360-270 B.C.) nor the basis for founding the sceptical movement or school was clearly stated by Theodosius.[6] Diogenes Laertius provides considerable evidence for many earlier thinkers who had formulated sceptical doctrines. The feature characteristic for the period under discussion is that the Sceptics emphasized on the abstract intellectual level a distrust of science and of the other disciplines which needed stable and dependable social circumstances in order to flourish.

The Hellenistic retreat from uncontrollable cultural circumstances brought about elaborate refinements of the sceptical attitude. Basically the Sceptics of the Hellenistic period organized a practical epistemological system for use as a weapon with which to undermine established reliance upon knowledge. Aenesidimus of Cnossus (*ca.* 1st c. B.C.?), who taught at Alexandria, organized the arguments known as the ten tropes or modes by which suspension of judgments is brought about. True to the naturalistic tradition of Greek psychology, he used as a

[5] *Ibid.*

[6] Diogenes Laertius, *op. cit.*, ix, 70.

model the activity of persons with respect to things, and in consequence the first four of the tropes, according to Sextus Empiricus,[7] pertain to the knower, the seventh and tenth to the object, and the fifth, sixth, eighth, and ninth to the interaction of the knower and the known. What these tropes or modes are based on, Sextus sets forth as follows.

1. Based on the Variety in Animals
2. Based on the Differences in Human Beings
3. Based on the Differences in Sense Organs
4. Based on the Specific Personal Circumstances: Sleeping, Waking, Age, Motion
5. Based on the Positions, Intervals, and Locations of Things
6. Based on the Intermixtures of Things and their Media
7. Based on the Quantity and Formations of Objects.
8. Based on Relativity
9. Based on the Frequency or Rarity of Occurrence
10. Based on Customs, Legendary Beliefs, and Dogmatic Convictions

Although the separation of the so-called subject and object, and the relation between them, is a verbal device, it can frequently aid us by indicating the factors upon which the negating influences are primarily directed. For the most part we should modify the arrangement of Sextus and put the sixth and ninth tropes among the modes primarily affecting the object. Aside from the use made by Aenesidimus of the facts indicated in the modes to break down the absoluteness of knowledge, the set constitutes a good description of the factors involved in reacting to objects. Herein lies a paradox of the Sceptical position in that the enumeration of the negative conditions of knowledge really supports the validity of knowledge.

On the whole, the tropes or modes have to do with sensory reactions and sensory knowledge. The later Sceptics have piled upon the Ossa of sensory unreliability the Pelion of the weakness of the syllogism as a stronghold of knowledge. Thus, Agrippa questioned the validity of syllogism because the conclusions could be no better than the premises. Such Sceptics as Carneades also argued that all scientific proof involves a *regressus in infinitum*. Erdmann sums up Agrippa's five tropes or modes as follows.

> . . . the variety in the meanings of words, the progression of all reasoning to infinity, the relativity of all things, and their dependence on disputable assumptions, and lastly, the fact that all reasoning is circular.[8]

In the case of both the Cynics and the Sceptics we discern a wrecking instead of a complete rejection of the Hellenic philosophical tradition.

[7] *Outlines of Pyrrhonism* i, Ch. 14, 36-163.

[8] *A History of Philosophy,* Vol. I, 197 *f.*

The theme is still a sort of cosmos-embracing knowledge and a realistic objectivism that even seeks to go beyond events and their functional interpretations. The tribulations and eventual collapse of Hellenic civilization concomitant with the trying days of the Macedonian hegemony and its disintegration, favored the unsettled and hesitating philosophy represented by these schools.

STOIC COSMOPOLITAN CONSTRUCTION

Stoicism in its historical aspect represents a more definitely escapist philosophy than Epicureanism. In its development, the adaptational motive facilitated the construction of a cosmic order in which man could find asylum despite all the vicissitudes of economic and political life. The dream of the Stoics involved a universal rational society and a world state that could help man to adapt himself to the kind of cosmopolitan world which the Hellenistic and Roman empires brought into being. The construction of such a universal society, the Stoics thought, required little more than the exercise of the sagacity which the reasonable man could readily muster. In such a state it was easy to find a place for oneself, be one an abject slave, ordinary citizen, or emperor. On the other hand, such a universal state afforded one sufficient room to withdraw from the company of this or that local group.

Helpful for the bipolar development, both adaptational and escapist, of Stoic universalism is the historical change from a cosmic to a more personal type of philosophy. In the early period, in the days of Zeno of Citium (340-265 B.C.) and his successors Cleanthes of Assos (*ca.* 250 B.C.) and Chrysippus (280-209 B.C.), Stoicism was greatly influenced by the Alexandrian astronomers, especially Aristarchus (*ca.* 310-230 B.C.) and Eratosthenes (*ca.* 273-195 B.C.). This connection lent a cosmic tone to Stoic ways of thinking. Stoic universalism was based on the immensities and grandeurs revealed by astronomical observation. But with the decline of social and political security an era of subjectivism arose. The harmony with nature and the notion of man as a microcosm corresponding to the astronomical macrocosm gave way to ideas of man as opposed to nature and society. The reliance upon judgment, based on knowledge and the discovery of the nature of things, gives way to the suspension of judgment and the submission to uncontrollable powers and things. By the time of Seneca (5-65) and Epictetus (*ca.* 1st c. B.C. ?) there is a retreat to conscience, some inner solipsistic process, as the criterion of morality and wisdom. An excellent illustration of this is the submission of Marcus Aurelius (121-180).

All that is in tune with thee, O Universe, is in tune with me! Nothing that is in due time for thee is too early or too late for me! All that thy seasons bring, O Nature, is fruit for me! All things come from thee, subsist in thee, go back to thee.[9]

To the historian of science, of course, the greatest significance of Stoicism is its long life, which contributed markedly to cultural continuity. Here is a social institution, created out of innumerable previously existing cultural factors, which lent itself to many changes so as to comport with the ever-changing social and political circumstances of its votaries. Early Stoicism was founded upon the naturalistic traditions of Hellenic Greece. With the changes of human circumstances in Hellenistic and Roman times, later Stoicism still remains naturalistic, although it is now deeply affected by the subjective and egocentric patina with which it is overlaid and which made it into potential material for the spiritual transformation to be wrought by the thinkers of the approaching Christian period. When Plotinus appears upon the scene a tremendous leap will be taken toward a mystical transmutation of Greek thinking, and by the time of Augustine little will be left of the naturalism so laboriously constructed during the heyday of Hellenic culture.

Stoicism obviously is a very elaborate cultural complex. It can readily be analyzed into a variety of philosophical doctrines, ontological, epistemological, and ethical. All these have their outlet in a series of psychological doctrines which, informal and unorganized as they may be, have exerted a great influence upon the development of spiritistic psychology. But Stoic psychology is in itself not spiritistic. It maintains the naturalistic characteristics of Hellenic thinking, howsoever far it departs from effective description of actual psychological behavior. As primarily philosophers or humanists, and not scientists, the Stoics maintain the division of the intellectual domain into logic, physics, and ethics. While psychology entered somewhat into all three, its primary and perhaps most humanistic place is in the ethical division. In the treatment of good and evil, conscience and duty, the behavioral aspect of psychological doctrine has its most ample habitat. In the ethical domain the Stoics could come close to actions and passions, to the significance of life, and to the place of man in the scheme of nature.

If we recall how ample and firm is the structure of the Aristotelian psychological corpus, it is not unfair to characterize Stoic psychology

[9] *The Communings with Himself of Marcus Aurelius Antoninus* iv, 23.

as an incoherent assemblage of vague verbalism. It is not untrue, either, to look upon it as a decided regression to pre-Aristotelian cosmic speculation. The primary emphasis in Stoic psychology is substantive, and the factor which the Stoics favored was the *pneuma.* Cosmically regarded, *pneuma* was like the fire of Heracleitus and, at the same time, the basis and reason for all things, as well as the effective element initiating and regulating all motion, action, and change. Since the psychological action of individuals mirrors cosmic reason, all psychological action is ultimately part of the action of cosmic reason, or the universal *pneuma.*

In consonance with Greek naturalism, *pneuma* is only a more refined substance than those which it sets into action. This view is obviously reminiscent of the doctrine of Anaxagoras and the other Greek philosophers who sought to explain the differentiations in the unitary cosmic stuff. Fanciful as this way of thinking is, it comports with the naturalistic attitude. Even in the late days of Stoic thinking, as, for example, in the distinction Panaetitus (*ca.* 185-109) makes between natural and unnatural pleasures as motives of men, or Posidonius' (135-51 B.C.) separation of the irrational emotions from rational judgments, and, finally, Seneca's complete dichotomization of man into flesh and spirit, the naturalistic view still held sway.

Pneuma for the Stoics is some form of warm, diffuse air which in organisms is connected with blood and breath. Generally speaking, *pneuma* is the principle or spirit of living things and corresponds to other principles such as earth and water, which form the basis for the existence and growth of all nonliving things. In its cosmic dimensions *pneuma* is much like the air, which Anaximenes regarded as the foundation of all that is and acts. One can hardly find fault with Siebeck's attempt to relate *pneuma* to all sorts of commonsense observations about physiological processes.[10] Thus, *pneuma* is associated with respiratory and circulatory functions, with actions of the heart, arteries, veins, lungs, larynx, and so on. Siebeck shows not only the connection of *pneuma* with the various forms of elements that the cosmological philosophers dealt with but also its relation to processes proposed by medical doctrines from the time of Hippocrates to Galen.

It would be vain to look for specific descriptions of psychological actions among the Stoics, even if better samples of their writings were available. Still, it is worth noting that, in consonance with the general humanistic tone of this type of doctrine, the Stoics, like the Epicureans,

[10] *Geschichte der Psychologie,* Vol. II, Ch. 1.

place great stress upon the affective types of behavior as well as on the various cognitive actions. In general, however, the Stoics are influenced by the kind of psychological doctrines which Aristotle developed. For example, they accepted the notion of the primacy of touch among the sensory activities, and the idea that visual and auditory responses were mediated by light and air.

EPICUREAN ADAPTATION TO SOCIAL CHANGES

The durable and important philosophical tradition called Epicureanism illustrates most effectively the transition in doctrine from Hellenic to Hellenistic times, since Epicureanism in all its phases is above everything else a humanistic philosophy which stresses the well-being of men through their effective orientation to nature and to society.

For Epicurus (341-270 B.C.) and the Epicureans science and philosophy can be divided into three phases: canonics, physics, and ethics. By canonics they understood the study of assumptions or first principles. There it is laid down that the basis and standard of knowledge are sensory encounters with things, preconceptions, and the feelings. By preconceptions they understood general ideas or principles derived from encounters with things. Feelings consist of the two states, pleasure and pain. Physics for Epicurus was the general discipline which treated everything in nature. Epicurus himself devoted thirty-seven books to this aspect of his philosophy in addition to monographs on special scientific topics. The ethical aspect of Epicureanism, according to Diogenes Laertius,[11] is devoted to facts of choice and aversion. Basic to these facts, of course, are the principles of pain and pleasure. Epicurean ethics is essentially hedonistic.

On the whole, of course, all learning and all science have one fundamental goal according to Epicureanism. Why should one investigate the terrestrial and cosmic operation of the atoms and the void which are the basic data? It is to achieve the calm certainty and confidence needed to adapt oneself to personal, social, and political conditions. The ethical aspects of life are the important ones; everything is subordinated to them. Epicureanism reflects accurately the turmoil and violent changes of the fourth and third centuries B.C.

Learning, science, and wisdom can serve to free the individual from fear and the evil effects of intolerable social conditions. The height of wisdom is to withdraw as much as possible from commerce with and the control of the state. Epicureanism, too, is a positive formulation

[11] *Op. cit.*, x, 30.

definitely directed against religious and pseudo-theological institutions. Like all Greek philosophers, the Epicureans regarded themselves as charged above all with the liquidation of superstition. By the time of Epicurus the dangers of mysticism and superstition were proliferating and it was the office of philosophy to rid the world of them.

The wise man can withdraw from undesirable contacts with improper dominant institutions and conventions by choosing and adhering to the right pleasures, which make for happiness. And what are these proper pleasures? Not what the traducers of Epicureanism say in their vindictiveness, but rather the satisfying pursuit of knowledge and the appreciation of the significance of things and events, the joys of witty and informing social life, and the harmonious configuration of the various factors making up the natural and conventional patterns of human living. To a great extent, all the human benefits the wise man seeks are to be gained by retreat and resignation. Desires must be moderated and curbed.

By Lucretius, the Roman (99-55 B.C.), we are again reminded how important it is for Epicureanism to serve as a definitely utilitarian philosophy. The purpose of the *De Rerum Natura* is to save men from the superstitions of religion and to free them from the unwarranted fear of death. If there is no mention of the terrors of social and political vacuity or economic disability, it is because Rome still provides a considerable measure of security. Doctrinally, this security is expressed in the formula of a concretely infinite universe in which the Democritean atoms and the void are the tangible basis for everything.

Not the least interesting thing to the historian is the pagan and naturalistic character of the *De Rerum Natura*. It is small wonder, then, that so striking a document should be the victim of the calumnies of such representatives of another world of thought as Lactantius (*ca.* 250-317).[12] It is important to distinguish Epicurean doctrine from what has been called, after the establishment of dualism, materialism. Neither Epicurus nor Lucretius had any notion of the spiritual-material dichotomy, so that they could not have rejected the former or made the latter dominant. In their day and under the cultural conditions in which they lived, they had only ignorance and oppression to combat, not spiritual powers or forces.

Fitting well into the structural pattern of the *De Rerum Natura* are the primary tenets of Greek objective psychology. We have already

[12] *Cf.* Sarton, *A History of Science,* Vol. II, p. 276.

mentioned that there is no transcendent mind in the system. The sections on soul are consonant with those on astronomical, physical, biological and other kinds of events. In the footsteps of Anaxagoras, Democritus, and other naturalistic Greek philosophers, Lucretius thinks of soul stuff as made up of atoms similar to that of other stuffs; only the soul is made of smaller, more refined, and roundly-shaped atoms.[13] Despite the complete absence of a systematic organization of psychological data, Lucretius presents a number of details about sensory and imagery responses, as well as others, all in a poetic, philosophical style. In the first century B.C., we find that in the last relatively stable community in the ancient world naturalistic doctrines are still maintained; thereafter they disappear from Western Europe. In the excerpts from Lucretius to be given below we have the last ancient attempt to state psychological problems in an objective form. Here is the call of Rome that was to be echoed only in the twentieth century.

THE PSYCHOLOGY OF LUCRETIUS

MIND: A PART OF MAN. Mind or intelligence, which is the source of guidance and the control of life, is an essential part of man, as are the hands, feet, and eyes. All are parts of a whole living creature. Lucretius specifically rejects the notion that mind is a harmony, a condition of the organism instead of a definite substantive part. As a controlling and directing part of the organism, mind is localizable in the mid-region of the breast, and is one with the vital breath and heat which permeates all parts of the organism as long as it is alive. In a sense, the vital spirit animating the veins, flesh, sinews, and organs of the animal obeys the dictates of the mind.

MIND AND SPIRIT BOTH REFINED ATOMS. To begin with, mind and spirit are bodily and organic. This is clearly argued by Lucretius in the following.

We see them propelling the limbs, rousing the body from sleep, changing the expression of the face and guiding and steering the whole man—activities that all clearly involve touch, as touch in turn involves matter. How then can we deny their material nature? You see the mind sharing in the body's experiences and sympathizing with it. When the nerve-racking impact of a spear gashes bones and sinews, even if it does not penetrate to the seat of life, there ensues faintness and a tempting inclination earthwards and on the ground a turmoil in the mind and an intermittent faltering impulse to stand up again. The substance of the mind must therefore be material, since it is affected by the impact of material weapons.[14]

[13] *De Rerum Natura* iii, 177-180.
[14] *Ibid.*, iii, 162-176.

Now, because the action of the mind is so smooth and swift it must be composed of exceedingly minute spherical particles. The arguments to support this view Lucretius takes from commonsense observations. Water flows so easily and so quickly because its atoms are small compared to those of sluggishly acting honey. Poppy seeds can be disturbed by a light puff of breeze, but not stones or ears of corn.

MIND COINCIDENT WITH LIVING. As part of the total organism mind exists only as long as the organism is intact and alive. Lucretius stresses the mortality of man in all its phases in consonance with his desire to show that nature offers no support for any superstition or terror. To this end he marshals numerous evidences that mind and other parts of the organism are born together, grow up together, and decay and become dissipated together.

THE SENSORY PROCESS. The phantastic, though mechanical sensory psychology of Lucretius is based upon an analogy between the never-ceasing movement and impacts of atoms and the similar motions of images, simulacra, or films emanating from the complexes of molecules which constitute things or sensory objects. Using many analogies, Lucretius argues the possibility that objects can give off floating particles which come into contact with the sense organs. As examples of the gross shedding of simulacra, he cites the cicadas throwing off their coats in summer, the calves shedding their cauls, and the serpents their outer skins. The films, complete with shapes, sizes, and colors, emanating from objects are simply exceedingly smooth complexes of atoms too tiny to be directly sensed, but effective in their mass impact upon the sense organs.

Atoms, out of which all things are made, in themselves contain none of the properties which have historically been called secondary. They possess only size, number, spatiality, motion, shape, solidity, hardness, and indestructibility. They are colorless, odorless, tasteless, and soundless. But the properties they do have, and the results of the commingling of various atoms eventuate in the appearance of secondary qualities or properties. An added property of atoms is that they sometimes impinge upon animate and sentient creatures.

To illustrate the production of secondary qualities by the churning up and reshuffling of atoms, Lucretius naturally stresses the production of colors. He asserts that the whole range of colors depends upon the combinations, positions, and reciprocal motions of variously shaped atoms.[15] For example, the ruffling of the sea surface by a fresh breeze

[15] *Ibid.*, ii, 730-833.

produces whiteness of a marble lustre. Again, the brightest of crimson or scarlet color is dissipated by increasingly dividing the substance in which it inheres. Light and especially changes of light produce and modify colors, according to whether the beams strike them vertically or obliquely.

> Observe the appearance in sunlight of the plumage that rings the neck of a dove and crowns its nape: sometimes it is tinted with the brilliant red of a ruby; at others it is seen from a certain point of view to mingle emerald greens with the blue of the sky. In the same way a peacock's tail, profusely illumined, changes colour as it is turned this way or that. These colours, then, are created by a particular incidence of light. Hence, no light, no colour.[16]

What is true of color is true of odors, tastes, sounds, and other sensory qualities. All depend upon the size and shape of the sense-producing atoms and on their appropriate motions, arrangements, and positions.

IMAGINATION. By comparison with ordinary truth-providing sensory activities, the phantastic activities in which centaurs, mermaids, the many-headed Cerberus, and the phantoms of the dead play a part require special explanation. But for Lucretius there is no need to go beyond the film and images of things and the refined atoms that constitute the source of sensing and reasoning processes. There are, of course, the different ways of contact between sensing and imaging. Whereas in sensing the films or images thrown off by things penetrate to the organism's refined atoms through definite sense organs, in imaging they reach their goal through the interstices of the body in general. In the case of imagination, too, there are unique images which are formed not from objects, but produced spontaneously in the air itself.[17] On the whole, however, what is seen by the mind directly is similar to what is seen by means of the eyes. When the surface images of a horse and of a man encounter one another they amalgamate like gossamer or goldleaf, and we see a phantastic centaur.

The imaginative processes while sleeping are extremely vivid, since they lack the competition of the sensory organs and the critical vigilance of memory; thus, we may be convinced that we are seeing someone who has died and turned to dust. By the same processes we may observe the transformed object, as when a woman becomes a man or an aged person a youth.

THINKING AND IMAGE CONTROL. On the whole, Lucretius regards the

[16] *Ibid.*, ii, 801-809.
[17] *Ibid.*, iv, 736.

imaginative process as a relatively passive way of behaving. While all psychological activities occur as interactions of external images and the refined internal atoms, in the case of imagination the organism is relatively quiescent. It is primarily the images that bring about the phantastic results. In thinking, on the contrary, the organism is extremely active. It is true that both kinds of action presuppose the presence of an enormous number of films or images of all sorts that move about very rapidly. But in thinking and recollecting the mind is extremely attentive and selective. It is this activity that gives order, propriety, and effectiveness to a dance of images so swift and so numerous that only reason can recognize them and not direct and immediate perception.[18] The active process of thinking makes it possible for persons to react to assemblages of men, processions, battles, and other complex objects instead of to phantoms.

VOLITION AND MOTION. What are the mechanisms for the many actions and gestures of the limbs and for the locomotion of the heavy human organism? First, images of motion or walking impinge upon the inner refined atoms which are the mind. This constitutes volition or will, which invariably and necessarily precedes any action. Such anticipations of action immediately are propagated through every limb and organ of the body, since the motions of the mind atoms are intimately connected with the vital spirits of the body. It is through the action of the vital spirits that the mass of the body is pushed forward and set in motion.

LANGUAGE-SPEECH. Of especial interest to modern students of psychology are the discussions of Lucretius concerning language and speech.[19] For one thing he offers a completely naturalistic theory of the origin and development of speech. Again, he anticipates what in recent times has been hailed as an excellent hypothesis—namely the evolution of human speech from the common biological source of animal cries and gestures.

The sounds of spoken language originated in the natural conditions of man, and the specific forms of the names of objects grew out of practical convenience. Lucretius expressly rejects the view that a particular individual invented the names of things and then passed on this boon to others. Such a view is stark madness. When need arose, persons made use of the organic facilities which they had previously developed in the way of voice and tongue in order to produce sounds.

[18] *Ibid.*, iv, 795-801.
[19] *Ibid.*, v, 1028-1090.

Language thus is a common or universal development. Here, we may well recall Lucretius' emphatic declaration that the tongue and voice were not developed for speech, that the ears were created before a sound was heard.

. . . since nothing is born in us simply in order that we may use it, but that which is born creates the use.[20]

Few are the details that Lucretius suggests for the development of speech. But he does make the general point that distinctive utterances were developed to aid in distinguishing one thing from another. He takes as the primordia of speech the utterance by animals of different cries as expressions of different feelings.

SLEEPING AND DREAMING. Knowing that systematic psychology had disappeared from the intellectual institutions of Western culture several centuries before Lucretius, we cannot expect anything more from him than the more or less sketchy treatment of isolated topics. We must be grateful, then, for his inclusion of sleep and dreams in his great work.

Sleep occurs when the vital spirit which permeates the body is discomposed. Basically, of course, this modification of the organism's condition is to be carried back immediately to changes in the refined atoms of the mind as well as in the cruder ones of the organism in general. The various atoms are dislocated so that the regularities of action are interfered with. The limbs slacken, arms and eyelids droop, and the confusion of atoms makes for a slumping and instability of action.

With the normal oriented and adjusting actions in abeyance, the subtle phantastic actions take over and dreams become powerful and often disturbing. The individual, withdrawn from his usual responsiveness to routine and necessary objects and conditions, behaves spontaneously and without intimate control of the environment. What the individual dreams about must, of course, depend upon his usual occupation, but it is greatly exaggerated and free from reasonable constraint.

Lawyers argue cases and frame contracts. Generals lead their troops into action. Sailors continue their pitched battle with the winds. And as for me, I go on with my task, for ever exploring the nature of the universe and setting down my discoveries in my native tongue.[21]

The massiveness and even violence of dreaming action Lucretius describes excellently.

[20] *Ibid.*, iv, 834-835 (quoted from W. H. D. Rouse translation [Loeb Classical Library], London, Heinemann, 1943).

[21] *Ibid.*, iv, 966-970.

Kings take cities by storm, are themselves taken captive, join in battle and cry aloud as though they felt the assassin's dagger—and all without stirring from the spot. There are many who fight for their lives, giving vent to their agony in groans or filling the night with piercing screams as though they were writhing in the jaws of a panther or a ravening lion. Many talk in their sleep about matters of great moment and have often betrayed their own guilt. Many meet their death. Many, who feel themselves hurled bodily down to earth from towering crags, are startled out of sleep; like men who have lost their wits, they are slow in returning to themselves, so shaken are they by the tumult of their body. The thirsty man finds himself seated beside a river or a delectable spring and is near to gulping down the whole stream.[22]

Though the psychology of Lucretius marks the end of the era in which psychological events are treated naturalistically, the light of science continues to shine brightly on other subjects. Mathematics, physics, astronomy, and the anthropic sciences reach their highest peak in the environment of Alexandria. In that city a cultural situation arises which will foster for several centuries marked improvement in the nonpsychological studies. In contrast, psychology degenerated. In the next chapter we will survey briefly the development of science in the Museum and Libraries of Alexandria.

[22] *Ibid.*, iv, 1013-1025.

SECTION FIVE

THE HELLENISTIC EXPANSION AND DIFFRACTION OF SCIENCE

CHAPTER 12

ALEXANDRIA: THE MUSEUM AND THE LIBRARIES

HELLENISTIC INTERMIXTURE OF CULTURES

THE HELLENISTIC PERIOD stands out strikingly in the history of European civilization. Politically this interval is marked by the campaigns and conquests of the two famous Macedonian rulers, Philip the Second and his more eminent son, Alexander, accomplishments which took on even greater significance during the dominance of their successors. Obviously, the political and military happenings that occurred in the period were accompanied by many other, diverse events, but the historian of science can do no better than to focus upon the changes that took place when the Greeks and their civilization became drastically intermixed with the peoples and cultures of the Near East.

These changes affected every phase of the lives of the various populations concerned. With the removal of the barriers between different and formerly autonomous national units, opportunities arose for the expansion of political, industrial, commercial, and social affairs and for the development of new ways of living, including moral, religious, and philosophical activities. Probably the greatest cultural changes may be traced to the intermixture of the intellectual equipment of the fourth-century Greeks with that of the nearer Oriental peoples. Early in the period we can discern the comparatively great expansion of the intellectual horizons of the Greeks—the opening up of their restricted outlook, which had been confined to a relatively limited world of things and events. Speculation became freer, and scholars, learning the technique of manipulating language, acquired the ability to roam widely into regions which they themselves created. As to the Easterners, their philosophies were presumed by the Greeks to form a firmer anchorage for men than was possible by means of science and to bring to things the criteria of graded existence and of greater or lesser approximation to reality.

SOCIAL AND INTELLECTUAL CONSEQUENCES OF HELLENISTIC IMPERIALISM

It is doubtless true that some of the early consequences of Alexander's conquests and the resulting imperialism were fraught with substantial benefits from a commercial and political standpoint. Certainly, the levelling of boundaries and barriers increased the scope of traders and transporters. These benefits perhaps are most clearly seen from the angle of the conqueror nations, but all those states which adapted themselves to the fusion made substantial profits. Empires provide many advantages for those who need to have open paths for the exchange of goods or to relieve themselves of the need to be constantly guarding their borders.

However, the scientific and philosophical institutions of the European peoples did not achieve any lasting benefits from the imperial conquest. In fact, when we take as our vantage point the most systematic and objective results attained by Hellenic intellectual workers, the constant deterioration is all too definitely marked. As Bury put the matter, the later Alexandrian period shows a distinct failure of nerve.[1] In the same sense, the Roman period which succeeded it represents a failure of inspiration, while the following medieval age reveals an almost complete fading out of knowledge.[2]

Basic to this sad record of intellectual deterioration are the cultural changes which mark the loss of social security on the part of individuals when empires absorb other political entities, especially when the nations absorbed are such intimate and accessible ones as the Greek city states. The effect of having to face a massive and unmanageable society is that man turns within himself to find his anchorage and stability. In this period we have a second stage of development—one that follows on that which has given rise to the universal perspectives of the Stoics, Epicureans, Cynics, and Sceptics.

As imperialism expands and becomes intensified, the return into oneself gives rise to projections more and more remote from natural things. While the Athenian Stoics and Epicureans could still base themselves upon natural events, in the Hellenistic period there is the beginning at least of the attempt to break through the confines of practical and amenable space-time in order to reach for the nonexistent. The technique, of course, is the sophisticated use of language. As we shall see, this is a period characterized by the composition of treatises and commentaries. In the following sections we will trace the great

[1] See Murray, *Five Stages of Greek Religion*, p. xiii.
[2] Singer, *A Short History of Science to the Nineteenth Century*, p. 55.

scientific expansion in Alexandrian times, along with the development of many new intellectual institutions. The Hellenistic era is a lofty peak and at the same time a valley which marks the devolution of the naturalistic and scientific attitudes of European culture.

HELLENIC AND HELLENISTIC SCIENCE

As we know, the development of psychological science ceased even before the decline of Greek science. The explanation for this must undoubtedly be sought in the particular social and economic circumstances of the time. The historian of science can only record that in the Hellenistic period there was a flare-up of scientific institutions. Not only was there a great increase in the number of scientific centers, but the work in each, whether Pergamum, Antioch, Rhodes, Alexandria, or Athens itself, became intensified. In particular, the great concentration of social and economic life in the world-trade center of Alexandria favored the development of astronomy, medicine, mathematics, physics, and some branches of biology, but not of psychology. This surge of scientific development, to be sure, was only a prelude to a decline and a temporary extinction. But while it lasted, it illuminated the scientific scene and provided the seeds which grew into a number of still-flourishing scientific institutions.

There is nothing mysterious about the expansion of Hellenistic science. All the favorable participating factors were ready at hand. On one side were all the advantages of a great and growing population with a heterogeneity born from the free intercourse of extremely different members of a unique community. Then there were the riches concentrated in favored centers of industry, trade, and regal grandeur. Not to be slighted is the appearance of new geographical and political establishments which were unhampered by traditions hallowed by lengthy survival. These stirring circumstances provide a double advantage: first, the absence of hindering institutions and, second, the scientific potential residing in the varying intellectual resources of different cultures. Alexandrian science is based upon intellectual materials derived not only from Ionia, Attica, Egypt, and Mesopotamia, but also from Syracuse, Crotona, and other western scientific outposts.

ALEXANDRIA'S INFLUENCE ON SCIENTIFIC TRADITION

The great significance of Alexandria with its Museum and Libraries for the history of science is that it helped to establish many of the scientific institutions of Western civilization. This result was brought about in two ways. First, by the actual promotion of various branches of science, notably mathematics and astronomy, and second, by segregating concrete investigative disciplines from what had been primarily speculative exercises.

It is not misleading to consider that the Alexandrian Museum was in design and function much like a modern university. Essentially, it consisted of a set of buildings which housed the groups of scholars and scientists brought together to carry on their intellectual labors, and which included facilities for various kinds of scientific and other intellectual work. We are hardly forcing the point if we say that the campus was fitted with halls of residence, and refectories, as well as buildings for library, observatory, and laboratory work.[3] The founders were Ptolemy I (Soter) and II (Philadelphus), who reigned in the early part of the third century B.C. With great variations in production, usefulness, and general prosperity the Museum endured for seven or more centuries.

HELLENISTIC SCIENTIFIC SPECIALIZATION

Doubtless, one result of the assiduous acquisition of knowledge and the development of new phases of science was the increase of specialization, exemplified by a great proliferation of disciplines devoted to particular kinds of data. From the Alexandrian period dates the institution of such specialized sciences as number theory, geometry, geography, conic sections, astronomy, algebra, mechanics, and various branches of biology such as anatomy and physiology. Obviously, there are already rudiments of particularization present in the specialized treatises of Aristotle and the members of the Peripatetic school. But in the Alexandrian period begins the intensive preoccupation of individuals with specialized studies.

One of the most fundamental innovations was the differentiation of humanistic from nonhumanistic studies. Especially important is the development of anthropological and linguistic sciences. The propagation of humanistic studies clearly follows from the observation of differences in the various peoples who came together to form the great society of Indians, Persians, Syrians, Babylonians, Egyptians, Jews, and the many other groups of the Hellenistic kingdoms. Linguistic studies obviously were promoted by the problems of the concentration of so many different languages in the cosmopolitan centers, especially Alexandria. The two scientific trends which developed in Alexandria were destined to have a great influence on the intellectual development of Western Europe. The nonhumanistic trend, of course,

[3] *The Geography of Strabo,* xvii, 1, 8.

was extinguished to be revived only after many centuries. The humanistic trend made it possible to dispense with the study of inorganic nature and, further, to build up intellectual techniques and system-products which are still viable and which have made possible the nature-spirit bifurcation of Western European culture. The linguistic principles developed in Alexandria became intimately linked with the tradition of constructing systems of propositions based more on the autistically created foundations of socially influenced thinkers than on the intimate contacts of observers with independent things and events. Humanistic science was concerned with allegory, symbols, and with general linguistic constructions.

HELLENISTIC NONANTHROPIC SCIENCES

The Hellenistic period stands out starkly in the history of science and scientific institutions because it marks both a high point and a turning point in the development of knowledge. The height of Hellenistic scientific eminence may be gauged by the achievements of the Alexandrian and other workers in this period. What Euclid, Archimedes, Apollonius, Pappus, and others achieved persist as scientific institutions. To cite a few examples, even if Euclid only synthesized geometric wisdom he wrought marvellously in his chosen field. Consider also that Descartes' researches on analytical geometry may have had their starting point in the famous problem of Pappus on geometrical loci.[4]

The significant turning point in Hellenistic science is the movement of scholars away from persistent, direct contact with events to a procedure of arbitrary construction and cherishing of propositions. During the Hellenistic period the interest in events faces the strong competition of personal problems until natural science eventually becomes altogether extinct in the Western European tradition, and will persist only in a diluted form among the scholars of the "Arab" tradition.

As to the value of Hellenistic science historians are not agreed. Some stress the sheer advancement of knowledge itself whether it be concerned with abstract mathematical things or technological objects such as primitive steam engines, inclined planes, the lever, and so on. Others emphasize the development of methods and principles. It is said, for example, that Hellenistic scientists, especially mathematicians like

[4] Reymond, *History of the Sciences in Greco-Roman Antiquity,* p. 98; Bell, *Development of Mathematics,* p. 549.

Euclid, have achieved their goals by rationalizing, by deducing from certain postulated principles the irresistible sequence of mathematical propositions.[5] For our part we refrain from overstressing either of these modes of evaluation; both proceed on the basis of abstracting from a complex situation. We plan to indicate the features characteristic for the various scientific activities and accordingly we present a number of samples of development taken from the great complex of enterprises that flourished in the Hellenistic period.

Mathematics

By common consent Greek mathematics constitutes the highest attainment of the Hellenistic period because it displayed both a diligence in summarizing what had previously been achieved and in originating new ideas. So far as lines of work are concerned, the theory of numbers and, of course, geometry are emphasized, although, when Diophantus is taken into account, one cannot undervalue the algebraic accomplishments. In consonance with our sampling procedure we examine Hellenistic mathematics by the consideration of several outstanding writers of the time.

Euclid (330-260 B.C.). Whether or not it is true that Euclid intended his *Elements* to combine the theories of proportions worked out by Eudoxus and Theaetetus with Plato's theory of the five regular bodies,[6] his work is basically naturalistic, as are the writings of the earlier three authors. His logic, as represented by the organization of definitions, postulates, axioms, and theorems, clearly reveals the derivation of the entire system from commonsense considerations. Geometry for Euclid is clearly based upon contacts with tangible and visible objects. The abstracted relations stand close to problems of land areas, crude dimensional analysis, and inferences derived from dealings with everyday things and their interrelations.

It is characteristic of Euclid that he carries over into the Hellenistic period the basic fixity, rigidity, and simplicity of the systems of the Hellenic age. Whatever flexibility, daring, and free creation entered into his tight system were thoroughly assimilated into the style favored by Athenian culture.

Apollonius of Perga (260-170 B.C.). Apollonius excellently represents Hellenistic mathematics. An outstanding achievement is his effective gleaning of facts and principles from the work of his predecessors (Menaechmus [375-325 B.C.], Euclid) and contemporaries (Nicoteles

[5] *Cf.* Reymond, *op. cit.*, p. 67.

[6] Struik, *A Concise History of Mathematics,* Vol. I, p. 61.

of Cyrene, Conon, Thrasydius)[7] in order to shape them into a definitive treatise. The final result is his great work on conics. The importance of this mathematical treatise may be assessed by considering the question whether or not it marks the establishment of analytic geometry. Coolidge, the historian of geometrical method, writes,

> My thesis, then, is that the essence of analytic geometry is the study of loci by means of their equations, and that this was known to the Greeks and was the basis of their study of conic sections.[8]

Similarly, Struik credits Descartes only with the merit of influencing the later development of analytical geometry, which Struik traces back to Apollonius and Pappus.[9]

Apollonius stands always as a firm supporter of the synthetic deductive method of Hellenic geometry. He is credited with a desire to confine his mathematical constructs to situations actually encountered and to limit the number of fundamental propositions.[10] By stressing organization and synthesis, Apollonius merges his own original ideas with the creative products of other thinkers and thus produces substantial mathematical achievements.

Archimedes (287-212 B.C.). Not only is Archimedes awarded the palm for being the greatest mathematician of antiquity, a worker of rigor, great scope, originality, and power, but he is also probably the last representative of the intellectual enlargement of Greek civilization. The breadth and depth of his work indicate an acquaintance with all the scientific attainments of the Hellenic and Hellenistic eras. Born in Syracuse, he studied in Alexandria, and his mention of the work of Democritus shows his knowledge of the science and mathematics of Hellenic times. All historians of science marvel at Archimedes' extreme versatility; he is credited with the invention of many machines —compound pulleys; screws of various sorts, including endless and hydraulic ones; burning mirrors; planetaria; and many others. In mathematics he was a geometer, computer, arithmetician, and analyst. This versatility signalizes a pragmatic and naturalist approach to science and encourages the tendency to envisage mathematical problems in a broader and bolder way than was the case before Alexander's conquests. Some mathematical historians like to think of this versatility as a repudiation of Platonic thinking with its remoteness, absolutism, and utter fixity.[11]

[7] See Preface to Book iv of the *Treatise on Conic Sections.*

[8] Coolidge, *A History of Geometrical Methods,* p. 119.

[9] Struik, *op. cit.,* p. 134.

[10] See Reymond, *op. cit.,* p. 78

[11] Bell, *The Development of Mathematics,* p. 68 *f.;* Struik, *op. cit.,* p. 65.

Probably the best demonstration that Archimedes was an original mathematician and an initiator of modern mathematics lies in his practical preoccupation with infinites. We accent the word practical because, as already indicated in Chapter 6, Archimedes, no more than any other Greek, concerned himself with such indefinite and impalpable entities as infinites. As Heath points out, Greek geometers must have arrived in practice at infinites "in the case of the proposition that circles are to one another as the squares on their diameters."[12] Although Archimedes really carries out integration processes and "performs the first summation of an infinite series in history"[13] he disguises his work as methods of exhaustion. The explanation for this is that even though Archimedes has reached in his technical pursuits an enormously enlarged intellectual perspective, his general frame of reference remains that of the Hellenic Greeks. One might envisage Archimedes' predicament as a slight clash of cultural attitudes. Solid and safe classical geometry may have appeared as a refuge of certainty in Hellenistic times, although the current scientific, political, and economic conditions were bringing in their train their own pertinent methods, processes, and results.

Diophantus (2nd half of 3rd c. B.C.). This Alexandrian demands mention among the great Hellenistic mathematicians not only because of his technical merits, but also because he symbolizes the enlargement of the Greek mathematical scene to include algebra in addition to geometry. This fact appears to be so radical a change from the essentially geometrical culture of the Greeks that it raises a number of crucial questions. For example, did Diophantus originate his algebraic methods or did he derive them from Babylonian writers? The latter supposition would be strengthened if it could be proved that Diophantus himself was, as has been suggested, a Hellenistic Babylonian.[14] On the other hand, it is asserted that Diophantus' work is not up to the standard of the Babylonians of a much earlier period.[15] The question could also be raised as to why, if Mesopotamian algebra was so good and potentially available, did the Greeks not take to the subject before the Hellenistic period, and not generally even then? Here among the many possible explanatory factors that could be cited, the difficulties of the Akkadian language, particularly of its forbidding script, deserve special mention.

[12] Heath, *The Works of Archimedes,* p. cxliii.
[13] Bell, *op. cit.,* p. 71.
[14] Struik, *op. cit.,* p. 74.
[15] Bell, *op. cit.,* p. 37.

What is significant for us in the consideration of Diophantus and his algebraic and arithmetic achievements is the unmistakable mixture of atypical and presumably foreign elements in Hellenistic culture. Though the present example pertains to mathematics, it obviously reflects a general condition which presages great intellectual changes at every point.

Simply by way of emphasizing the culminating peak attained by Hellenistic science, we may list other mathematicians of outstanding merit and achievement. First, we mention the friends and correspondents of Archimedes; for example, Dositheus, Eratosthenes, and Conon, the last recorded by Archimedes as an admirable mathematician.[16] Next, we name Pappus of Alexandria, not only for his own mathematical work, but for his *synagoge* or mathematical collection, which is a valuable source of mathematical history.

Astronomy and Geography

Many scholars have referred to and condemned what they envisage as the aloofness of the Hellenic intellectual or philosophical culture. They have formulated a notion of Platonic transcendence or prudery that disdains contact with earthy things. Whether this view is justified or not, it has no application to the Hellenistic age. In this period there is no disdain of applied mathematics, of interest in the minutiae of everyday living. Surely the social and political circumstances of the Hellenistic world stimulated an intense interest in the earth and its relation to the stars and other planets. The Hellenistic enlargement of the intellectual horizon is certainly in part accounted for by the expansion of industry and commerce, by the competition of the states belonging to Alexander's successors. A most interesting story is thus unfolded in the expansion of geography and astronomy, which we sample by the presentation of some of the outstanding writers.

Aristarchus of Samos (310-230? B.C.). Aristarchus is justly celebrated as one of the greatest astronomers and mathematicians of antiquity. His career effectively mirrors the evolution of Greek science. As pupil of Strato, the leader of the Athenian Lyceum, he stems from the authentic Hellenic culture; and as an innovator in the Alexandrian period he helps to carry forward the naturalistic tradition to its peak.

What appears as the most impressive of his achievements is the anticipation of the heliocentric theory of Copernicus. Apparently this hypothesis was presented in a work that has not survived. But an ex-

[16] Heath, *op. cit.*, p. 233.

cellent witness to Aristarchus' achievement is Archimedes, who sets forth his testimony in the *Sand Reckoner* addressed to Gelon the Second, king of Syracuse.

Now you are aware that 'universe' is the name given by most astronomers to the sphere whose centre is the centre of the earth and whose radius is equal to the straight line between the centre of the sun and the centre of the earth. This is the common account, as you have heard from astronomers. But Aristarchus of Samos brought out a book consisting of some hypotheses, in which the premisses lead to the result that the universe is many times greater than that now so called. His hypotheses are that the fixed stars and the sun remain unmoved, that the earth revolves about the sun in the circumference of a circle, the sun lying in the middle of the orbit, and that the sphere of the circle in which he supposes the earth to revolve bears such a proportion to the distance of the fixed stars as the centre of the sphere bears to its surface.[17]

It is no wonder that Aristarchus commands the admiration of modern students even though he himself vacillates in his adherence to the

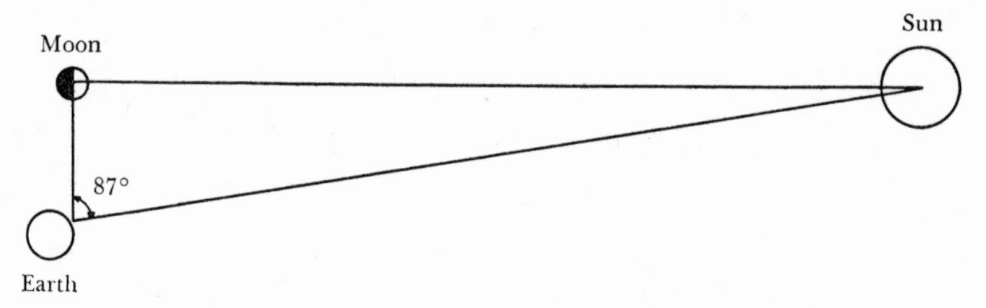

FIG. 17. ARISTARCHUS' METHOD FOR MEASURING ASTRONOMICAL SIZES AND DISTANCES

hypothesis, as, for example, when he attempts to determine the magnitude of the sun and moon and their distance from the earth. Nor does his great fame suffer diminution because Philolaus (5th c. B.C.) and Heraclides of Pontus (388-310? B.C.), as pupils of Plato and Aristotle, had previously proposed a similar way of thinking.

Another outstanding contribution of Aristarchus was his inauguration of quantitative procedures, as in his attempts to measure the relative sizes and distances of the sun, earth, and moon, and their relative distances from each other. This method, of course, was the ubiquitous geometric one, though in its application he attained a close approximation to trigonometric principles. The accompanying diagram (Fig. 17) illustrates his procedure.

The basis of the method is the assumption that at the period of half moon the angle EMS must be a right angle. If, at such a time the

[17] *Ibid.*, p. 221 *f.*

angle MES could be measured, the result would give the relative distance of the sun and moon. As we know, his estimates and calculations were full of errors and so, while his method was excellent, he still did not achieve his goal. The following table (Table III) indicates the deviation of Aristarchus' results from those accepted today.

TABLE III. COMPARATIVE RELATIONS BETWEEN THE MOON, SUN, AND EARTH ACCORDING TO ARISTARCHUS AND MODERN ASTRONOMERS[18]

Quantity	*Aristarchus*	*Modern*
MES angle	87°	89° 50′
Distance ratio of $\frac{EM}{ES}$	$\frac{1}{19}$	$\frac{1}{400}$
Ratio of volume of $\frac{M}{E}$	$\frac{1}{17}$ to $\frac{1}{31}$	$\frac{1}{49}$
Diameter ratio of $\frac{M}{S}$	$\frac{1}{19}$	$\frac{1}{400}$
Ratio of volume $\frac{M}{S}$	$\frac{1}{5832+}$ to $\frac{1}{8000-}$	$\frac{1}{106,600,000}$
Ratio of $\frac{\text{M diameter}}{\text{M orbit}}$	$\frac{1}{26\frac{1}{4}}$	$\frac{1}{110.5}$
Diameter ratio of $\frac{E}{S}$	$\frac{1}{6.75}$	$\frac{1}{109}$
Volume ratio $\frac{E}{S}$	$\frac{1}{311}$	$\frac{1}{1,300,000}$
Diameter ratio $\frac{M}{E}$	$\frac{1}{2.85}$	$\frac{1}{3.7}$

[18] Data from Sarton, *A History of Science*, Vol. II, p. 54 *f*.

Eratosthenes of Cyrene (1273-195? B.C.). Although the Hellenistic period is definitely an age of great intellectual specialization it is not at all surprising that the outstanding figures of the time defy rigid classification. And so, despite the fact that Eratosthenes is called primarily a geographer, this does not mean that he lacks merit as a mathematician, astronomer, grammarian, and so on. When the various disciplines are themselves not sharply separated, it is impossible to follow strict lines of specialization. As chief librarian of Alexandria, Eratosthenes must have developed a wide horizon of interests, and he is credited with a number of achievements, for example, the sieve for separating out the prime numbers, a method of geographic mapping which suggests coordinates, and a great many others.

By far his most important achievement as a representative of Hellenistic science was his method of measuring the circumference of the earth. He ascertained that, while at noon in Alexandria at the time of the summer solstice a vertical rod casts a shadow indicating that the distance of the sun from the zenith is one fiftieth of the circumference of the heavens, at Syene (Aswan) at the same moment the sun is at the zenith, since a gnomon casts no shadow and the bottoms of wells are perpendicularly illuminated. Fig. 18 illustrates the simple procedure Eratosthenes used to arrive at his determination of the earth's circumference. His problem was to determine the angle at the center of the earth subtended by 5,000 stadia, the distance he accepted as separating Alexandria from Syene. The two cities he assumed to be in the same meridian. A simple calculation should be that the earth's circumference was 50 × 5,000, or 250,000 stadia. This number he later raised to 252,000. If it is assumed that a stadium equals 517 feet his result would be 24,675 miles as compared with the accepted value of 24,875 miles. Eratosthenes' method demonstrates the progress made in the Alexandrian period in determining the dimensions of the earth. The previous estimates of 400,000 stadia made by Aristotle and that of 300,000 stadia made by Archimedes, probably on the authority of Dicaearchus of Messina,[19] seem less adequate, though there is uncertainty as to the stadia scales used.

Hipparchus of Nicea (3rd c. B.C.). Even if it is not true that Hipparchus is one of the greatest astronomers of all times, he assuredly was the greatest of the Hellenistic period. Certainly he is a model scientist in the sense of keeping close to astronomical events and performing observations and calculations which increase considerably the

[19] Dreyer, *A History of Astronomy*, p. 173.

stock pile of scientific results. No greater commendation can be made of him than to point to his work as one of the highest achievements of a scientific era which was itself a paragon not to be equaled until science was revived many centuries later.

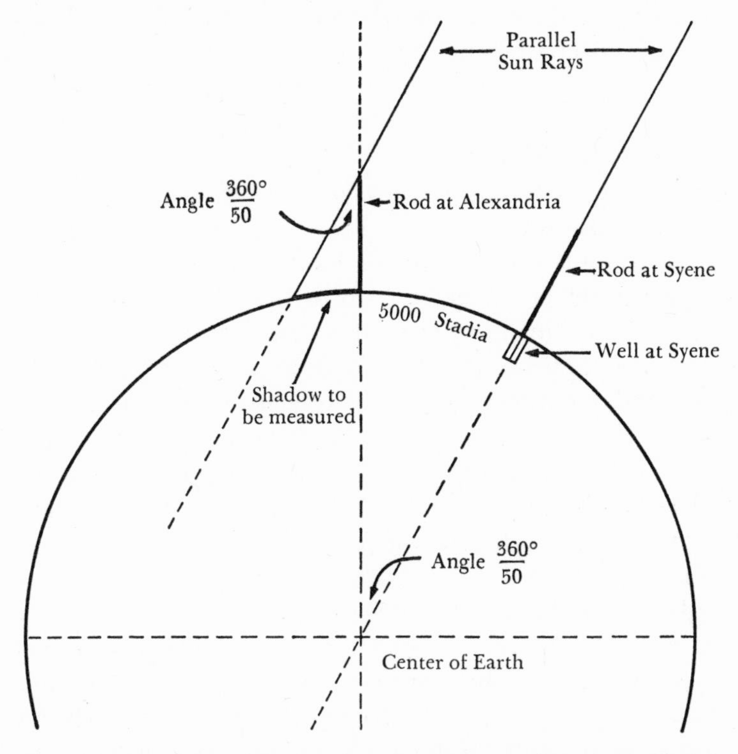

FIG. 18. ERATOSTHENES' METHOD FOR MEASURING THE SIZE OF THE EARTH

The character of Hipparchus as an investigating astronomer is shown by the observations he made in the observatory that he built at Rhodes and by his zeal in searching out the records of the positions and motions of the stars left by the Babylonian astronomers. As a meticulous observer, it was almost inevitable that he should prepare a list of stars giving accurate determination of the position and magnitude of eight hundred and fifty stars. In making these determinations he helped to establish a celestial system of coordinates comparable to the terrestrial longitude-latitude systems. Hipparchus also attempted, though without success, to correct the estimations of Aristarchus concerning the sizes of the sun and moon and their distance from the earth.

With one voice, historians of astronomy acclaim Hipparchus for his establishment of the facts of equinoctial precession. To discover the precession he had at hand the necessary data gleaned from Babylonian observers, but the comparisons had to be made upon the basis of data achieved by his own careful observations. The studies of Hipparchus which led to the discovery of the precession of the equinoxes were influential in redetermining the positions of the stars. For example, Hipparchus compared his observations on Spica with those of Timocharis of Alexandria made about one hundred and fifty years earlier. While Timocharis had found Spica to be located eight degrees from the autumnal equinox Hipparchus located the star as only six degrees from the same position.[20]

That Hipparchus was able to aid Hellenistic astronomy to reach its peak can certainly be in part accounted for by the attitude and instruments he could bring to bear upon astronomical work. Commendable is his view that astronomical observation was a definite task to be performed, and one which was subject to many errors. Such errors he believed to be constant factors in the scientific situation so that they have to be studied and understood in order to be avoided or at least minimized. The instruments Hipparchus developed or used may be divided into two types, the mathematical and the observational. The subject of trigonometry, which Hipparchus is credited with inventing, is certainly one of the most effective tools in his equipment. Without spherical trigonometry astronomical progress would have been difficult to achieve. Among the observational instruments used by Hipparchus were a celestial sphere, an improved type of diopter or sighting instrument, a meridian circle, and, of course, the universal *astrolabon organon*.[21]

Claudius Ptolemy (2nd c. A.D.). The last and best known of the Alexandrian astronomers was separated from Hipparchus by almost three centuries. Although Ptolemy merits acclaim because of his original contributions, his superb astronomical synthesis, and because he preserved in his famous *Almagest* the record of astronomical development at the hands of his predecessors, especially Hipparchus, he has become infamous for his espousal of the geocentric theory.

Since Ptolemy is known less as a person than as a great volume of thirteen books, we can sum up his contribution, as well as Hellenistic astronomy, by briefly mentioning its contents. Following a prefatory explanation of the value of astronomy, Ptolemy proceeds in his first

[20] Dreyer, *A History of Astronomy*, p. 203.

[52] *A Treatise on the Natureof Man,* Ch. 20 (p. 295).

two books, as does Euclid in his great counterpart, to give his definitions and general theorems. Aside from a discussion of many technical points like the sphericity of the earth and earth-directed gravity, the position of the ecliptic, and the location of the inhabited regions, he commends the soundness of his work because it is based upon observation and geometric methods. In the next two books he studies the motions of the sun and moon. In the former he is concerned, too, with the length of the year. The sun, of course, has lost its centrality and especial significance in astronomical thinking. In the latter of these two books Ptolemy develops his constructs of epicycle, deferent or eccentric, and other elements of his system. The fifth and sixth books are largely concerned with new instruments and observational methods. He describes the astrolabe and the mural circle and discusses problems of map making which, of course, must begin with proper coordinates, and the parallax method for working out problems of astronomical distances. In the sixth book he also includes his method for calculating eclipses.

Books seven and eight are devoted to the study of the star catalogue, which contains 1,022 entries. It is assumed that this is a corrected version of Hipparchus' catalogue, which is known only through Ptolemy. The remaining five books are devoted to Ptolemy's theory of the planets, which includes the view that the planets are closer to the earth than the fixed stars and farther away than the moon. This theory is assumed to be the most original contribution of the author,[22] especially because Ptolemy contributes some original observations concerning several inequalities in the moon's motion. The exposition of plane and spherical trigonometry in books nine and eleven is highly lauded.

An evaluation of Ptolemy's work suggests at once a zealous and extremely competent interest in astronomical, mathematical, geographical, and other scientific fields, including optics. There is, too, a special emphasis upon organization and encyclopedic survey of facts. However, this marked interest in synthesizing is a definite symptom that the great naturalistic era with its assiduous effort to penetrate deeply into events is coming to an end.

Physics and Mechanology

Historians of science who stress the decline of scientific work and achievement in the Hellenistic period point out that aside from the

[22] Abetti, *The History of Astronomy*, p. 45.

principles that Archimedes established with respect to the lever, centroid, and floating bodies, there was little development in physics. Instead, the achievements in this domain were technological, oriented especially toward the development of mechanisms, apparatus, and tools needed in the practical affairs of the cosmopolitan societies that were flourishing at the time.

As an excellent indication of the Archimedean contribution to physics we cannot do better than to set down the postulates he formulated in his *On the Equilibrium of Planes* or *The Centres of Gravity of Planes.*

1. Equal weights at equal distances are in equilibrium, and equal weights at unequal distances are not in equilibrium but incline towards the weight which is at the greater distance.
2. If, when weights at certain distances are in equilibrium, something be added to one of the weights, they are not in equilibrium but incline towards that weight to which the addition was made.
3. Similarly, if anything be taken away from one of the weights, they are not in equilibrium but incline towards the weight from which nothing was taken.
4. When equal and similar plane figures coincide if applied to one another, their centres of gravity similarly coincide.
5. In figures which are unequal but similar the centres of gravity will be similarly situated. By points similarly situated in relation to similar figures I mean points such that, if straight lines be drawn from them to the equal angles, they make equal angles with the corresponding sides.
6. If magnitudes at certain distances be in equilibrium, (other) magnitudes equal to them will also be in equilibrium at the same distance.
7. In any figure whose perimeter is concave in (one and) the same direction the centre of gravity must be within the figure.[23]

We have already mentioned the engines and other machines attributed to Archimedes. There are other prominent figures in this phase of Hellenistic science. We may mention in order Ctesibius of Alexandria (2nd c. B.C.), Philo of Byzantium (2nd c. B.C.), Hero of Alexandria (1st c. A.D.), and Vitruvius (1st c. B.C.). Ctesibius is reputed to have invented a force pump, water organ, and water clocks, among other things.[24] The water clock included a means of regulating the flow of water and, in consequence, the passage of time.

Philo of Byzantium is credited with the development of numerous types of new engines as well as a complete treatise on the type of mechanical engineering known at the time. Hero of Alexandria invented both gadgets and more consequential apparatus. We mention a

[23] Heath, *The Works of Archimedes,* pp. 189-190.
[24] Sarton, *A History of Science,* Vol. II, p. 344.

magic jug, which poured or not depending on the covering or uncovering of a hole in the handle (Fig. 19, A). His most striking invention is the steam engine—a globe pivoted on tubes arising from the lid of a vessel in which water is heated. Two oppositely projecting tubes emit steam, which upon striking the air, makes the globe revolve (Fig. 19, B).

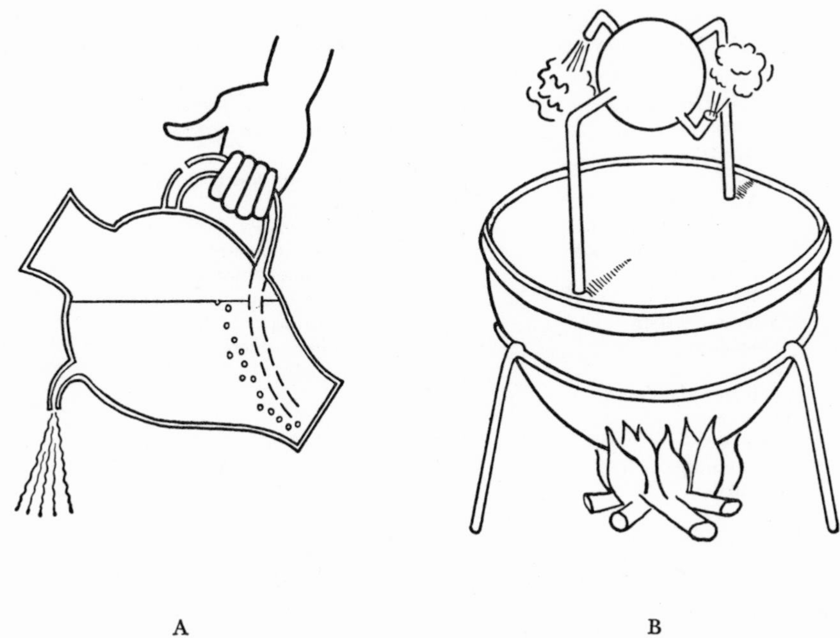

A B

FIG. 19. THE MAGIC JUG (A) AND STEAM ENGINE OF HERO (B)

Vitruvius is extremely well known through his famous treatise on architecture.[25] Despite the title the book covers not only architecture, including building materials, constructional methods, and engineering, but also town planning, astronomy, practical mechanics of all sorts, and even aspects of medical hygiene. He describes an immense variety of machines and apparatus, both historical and current.

Biology and Medicine

Although Alexandrian scholars distinguished themselves by many discoveries, their achievements in biology, with a few exceptions, hardly match those in mathematics and astronomy. When we take Aristotle's biological accomplishments as a standard, we must conclude that there is a sharp drop in biological and medical evolution in the Hellenistic period.

[25] *De Architectura.*

As to the actual attainments of this period in biology, historians are agreed that they center in the anatomical studies of two Alexandrian workers. Herophilus of Chalcedon and his pupil, Erasistratus of Chios, made a number of valuable discoveries in human anatomy. Since these are the main Hellenistic achievements in biology, it might be well to summarize them in a comparative table (Table IV).

TABLE IV. THE ACHIEVEMENTS OF HEROPHILUS AND ERASISTRATUS IN ANATOMY[26]

Herophilus	*Erasistratus*
Described:	Described;
Brain (in detail)	Chyliferous vessels (Mesentery)
Meninges	Epiglottis
Torcular Herophili	Auriculoventricular valves
Calamus scriptorius	Cerebral convolutions
Optic nerves	Physiological functions of brain
Retina	Relation of muscles to motion
Vascular system	Metabolism
Duodenum	Lymphatic ducts
Liver	
Salivary glands	
Pancreas	
Prostate	
Genital organs	
Lacteals	
Distinguished	Distinguished
Cerebrum from Cerebellum	Motor from sensory nerves
Nerves from tendons	Cerebrum from Cerebellum
Arteries from veins	(more distinctly than others)

An indication of the zeal of these two anatomists in the study of human anatomy is the accusation, albeit false, that they practiced human vivisection. Erasistratus is credited with the greater interest in physiology, though his biological results consist only of the localization of actions in anatomical parts. For example, the blood circulatory functions are connected with veins. The heart is the organ which transforms the air, which is taken in by the lungs, into vital spirits which the arteries carry to various parts of the body. The brain produces a second kind of *pneuma,* the animal spirits, which the hollow nerves distribute. It is the animal spirits which are concerned with sensitivity and motion, while the vital *pneuma* mediates the vegetative activities. Herophilus is credited with correcting one of Aristotle's worst errors; namely, the localization of intelligence in the heart.[27] Herophi-

[26] This material is derived from Singer, *A Short History of Science,* p. 61 *f.* and from Sarton, *A History of Science,* Vol. II, p. 132 *f.*

[27] Singer, *A Short History of Medicine,* p. 37. Sarton, *op. cit.,* p. 131.

lus goes back to Alcmeon, who located intelligence in the brain.[28]

Aside from human anatomy with its connection with medicine, there is little cultivation of the biology of either animals or plants, though it would be a great error to assume at any time there could be a complete lapse of interest in animals and plants. However, records of scientific achievements in those directions are lacking.

As we have already pointed out, the high attainments of Aristotle in psychology are completely lost, not to be recovered until the thirteenth century. The anatomical notions of the brain developed in the Alexandrian period signify little or nothing so far as psychology is concerned.

The work of the Alexandrian anatomists may be counted as gains for medical science. Even so, the sharp turn downward from the Hippocratean peak is clearly evident. Medical historians can easily muster long rolls of prominent names, such as Philinus of Cos, Serapian of Alexandria, Glaucias of Tarentum, and Asclepiades of Bithynia, but the medical field becomes in the Hellenistic period mostly a hedged-in and fossilized subject in which good and not-so-good medical institutions are cherished and handed on. At once we think here of Galen (130-200), who played so large a part in Greco-Roman medical history, and of the earlier work of Celsus (25 B.C.-?).[29]

HELLENISTIC ANTHROPIC SCIENCES

The Literary or Humanistic Specializations

That Alexandria could boast of a Library as well as a Museum is an extremely significant fact for scientific history. The existence of these two separate, though interrelated institutions indicates the separation and specialization of studies that developed in the Greek world. Surely there is a significant connection between the facts that the sciences of nature show such a decline from the standpoint of the early Hellenic period while there was a great upsurge of investigations involving *words,* such as the study of language, literature, and grammar. Despite the intimate interconnection of the Museum and the Library at Alexandria, the existence of large collections of books actually symbolizes an extreme preoccupation with verbal substitutes for things. At once we must distinguish between two kinds of books and book use. The first type consists of collections of data, that is records of contacts with

[28] Here is an instance of the characteristic attribution of later ideas to writers who entertained quite different views. Singer and Sarton think in terms of *psychic functions,* which had no place in either Hellenic or Hellenistic science.

[29] *De Medicina.* These writers are considered in a later section; cf. below pp. 212-13.

events, and as such may be regarded as parts of the paraphernalia of scientific investigation. The second may be characterized as incorporations of tradition, treasuries of the opinions of authorities which may or may not have been based upon research but which now serve to prevent contacts with things and events. This latter kind of book is used to perpetuate misleading systems of thought and practice. Examples are the Aristotelian books, which had been used as substitutes for observation in physics, and the Galenic texts, which made unnecessary the study of patients. It is unfortunate that the Library of Alexandria became an instrument for the eventual dethroning of scientific investigation in the Dark and Middle Ages.[30]

In the Alexandrian period, however, the Library was still a symbol of the growth of the sciences, especially the humanistic sciences. The zealous preservation of writings, not only of the literary sort but also on history, agriculture, and medicine still served investigative purposes. Eventually, however, the great development of the scriptural phase of culture led to the cultivation of respect for the written word, for authority, for tradition. Here lies the authentic basis for the conflict between the humanistic and the natural sciences. That conflict does not really center around the relative merits of cultural and noncultural things, but rather the departure from both kinds of things to cherish the *word* and the *tradition*. Incidentally, of course, the separation and specialization involved in the dichotomy become intricately involved with all sorts of human problems and conflicts. History is replete with the use made of particular scriptural interpretations to foster particular kinds of religion, science, politics, and economics.

From a technical psychological standpoint we may describe the final outcome of the new humanistic development as a turning away from interbehavior with things in order to overvalue and even glorify conventionalized responses. What becomes important is the view taken of things, the beliefs about them. In the extreme, things can be dispensed with altogether, and then one is preoccupied entirely with words. An excellent example is the turning from actual things, their characteristics, and their interrelations to a hypothesized generator or creator of them. Overlooked in such cases are the questions concerning the nature or even the very existence of the items under consideration.

The Institutionalization of Linguistics

Interest in speech and intercommunication is a perennial one and could not be otherwise in view of the omnipresence of language be-

[30] Obviously it was only one of many factors which tended toward the final result.

havior. So we may justly celebrate as a great achievement the inauguration of the systematic study of linguistics in Alexandrian times. The polyglot conditions prevailing in Alexandria and other great centers of trade must have been important catalysts for this development. Another large predisposing circumstance lay in the confrontation with many different literary documents representing not only the literatures of different cultures but also the sacred and cherished books expressing the essential values of the various cultural groups congregated in Alexandria. Accordingly, it is possible to find in Hellenistic times movements analogous to such ones as linguistic analysis and logical positivism, though we must distinguish between the details of the modern and ancient concern with linguistic problems.

GRAMMATICAL ANALYSIS. When the scholars of the Alexandrian period reached the stage of formal linguistic analysis and made speech and writing a distinctive and stable subject matter, the way was cleared for all sorts of investigations. Language became sharply distinguished into things and acts, and the latter lent themselves to all sorts of analyses. We take the term "grammatical analysis" to be the dissection and consideration of the formal and fixed aspects of speech. Sarton aptly compares a grammar with anatomy; both arose in the Alexandrian era and both consist of a kind of dissection and dismemberment of the morphological aspects of language or bodies.[31]

Grammatical analysis obviously must have had informal beginnings before the Alexandrian period, but it was at this time that formal grammatical study became established for Western culture. Among the outstanding early scholars are to be mentioned Aristophanes of Byzantium (257-180 B.C.) and Aristarchus of Samothrace (220-145? B.C.), who analyzed eight parts of speech.[32] The first Greek grammar is attributed to Crates of Malis,[33] while the earliest Greek grammar preserved to us is, of course, that of Dionysius Thrax.

The historical and social effects of grammatical study are to hypostatize behavior. Acts, in the first instance speech or communication, and later usage and custom, that is, style of speech, become frozen. But since speech is both the implicit and overt means of referring to belief, thought, and remembering behavior, these activities themselves become, through the medium of crystallized speech, palpable institutions. "It is written," "So saith the Lord," illustrate the substitution of words for actual or putative things and events. The institutionalization

[31] Sarton, *op. cit.*, p. 155 *et passim.*
[32] *Ibid.*, p. 492.
[33] *Ibid.*, p. 155.

of grammar, which marks a tremendous achievement in the understanding of speech as an important feature of human behavior and the literary arts, carried within it the possibility of humanistic disease. Linguists justifiably complain about the evils done to grammatical study by the acceptance of Dionysius Thrax' grammar as the ultimate model. But this is a minor difficulty in contrast to a basic misunderstanding of language and its function. What if in a much later period Donatus (4th c. A.D.) or Priscian (6th c. A.D.) forced Latin into the mold of the established Greek system? This is as nothing compared to the evils of removing language from the context of concrete interbehavior of either persons with things or with one another. Even St. Paul complained that "the letter killeth."[34]

SEMANTIC ANALYSIS. Although the term semantic analysis is comparatively new, the problem it refers to, namely, the interpretation of texts, was thoroughly established in the Alexandrian period. The Hellenistic thinkers faced fundamental questions as to the meaning or significance of the writings that had come to them. And obviously in such a complex and culturally mixed center they had to face competing doctrines. Hence, a basic motive was the reconciliation of writings derived from various civilizations. But what loomed largest from the standpoint of scientific history was the collation of the sacred and the profane. How could the reports of scientific observation be harmonized with the established scriptures? The technique of interpretation became, as history demonstrates, a most efficient tool for making the humanistic texts dominate and suppress scientific findings. A good illustration of the vagaries of exegesis or semantic analysis is the interpretation by Justin Martyr, Clement, Philo, and others of the Hebrew scriptures as the source of the doctrines of Plato and Aristotle.[35] If we define language as immediate activities of persons, and literature as the thing-products of such activities, we can then separate the various linguistic functions and consequently evaluate properly what is legitimate interpretation.[36]

Language is both descriptive and referential. Linguistic activity is a process of referring to things for the purpose of clarifying something to oneself or to inform someone else about the thing. A more complex variation of the process is to refer to a selected feature of something, or to indicate the relations of something to other things. Note, however, that in this case the activities mentioned can also be performed in the

[34] II *Corinthians*, 3, 6.
[35] Cf. Sarton, *op. cit.*, Vol. II, p. 246 *f.*
[36] See Kantor, *An Objective Psychology of Grammar.*

absence of the original things. By analogy and substitution persons can build up enormous language structures. This is the mythopeic procedure. It is easily seen how helpful written materials can be for the purpose of substituting interpretation for reference and description.

As we shall see, a great portion of the history of psychology consists of culturally determined interpretations, not descriptions of events confronted in actual observation. Such interpretations are the linguistic formulations of things believed. Literary elements, writings, documents, words, become symbols. But these symbols are arbitrarily manipulated; hence nature is made into a creational product sometimes distinct from the creator and sometimes identical with it. The creator may be verbally made into a person or into an impersonal power.

LOGOS EVOLUTION. A brief examination of the historical changes that have taken place in the handling of the term *logos* in varying cultural situations illustrates the word-hypostatizing process. The word *logos* was originally used as a descriptive term for observed natural processes and then in turn became a name for putative principles; finally in the Hellenistic-Roman era it became the symbol for an autistically constructed personal creator or engendering power. Because of the autistic employment of the term *logos* it is readily understandable why there should be as many as seventy interpretations of the term.[37]

Heracleitus. An early exploitation of the term *logos* is that connected with the sixth-century B.C. philosopher Heracleitus. Impressed by the ubiquity and essentiality of change and transformation, of both the partial and temporary and the complete and permanent form, he assumed that there was a law or principle which governed and ordered such changes. The natural model for the rhythmic activity of becoming and passing away he found in fire. In the age in which he lived it was not anomalous for Heracleitus to generalize all substances and their changes as manifestations of fire. Fire was at one and the same time a kind of thing and an effective process. This mode of thinking was entirely consonant with the primitive commonsense attitude of the time. Since the vibrant, cyclic fire-process was the all-pervading basis of order and control Heracleitus regarded it as the *logos*—the reason of all things. It was this governing and ordering *logos* or reason which made manifest all the appearances and disappearances of the observable world of nature.

The Stoics. Philosophizing in a context of greatly advanced knowl-

[37] See Liddell and Scott, *A Greek-English Lexicon.*

edge, the Stoics transformed the term *logos* to fit into a doctrine specifying a principle far removed from a simple process rooted in observable things. For them the *logos* symbolized an extremely abstract, rationalized power which ordered events in an interrelated and regulated cosmos. *Logos* is not merely a principle of determination, a causal principle, but also an actively productive and formative power; so the term became enlarged to *Logos Spermaticos*. The Stoics simply assumed that events presuppose prior causal principles which account for them. In an unalterable way those prior causes were determined by still earlier causes in an endless chain of past, present, and future. Taken all together the *logos* constitutes both a world-ground and world-reason which eventuate in a coherent and unified universe. It is clear that by now the word no longer serves even a vague descriptive function but is made to carry the products of autistic attitudes.

Philo Judaeus (ca. 25 B.C.–?A.D.). In the hands, or perhaps we should better say in the mouth, of Philo of Alexandria the *logos* doctrine takes on a personal and allegorical character. For Philo the *logos* was no longer an impersonal system of cosmic determiners but a symbol of the existence and activity of a personal God. On the one hand the *logos* is the sum total of divine wisdom and the supreme rational power of the personal God of the Hebrew scriptures; on the other, it is "uttered reason" emanating from God. In line with Philo's personalism this immanent *logos* is envisaged as the Son of God through whom God the Father carries out his creative and preservative acts. Clearly, with Philo the arbitrary allegorical interpretations reach an exalted mystical peak, and words become in some way derived from God himself and serve as His means of creation.

Christian Theologians. The early Christians transformed and elaborated the process of allegory and interpretation so that it became ultimate revelation. Linguistic power reached its peak when it produced the new interpretation of *logos,* according to which all wisdom and all reality became revealed through Christ, who is the rational nature of the universe and the second God. This linguistic power maximizes the capacity of the autistic thinker, who can draw from his own personal resources the ultimate truth of all existence and of all reality. Revelatory reason completely negates all knowledge based on natural reason and thus elevates belief and faith to a peak utterly unobtainable by science and its methods based upon contacts with things and events.

The *logos* doctrine of the Church Fathers brought in its train the immediate implication that man with his natural means of knowing was utterly incapable of attaining the truth and reality so essential at this time for the achievement of his ultimate destiny. Accordingly, the way is opened for a spiritistic psychology operating entirely within a mystic context. The essence of man is a soul or principle which transcends nature. This transcendence of nature applies also to the things upon which the soul operates.

St. John. The full development of the mystical *logos* doctrine is reached in the Johannine gospel. "In the beginning was the *logos* and the *logos* was with God and the *logos* was God." Reason, which was for the Hellenic thinkers an objective basis of order and system in the aggregation of things, has become a personal deity, and this deity is also a word. What is of basic significance in this version of the *logos* doctrine is the arbitrary use of terms. Here, clearly, words are arbitrarily manipulated so as to serve a purpose dictated by the cultural conditions and necessities of the time.

Further Embellishments. The multitude of writers who lived after the humanistic victory over science originated and disseminated many new interpretations of the *logos* doctrine. Notable among them is the version of Plotinus, in which he attempts a detailed treatment of the emanation of things from the ultimate transcendent *logos,* which for him bears the name, the *One.*

The evolution of the *logos* doctrine is obviously much more than an item in the history of the anthropic sciences. Important as the development of technical linguistics is for our culture, it is greatly overshadowed by the clue that study of the varying interpretations of *logos* provides to the function of language in the evolution of scientific institutions. As we shall see, throughout our study of scientific development as a whole and of the development of the science of psychology in particular, linguistic factors are the primary means for establishing and maintaining theories underived from the investigation of events. In psychology, such terms as "soul," "mind," "consciousness," and "sensations" have exerted a tremendous influence for aligning the discipline with cultural beliefs rather than with investigative findings. The foundation for this linguistic situation was laid in the Alexandrian era, as we have illustrated in this excursus on *logos.*

Historiography

It is in no sense surprising that among the great humanistic specialities to develop in the Alexandrian era historiography should take a prominent place. In the presence of so many great changes in the fortunes of nations how could reflective persons refrain from inquiring concerning the nature of such facts and how they have come to be? But there is something in historiography beyond the mere interest in the behavior of groups of men; annals, or other records of past happenings, are not history. Historiography is nourished by a persistent pursuit of the processes, actual or invented, which make things happen. A knowledge of such processes not only unifies human experience but aids in foretelling the future; even more significant is the ability it provides for controlling present conditions, which may lead to success in shaping future events.

The profusion of historical writings of various forms justifies the assertion that the Hellenistic period marks the advent of historiography as a specialized discipline. From Hellenic times, of course, the great masters Herodotus and Thucydides stand out as superb writers of history. But now there are long lists of historians, Greek, Latin, Christian, comprising philosophers (Plutarch, Polybius, Panaetius, Posidonius), generals (Caesar), politicians (Tacitus, Livy, Suetonius, Cato, Dio Cassius, Josephus, Sallust), scientists (Strabo), and churchmen (Eusebius).

The fundamental significance of Hellenistic historiography lies not in its quantity but in its quality. A glance at the development of historical writing shows on the surface a transformation that reflects completely new attitudes toward the meaning of the events recorded in historical writings. Basic to the Hellenistic interest in historical events is the search for an inner meaning not revealed to the classical historians, especially Thucydides. In this period the envisagement of history as a complex of interrelated happenings changes to the view of it as a manifestation of the thought and will of personal powers. Murray asserts that for Sallust

> . . . the whole material world is only a great myth, a thing whose value lies not in itself but in the spiritual memory which it hides and reveres.[38]

An effective way to assess the changes that history has undergone from Hellenic to Hellenistic times is to leap over the three centuries that separate Herodotus and Thucydides from Polybius and to examine the changes in the work subsequent to that of Polybius. Historians acclaim him as a faithful follower of Thucydides or even as somewhat superior, inasmuch as his cleaving to facts prevents him from constructing speeches for the persons he describes.[39] In contrast later historians fall far below him because of their lack of faith in actual

[38] *Five Stages of Greek Religion,* p. 158.
[39] Sarton, *op. cit.,* Vol. II, p. 438.

events and their assumed freedom to prescribe instead of describe. Here, it is in order to look ahead for a moment to a towering figure in historiography, namely, St. Augustine. For Augustine, recorded events are simply manifestations of divine necessity, each item of which bespeaks the detailed scrutiny of God. History is concerned not with a past which evolves and influences the present and future, but with a closed system of foreknown and foreordered happenings.

THE ROMAN CODIFICATION OF GREEK SCIENCE

There is hardly a cliché concerning national or ethnic characteristics to match in applicability the formula which makes the Romans into the greatest of engineers, builders, and organizers. Certainly that is their role in science. They hardly have a place among the scientific originators and discoverers, but they do stand out for their magnificent syntheses and compilations. They did not continue the investigations of the Alexandrinians, but they enshrined in their writings the results achieved by Hellenistic and earlier Greek science. Such authors as Varro (116-27 B.C.), Celsus (25 B.C.-?A.D.), Pliny (23-79 A.D.), and Galen (131-200 A.D.) are known for their incomparable collections and encyclopedias. Whether they write on agriculture, natural history, engineering and architecture, or medicine, they establish a new genre of scientific literature. In science they collect, arrange, and codify as effectively as other Romans did in the fields of law and the usages of practical life. It will serve our illustrative purpose simply to introduce some of the outstanding Roman encyclopedists.

Varro (116-27 B.C.). For a Roman who participated in the conflicts and conquests of Pompey, Caesar, and Augustus it was nothing to seize upon all available knowledge, assimilate it, and organize it according to a plan modified from earlier paradigms. Thus it seemed natural for Varro, after returning from his more active political and military pursuits, to labor in the library, first of Caesar, and later of Augustus.

Apparently Varro intended to encompass in his writings the whole of knowledge. Of his seven main works those outstanding for their range, importance, and influence are (a) the treatise on human and divine antiquities, (b) the book on the Latin language, and (c) the encyclopedic work called the *Disciplines.* The last is a coverage in the grand manner of almost all the intellectual institutions of Western civilization. The nine books are named as follows: (1) Grammar, (2) Dialectic, (3) Rhetoric, (4) Geometry, (5) Arithmetic, (6) Astrology, (7) Music, (8) Medicine, and (9) Architecture. As Sarton points out, the first seven of these cover the materials of the seven liberal arts.[40]

Celsus (25 B.C.-? A.D.). The man Celsus and his great work *De Medicina* are matchless symbols of the organizational capacities of Roman culture. Like a Roman road or an aqueduct, the product of Celsus' planning and construction stands intact and admirable by itself without known connections with other things. Hardly anything is known of the man, not only personally—his exact name, where and when he was born—but about his work. Was he a physician or a layman? Did he indeed write the *De Medicina* or was he a translator or adaptor of a Greek medical treatise? Still the work stands as a competent survey or encyclopedia of theory and practice, of materia medica, diagnoses, treatment, classification of diseases as general or specific, and so on.

From the standpoint of Roman encyclopedism, one of the outstanding features of the *De Medicina* is that it is itself only a part of a larger encyclopedic enterprise. Jones states that it is likely that the medical book is only the second part of a six-part treatise which included 1) agriculture, 3) military arts, 4) rhetoric, 5) philosophy, and 6) jurisprudence.[41]

Pliny (23-79). The thirty-seven books of Pliny's *Natural History* demonstrate the supreme urge to bring together in one grand system all knowledge and opinions concerning the celestial and terrestrial worlds, including plants and animals along with the nature and cultures of mankind. An excellent description of Pliny's encyclopedia is given by Littré in his book on Pliny. He says:

The author begins by setting forth ideas on the universe, the earth, the sun, the planets, and the remarkable properties of the elements. From this he passes to the geographical description of the parts of the earth known to the ancients. After the geography comes what we should call natural history, to wit, the history of terrestrial animals, fishes, insects and birds. The botanical section which follows is extensive, the more so because Pliny introduces much information on the arts, such as the manufacture of wine and oil, the cultivation of cereals, and various industrial applications. The botanical section concluded, he returns to the animals in order to enumerate the remedies which they supply. Finally he passes to mineral substances and, in what is one of the most interesting parts of his book, he gives at once an account of the methods of extraction of these substances and of the painting and sculpture of the ancients.[42]

In the Preface to his *Natural History* Pliny quotes Domitius Piso as saying that it is not books but storehouses that are needed. Accord-

[40] *Op. cit.,* Vol. II, pp. 310-312.
[41] Introduction to *De Medicina.*
[42] Quoted from Farrington, *Greek Science,* Vol. II, p. 133.

ingly he has collected twenty thousand noteworthy facts from a perusal of two thousand volumes, very few of which are ever handled by students. These facts have been obtained from one hundred authors. At the end of each book Pliny cites his authorities. Sarton states that these number one hundred and forty-six Roman and three hundred and twenty-seven Greek writers.[43]

Galen (129-200). The inclusion of Galen among the Roman encyclopedists brings to the front a number of questions. In the first place, his life and work fit better under the heading of Greek than Roman. Then, too, his writings are not primarily those of a compiler, as he is reputed to have been a physician and surgeon of great capacity. Again, insofar as he did summarize and codify Greek knowledge he acted as a specialist and covered mainly medical theory and practice.

Despite such questions Galen belongs to the line of Roman encyclopedists because of the role of his writings, especially his work on the natural faculties. Although Galen himself was a scientific biologist, having achieved a high place for himself as an anatomist and physiologist, his institutionalization of biological and medical truths and errors operated to fossilize learning and discourage scientific work and progress. It must be made clear that Galen himself is in no sense personally responsible for this result. His own vigorous and authoritative style of writing only contributed to the falling away of the investigative enterprise. The total result was contingent upon many factors making up the cultural conditions of European man at this date.

The significant point about the Roman encyclopedic writers and their works is that they have, intentionally or not, produced a new genre of scientific and medical literature. Even when the authors intend their writings to be references to and descriptions of general scientific or medical facts, the historical result has been that their productions took on the form of authoritative and dogmatic works that interfered with the direct contacts of scholars with things and events.

Thus, the Roman encyclopedists through the very codification which in one sense preserved Hellenistic science, or at least the knowledge it had acquired, made impossible the continued prosecution of that first-hand research by which the scientists of Alexandria had achieved their outstanding successes.

[43] *Introduction to the History of Science,* Vol. I, p. 249.

SECTION SIX

THE HELLENISTIC-ROMAN RETREAT FROM NATURE

CHAPTER 13

HELLENISTIC-ROMAN PERSONALISM

THE DECLINE OF SCIENCE AND HISTORICAL CONTINUITY

THE INTENSE STRESS which we place upon the great decline of scientific work following the Alexandrian period arises from our interest in the evolution of psychology as a science. But we do not forget that the history of a particular society or civilization is continuous. The decline of science simply signifies the development of a new phase of civilization. The historian is forever caught up in the swirl of rise and decline. In the inevitable changes in human living and social organization every decline is a rise and vice versa. The decline of science during the period of the Roman Empire parallels a new life and a new society. No matter how much this civilization is made up of institutional elements derived from other societies, from China, India, Persia, Mesopotamia, Syria, Palestine, Egypt, Carthage and the western centers, there is a unique fusion and conglomeration.

From a scientific and general intellectual standpoint, the primary Roman trait is the receiving and tolerating, if not welcoming, of all sorts of doctrines, beliefs, and other attitudinal institutions .which are more or less completely assimilated and integrated. This expansion and modification of Roman culture follows upon military conquests and political fortunes. Rome has possessed Sicily, or at least Syracuse, since 212 B.C., Carthage and Greece since 146 B.C., Mesopotamia and Syria since 64 B.C., and Egypt since 30 B.C. Each date marks an influx of new foreign elements.

Outstanding in the career of Rome is its service as a holding company harboring the established secular and pagan civilization, as well as one of a new type. Rome is the locus of a new way of living and thinking which evolves into spiritualism. There is nothing more impressive in history than the evolution of Rome into Byzantium. Rome was to become a Christian community, the home of scientific and political institutions that are partially naturalistic but mostly otherworldly. The Rome of the Caesars was to become the City of God. For the history of science, it is of the greatest importance that Rome became metamorphosed into the Holy Roman Empire. It is this metamorphosis which gives us the key to the new transcendental intellectual institutions—the institutions of Personalism.

The student of psychology and the other sciences finds the significance of the Roman period to lie in the opportunity it offers for the evolution of new assumptions and postulates. In the new way of thinking personal attitudes toward events outweigh the objective traits of the events. Basic categories are constructed without direct regard to the characteristics and relations of things. Within the confines of the Roman Empire there developed a definite matrix for intellectual institutions which contrast sharply with those of the Hellenic era.

PERSONALISM: ITS SCIENTIFIC SIGNIFICANCE

Basically, Personalism is an early stage in the development of soul and spirit. At first Personalism is merely a kind of subjectivism, a lack of interest in the nature of things. It contrasts with the authentic Greek and Roman attitudes toward nature as symbolized by the Roman, Lucretius. That attitude constitutes an attempt to take things on their own terms. As Lucretius and his master, Democritus, expressed the matter, the objective attitude holds in check the personal attitudes of individuals—their hopes and fears. Subjectivism or egoism, on the other hand, is a process of seeing things in the light of personal needs, of private wants and desires. Of course, the latter are institutionalized and thus made common or universal. What originates as the attitude of an individual, his ineffacable craving for security, results in the invention and imposition of qualities and characteristics upon things. Hence arise the arguments concerning the inability to know things in their ultimate nature and in their absolute "reality." The final stage of this development is the creation of *spirit,* a substance and a source of existence which transcends the observed characteristics of actual things and the changes resulting from their contacts with each other.

Personalism is, of course, at one and the same time, an extreme individual assertiveness and a renunciation. The development of Personalism is extremely well demonstrated in the writings of Tertullian, the celebrated Roman-African Church Father. This skilled practitioner of Roman law and rhetoric declares,

> The fact that Christ rejected an earthly Kingdom should be enough to convince you that all secular powers and dignities are not merely alien from, but hostile to God.[1]

[1] *De Idolotaria* 18 (quoted from Cochrane, *Christianity and Classical Culture,* p. 213).

This is the argument for withdrawing from and renouncing the established Roman order. To Tertullian and those who accept his way of thinking there is another order—a transcendental one and the two are inharmonious.

> . . . there can be no reconciliation between the oath of allegiance taken to God and that taken to man, between the standard of Christ and that of the devil, between the camp of light and that of darkness. *Non potest una anima duobus deberi;* it is impossible to serve two masters, God and Caesar.[2]

How aggressively personal one can become is shown by the degree of the renunciation of secular society. Tertullian says,

> For us nothing is more foreign than the commonwealth. We recognize but one universal commonwealth, viz., the world.[3]

> I owe no obligation to forum, campus, or senate. I stay awake for no public function, I make no effort to monopolize the platform, I pay no heed to any administrative duty, I shun the voter's booth, the juryman's bench. . . . I serve neither as magistrate or soldier, I have withdrawn from the life of secular society (*secessi de populo*). . . . My only concern is for myself, careful of nothing except that I should have no care. . . . No man is born for another who is destined to die for himself.[4]

FACTORS LEADING TO HELLENISTIC-ROMAN PERSONALISM

IDEATIONAL IMPACTS AND FUSIONS. Anyone inclined toward analogical forms of historical description can construct an impressive similarity between the clash and cohesion of ideas in the Greco-Roman period and the thermodynamic behavior of molecules in a container. The political and military events of the time contributed to the coming together of extreme intellectual attitudes from the western and eastern regions of the great empire. The result was a tremendous fermentation and intermixture of ideational institutions. One of the most striking examples is the juxtaposition of Greek and Eastern world views. The generally self-satisfying ideas of the Greeks, safely anchored in observable things confronted Eastern dissatisfaction with the current and immediate affairs of life. Greek self-reliance clashed with the Indian struggle for the unattainable. Greek satisfaction with things of sense met its opposite in ideas of *maya* and *nirvana.* The pouring of all the different elements into one cauldron resulted in compromise, equation, and fusion.

An outstanding illustration of the dissolving and fusing process of

[2] *Ibid.,* 19 (quoted from Cochrane, *op. cit.*)
[3] *Apologia* 38 (quoted from Cochrane, *op. cit.*)
[4] *De Pallio* 5 (quoted from Cochrane, *op. cit.*)

this time is the attitude of Philo. It was he who sought to conflate the doctrines of Hebrew scripture with those of Plato and other Greeks. To a great extent such fusion was possible for Philo because he believed that, after all, the wise men of Greece had drawn their inspiration from Mosaic doctrines.

For the historian of psychology the important point is that an ideological background is being prepared which will have a powerful influence on psychological development. A set of potent and lasting institutions of a verbal or linguistic sort is being built up. These institutions will in later ages serve as powerful instruments to help to withdraw men from the concrete events that are central in scientific work and to move them in the direction of entities arbitrarily constructed with the aid of traditional writings.

HELLENISTIC SPECIALIZATION AND BIFURCATION. Despite all the features of social and political life common to the peoples of the Hellenistic age, there developed an extreme specialization in the more exclusive aspects of scientific and intellectual culture. In the preceding chapter we have already shown that the Alexandrian scholars widened the cleft between humanistic and nonhumanistic scientific studies. Within each they set up further specializations. Astronomy was widely separated from mathematics and both from the biological disciplines. On the humanistic side specialized linguistic disciplines assumed great importance and became the central occupations of learned men. What in Greek times had loomed so important as rhetoric, the art of public disputation and conviction, now became a problem of textual analysis and exegesis. It is no accident that the Alexandrian school brought its humanistic studies to a climax with Dionysius Thrax' analysis of the meanings underlying the structures and forms of language. By the second century B.C. it was clearly evident how rapidly Hellenistic thinking was moving toward the extinction of interest in the events of the surrounding world. This change paralleled a change in problem and situation. While the Hellenic writers intended to control current affairs so as to favor themselves, whether properly or improperly, the promoters of the Hellenistic version of eristics were bent upon the establishment of majestic doctrines about the universe and its creator.

The difference between Hellenic and the subsequent Hellenistic period can be symbolized by the contrast between wisdom and revelation. Howsoever quickly and deeply the great tradition of Near Eastern and Greek science fell away toward oblivion, it maintained, even during its descent, a definite connection with things and events. But the value of such contacts with events rapidly became less appreciated.

What was increasingly valued was the *word* and what it revealed of the deep-seated reality assumed to lie behind things, as we have already pointed out in our discussion of the *logos* doctrine in Chapter 12. The Greco-Roman period was an age of creatures which are as nothing compared with their creator or creators.

PARABLE AND ALLEGORY: MECHANISMS FOR ENGENDERING PERSONALISM

Of extreme importance in the history of psychology is the Hellenistic-Roman preoccupation with words and symbols instead of with things. A preoccupation with words and symbols is, of course, a preoccupation with products of behavior which are themselves events. But the difficulty is that words can be reified into pristine events. It is this procedure, perhaps, which lends credence to the view that mythology and metaphysics are diseases of language.[5] As is obvious, this is the method which has been so effective in building up the theistic universe of our European culture.

Without exaggerating the importance of Philo Judaeus as a thinker or a cultural innovator, we may regard him as a fitting symbol of the changing character of our culture, one marking the transition from the classical period of Greece to the still prevailing theocentric period. We have already seen in Chapter 12 that it was Philo who transformed the *logos* of Heracleitus, which signified only that fire is a basic principle in nature, into *logos* as the word and wisdom of God. This supreme being became increasingly personalized by the verbal fiat of such mystical philosophers as Philo.

As linguistic behavior, parable-making is a deliberate act of myth creation undertaken for a particular purpose by the myth maker. It contrasts with the group construction of a proverb, folk tale, or similar linguistic product the origin of which cannot now be traced or controlled. Although it is affirmed that Philo did not originate the allegorical method but learned it at the Alexandrian school of Jewish allegorists,[6] he certainly elaborated it and employed it most extensively. By its use he could achieve all he desired in the discovery of the underlying or symbolic meaning of the scriptures as compared with their literal or obvious meaning. What could be a more effective instrument to fuse Greek science with Jewish ideas of divine perfection and pervasion of the universe? Here are bold and effective steps in the creation of a spiritual realm which is set up to contrast with the world of nature, even though the latter encompasses the myth maker and everything he projects by his verbological process.

[5] Spencer, *Principles of Psychology*, Vol. II, p. 502.
[6] Lewy (ed.), *Philo, Philosophical Writings*, p. 13.

HELLENISTIC THEOCENTRICITY: FROM PERSONALISM TO SPIRITUALISM

The construct of spirit, which has had so fateful an influence on psychology, grew mainly in the soil of theism. Theism, of course, may be regarded as a perennial feature of all intellectual civilization. But it differs in its fundamental character, according to the specific circumstances of those formulating it. In the beginning of the particular episode under discussion, it is still abstractive and remote. But this is only the beginning. The circumstances of the Hellenistic period simply promoted a belief in a benevolent and helpful power which later developed into one of an all-embracing and even thoroughly immanent essence of all things and events.

As a Hellenistic Jew, Philo refers to the atheism of the Egyptian people and asserts that Moses specified three grounds for this atheism: first, the Egyptians value earth above heaven; second, they prefer things that live in the land to those that dwell on high; finally, they value the body above the soul.[7] What this amounts to is simply the expression of a prejudice against a particular mode of life and manner of thinking in favor of an interpretation of religion and godhead which belonged to another culture resident in the same geographic location. Philo's views illustrate the swift growth of what will become a full-fledged spiritism when the fullest abstractions are reached. Such spiritism will evolve into the notion that man is at least in part a spiritual being and will make possible the constructions of *experience* and *consciousness*, creations which will infiltrate into the channels of science when it is reestablished after the long, silent, dark night of the spiritistic reign.

MONOTHEISM AND GRECO-ROMAN SPIRITUALISM

Undue emphasis on humanistic interests as compared with scientific ones betokens a social condition in which personal security and safe social anchorage are shaky, if not entirely lacking. Also, a turn toward a theistic philosophy reflects an intensification of the unsatisfactory conditions of human life for a particular group.

During the Hellenistic period we find a distinct social influence upon technical thought. It is the spread of monotheistic beliefs. The fusion of Greek and oriental cultures in the Hellenistic kingdoms made available, among many other religious ideas, the monotheistic doctrines developed by Zoroaster and by the Hebrew prophets, the latter undoubtedly being the more influential.[8] Monotheism as promoted by

[7] Wolfson, *Philo*, Vol. I, p. 30.

[8] Cf., for example, Gressmann, *Die orientalischen Religionen im hellenistischrömischen Zeitalter;* Henning, *Zoroaster: Politician or Witch-doctor?;* Weindl, *Monotheismus und*

Philo and the early Christians of the Roman Empire answers to the need for a single savior, valued principle, or other symbol of expanded social and political life. Imperialism gives particular scope for a great or universal god.

THE PERSONALIZATION OF THE GODS AND SPIRITUALISM

Spirituality is greatly accelerated by intolerable conditions of life. It is possible to correlate the change from the belief in objective gods, such as that entertained by the Greeks of the classical period, to a growing institution of a spiritual and anthropomorphized or personalized god with the increasingly bad social and economic conditions of the later Hellenistic period. Personal security was in constant peril. One might be taken prisoner of war or kidnapped by pirates to become permanently a slave.[9] In addition to the loss of social and political security there were in the second and first centuries B.C. intolerable economic conditions. Great hardship was experienced because of small incomes and high prices.[9] Such conditions make fertile soil for the development of spiritual and otherworldly refuges for troubled man.

The spiritualistic way of thinking which germinated in Alexandria and elsewhere in the Greco-Roman world develops by leaps and bounds as the history of Europe goes through its cycles and transformations. More and more will man turn away from nature and its happenings toward a spiritual world created as a putatively more sympathetic environment and as a more promising source of adaptation and adjustment.

As European culture moves on in time and spreads throughout the great Roman Empire and eventually beyond its crumbling borders, there will be built up beliefs in the existence of an anthropomorphic deity to whom man can appeal for personal help and who can serve him in his everyday conflicts and tribulations. In the Hellenistic-Roman period is evolved a god with magnified human traits who serves as a Paraclete to whom men can turn for their urgent needs. This social institution becomes enlarged to include a series of intercessors. The whole system is clearly designed as an instrument to preserve man and cater for his necessities.

As the raw material for this elaborate constructionism the men of the Hellenistic-Roman period found ready at hand the anciently de-

---

Dualismus in Indien, Iran und Palästina; von Wesendonk, *Urmensch und Seele in der iranischen Überlieferung* and *Das Weltbild der Iranier.*

[9] See Rostovtzeff, *The Mentality of the Hellenistic World and the After-Life,* p. 18 *f.* See quotation on p. 158 above.

veloped *pneuma*. That substance because of its various forms—wind, air, and breath, with its invisibility and its close connection with life could easily be transformed into spirit or invisible power or intangible forces conceived of as supernatural and transpatial. Because of the elusiveness of God it was easy to personalize *pneuma*. In order to attain to whatever infinities and ineffable properties their doctrinal constructions required, the theologians made the most of the God-Son-Spirit trinity to cross the boundaries of space and time. It is interesting here to recall Justin Martyr's explicit denial that spirit was Heracleitan fire, Stoic *pneuma,* Hippocratean blood, or any of the other entities which the pagans had believed it to be.

SPIRITUALISTIC ANTHROPOLOGY

When psychology disappeared as a scientific study during the Alexandrian period this circumstance obviously could have had no effect on the interest in man. As we have noted, it is a striking item in the fortunes of psychology that its scientific decline coincides with an increased general interest in man. The decline and disappearance of scientific psychology goes hand in hand with the separation of man from the other animals and with an intensified concern for man's social and political welfare. To satisfy these needs, the thinkers of the post-Hellenic period created properties and characteristics for man; in particular they endowed him with a spiritual nature which separated him from the other animals. At this point we have the birth of spiritistic anthropology. The key assumption in this science of man is that the human being is composed of a material body and a supernatural soul. It is only to be expected that the creators of the doctrine of the soul would not agree upon its properties and the circumstances of its existence. On the whole, however, those who constructed a soul for man ascribed to it the properties of simplicity, incorporeality of substance, rationality, and immortality. It was necessary to adopt in modified form theories developed earlier. For example, the Hellenic notion that soul or *psyche* is the essential activity of an organism was transmuted into the dogma that the soul is a dominating, controlling, and thinking substance.

When we seek the institutional roots of spiritistic anthropology we inevitably think of Socratic anthropology. And this is a salutary historical exercise since at once we observe the great contrast between Socrates' analysis of man and that of the spiritistic Personalists. As we have seen in Chapter 7, for Socrates the soul is a refined aspect of man's behavior. Soul is that behavior which lends worth and dignity to man, and care for soul leads him to regulate his life according to criteria which would foster harmony and intellectual growth. The ideals of an Athenian Greek were rooted in and remained a part of human nature.

Quite the opposite is spiritistic anthropology. Even at its best it tears man out of his natural context and endows him with supernatural properties. Soul is obviously a constructed entity designed especially, if not deliberately, to help man escape from the actual conditions under which he has to live and which he finds intolerable. It is impossible to overlook the difference between the ideals based upon an adjustment to the things and conditions with which one is in contact and the verbal creation of things and conditions by the extreme attenuation of actual things.

Any attempt to link Socratic doctrines with those of the spiritual personalists yields nothing but unsatisfying verbal results. The only links between the two types of analysis are that each has a problem concerning man and each gives a solution in terms suitable to the life conditions prevalent at the time. What are continuous throughout history are the human beings, their sciences and political circumstances, and an intellectual interest in all of those subjects.

EVOLUTION OF SOUL CONSTRUCTIONS

The processes of constructing souls and the created products comport at every period of history with the general cultural and specific intellectual institutions, including philosophy, prevalent at the time. In the period of Hellenistic-Roman Personalism the novel feature of the constructing process is the development of transcendental properties and their assignment to the soul entity then being invented.

Generally speaking, soul in this period was regarded as a spaceless and timeless substance with which the creator endowed human organisms. Soul was the source of knowledge and feeling, as well as the enduring entity which underwent the punitive and purifying sufferings in the afterlife. Another special trait of the soul was the link it provided with the creator. By sharing this spiritistic essence with God man gained in dignity and provided himself an avenue of escape into a secure eternal life.

To a great extent the Patristic constructors of soul borrowed traditional names such as *psyche* for use in the new cultural conditions. Assuming a spiritual base for the soul, writers of the various Personalist schools look upon soul properties as corporeal or incorporeal and attribute to soul forms and functions to suit their own particular intellectual loyalties.

CHAPTER 14

PATRISTIC TRANSCENDENTALISM

SACRED SCIENCE AND THE CHRISTIAN COMMONWEALTH

THE GREATNESS of Rome consists in large measure of its capacity to encompass not only numerous but contradictory features. The name Rome blankets strength and great weakness, power and impotency, organization and chaos, eternity and great change, as well as utter dissolution. Rome is a multiplicity within a definite unity. What interests us at this juncture is the fact that within the Roman Empire it was possible for a new type of society and a new civilization to grow even though it contrasted markedly with the older institutions. For the historian of psychology it is of primary importance that in the Roman period there developed the great dualism which has exerted so mischievous an influence on the evolution of scientific psychology.

From a social and political standpoint the new civilization evolved as a Christian commonwealth, a set of institutions which stands at the opposite pole from the naturalistic culture so characteristic of the Hellenic world and of pagan Rome. The intellectual aspect of this new culture, Transcendentalism, is well named since its votaries built their doctrines and beliefs on the premise that they were in contact with a reality which transcends the things and events of everyday life, and which is known by means that contrast with observation and observational inference, the stand-bys of ordinary scientific investigation.

This new Transcendentalism is, of course, an outgrowth of Personalism and other departures from naturalistic ways of thinking. In general, Transcendentalism with its turning inwards and retreating from actual events represents an intensification of the attitudes of escape from the pressures of intolerable social circumstances. Probably one of the most outstanding differences between Personalism and Transcendentalism, the relatively passive attitudes of the one and the more assertive ones of the other, arose from the active and persistent constructional work of a number of specialized professional writers. It is these Church Fathers, or Patristics, who set up models of reality influenced by dissatisfaction with things as they are and the desire to replace bad conditions with ideal ones.

Human beings, even those who establish the most far-fetched transcendentalisms, take their departures, of course, from the everyday facts of life. But in creating a spiritualistic civilization they make themselves oblivious to the details of their actual living and construct literary or verbal products that replace actual things. Such thinkers concern themselves with the word of God, with God's creative powers and results. They act according to God's dictates and not those of social customs or arbitrary personal whims. We speak of this transcendentalism or supernaturalism as Patristic because in this age we have as spokesmen of knowledge, or wisdom the Church Fathers, who at first compete with the scientists and later supersede them entirely. This is the age of belief, of authority, of submission, of acceptance. Although faith was established in the interest of religion or sacred doctrine, it later conquered all of the intellectual domain.

When items of Greek wisdom seemed too valuable to be discarded, they were endowed with supernatural validity by ascribing them to the shadowy activities of the divine Logos in the gentile world at large prior to the rise of Christianity.[1]

SACRED CHURCH AND SECULAR STATE

To seek the cultural roots of transcendentalism and supernaturalism, one must turn to the evolution of the church which grew up in the Roman state, competed with it, and replaced it in the history of Western Europe. From the Christian standpoint it was not an idle thought that the existence and triumphs of the Roman Empire were foreordained preparations for the coming of the Holy Church, its doctrines, and its way of life. Indeed Prudentius is only one of many writers who referred to this idea:

O Christ, sole deity, O Splendour, O might of the Father, O maker of earth and sky, builder of these walls, who hast set the sceptre of mankind on the hill of Rome, and dost ordain that the whole world should serve the Roman *toga* and yield to Roman arms, that thou mightest bring under one law the customs and the ways of differing nations, their tongues, their genius, and their faiths.[2]

But the growth of the church was neither rapid nor painless. Five centuries of strife and struggle were required before it attained doctrinal acceptance and political dominance, although in the interval many and sometimes marked developments occurred in local centers and in doctrinal growth. In the beginning, of course, Christianity de-

[1] Case, *The Origins of Christian Supernaturalism,* p. 224 *f.*

[2] From Glover, *The Ancient World: A Beginning,* p. 312.

veloped only through the conversion and adhesion of humble folk until it became so widespread as to attract the attention and opposition of emperors and other rulers before ultimately being accepted by them. Always during this development the civil strife and bad economic and social conditions that disturbed the Roman Empire at various times were a powerful impetus. For example, a relatively rapid expansion of Christianity took place at the time of the accession of Commodus in 180 A.D.[3]

Both the struggles and the triumphs of Christian culture are symbolized by the numerous persecutions it suffered before it reached the status of the official church under Constantine in the early years of the fourth century. When we glance at the long list of Roman emperors who engaged in major persecutions of the Christians, we obtain a fair estimate of the troubles the latter had in getting themselves and their movement appreciated. The list includes Nero, Domitian, Trajan, Hadrian, Marcus Aurelius, Septimius Severus, Maximinus the Thracian, Decius, Valerian, and Diocletian.[4]

It is said that when Paul stood on Mars Hill below the Acropolis in Athens, pleading for a wholly new view of life, and told about a dead man who rose from the grave, his listeners laughed.[5] For this new way of life involved a complete revolution in thinking and believing with respect to man and his world. It entailed the notion that man is not only a reacting and adapting organism made up of bone, muscles, and nerves, but also a partially transcendent entity independent of the laws of nature. The transcendent part of man—his soul—is unlike anything one could ordinarily know or understand, a direct creation of the deity. Other Christian doctrines referred to what had hitherto been thought to be impossible, a world invisible and intangible that can only be believed in but not approached and examined. It is little wonder that Paul and his friends were denounced as the men who had turned the world upside down. For they propagated the view that the greatest and most authentic realities are those that cannot be grasped, pictured, or understood. It is such realities that are of prime interest to Christianity in its philosophic aspects. And it was interest in these realities that engendered the Christian scorn for evidence and reasoning based upon observation.

With this type of cultural background it is easy to see how bold and

[3] See Latourette, *A History of the Expansion of Christianity*, Vol. I, pp. 68, 85.

[4] Uhlhorn, *The Conflict of Christianity with Heathenism*, pp. 235-237 and Latourette, *op. cit.*, Vol. I, p. 136.

[5] Glover, *op. cit.*, p. 301.

original the thinkers of this period could become. Armed with the weapons of an intimate god and with the power of intuition and inner revelation, the Church Fathers could transform their world freely and in their own way. Here is the source of the *Credo quia absurdum* mode of thinking. If the doctrines developed do not accord with events, so much the worse for the events. The irrepressible Tertulian lays bare the power of belief against the records of fact and the criteria of reason.

> . . . can any of them be so foolish as belief in God who was born, born moreover of a virgin, born with a body of flesh, God who has wallowed through those reproaches of nature?
>
> The Son of God was crucified: I am not ashamed—because it is shameful. The Son of God died: it is immediately credible—because it is silly. He was buried, and rose again: it is certain—because it is impossible.[6]

The central theme of Christian philosophy is the invisible and unknowable creator of the universe, the basis of all that is or could be. The uniqueness of the Christian God is His transcendence or hiddenness which necessitates a great deal of verbal mediation if he is to be approached at all. It is this unknown being or power that explains everything provided that one has sufficient faith to accept him. But for those who do have that faith God is both foundation and superstructure of everything; His very immensity explains His unknowability. This way of thinking about Him is excellently described by Minucius Felix:

> God cannot be seen—he is too bright for sight; nor grasped—he is too pure for touch; nor measured—for he is beyond all sense, infinite, measureless, his dimensions known to himself alone. Too narrow is our breast to take him in, therefore we can only measure him aright in calling him immeasurable. As I feel, so will I speak; he who thinks he knows the greatness of God, makes it less; he who would not lessen it, knows it not.
>
> Seek not a name for God: God is his name. Terms are needed when individuals have to be distinguished from the mass, by proper marks and designations: for God, who alone is, the term 'God' sums all. Should I call him 'Father,' you would think of flesh; or 'King,' you would reduce him to this world; or 'Lord,' you will surely deem him mortal. Away with names and appanages, and you will see him in his splendour.[7]

SOTERISM REPLACES INVESTIGATION

To the question of why secular wisdom loses its value and suffers replacement by supernaturalism, the historian has a ready answer.

[6] *De Carne Christi,* Ch. 4, 41-43 and 5, 23-26.
[7] *Octavius,* Ch. 18, 8-10.

Essentially the establishment of Patristic transcendentalism is a factor in Roman society along with and conditioned by the political isolation, economic deprivation, and other vicissitudes of the time. The dissipation of interest in science is explained by the insecure and hopeless outlook upon life arising when men possess only a vague and loose connection with an impersonal and gigantic society, a society lacking completely the stability provided by the homogeneous institutions of a precisely bounded and unified community. Added to this was the strain caused by the dissolution of the enormous nebulous political structure of the Roman Empire. Facing such circumstances of life, the people of Western Europe turn completely to problems of personal salvation. The worldly wisdom of the Greeks is abandoned in favor of a superior type of knowledge, namely, revelation. No longer do the men of this age seek to know the composition and operation of their surroundings. They are interested only in their own inner life, which, however, they think of as rooted in a divinity far more important than the things about them.

The nature of the change from science to soterism and the consequent effects on culture have often been described. But no one has characterized it more accurately than Murray, who calls it a failure of nerve.

Anyone who turns from the great writers of classical Athens, say Sophocles or Aristotle, to those of the Christian era must be conscious of a great difference in tone. There is a change in the whole relation of the writer to the world about him. The new quality is not specifically Christian: it is just as marked in the Gnostics and Mithras-worshippers as in the Gospels and the Apocalypse, in Julian and Plotinus as in Gregory and Jerome. It is hard to describe. It is a rise of asceticism, of mysticism, in a sense, of pessimism; a loss of self-confidence, of hope in this life and of faith in normal human effort; a despair of patient inquiry, a cry for infallible revelation; an indifference to the welfare of the state, a conversion of the soul to God. It is an atmosphere in which the aim of the good man is not so much to live justly, to help the society to which he belongs and enjoy the esteem of his fellow creatures; but rather, by means of a burning faith, by contempt for the world and its standards, by ecstasy, suffering, and martyrdom, to be granted pardon for his unspeakable unworthiness, his immeasurable sin. There is an intensifying of certain spiritual emotions; an increase of sensitiveness, a failure of nerve.

Now this antithesis is often exaggerated by the admirers of one side or the other. A hundred people write as if Sophocles had no mysticism and practically speaking no conscience. Half a dozen retort as if St. Paul had no public spirit and no common sense. I have protested often against this exaggeration; but, stated reasonably, as a change of proportion and not a creation of new hearts, the antithesis is certainly based on fact. The historical reasons for it are suggested above, in the first of these essays.

My description of this complicated change is, of course, inadequate, but not, I hope, one-sided. I do not depreciate the religions that followed on this movement by describing the movement itself as a "failure of nerve." Mankind has not yet decided which of two opposite methods leads to the fuller and deeper knowledge of the world; the patient and sympathetic study of the good citizen who lives in it, or the ecstatic vision of the saint who rejects it. But probably most Christians are inclined to believe that without some failure and sense of failure, without a contrite heart and conviction of sin, man can hardly attain the religious life. I can imagine a historian of this temper believing that the period we are about to discuss was a necessary softening of human pride, a *Praeparatio Evangelica*.[8]

Because Christian culture was born out of poverty, need, and the perennial hope of a better life, it is no surprise that its characteristic cry is "What can I do to be saved?" And the need for salvation was not thought to be connected with the discovery of the nature of things. All important for a Christian is the revelation that God is the source of all things, including the inner essence of man, since man is the creation of God and the recipient of His grace and beneficence. Many of the Church Fathers have emphasized this simple pietistic philosophy, but none better than St. Augustine. In his *Confessions* he marvels at the contrast between the search for self-understanding and the interest in the works of nature.[9] Similarly, in his *Enchiridion* he contrasts the dispensability of science with the necessity for the beliefs of religion.

Wherefore, when it is asked what we ought to believe in matters of religion, the answer is not to be sought in the exploration of the nature of things [*rerum natura*], after the manner of those whom the Greeks called "physicists." Nor should we be dismayed if Christians are ignorant about the properties and the number of the basic elements of nature, or about the motion, order, and deviations of the stars, the map of the heavens, the kinds and nature of animals, plants, stones, springs, rivers, and mountains; about the divisions of space and time, about the signs of impending storms, and the myriad other things which these "physicists" have come to understand, or think they have. For even these men, gifted with such superior insight, with their ardor in study and their abundant leisure, exploring some of these matters by human conjecture and others through historical inquiry, have not yet learned everything there is to know. For that matter, many of the things they are so proud to have discovered are more often matters of opinion than of verified knowledge.

For the Christian, it is enough to believe that the cause of all created things, whether in heaven or on earth, whether visible or invisible, is nothing other

[8] *Five Stages of Greek Religion*, p. 119 *f.*

[9] See Ch. 15 below.

than the goodness of the Creator, who is the one and the true God. Further, the Christian believes that nothing exists save God himself and what comes from him; and he believes that God is triune, i.e., the Father, and the Son begotten of the Father, and the Holy Spirit proceeding from the same Father, but one and the same Spirit of the Father and the Son.[10]

CHRISTOLOGY: THE NEW SCIENCE

The retreat from science is perhaps not the most significant thing about the Patristic period. It is rather the great preoccupation with diction and with dogma. In fact, as the Hellenistic-Roman population relinquished the study of the natural sciences so ably cultivated in the Hellenistic period, it substituted for them Christian theology. As the name indicates, this study was claimed to be a science by its votaries. They thought that they were developing a science more worthy than the old learning. They regarded themselves as studying the origin, changes, and relationships of things and processes quite in the manner of any scientist. They insisted, in other words, that the object of their studies was an independently existing thing or power and not merely institutionalized behavior, that is beliefs, faiths, hopes, and assertions. What the natural scientists were interested in and described, the theologians took to be symbols of and approximations to the "essential reality" which events suggested or revealed. On the whole, modern scholars of the Western tradition grant that theology is a science only in so far as it is an interest in what men believed and wrote within a religious or theological context. However, if, indeed, the institutions of argument or the development of propositions and systems of sentences can be called science, then the men of this age did develop a new science. But instead of studying stars, plants, animals, mechanics, or disease, they study the nature of Christ, His transcendental qualities and His relation to the all-pervading spiritualized God of whom they spoke.

Who is to be credited with the detailed inauguration of this new discipline of science? This is surely a difficult question to answer, and perhaps of no great moment. It is certain that in this case, as in that of all other cultural origins, many factors are involved. There are doctrinal elements derived from the earlier civilizations of the Greeks, Syrians, Persians, Indians, and others, along with innumerable factors residing in the social, economic, and political situations of the Hellenistic and Roman periods.

Writers on theological history credit Justin Martyr (100-165?) with

[10] Ch. 3, 9.

the primary establishment of Christian theology,[11] while others assert that it was Origen (185-254?) who accomplished it on the basis of inspiration received from the Catechetical school developed by Clement of Alexandria (*ca.* 150-218).[12] Basically, however, the establishment of Christian theology must be regarded as an intellectual representative of a new and different civilization which has replaced the naturalistic and scientific culture of the Greek world. This is not merely a shift of attitude from an interest in nature to the study of an anthropomorphic god but also a change of culture, which may be characterized as the spiritualization of the universe. The reaction to the suppression and dislocation of individuals, to political disorientation and the loss of personal safety was so great as to give rise to a paradoxical self-aggrandizement achieved by the verbal creation of an infinite, ineffable being as cause and creator of the universe.

It is a commonplace that Christian Transcendentalism, with its unique dichotomy of the thinker's environment into God and the world, into spirit and nature, centers around the entity called Christ. As a recent theological writer aptly says:

> Ideally, in tracing its effects, Christianity would seem best described as the continuation of the impulse given by the life, teachings, and death of Jesus, and by the convictions held by his immediate disciples concerning his resurrection.[13]

It is through the constructions made about Jesus that the Christian tradition built up the super-spatial universe that offered such effective escape from the poverty and perils of the social system in which the builders found themselves. As we have already pointed out, transcendental ideas were derived from a matrix of Personalism. Accordingly, it is through Jesus, the man-God, that the faithful can penetrate into the transcendent world. As Windelband puts the matter:

> Christianity, as a living religion demands a *personal relation of man to the ground of the world conceived of as supreme personality,* and it expresses this demand in the thought of the divine sonship of man.[14]

From this kind of source has arisen the notion of the duality of man and the superiority of his transcendental over his natural character. Through his transcendental nature man can attain salvation and resurrection and move from the vale of agony to heavenly glory.

As to the intellectual process of dealing with the transcendental

[11] See von Campenhausen, *Die Griechischen Kirchenväter,* p. 14.
[12] Windelband, *History of Philosophy,* p. 217.
[13] Latourette, *A History of the Expansion of Christianity,* p. 240.
[14] *Op. cit.,* p. 238.

world, that requires a new type of science, or perhaps we should say, a new type of intellectual orientation. It can be summed up on one hand as the belittling and renouncing of things and events and on the other as the thorough embracement of autistic creations achieved by manipulating words. With this technique it became easy to create the realm of the supernatural, to despise all the host of events to which man inevitably must bow. Tertullian, especially, undertook to supply a cognitive technique for handling the invisible and inscrutable mysteries of the soul and other transcendental entities. Because Tertullian could not abide the Socratic view of soul as a natural fact, he does not hesitate to ascribe to Socrates an intentionally assumed indifference to the truths of revelation.

For, who can know truth without the help of God? Who can know God without Christ? Who has ever discovered Christ without the Holy Spirit? And who has ever received the Holy Spirit without the gift of faith?[15]

PATRISTIC DOCTRINES AND DOGMAS

It is decidedly outside the scope of this book to enter in detail into the quarrels and triumphs of the Church Fathers with respect to the dogmas that became the intellectual foundations of Christian civilization. Nevertheless, in view of the fact that these doctrines and dogmas have maintained a perennial influence upon technical psychology, we must at least remind ourselves of the way this influence was exerted.

The Existence of God. By the time of the Church Fathers the institution of a spiritual god was firmly entrenched in European culture. Whatever may have been the elements out of which this construction was built, whether ideas and propositions of Greek or oriental civilizations, the central theistic notion was taken for granted. Naturally there still remained a variety of attitudes and modes of reference. For example, the Fathers disagreed among themselves as to whether God could be positively characterized despite the acknowledged feebleness of man, or whether He had to be described in negative terms—in the sense of negative theology. It is safe to say of both parties that they accepted the doctrines that God is a personal being, a creator Who maintains a personal interest in His creatures. Despite all the difficulties involved, the Church Fathers were united in the belief that the transcendent God is also an immanent being Who not only has created the universe and all that is in it, but Who continues to operate within it. On this basis,

[15] *De Anima,* Ch. 1, 4.

the panorama of human history may be conceived as a record of the divine economy, the working of the Spirit in and through mankind, from the creation of the first conscious human being to its full and final revelation in the Incarnate Word.[16]

The Divinity of Christ. Since Christianity centers around the personality of Jesus it was, of course, inevitable that Christ should be divine. But since Jesus was also taken to be a man the problems and the paradoxes that arose from this duality could hardly be ignored. To be sure, divine men were well-established institutions in the oriental cultures—kings and emperors were regularly deified. But that took place under different civilizational auspices. Christianity belongs to a transcendental civilization—God transcends time and space, He has become ultimate and separate. He is so far removed from actual events as to create insoluble problems for the believers. Moreover, the current monotheism calls for a singleness and comprehensiveness of the divine which allows for no addition or multiplication. Great conflicts existed between the dogma of an ineffable and remote God and the dogma of the Savior and Redeemer, the exalted Being who is concerned with the affairs of individual persons. It was necessary to harmonize within one system elements of varying character and origins such as the ideas of a supreme god as developed by the Hebrew prophets and the changing conceptions of a messiah, becoming increasingly transcendental as Jewish hopes for political salvation were repeatedly disappointed. The unifying principle by which such conflicts were resolved was the escapist goal of Christianity, for it was even more a cultural system concerned with the destiny of man than a religion of moral and social control.

The entire man-God drama is summed up in the universally known great Arian controversy of the fourth century. Arius argued that if Jesus was the incarnate word of God he must be something less than God, a radiation out from God, but still not the basic supreme spiritual creator.[17] His primary opponent, Athanasius, argued for the true and absolute identity of Christ and God. Christ is *homoousious* with God, of the same substance with Him, the difference between them as of Father and Son does not make the latter simply *homoiousious.* As everyone knows, the Council of Nicea called by Constantine and participated in by about three hundred bishops settled the controversy in favor of Athanasius. The *homoousian* dogma became codified as the

[16] Cochrane, *Christianity and Classical Culture,* p. 367 *f.*
[17] See Goodenough, *The Church in the Roman Empire,* p. 47.

permanent doctrine of the Church. It was this doctrine that provided the basis for the resurrection and immortality of the individual Christian, because through it he could become deified by partaking in the eucharist of the body of Christ, Who was fully God.

The Holy Spirit. The historians tell us that between the years 325, when the Council of Nicea was held, and 381, when the great synod of Constantinople was called by the emperors Gratian and Theodosius, the bishops had to face the problem of the Holy Ghost as the third person in the Trinitarian dogma. The synod concluded that the divine nature is represented by three persons—God the Father, God the Son, and God the Holy Ghost. Each of these is fully God, but there is only one God. The equation for the Trinity is $X = 3X$. The doctrine is that only one God exists, but He is a personal presence in the world, guiding men, loving men, and making Himself available for the prayers of men.[18] Admittedly there is a profound mystery here, but the nature of religious thinking is such that it is incomprehensible to the nonrevelatory cogitation of scientific thought.

The whole set of Christian doctrines and dogmas with their problems concerning the relation of the man-God to God and the triune God to man, formed a basis for the dual character of man so that, on the one hand, he is a natural being, a biological organism, and, on the other, a creative soul, a psychic substance, and a set of mental functions.

PATRISTIC TRANSCENDENTALISM AND MODERN PSYCHOLOGY

The study of the history of science cannot fail to take account of the enormous role which theology played not only in the political, economic, and other post-Greek phases of culture, but also in the general intellectual, philosophical, and scientific aspects as well. There is a spiritualistic as well as a materialistic component in every aspect of our civilization, whether or not we regard such components as determiners.

The historical period which we have just been examining begins a stage in which theology, so to speak, drives science off the platform of significant enterprises. But even when natural science becomes cultivated again after many centuries, theology maintains its place in the intellectual life of Western Europe. We need only remind ourselves of the general sentiment prevailing among scientists in the seventeenth century that the study of nature accrued first to the greater glory of

[18] *Ibid.*, p. 63.

God and only second to the good of mankind. In Bacon's words, the true end of scientific activity is the "glory of the Creator and the relief of man's estate." What is perhaps more important than the general incorporation of science in a theistic structure is the importation of theistic principles into the concrete study of events, either by means of hypotheses or of descriptions and interpretations. Examples of such influences are the teleological ideas in general biology or the notions of determinism and predestination in genetics. In physics the example is the infiltration of theistic ideas into the terrestrial and celestial mechanics of Leibniz, Newton, and the other great scientists of the seventeenth century and later.

Accordingly, the historian of scientific psychology is not completely out of his depth when studying Patristic Christology. What has psychology to do with the doctrines of the Church Fathers, of the Christologists? The answer is plain. Although we are at this point completely outside the range of the behavior of organisms and are in touch only with the inventions of the Christian masters of the word, we still remain close to the materials of developing psychology. It may be humiliating to acknowledge the fact, but psychology has for most of its past been made up of two incongruous ingredients. In addition to its inescapable contacts with behavior, it has carried with it on the interpretational side a heavy load of traditional verbal creations. To the overpowering influence of theology may be attributed all doctrines of mind and body, as well as the persistent preoccupation of psychologists with a transcendent ego or mentality and with psychic processes like sensations, mental images, consciousness, experience, intelligence, and other native or acquired powers and with, finally, the correlation and dependence of mental powers with and upon a brain. Here we must bring into play our most critical and analytical powers. Even if we cannot immediately accept the hypothesis that many of the best-established constructs, such as those just mentioned, are directly connected with the transcendental constructs of the Patristic period, we certainly are obligated to consider the possibility that the historical continuity of Greco-Roman and modern civilization, which, as is universally accepted, so greatly influenced our law, art, social organization, and languages, also affected enormously our philosophy and our science. In fact, there is hardly a doubt that the basic constructs of psychology have been evolved from inventions developed in the theological era of Western culture.

Now it is clear how justified is the statement that psychology as a science was lost from our culture, not to be regained for many centuries. The many works of the Roman imperial period entitled *De Anima* discuss very different topics from those in Aristotle's book whose title, *Peri Psyches,* is similarly translated. We may take Tertullian's effort as typical. He is dealing with an *afflatus dei,* a breath which God breathes into man so as to give him the qualities which he possesses that are like unto God's. The subject matter discussed in this period is frankly not reported observation but a set of constructions developed in a mystically-dominated culture. What the Patristics write about are unknown entities asserted to perform important functions; thus, the soul is man's instrument of knowing and willing. The soul is transcendent but can be written about because the writers possess the power to intuit what is revealed to them.

The basic significance of the Patristic period is that it erected a *soul* institution which persisted as a heritage of European culture and provided a source of doctrines that influenced psychological thinking throughout the centuries. In the following paragraphs we examine some samples of Patristic psychology formulated by representative Church Fathers.

Justin Martyr (100-165?). Whether or not Justin actually prepared a treatise on the soul, no such document is extant. Nevertheless, this early Greek Father can be included among the succession of writers who helped to formulate the doctrines of the Church concerning the soul. This is possible because Justin's views concerning the soul of man can be gleaned from his numerous writings. As a converted heathen who stressed a deity lacking all material qualities, Justin assumed that the soul's immortality is not inherent in it but is a result of the free power and grace of God's will.[19] Contrary to the teachings of other writers Justin denied to the human soul any participation in God's essential nature.

Clement of Alexandria (150-215?). As in the case of many other early Church Fathers, an adequately detailed discussion of Clement is excluded by lack of data. Little is known about his life or even about the details of his ideas. However, it is certain that, even if he was not an Athenian by birth, he did make use of classical writings; in particular he bolstered his mystical beliefs with the authority of a spiritualized Plato. In his role of teacher at Alexandria Clement strongly advocated the building of a bridge between Christian truth and the wisdom of

[19] Siebeck, *Geschichte der Psychologie,* Vol. II, p. 365.

the Greeks, between Christianity and science.[20] With his firm belief that Christ is the reason for the world—the source of all truth[21] he saw no objection to the assumption that the philosophy of the Greeks is derived from a partially divine revelation. Probably he found support for this view in his other belief that, after all, Greek wisdom was a plagiarism from the Hebrew prophets.[22] Despite Clement's toleration of Greek thought, his actual interest in it is limited mainly to its ethical aspect. As a Christian interested in salvation and redemption, he attempted to equate the nature and destiny of man with the ethical principle at the center of the universe. To achieve everlasting life and spiritual perfection is to know the good and make it prevail over every type of evil.

Emerging from this moral and mystic background is Clement's religious psychology. There is no hint in it of the scientific wisdom which the Greeks developed about human behavior. For Clement, behavior merges with inner processes described as intuitive cognition. The soul of man is single and integral, existing in some indefinite correspondence with the body. But despite this unity the soul is differentiated into two parts or phases. The rational phase is divine in its origin and essence, and constitutes the link between man and God. In this phase of man's soul lie his claims to perfection and superiority over the rest of the created or emanated beings. The irrational phase of the soul links man with the flesh or body. It is the latter that gives man his place in nature and constitutes the base for his everyday knowledge, feeling, and willing, which lead to his good and evil adjustments to other men and inanimate things.

Origen (185-254?). Historians of the Patristic period agree upon the great importance of Origen, the first Christian-born Church Father, as one of the founders of the Christian theological system and his work is, in addition, significant for the history of psychology. This is not because he has produced a clear-cut document concerning psychological subjects, but rather because he illustrates in his own intellectual career the process by which intellectual institutions become established and persist. Yet Origen, despite his vast learning and voluminous production, could hardly be expected to systemize what is nothing more than a fardel of the most varied beliefs and a plethora of personal verbal utterances. That he did after all accomplish this feat is supported

[20] *Stromata,* Ch. 6, 10.
[21] Harnack, *History of Dogma,* Vol. II p. 324.
[22] See Fisher, *History of Christian Doctrine,* p. 94.

by his great reputation as a wise and learned man. Harnack calls the tradition that Origen's writings numbered six thousand only an exaggeration.[23]

Origen's work produced the impression that Christianity is something more than a fragile conglomeration of personal beliefs and practices; that it is, in fact, a unified body of doctrine, a philosophy, and as theologians say a science. It is this intellectual structure of Origen that appeared palpable enough to support the burgeoning religious and political institution, the Church. The effectiveness of Origen's writings stems from the alleged fact that, as a profoundly learned man, he was able to evaluate the work of Greek philosophy and science and to point out the obvious superiority of the Christian modes of thinking that had been established by Clement and numerous other inspired thinkers. What Origen actually built upon were the various systems of mystical philosophy developed by the Neoplatonists, the decaying Stoics, and other Pagans who were constructing a spiritistic universe to parallel or absorb natural events. Probably the most fundamental feature that Origen helped to establish was the utter absorption of science by mystic and assertional revelation. Origen played too, upon the theme of the personal salvation of each man through his development of his inner essence, his soul, which constitutes the gateway to the universal soul, namely, God. What Origen, among others, accomplished in the last analysis was to establish a transcendental world for believers. Windelband asserts that through Origen Christian philosophy completed the metaphysical *spiritualizing* and internalizing or idealizing of the world of the senses.[24]

As to specifically psychological or soul doctrines, we may echo the complaint of Brett that they can only be gleaned from scattered writings, since Origen did not concentrate his doctrine in one treatise.[25] According to these gleanings the essence of man is his reasonable soul, which has fallen from the transcendental world. The soul thus preexists and outlasts the body. Through the animal soul which has blood as its substratum the rational soul is united with the body. Insofar as man suppresses his instincts and passions he becomes more and more like God and consequently becomes worthy and capable of salvation and redemption.

Gregory Thaumaturgus (205-265?). The orderly collection of psychological doctrines which was lacking in Origen, the master, is fully

[23] "Origen," *Encyclopedia Britannica*, 13th ed., Vol. XX, p. 271.
[24] *History of Philosophy*, p. 253.
[25] *History of Psychology*, p. 277.

supplied by his pupil Gregory. In his topical discourse *On the Subject of the Soul* Gregory gives a succinct statement summing up the characteristics of the soul. In his own words,

I shall propose to inquire by what criterion the soul can, according to its nature, be apprehended; then by what means it can be proved to exist; thereafter, whether it is a *substance* or an *accident;* then consequently on these points, whether it is a body or is incorporeal; then whether it is simple or compound; next, whether it is mortal or immortal; and finally, whether it is rational or irrational.[26]

His answers to these questions are as follows: The soul being apprehended by thought is unknown in itself, and hence can only be known by its operations or its effects. The existence of the soul is demonstrated by the fact that human bodies cannot be put in action externally like soulless or inanimate things which move by impulsion or traction. Moreover, human bodies do not act by inner nature, as in the case of fire, for fire never loses its action as long as there is fire. But the dead body exists, though without action. Hence it must be the soul which is known through its actions, one of which is the provision of life for the body.

The soul is a substance because only substances can persist and successively take on various and contrary accidents or characteristics. The soul can be righteous or unrighteous, courageous or cowardly, temperate or intemperate. Again, since the soul imparts life to a substance, it must be a substance itself. Because the soul lacks color, quantity, and figure and is not maintained by nature like the body but by reason, it is incorporeal.

Since the soul is not a body, it is not compounded or made up of single substances and so is simple. It necessarily follows that simple things are not subject to corruption and decay, and thus are immortal. Gregory contends that the soul is rational on the basis of several arguments. In the first place, the soul has discovered the arts that operate in the service of human life. Again, the senses are insufficient for the knowledge of things and also misleading; then it must be by the intellect that things are known as they actually are. Finally, it is through reason that man is able to exercise the process of active judgment and to make the comparisons needed for discriminating differences in otherwise similar things.

In this brief work on the soul Gregory lays down views and arguments that have served as definite and enduring institutions throughout the entire history of transcendental psychology.

[26] Roberts and Donaldson, *The Ante-Nicene Fathers,* Vol. VI, p. 54.

Tertullian (160-240?). The great significance of Tertullian, the first of the outstanding Latin Fathers, for psychological history lies in his attempt to formulate a Christian doctrine concerning psychology. Naturally, this violent opponent of natural science and Greek learning did not set up a definite system, but rather emphasized the theme of the soul in order to refute and reject the knowledge of human behavior known to him from the Greek tradition. Of the philosophers he chooses to refute, Socrates, Plato, and Aristotle are most frequently mentioned.

In typical theological fashion Tertullian discusses first the origin of the soul rather than its nature. How and where the soul originates is, of course, a foregone conclusion. It arises from the "breath" of God and not from matter. Revelation is the authority for this view.

As to the nature of the soul, the first point is that it is corporeal. One proof of this is the mutual influence of soul and body.

> . . . the soul shares the pain of the body when the latter suffers from bruises, wounds, or sores, and the body will reflect the disabilities of the soul under the influence of anxiety, worry or love by a parallel weakness, as when the body testifies to the presence of shame and fear in the soul by blushing or growing pale.[27]

Then there is the testimony of the Scriptures. The sufferings of souls in hell prove that they must be bodies. Also, Tertullian cites as evidence the ecstatic vision of a soul as reported by a Montanist sister:

> I have seen a soul in bodily shape and a spirit appeared to me, not an empty and filmy thing, but an object which could be taken in the hands, soft and light and of an ethereal color, and in shape altogether like a human being.[28]

He asserts that the soul has external form and triple extension—length, breadth, and height. Still it is a simple substance without parts, as otherwise it would not be immortal. What are assumed to be parts of the soul by various philosophers are really powers, capabilities, or operations; for example, the traditional five senses—sight, hearing, taste, touch, and smell. The soul's sensory activities are all functions of the soul and not parts, though each has a definite portion of the body assigned to it.

Although Tertullian's *De Anima* is a lengthy document, it is in no sense a systematic one. He merely treats a number of topics with the single motive of supporting his theological beliefs. Thus in discussing

[27] *De Anima,* Ch. 5, 5.
[28] *Ibid.,* Ch. 9, 4.

the question of the relation of mind to soul he favors the primacy of the soul, as that is more in line with God's testimony. Mind is a function of the soul, and derives its capacities from its relation to the soul. If the mind is capable of suffering that is because the soul is subject to torment in hell. Tertullian can even acknowledge some agreement with Plato concerning the rational-irrational duality of the soul since Plato is in consonance with revelation on that point.[29] The irrational phase of the soul, though not a separate entity from the rational which is informed by God, is influenced by the devil.

Though the soul and the body are absolute correlates, Tertullian asserts that the actual seat of the soul is in the heart, not in the brain as Hippocrates taught, nor around the base of the brain as with Herophilus, nor yet in the outer membrane of the brain as Strato and Erasistratus believed. Tertullian quotes with approval from "the verse of Orpheus or Empedocles" that "the seat of sensation lies in the blood around the heart."[30] And since on this point he is supported by Protagoras, Apollodorus, and Chrysippus he says,

> . . . let Asclepiades go searching for his goats who are bleating without hearts and his flies flitting around without heads. And as for the rest of them who try to argue to the nature of the soul from their experiments on animals, you can tell them that they are the ones who are 'living' without ears or heads.[31]

A remarkable feature of Tertullian's *De Anima* is that in the interest of theology and salvation he argues quite naturalistically against those who minimize the senses and impeach their veracity as compared with that of abstract reason. Tertullian proceeds to explain in terms of media, environment, and other conditions why the oars in the water appear bent, the distant square tower round, the walls of the long corridor convergent, and thunder like a cart rumbling. Again, he knows that an excess of bile or jaundice makes everything taste bitter. He also refers to madness as a basis for illusions as well as delusions, since the senses are closely associated with intellect or judgment. He is strongly opposed to a separation of intellect or reason from the senses because the senses form the basis for the intellect.

> Isn't it true that to feel is to understand and to think is to have sensation. For, what else is sensation than the perception of the thing felt? Or what else is understanding than the perception of the thing known? Why, then, all this torturing of simple truth into obscurity? Can you show me a sensation

[29] *Ibid.,* Ch. 16. On Tertullian's attitude toward Greek philosophy see Quasten, *Patrology,* Vol. II, p. 320 *f.*

[30] *Ibid.,* Ch. 15, 5.

[31] *Ibid.,* Ch. 15, 6.

which does not understand what it feels or an intellect which does not perceive what it knows, so as to prove to me that one can get along without the others?[32]

To impugn the veracity of the senses may result in a denial that Christ really saw Satan cast down from heaven. "The witness of St. John is false if we cannot believe the testimony of our eyes, our ears, and our hands."[33]

We have still to mention Tertullian's insistence that the soul is a free agent with characteristics inherent in it through its divine creation. This means that it has in it a directive faculty, and that this is the basis for man's moral character and moral responsibility. Nonetheless, it remains a fact that human intellect is conditioned in its development by many factors, including such environmental ones as geographical location, social background, bodily health, and obesity. Tertullian enumerates also a set of behavioral conditions; for example, sustained study, laziness, idleness, and vice.[34]

So far, Tertullian has been discussing the nature of the soul. He goes on to the consideration of its origin and destiny. Also, he treats the subjects of sleep, dreams, and death. But before doing so he sums up as follows his views so far.

The soul, therefore, we declare to be born of the breath of God, immortal, corporeal, possessed of a definite form, simple in substance, conscious of itself, developing in various ways, free in its choices, liable to accidental change, variable in disposition, rational, supreme, gifted with foresight, developed out of the one original soul.[35]

The soul originates simultaneously with the body at conception. They coexist together until death, which is essentially a parting and separation of the two substances. This view precludes the acceptance of Plato's doctrine of reminiscence as well as that of transmigration. As to the disposition of the immortal souls after death, Tertullian consigns them all to hell, there to undergo punishment or reward.

Concerning sleep, Tertullian agrees with the Stoics that it is a suspension of sense activity since it brings quiet to the body, but not to the soul. It is certainly not a temporary separation of body and soul. The business of sleep is dreaming. It is a proof both of the divinity and immortality of the soul that it is uninterruptedly active. It can thus be influenced in four ways to dream: by God; by the devil; by its own

[32] *Ibid.*, Ch. 18, 7.
[33] *Ibid.*, Ch. 17, 14.
[34] *Ibid.*, Ch. 20.
[35] *Ibid.*, Ch. 22, 2.

attentive contemplation of surrounding things; and by ecstasy, a kind of madness or inspired turbulence.

Hippolytus (170-236?). Whatever uncertainties and mysteries may surround the life and literary productions of Hippolytus, they all recede into the background beside his positive views concerning science in general and psychology in particular. In his *Refutation of All Heresies* Hippolytus, a Greek who is the first great Christian Father with a Roman background,[36] employs a weighty implement of learning to clear away the doctrines of the Greek and Roman natural and moral philosophers, in order to replace them by Christian dogma. He begins his attacks with a diatribe on Thales and continues until he has refuted all his non-Christian predecessors in the history of thought. What is of special interest to the student of psychological history is his attack upon Aristotle's *De Anima.* Hippolytus objects to Aristotle's attribution of mere permanence but not immortality to the soul.[37] In general, Hippolytus could make very little out of Aristotelian psychology. He declares,

> His work, however, (styled) *Concerning the Soul* is obscure. For in the entire three books (where he treats of this subject) it is not possible to say clearly what is Aristotle's opinion concerning the soul. For as regards the defintion which he furnishes of soul, it is easy (enough) to declare this; but what it is that is signified by the definition is difficult to discover. For soul he says, is an *entelecheia* of a natural organic body; (but to explain) what this is at all, would require a very great number of arguments and a lengthened investigation.[38]

There can be no clearer indication of the cultural changes from Athenian to Patristic times. The mundane description and interpretation of the complexities of an organism's behavior were as nothing to Hippolytus besides the intuitive revelation of the simplicity of the soul which could be immortalized and redeemed. Hippolytus may be literally as well as doctrinally following Irenaeus in distinguishing between the temporal, organic breath of life and the eternal animating spirit.

Athanasius (296-373?). Although Athanasius is best known as the political and ideological shaper of Christian doctrine, he is also worthy of a place in psychological history for two reasons. First, he offers in the second part of his *Contra Gentes* a brief but unique statement of psychological doctrine. Second, he illustrates well the attempts of the

[36] Coxe in Roberts and Donaldson, eds., *The Ante-Nicene Fathers,* Vol. V, p. 3.
[37] *The Refutation of All Heresies* i, Ch. 17.
[38] *Ibid.,* vii, Ch. 7.

Church Fathers to establish Christian dogma by parading factual evidence.

Athanasius' method of glorifying the immortal, rational, and intellectual soul of man is to declare that it can know God by its own power if it keeps itself free from sin. That the rational soul exists is proved by the difference between man and the brutes, and by its superiority and control over the senses and the instincts. Furthermore, because of his rational soul man can think of things not present, this being the basis for memory and for the contemplation of all sorts of things, even of what goes on in the heavens. Such activities surpass anything that the body can do. How far the soul can go beyond bodily behavior is demonstrated by the elaborate dreams that happen while the body is quiet and at rest during sleep.

Conclusive proof for the immortality of the soul Athanasius finds in its thorough distinctness from the body, in its role as the originator and basis of action, and in its power to go beyond the body in imagination and in thought.

Lactantius (260-330?). Probably one of the most outstanding traits of Lactantius is his practical and naive attitude toward God, man, nature, and society. Of course he was as ardent a Christian as any convert, but he was not a worshipper of a remote and distant God. Lactantius was on decidedly intimate terms with the divine creator and believed that there was a manifest affinity between man and God.[39] Indeed God contrived the world for the sake of man and created man with judgment, thought, prudence, and the tongue, the interpreter of thought, that he might be able to declare the majesty of the Lord.[40] In the *De Ira Dei* Lactantius writes as though God is somewhat the creature of man and that hence his mental life is known to man. God is not without emotions; were he not angry he would not be moved to punish sinners.

On the whole Lactantius is concerned with moral problems. His principal work is greatly concerned with the nature of righteousness, the punishment of the wicked, and the reward of the righteous. Cochrane affirms that in his *Divine Institutes,* his object was precisely that of Cicero in his generation, to serve as a *De Officiis* for the Constantinian age.[41] Lactantius concentrates most of his specifically psychological ideas in a work entitled, *On the Workmanship of God or The Forma-*

[39] *De Ira Dei,* Ch. 7.
[40] *Ibid.,* Ch. 14.
[41] *Christianity and Classical Culture,* p. 191.

tion of Man. In this treatise addressed to a pupil he undertakes to justify the work of God in making man what he is and in giving him features contrasting with those of the other animals. Because God provided man with an immortal soul he did not need to endow his body with claws, horns, hooves, or tusks. Lactantius thinks it quite appropriate for an intelligent being like God to give man perception and reason.

Central to Lactantius' psychology is the incorporeal soul, a substance akin to the spirit of God. The soul is, of course, imperceptible to the senses. It is not, however, unconditionally immortal, as a wicked man dies in both body and soul. The soul is not derived from the parents, as that would involve some sort of partition. The soul is concerned with affections as well as reason, and the senses through the sense organs of the body operate as instruments of the mind. The soul, too, is the source of the virtues, while the vices stem from the body. Although the body is very different from the soul, its primary function is to serve the latter even if the method is unknown. Thus the head of the erect, bipedal man as the highest part of him, the part nearest heaven, is the proper home of the thinking soul. Though the purposes of some of the viscera, as the spleen, liver, and gall bladder, are unknown to Lactantius, he believes that they too are connected with the soul, their office being to retain it in the body.[42]

Gregory of Nyssa (335-395). Like other Church Fathers, Gregory developed his psychological views in the interest of the Christian faith and the regulation of the church. As a Cappadocian bishop Gregory labored politically at various synods to establish the church on Nicean lines, and as a scholar he worked diligently to make philosophy the handmaiden of theology. As a zealous builder of Christian theology, of which his psychology is really a part, he borrows from various sources—the Greek philosophers, the Scriptures, and, of course, Christian writers—with a transparent disregard of contradictory argument or even of the taint of unorthodoxy.

Gregory's psychological views are to be gleaned primarily from two works which, though independent, fit into a general theological scheme. These are *On the Making of Man* and *On the Soul and its Resurrection.* The former is designed to establish the place of man in the scheme of creation, while the latter treats of his destiny. In both there are copious evidences of the difficulties of fitting together a scheme of

[42] *On the Workmanship of God,* Ch. 14.

accepted spiritualism with everyday observations about man and the teachings of the Galenic physicians.

Gregory's views may be organized around his definition of soul.

The soul is an essence created, and living, and intellectual, transmitting from itself to an organized and sentient body the power of loving and of grasping objects of sense, as long as a natural constitution capable of this holds together.[43]

The soul just described is the superior part of man and was created as a link between the purely intelligible God and material things. It is through the soul that man is an image of God, while his body attests kinship with the lower animals and with matter in general. In this sense man is a microcosm carrying within himself all the elements which go to complete the universe.[44] But man is unlike God in that he has to depend upon his senses for knowledge of things. Man, then, was created as mind and body; the body was designed as the instrument of the mind. It is through the senses that the mind apprehends the things external to the body. In the case of sight the mind draws to itself the images of things and marks in itself their impressions.[45]

Soul and body are both transmitted in the generating seed. Thus the soul is not preexistent, but it is immortal and outlasts the body. In general both the soul and the body cooperate in the sense that there must be a compresence of the two. Usually the soul influences the actions of the body, but sometimes the body takes the lead and the soul becomes the servant of the bodily impulses, as in the case of pain and the desire for pleasure.[46] Gregory discusses at length a number of bodily conditions which influence the working of the mind or soul and refers to the researches and opinions of medical men.[47]

Man for Gregory is a composite of a rational soul and a complex integrated body. In this he differs from the brutes who are limited to nutritive and sensitive "souls," also, of course, possessed by man. However, the only authentic soul is the intellectual or rational one. The nutritive and sensitive "souls" are really forms of vital energy. Such are the functions of nutrition, respiration, and production of vital heat carried on by the stomach, lungs, and heart respectively. Obviously, Gregory is here having great difficulty in dancing between the eggs of common-sense fact, reinforced by the teachings of the physicians, and

[43] *On the Soul,* p. 433.
[44] *Ibid.,* p. 433.
[45] *On the Making of Man,* Ch. 10, 3.
[46] *Ibid.,* Ch. 14.
[47] *Ibid.,* Chs. 12-14.

those of the spiritualistic doctrines of religion. This difficulty becomes calamitous when he faces the question of how the soul is related to the body. This relationship, Gregory frequently asserts, is a mysterious and indescribable one.

Because Gregory is a builder of official doctrine it is permissible to point out his technique of transferring the naturalistic knowledge of and beliefs about man into items of a spiritualistic theology. Gregory is acquainted with the attempts made to localize psychological activities in the heart because it is centrally situated, or in the brain as the citadel of the whole body, and he rejects such views. Clearly, his theological interests demand that the soul should be so absolutely different from the body as to be spatially unlocalized. He can go only so far as to say that the mind is not restricted to any part of the body but is equally in touch with the whole.[48] As to the exact relationship Gregory declares,

> . . . the union of the mental with the bodily presents a connection unspeakable and inconceivable,—not being *within* it (for the incorporeal is not enclosed in a body), nor yet surrounding it without (for that which is incorporeal does not include anything), but the mind approaching our nature in some inexplicable and incomprehensible way, and coming into contact with it, is to be regarded as both in it and around it, neither implanted in it nor enfolded with it, but in a way which we cannot speak or think, except so far as this, that while the nature prospers according to its own order, the mind is also operative; but if any misfortune befalls the former, the movement of the intellect halts correspondingly.[49]

In the framework of his theological psychology Gregory attempts to fit in the facts of everyday behavior. Man was created in the image of God, and all his goodness and right conduct can be attributed to his resemblance to his divine maker. But man also resembles the brutes, and from them he took over the passions. This is the consequence of sin, which is basically the process of dragging down his reason to become the servant of his passions. But if man wills that reason should assume mastery over his passions, each of them can be transmuted to a form of virtue. From anger arises courage, from terror caution, from fear obedience, from hatred aversion to vice, from love the desire for the truly beautiful.[50] Clearly, Gregory has prepared thoroughly the basis for the gradual evolution of spiritistic doctrines in psychology.

Nemesius of Emesa (4th c.). We round out our sampling of the

[48] *Ibid.*, Ch. 14, 1.
[49] *Ibid.*, Ch. 15, 3.
[50] *Ibid.*, Ch. 18, 5.

Church Fathers with the work of the Syrian Nemesius, first, because his book, *A Treatise On the Nature of Man,* resembles a conventional psychological treatise more than any other work of a churchman; and second, because the doctrines it contains admirably illustrate the transformation of naturalistic descriptions into spiritistic dogmas.

Telfer, the editor and biographer of Nemesius, tells us that he was probably an amateur student of medicine and in some sense a follower of Hippocrates after whose treatise Nemesius named his own work.[51] Nemesius appears to have had considerable acquaintance with Plato and Aristotle as well as with Galen and Plotinus. His work can probably be best summarized by means of a series of statements giving his basic propositions.

Proposition 1: *man is composed of an understanding soul and a body.* Of the two components the soul deserves more regard. The body is an instrument employed by the soul. Nemesius assumes that he is following a well-trodden path in setting forth this proposition, even mentioning Aristotle as a forerunner. Nemesius fails to realize, of course, that he himself springs from a different cultural soil, that he is a Christian apologist concerned with verbally-constructed entities and not a biologist studying behavior.

Proposition 2: *the incorporeal soul sustains a unique relation to the body; it is neither united, juxtaposed, or mixed with it.* Here there is a frank recognition of the insoluble mystery of how two such utterly different entities can be conjoined. Nemesius follows Ammonius and quotes in his own work the latter's statement that:

> . . . it is in the nature of intelligibles both to be capable of union with things adapted to receive them, just as much as if they were things that would perish with them, and to remain, nevertheless, unconfused with them while in union. . . .[52]

Proposition 3: *the body is composed of the four elements, fire, air, earth, and water, as are inorganic things; but also as living things of the four humors, blood, phlegm, choler, and black bile.* Here the primary point for the historian is that Nemesius appears to be acquainted with the theories of the Greek physicians and scientists, a fact which gives added emphasis to his attempt to combine classical learning with religious and spiritual interests. He discusses the creational problems suggested by the Scriptures before he moves on to his next psychological proposition.

Proposition 4: *the soul is divisible in various ways.* One way is to

[51] Telfer, *The Library of Christian Classics,* Vol. IV, p. 212 *f.*

[52] *A Treatise on the Nature of Man,* Ch. 20 (p. 295).

distinguish between the three faculties of imagination, intellect, and memory. These can be related to various parts of the body, the instrument of soul.

Imagination is a faculty of the irrational soul and acts by means of the sense organs. Perception is a simple faculty, but through the five sense organs the soul takes notice of what goes on in the four elements or combinations of them. Nemesius adorns his exposition with many common-sense observations. The senses have their sources and roots in the front ventricle of the brain.

The intellectual faculty covers the subdivisions of judging, approving, refuting, deliberating, choosing, and assaying. Through dreams, intellect divines the future. "The organ of the faculty of intellect is the middle part of the brain and the vital spirit there contained."[53]

The memory faculty is cause and storehouse of remembering and recollection. As Origen says, memory is an image left on the mind from perceiving something actually taking place.

Memory, then, is of things no longer present, and it is certainly not caused by those past events themselves.[54]

The recreation of a faded or forgotten memory is recollection. The location of the memory faculty is the cerebellum, called the hinder part of the brain. Nemesius argues for his brain localizations on the basis of case histories of lesions of the particular parts of the brain supporting the mental action.[55] In this he, of course, follows Galen.

Proposition 5: *another way of dividing the soul is into the rational and irrational parts or forms.* This is the division which Aristotle makes in his *Ethics.* The rational soul consists of imagination, thought, and memory, and has already been treated. The irrational parts are the passions.

Proposition 6: *some irrational parts of the soul are controllable by reason.* There are two classes of these, anger and concupiscence. The origin of anger is the heart. The origin of concupiscence is the liver.

Proposition 7: *there are various ways of defining the passions.* Firstly, passion is any change induced by one thing in another. Secondly, passion is an irrational movement of the soul caused by apprehending something good or bad. Thirdly, passion is a movement of the faculty of appetite upon perceiving an image of something good or bad.

Proposition 8: *concupiscence divides into two passions: pleasures and griefs.* When fortune favors our desire, it ministers pleasure; when

[53] *Ibid.,* Ch. 32 (p. 338).
[54] *Ibid.,* Ch. 32 (p. 340 *f.*).
[55] *Ibid.,* Ch. 32 (p. 341 *f.*).

fortune frowns on our desires, it causes grief. Pleasures are of three kinds: purely spiritual, purely bodily, and mixed mental and bodily. Griefs are of four kinds: pain, trouble, envy, and commiseration.

Proposition 9: *the irrational parts of the soul not subservient to reason are the nutritive, the generative, and the pulsatory faculties.* The nutritive and generative faculties are called nature. The pulsatory faculties are called vital.

Nemesius' exposition of his psychology and biology presses home, of course, without his being aware of it, the transformation of Greek science into Patristic wisdom. In so far as Aristotle and Galen can be clear to him on the basis of common-sense observation and his knowledge of medical writings, he follows them as closely as he can. But the evident fact that he and his Patristic forerunners are dealing with altogether different things is clear in his descriptions.

Proposition 10: *acts are differentiable into involuntary and voluntary types.* Involuntary acts are done either under constraint or unknowingly. Voluntary acts are done neither under constraint nor unknowingly. Acts of free choice are voluntary, but not every voluntary act is an act of free choice. They are mixtures of plan, judgment, and desire.

As we should expect, Nemesius in his study of conduct depends less on technical psychology than on ethical considerations. From an Aristotelian or a modern objective standpoint this would not be a grave fault. But it is impossible for him to remain theologically neutral. Accordingly, the spiritistic halo is everywhere present and serves as a constant reminder of the intellectual distance that separates Aristotle from a Church Father, even from one who, like the medically-oriented Nemesius, respects and follows him as much as the cultural conditions allow. We need only add that the capstones of the *Treatise on the Nature of Man* are God's endowment of man with free will and the problems of providence and human destiny.

Though we did not stress the point, it is evident that a number of the later Church Fathers knew and were influenced by the pagan Neoplatonists, not only by Ammonius but also by Plotinus. Nevertheless, we have postponed our treatment of Plotinus until we have finished our discussion of the Church Fathers because we wish to accord him the accolade of treating his psychological problems without stressing the practical soteriological aspects of the post-Greek period. We turn now to a study of Plotinus as a factor in the development of scientific psychology.

CHAPTER 15

PLOTINUS AND ROMAN-AFRICAN CONVERSIONISM

PREPARATIO PSYCHOLOGIA

THAT PSYCHOLOGY is a continuing, though constantly changing item in Western civilization is the essential theme of psychological history. The traditional interest in the mativations and actions of human organisms, at least, continues without interruption. At this point we are concerned with the evolution of the mentalistic era which followed the extinction of the previous naturalistic era centered primarily in Athenian Greece.[1] We have discussed the role of Christian thought in the development of psychology and now must consider the contribution of pagan mysticism. There can be no doubt that both the Christian theology and the pagan philosophy of the third and immediately preceding centuries constitute the effective basis and preparation for the psychology of the future. Since technical psychological ideas are rooted in the prevailing intellectual or philosophical attitudes of their age, we shall do well to search in the mystical and subjective philosophy of the third century for the matrix of post-Greek transcendental psychology. This brings us at once to the consideration of the mystical philosophy represented by Plotinus' Neoplatonism.

It is impossible to overestimate the extreme importance of Neoplatonic philosophy in the history of Western civilization, in which it plays a double role. In the first place, like all systematic philosophies, it serves as a cultural matrix for the esthetic, legal, scientific, moral, and other attitudes of the social groups dominated by it. These intellectual items are just as definite and tangible as are the baskets, pots, tools, and other things making up the gross paraphernalia of the civilization, and they guide the individual and collective action of the group members. Such attitudes are the ingredients from which are derived the basic assumptions and postulates that govern the thought and practices of any given age or culture. Thus, in the late Roman period, Neoplatonism set the pace for the attitudes and postulates of all nonscientific society and later laid down the lines of interpretation for

[1] See Ch. 10 above.

scientific work when it came to be gradually resumed in the ninth and tenth centuries.[2] In its second role in Western culture, Neoplatonic philosophy is specifically concerned with psychology, for it serves as the means for maintaining the continuity of the psychological tradition, while at the same time transmuting its naturalistic content into mystic transcendentalism. Neoplatonism is a complete inversion of Hellenic ways of thinking. In the history of thought Plotinus stands out as a superb example of a complete converter of Hellenic thinking, of which his religious philosophy is in a genuine sense a continuation. For Plotinus may be still counted as an adherent of the Hellenistic Greek tradition, not only because he writes in Greek but also, and more significantly, because he takes his departure from and inverts Plato. Thus, it is easy to see how spiritistically-inclined writers can envisage Neoplatonic philosophy as a culmination of the intellectual institutions of Greece.[3] However, it is still easier to see that Plotinus, universally acknowledged to be the first essential mystic in the European tradition, belongs to an age in which social and political conditions are the precise opposites of those that fostered the naturalistic doctrines of Hellenic times. Think of the difference in human conditions between Athens in the fifth century B.C. and Rome in the third century A.D. Only those who accept spiritistic postulates can fail to evaluate Plotinus as the forerunner of a new age, one which will foster diaphanous constructs of escapism as though they were stable realities. It is in this sense that Plotinian Neoplatonism begins to exert a great influence upon the Church Fathers, for example, Basil, Gregory of Nyssa, and Nemesius, and becomes the basis for Augustinian doctrine. As we shall see, St. Augustine translates Plotinian cosmic spiritualism into a personalistic form of individual psychology.[4]

SOCIAL CONDITIONS UNDERLYING NEOPLATONISM

Granted that all doctrinal institutions, whether scientific, economic, political, or religious, must conform to the cultural complexes of which they are a part, it is still true that at some times these correlations are easier to observe than at others. In the case of Plotinus and his doctrines, we can readily see the definite correlations between the changes in both the Neoplatonic doctrines and the cultural background which they reflect. A similar advantageous situation awaits us in our

[2] Bréhier speaks of the persistence down to our day of the new type of idealism which Plotinus introduced; cf. *The Philosophy of Plotinus*, p. 182.

[3] E. Caird, *The Evolution of Theory in the Greek Philosophers*, Vol. II, p. 238.

[4] See below, Ch. 16.

study of the writings of St. Augustine. Both these writers lived in the intolerable conditions of the crumbling and decaying society centered in the Roman Empire, the empire which in more than a figurative sense explodes in the third century and becomes erased in the fifth.

The third century of our era is a time of political chaos and intellectually a dark age. Gone are the great cohesive conditions of the giant social structure represented by the *Pax Romana,* and with them the economic and political advantages which once made the Roman Empire strong and efficient. In this century emperor succeeds emperor, a sure sign of unstable and anarchic conditions. It is chiefly the army which makes emperors and unmakes them by the simple process of summary execution, so that in an interval of eighty-five years the Romans squandered the great quantity of thirty-seven imperial personages. Private vendettas among those ambitious for the purple also account for part of the carnage. As to the army, the proud Roman legions have long given way to alien and less cultivated manpower. At this time the Roman Senate itself consisted mostly of Africans, Syrians, and Illyrians. It is to be expected, of course, that under such anarchic conditions poverty should reach a high stage of discomfort. The glories that were reflected in architecture and public works are in shadow. The proud and shining cities are fast declining into rubble.[5]

Only by blinding oneself to the life conditions of the intellectual leaders of the past can one envisage their constructional products as the abstract and independent unfolding of cosmic events. The study of Plotinus and his doctrines cannot fail to show us that his mysticism was begotten of extremely troubled times. In such a degraded state of society as we have just sketched, the intellectual institutions of ancient Greece, once so assiduously cultivated, have no place. The philosophical doctrines of the early Stoics, the Epicureans, and the other Greek schools, which so warmly attested the reliability and grandeur of nature and man's place in it, were replaced by magical beliefs, by superstitions, by astrology, and by expression of personal hopes, fears, and desires for deliverance from the circumstances of a difficult time and life. The third century is intrinsically the century of mysticism. Thus Plotinus is the builder of transcendental institutions that were to be adopted and perfected by St. Augustine so as to accord with the complete replacement of the science of the Greeks and the technology of the Romans by Christian theology. In the hands of Plotinus and

[5] See Rostovtzeff, *The Social and Economic History of the Roman Empire,* Vol. II, Chs. 11, 12.

Augustine psychology, in particular, is transformed from the study of the behavior of individuals to a concern with invisible and intangible forces or processes of consciousness.

PLOTINUS: SYSTEMIZER OF SPIRIT

The Neoplatonic movement sums up the complete intellectual change occurring when Christianity was replacing classical culture. Though Plotinus was a pagan Greek of the Roman Empire, his views, which are sometimes regarded as antagonistic to Christian doctrine, actually not only lent support but also helped to establish Christian philosophy and religion. It is not only Augustine who was influenced by Plotinus and his Neoplatonism, but also numerous thinkers in the Christian and Islamic traditions throughout many centuries.

Plotinus was probably an Egyptian—he is believed to have been born in Lycopolis, modern Assiut, and had studied in Alexandria before he came to Rome at the age of forty in 244. Thus Plotinus, like the greatest contributors to Christian literature, was a North African, and this is more than incidental. Pagan and Christian thought developed, both literally and metaphorically, on common ground. As in the case of Christian thinking already discussed, the whole Plotinian philosophy may be rightly interpreted as a way of deliverance from the turmoil of chaotic living. The sagacious individual, whether Christian or pagan, finds refuge in his union and identification with the One. From this lofty and safely unlocalizable position, it is easy to look down upon the havoc being wrought on the last remnants of integrated political existence and to declare it as worth nothing.

> If the Proficient thinks all fortunate events, however momentous, to be no great matter—kingdom and the rule over cities and peoples, colonizations and the founding of states, even though all be his own handiwork—how can he take any great account of the vacillations of power or the ruin of his fatherland? Certainly if he thought any such event a great disaster, or any disaster at all, he must be of a very strange way of thinking. One that sets great store by wood and stones, or, Zeus! by mortality among mortals cannot yet be the Proficient, whose estimate of death, we hold, must be that it is better than life in the body.[6]

The evolution of spirit can no better be shown than by this verbal creativity of the Neoplatonic way of thinking. Only those who embrace the basic assumptions underlying the spiritualistic point of view can believe that Plotinus "ignored the chaos which surrounded his peace-

[6] *The Enneads,* Ennead i, Tractate 4, 7.

ful lecture room."[7] How is it possible that Plotinus, who laboured strenuously to free himself and rise above the bitter waves of this blood-drenched life,"[8] should not have left in his writings any trace of the external affairs of his time?[9] The fact is that his writings are nothing but a reflected chronicle of the affairs of his time and a verbal attempt to escape from them.

When we ask where Plotinus found the model for his imposing system we discover that, like the Christian writers of his time, he displays a decided preference for Plato as a source of acceptable doctrines. He converted such features of Platonic philosophy as seemed useful to the needs of the new times. This was no mean task. It demanded the construction of new postulates to replace unacceptable ones, and intellectual attitudes to fit the new age. Instead of a dialectic rooted in contacts with things, Plotinus had to forge propositions that in his estimation and in that of the time were sufficiently fluid and supple to deal with a reality that was unstable, growing, and diaphanous. Included in the Plotinian system was a new cosmology, a new ethics, and a new psychology.

Needless to say, Plotinian Neoplatonism required a tremendous verbal facility, a great power of translation, the use of analogy, and the development of a new vocabulary and a new technique of using and correlating words. We are reminded here of Goethe's commentary on the power of words.

> .....haltet euch an Worte!
> ....
> Mit Worten lässt sich trefflich streiten,
> Mit Worten ein System bereiten,[10]

PLOTINUS CONVERTS PLATO

How was it possible for Plotinus to create such a relatively elaborate and integrated system of philosophy when the materials he used were the nebulous fantasies of transcendent spirit? One ready answer is that he simply converted the well-structured thought of Plato. Another is that he had at hand the dire needs of men and drew upon the mass of current beliefs to bring about what he regarded as a satisfactory adjustment of man to his hostile and intolerable environment. Naturally, neither answer presupposes that Plotinus deliberately proceeded to

[7] Inge, *The Philosophy of Plotinus,* Vol. I, p. 27.
[8] Porphyry, *On the Life of Plotinus and the Arrangement of his Work,* Par. 23.
[9] Armstrong, *Plotinus,* p. 12.
[10] *Faust,* lines 1990, 1997-98.

create his system on these plans. Indeed Plotinus regarded himself as following Plato implicitly. The great mystic sincerely thought he was absorbing the best of Plato with the help provided by an objective order of intelligence and truth. Plotinus hardly thought of himself as a formal Plotinian, and it was far from his ideas to establish a Neoplatonic system. But the fact is that Plotinus was a child of his age, and he converted Plato in conformity with the intellectual conditions made necessary by the vicissitudes of the third century. His *Enneads,* arranged and edited by his pupil Porphyry, was published in 304 just when Christian thought was becoming formulated and disseminated. This is a significant coincidence for in content the *Enneads* fitted harmoniously with a period that included Constantine's elevation of Christianity into the official religion of the Roman Empire.

In order to present in a clear and concise way just what the Plotinian system means as a conversion of Platonic philosophy, we set up in parallel columns some indices of Platonic thinking and the Plotinian transformations of them.

TABLE V. COMPARISON OF PLATONISM AND NEOPLATONISM

Item or Topic	*Plato*	*Plotinus*
Philosophical Methods	A. Rational Dialectic B. Philosophers move from concrete nature to Forms or Patterns C. Constructs based upon observation and postulation	A. Mystical Intuition B. Philosophers know by identification with thing known C. Constructs based upon verbal argument; no authentic development in system
Model for relating Things and Constructs	A. Mathematical extrapolation B. Participation of individuals or integer in sum	A. Emanation of homogeneous states B. The Self-containment of All in One
The One	The highest or most perfect Form or Pattern	A mystic all-containing unity existing nowhere and everywhere
Nature of Man	Man a natural being in a spatio-temporal environment	Man partially not natural but partakes in the supernatural
Place of Forms	At the peak of the dialectic system, not transcending nature but only sensible objects	In the divine mind, in the *Logos*, the mind of God or the transcendent One, as previously said by Philo
Comparison of Values	Reasoning glorified in comparison with sensing	Transcendent Soul glorified in comparison with Body

PLOTINUS: INSTITUTOR OF SPIRIT

Obviously Plotinus was learned in the philosophies of the ancients and was interested in learning more;[11] the *Enneads* testify to this with the many references to the Greek philosophers. But it is also obvious that by his transformation of pagan doctrines, and his sensitivity to the conditions of the time and to the doctrines of the Christian sages, he not only became a formulator and founder of spiritual philosophy but also influenced all later thought, including the postulates of current philosophy and science. It is frequently pointed out how great an influence Neoplatonism exerted upon St. Augustine and St. Thomas. And since St. Augustine and St. Thomas are two of the important links in the chain of historical transcendentalism, Plotinus added force to the establishment and maintenance of spiritualism.

Probably the best way to envisage Plotinus' formulation of transcendence and spirit is to take his three primary hypostases as the center of his system. As the basic hypostasis he places the One, God, the Good, or the Absolute and Totality of Being and Not-Being, or what is to become. From the One is derived, by a sort of precipitation or emanation, the Universal Intelligence or world soul (*Nous*). This Intelligence Plotinus thinks of as the image of the One.[12] The third and final hypostasis is Soul. Soul on one side merges with universal contemplative Intelligence and on the other shades into individual soul as the highest feature of man. In point of fact, individual soul is for Plotinus so central a phase of emanation, with its connection with things, that it constitutes beside Universal Soul a fourth type of hypostasis, though Plotinus does not formally admit it. Scholars do not hesitate to say that the system does not stop at four hypostases but that Plotinus keeps multiplying them to accommodate things that appear important enough to be mentioned. We have already pointed out the role of words and linguistic processes in the construction of such systems. Here we must add that the linguistic tool primarily employed is that of negative assertion; namely, the attribution of ineffability to the system and its components. It is reputed to be beyond man's power to conceive and to describe what the One is, what Man is, or what the relations between them are.[13]

Is it possible that such a system of thinking should be continuously

[11] See Porphyry's account of how Plotinus joined the Emperor Gordian's expedition to Persia in order to carry out his ambition to learn about Persian and Indian philosophy (*On the Life of Plotinus,* Par. 3).

[12] *Enneads,* v, 1, 7.

[13] *Ibid.,* vi, 8, 13.

adopted down to modern times? The facts speak for themselves. The basic institutions which Plotinus has organized do continue, though the details vary with the march of time. The basic transcendentalism, the search for ultimate principles beyond everyday events, the existence of a unity, an absolute in which everything is contained, and in which all differences are obliterated and made to appear again, is a stable feature of modern philosophy and science. It is most interesting that the Plotinian merger of the knower and the known should become a basic tenet of the most recent developments of physics theory.

It is unnecessary to argue for the similarity of the mystic ways of thinking exhibited by Plotinus and by the writers of the European philosophical tradition. This is true not only for the avowed religious mystics such as Boehme, Tauler, and an enormous number of others, but also for those who claim to be rationalists, logical epistemologists, and dialecticians. The only question is one of specific influence. The hypothesis of the unbroken continuity of thought between Plotinus and his Patristic predecessors does not require the transmission of unmodified doctrine. On the contrary, we find it indispensable to take into account the greater or lesser variations in the grand theme of a transcendental universal that contains or parallels the work of nature. We must point out, too, that the similarity of doctrine extends to the notion that the transcendental world is the stable, dependable, authentic, and omnipresent existence. By contrast, the world of nature is imperfect, incomplete, ever in a nascent and changing form. One scholar asks if it is going too far "to suggest that Kant's distinction between the 'phenomenon' and the 'noumenon,' in spite of significant differences, descends from this tradition."[14] Of course not; the following is Plotinus' clear-cut statement of this type of duality:

> On the one hand there is the unstable, exposed to all sorts of change, distributed in place, not so much Being as Becoming; on the other, there is that which exists eternally, not divided, subject to no change of state, neither coming into being nor falling from it, set in no region or place or support, emerging from nowhere, entering into nothing, fast within itself.[15]

How close this view is to the Hegelian dialectic with its Unity, Absolute, and passage from one to the other, is clearly apparent. It is no less apparent how faithfully the whole tradition of Romantic philosophy mirrors the basic characteristics of Neoplatonic thought. Whether Bergson's philosophy is directly derived from Plotinus or

[14] Henry, "Plotinus' Place in the History of Thought," p. xxxix.
[15] *Enneads,* vi, 5, 2.

indirectly through the Romantics, Schelling, and Schopenhauer, there is no doubt that his anti-intellectualism and mystic intuitionism continue a tradition begun in the early centuries of our era.[16] Among more recent philosophical writings the following statement is irresistibly reminiscent of the Plotinian obliteration of the difference between the knowing soul and what it knows:

> The reader will recall that in our general procedure of inquiry no radical separation is made between that which is observed and the observer in the way which is common in the epistemologies and in standard psychologies and psychological constructions . . . nor is there any radical separation between that which is named and the naming.[17]

Whatever may be the case in the philosophical tradition, the influence of Plotinian transcendentalism on later ages is strikingly demonstrated by the attitudes adopted by contemporary physicists as a result of relativity and quantum mechanics theory. We may take as a satisfactory example the view of Bohr, who, when facing difficult and indeterminate situations, evokes the principle that after all there is no definite line between things known and the act of knowing. His formula is "that in the great drama of existence we are both actors and spectators."[18] When we seek the derivation of this type of view we should do well to look to traditional theory and not to anything that goes on in the laboratory.

PLOTINIAN PSYCHOLOGY

For Plotinus psychology consists of that series of human activities making up what we now call popular psychology. What interests him especially is the basis for these activities, and for him that is soul. Inevitably, Plotinus accepts the then current assumption that soul is a transcendental entity very different from body. Even though for Plotinus everything in the final analysis is spirit transcendent, he still proposes grades of being; the soul is a more glorified entity than the body. It is on this basis that Plotinus formulates and espouses a mind-body system. What Plotinus aims at above all in his psychological thinking is to prove within his theological and mystical framework that the soul had an independent existence of its own different from that of the body and other corporeal things.[19] The soul is divine. Porphyry tells us that Plotinus seemed ashamed of having a body. For this reason

[16] See Mossé-Bastide, *Bergson et Plotin, passim.*
[17] Dewey and Bentley, *Knowing and the Known,* p. 103 *f.*
[18] *Atomic Theory and the Description of Nature,* p. 119 *et passim.*
[19] See Whittaker, *The Neo-Platonists,* p. 42.

he never could be induced to speak of his parentage or birthplace. About to die, he declared, "I am striving to give back the Divine in myself to the Divine in the All."[20]

Because Plotinus is essentially a transforming philosopher, one who obviously is constructing a way of retreating from concrete events, including psychological ones, it is interesting to observe his intellectual behavior. On one hand, he builds a transparent system of soul constructions which deviates immeasurably from descriptions of the activities of organisms. But on the other hand, even while most active in producing his spiritistic inventions, he is still forced to deal with the concrete things and events from which he derives his constructs by verbal transformation and recreation. Both the creational and observational aspects of Plotinus' work will appear in the following exposition.

Characteristics of Soul

To begin with, of course, the soul for Plotinus is a unitary entity without parts, spatial distribution, or the properties of material things. Next, it is clear that the soul is incorporeal and without number, being both one and many. Again, the soul is simple, not composed of parts or combined with the body or any other form of nonspiritistic substance. And finally, the soul is indestructible and hence immortal.

While discussing the characteristics of soul, Plotinus considers the proposals of his predecessors of whom he has a keen awareness. He rejects the notion that the soul is a harmony, because primarily the soul is a substantive entity and not a property of something else—a conjoinedness of things. Neither is the soul an entelechy of the body as Aristotle taught, since that, too, implies the lack of substantivity and independent existence. Obviously, too, Aristotle's theory would subordinate the soul to material things. For the same reasons Plotinus also firmly rejects the Stoic notion that the soul is *pneuma* or anything short of transcendent spirit.

The Nature of Psychological Actions

Plotinus, the man and the scholar, can be clearly distinguished from the transcendentalist philosopher. In the former role he is a keen psychological observer on a common-sense level. He concerns himself with man and his adjustments. Accordingly he has left a record of appreciation of human behavior, though always with the expressed

[20] Porphyry, *On the Life of Plotinus,* Par. 2

intention of submerging such events in the great ocean of spiritistic verbalism. We consider, in order, the following topics, which he treats with consummate skill: sensing and perceiving; remembering; imagining; feeling or the affective processes; and thinking, reasoning, and comprehending.

SENSING AND PERCEIVING. Believing himself to be following in the epistemological and ethical footsteps of Plato, Plotinus spares no effort to denigrate the sensory processes. In line with his spiritistic premises he accounts for the low-grade character of sensing activity on the ground that the body participates in it and conditions it even more than the soul. Bodily organs are necessary. Soul without body can apprehend nothing on the sensory level.[21]

From the standpoint of psychological history it is a remarkable fact that Plotinus, the mystic, formulated the sensing and perceiving process in a way that has persisted down to our own time. His position is essentially that objects or their qualities become known to the soul by means of a positive act mediated by some bodily organ.

> The mind affirms something not contained within it: this is precisely the characteristic of a power—not to accept impression but, within its allotted sphere, to act.[22]

Plotinus repeatedly declares that impressions are neither made on nor left in the mind. Sensing is an active creative process based on the fact that there is some sort of sympathy between the objects seen, and the awareness of the objects.

> Perception of every kind seems to depend on the fact that our universe is a living whole sympathetic to itself.[23]

This notion of sympathy is probably borrowed from the Stoics and fits admirably the large mystic all-in-all which is the basic Plotinian construction. What, then, is the precise character of the sympathetic action of awareness? The answer is plain. It is a change in the soul which is well described by Plotinus as consciousness. It is an inexistent existence of things corresponding to bodily things which, on the perceptual level, stand at the opposite pole on the scale of being. In a sense, too, he thinks of perceiving as a judgment formed as a result of an object making an impression upon the body or special end-organ.[24]

We undoubtedly have here one of the earliest technical formulations

[21] *Enneads,* iv, 4, 24.
[22] *Ibid.,* iv, 6, 2.
[23] *Ibid.,* iv, 5, 3.
[24] *Ibid.,* iv, 3, 26.

of the now traditional inner life or inner principle concerned with psychological processes. This description of the soul or mind engaged in cognitive acts is a new verbal formulation which is employed even today. So novel is this idea when first enunciated in its technical guise by Plotinus that it is enlightening to look forward and see what Leibniz as well as other writers in the psychological tradition have done with it. This is none other than the conventional conscious mind or ego; when the soul is not cognizing we have the unconscious mind. As we shall see presently, Plotinus makes his inner actions, his soul energy, cover affective processes as well as cognitive ones.

It is most interesting that Plotinus, the mystic, carefully specifies the nature of the organs or bodily parts concerned in perceiving. It is the brain, a view which gives Plotinus a middle position between the long tradition of physiological psychology of the future and its Hellenic and Hellenistic forerunners. Plotinus is certainly aware of the anatomical and physiological advances made by Herophilus and Erasistratus.

> . . . a living body is illuminated by soul: each organ and member participates in soul after some manner peculiar to itself; the organ is adapted to a certain function, and this fitness is the vehicle of the soul-faculty under which the function is performed; thus the seeing faculty acts through the eyes, the hearing faculty through the ears, the tasting faculty through the tongue, the faculty for smelling through the nostrils, and the faculty of sentient touch is present throughout, since in this particular form of perception the entire body is an instrument in the soul's service.
>
> The vehicles of touch are at the ends of the nerves—which, moreover, are vehicles of the faculty by which the movements of the living being are effected—in them the soul-faculty concerned makes itself present; the nerves start from the brain. The brain therefore has been considered as the centre and seat of the principle which determines feeling and impulse and the entire act of the organism as a living thing. . . .[25]

The more we study the tortuous and sometimes contradictory, yet integral psychology of Plotinus, the clearer we see his emphasis upon the essentiality, primacy, and exclusiveness of spirit or soul. In perceiving, as in every other type of activity, everything ultimately arises from the many factors in the unity of the One. It is Plotinus who invents the introspective tradition of spiritistic psychology. In perceiving there can be no nonpsychic object which affects the soul directly. Neither can there be a secondary affection of the soul by the intervention of the change brought about in a bodily organ. No, in the final analysis, what is perceived consists of the things and their qualities which arise within the psychic system. This perceptive process may

[25] *Ibid.*, iv, 3, 23.

reach a degree of awareness such that the soul is conscious of the process, and this supplies an introspective form of self-consciousness, an awareness or appreciation of what changes have taken place in the soul. From the standpoint of Plotinus' cosmic system, the entire process of an object affecting the body and the soul thereupon appreciating the change in itself is a purely incidental situation mentioned only because of the need to consider man and his duality of mind and body. When the ultimate One is taken into consideration, no distinction exists between subject knowing and object known.[26]

REMEMBERING. In typical mystical fashion, Plotinus regards remembering as an activity of soul alone and not of man's mixed nature. Remembering, then, is a basis for the spirituality and the transcendence which is the realm where Plotinus likes to dwell. In his discussion of remembering Plotinus displays the cleft in his thinking between his preformed spiritualistic beliefs on one side and his observational knowledge on the other. He does not overlook the fact that the body, may be a hindering or a helping factor in remembering,[27] but maintains that, whatever may be the role of the mind-body complement in remembering, the body itself does not remember. Memory activities belong to the soul exclusively. To show how different the memorial activities are from the perceptual ones, including thinking, Plotinus says:

> The most powerful thought does not always go with the readiest memory; people of equal perception are not equally good at remembering; some are especially gifted in perception, others, never swift to grasp, are strong to retain.[28]

Remembering, then, is a self-contained activity of the soul. What it retains is a record of its own former activities. Even though these activities are more or less remotely connected with natural events, the psychic purity of remembering cannot be gainsaid. The salient point here is that soul and its actions can never be directly in touch with things. Again, the soul can remember only its own movements.

> . . . for example its desires and those frustrations of desire in which the coveted thing never came to the body: the body can have nothing to tell about things which never approached it, and the Soul cannot use the body as a means to the remembrance of what the body by its nature cannot know.[29]

[26] See for example, *ibid.*, iii, 8, 8; v, 3, 13; v, 8, 12; vi, 6, 6, *et passim.*
[27] *Ibid.*, iv, 3, 26.
[28] *Ibid.*, iv, 3, 29.
[29] *Ibid.*, iv, 3, 26.

In the interest of mystical transcendence Plotinus argues powerfully that remembering is purely psychic and only very distantly connected with things external to the soul. And yet this argument introduces a discontinuity in the universe which is wholly obnoxious to an apostle of unity such as Plotinus. Moreover, to his credit be it said, his flight into transcendence does not entirely extinguish his urge to analyze and to retain some contact with ongoing events. After all, the more detached a psychic being is from the world of everyday things, from events in space and time, the less need there is for remembering.

Now a memory has to do with something brought into ken from without, something learned or something experienced; the Memory-Principle, therefore, cannot belong to such beings as are immune from experience and from time.

No memory, therefore, can be ascribed to any divine being, or to the Authentic-Existent or the Intellectual-Principle: these are intangibly immune; time does not approach them; they possess eternity centred around Being; they know nothing of past and sequent; all is an unbroken state of identity, not receptive of change. Now a being rooted in unchanging identity cannot entertain memory, since it has not and never had a state differing from any previous state, or any new intellection following upon a former one, so as to be aware of contrast between a present perception and one remembered from before.[30]

IMAGINING. If remembering, though a purely psychic act, must pertain to things learned or experienced, then there must be a faculty or process by which such a pure psychic act can be involved with happenings that are really conjoint acts of soul and body. The bonding process which ties together the higher processes of remembering and the lower of sensing and perceiving is imagining. Here is Plotinus' statement.

. . . we may well conceive that where there is to be memory of a sense-perception, this perception becomes a mere presentment, and that to this image-grasping power, a distinct thing, belongs the memory, the retention of the object: for in this imaging faculty the perception culminates; the impression passes away but the vision remains present to the imagination.

By the fact of harbouring the presentment of an object that has disappeared, the imagination is, at once, a seat of memory: where the persistence of the image is brief, the memory is poor; people of powerful memory are those in whom the image-holding power is firmer, not easily allowing the record to be jostled out of its grip.

Remembrance, thus, is vested in the imaging faculty; and memory deals with images. Its differing quality or degree from man to man we would

[30] *Ibid.*, iv, 3, 25.

explain by difference or similarity in the strength of the individual powers, by conduct like or unlike, by bodily conditions, present or absent, producing change and disorder or not. . . .[31]

It is quite clear that Plotinus has achieved his goal of unifying the soul by restoring to a procedure which comes close to a simple invocation of common-sense observations. Remembering turns out to be a process of acting with reference to absent things. In the matter of regarding images as the basic feature of this process, Plotinus creates certain psychic entities (images) which become established institutions and maintain a prosperous existence during the entire tradition of spiritistic psychology.

According to Plotinus images and the faculty of imagination are extremely pervasive features of psychic existence and action. They not only aid in preserving sense knowledge but also assist the soul in remembering and mirroring its own states.[32] Thus the thoughts of the soul become objects for itself. Here is reached the peak of the introspective process where the soul apprehends its own psychic acts. Furthermore, the imaging faculty provides the psychic mechanism for the perduring intuition of the soul.

What may appear utterly surprising to find in such a mystical writer as Plotinus is his interweaving of verbal elements into the fabric of the imaging faculty. What, he asks, if there is no image to serve as a picture of the earlier thought? How can it be retained in the intellective or intuitive system? His answer, which is a tribute to his undeniable contact with actual human behavior, is that verbal formulae which accompany mental states (ideas or conceptions) serve to reveal them to the soul. The mental states which lie unknown below the level of apprehension are connected with the image-making faculty by the bridge of words.[33]

AFFECTIVE PROCESS. A reflective reading of Plotinian psychology indicates strikingly that Plotinus was not only a Neoplatonist but a Neoaristotelian as well. We have already seen that his treatment of perception is strongly reminiscent of Aristotelian psychology despite the conversion of sensing action into soul function. The same conversion dominates the Plotinian discussion of affective action. In both cases, however, the striking thing is that a mystic should be constrained to put so much emphasis on the bodily actions.

[31] *Ibid.*, iv, 3, 29.
[32] *Ibid.*, iv, 3, 30.
[33] *Ibid.*

Pleasure and pain and the like must not be attributed to the Soul alone, but to the modified body and to something intermediary between soul and body and made up of both.[34]

Students familiar with the James-Lange theory of emotions will be agreeably surprised to see how closely Plotinus anticipated this theory.

. . . anger follows closely upon bodily states; people in whom the blood and the bile are intensely active are as quick to anger as those of cool blood and no bile are slow; animals grow angry though they pay attention to no outside combinations except where they recognize physical danger; all this forces us again to place the seat of anger in the strictly corporeal element, the principle by which the animal organism is held together. Similarly, that anger or its first stirring depends upon the condition of the body follows from the consideration that the same people are more irritable ill than well, fasting than after food: it would seem that the bile and the blood, acting as vehicles of life, produce these emotions.[35]

By contrast with Aristotle's classification of psychological activities on the basis of the types of contact with the objects to which the organism adjusts itself, Plotinus sets up a distinction of higher and lower activities. The lower ones consist of psychic changes dependent upon bodily conditions. As we have seen, such activities include sense perception and imagination. To this list must be added psychic acts concerned with vegetation and generation. In the excerpt just presented we notice that the affective processes include desire.

Plotinus divides affective actions into desire and the two paired categories of pleasure and pain, and the emotions and passions, which can be briefly described as follows.

Pleasure and Pain. When Plotinus defines pleasure as "our perception of the living frame in which the image of the Soul is brought back to harmonious bodily operation,"[36] he appears to link himself on one hand with the objective thinkers, Socrates, Plato, and Aristotle, and on the other with the dualistic theorists who follow him in the mentalistic succession. It is undeniable that this definition does suggest some characteristics of affective events. More specifically Plotinian is the definition of pain as the perception of a body despoiled, that is deprived of the image of the soul.[37] Still, the suggestion that pain is somehow polar to pleasure-states ties Plotinus to his objective predecessors.

Emotions and Passions. Since Plotinus is not primarily interested

[34] *Ibid.*, iv, 4, 18.
[35] *Ibid.*, iv, 4, 28.
[36] *Ibid.*, iv, 4, 19.
[37] *Ibid.*

in psychological analysis but merely uses psychological data to establish his mystical philosophy and theology, we need not expect from him straightforward and precise descriptions of the various psychological activities. Indeed, on the basis of his fundamental assumptions and the knowledge of his time this would have been impossible. Still, we find him making the attempt to establish differences between differently named activities. Thus, he asserts that emotional states of mind are relatively more active and pertain to a lower phase of psychic existence than the passions. Emotions involve a striving,[38] while the passions, as the term implies, constitute more a form of suffering no matter how internal they may be. The intense passions may be regarded as the soul's retaliatory reaction to the wrong done it by the environment.[39] Throughout his discussion Plotinus does not fail to interrelate his descriptions of emotion and passion with pleasure and pain, discursive reason, and other processes.

DESIRE. Desires originate in modifications of the body, modifications contributing only slightly or not at all to awareness. Desire may be stirred by merely seeing something, and then arises a blind response or an automatic action.[40] In this way the body may acquire a restless movement which forces it

> . . . to aim at a variety of objects, to seek, as its changing states demand, sweet or bitter, water or warmth, with none of which it could have any concern if it remained untouched by life.[41]

Characteristically, Plotinus sets desire as well as all affective processes low in his levels of existence and finds a seat for these little-valued processes in specific parts of the body. Desire he localizes in a region about the liver,[42] and the passions in the bile or heart, the latter being expressly excluded as the seat of the soul.[43] It is apparent that Plotinus minimizes the sensory and affective processes as not articulating well with the essential activities of soul. Only the refined reasoning processes achieve that distinction.

THINKING, REASONING, COMPREHENDING. The higher psychic processes, that is those independent of the body, are of two sorts: those referred to the *logos,* which include opinion, volition, and discursive thought and, second, the still higher actions performed by the Intellect or Ego,

[38] *Ibid.,* iv, 3, 32.
[39] *Ibid.,* iv, 4, 28.
[40] *Ibid.,* iv, 3, 28.
[41] *Ibid.,* iv, 4, 20.
[42] *Ibid.,* iv, 4, 28.
[43] *Ibid.*

namely intuitive thought and true knowledge. In view of the basic mystical character of Plotinus' attitude his ideas of thinking and reasoning make them absolutely transcendent. The soul which performs such actions is definitely outside the range of human experience. Still, Plotinus appears to need such processes for completing his decriptions of concrete human actions. For example, thinking and reasoning participate in concrete actions of the individual, for example in performing passion processes like anger.[44] Though, as we have seen, Plotinus does localize some of the lower processes, he prefers not to connect the higher actions with bodily parts and their functions. He remarks that the "ancients" had, among all the organs, favored the brain as being somehow connected with deliberative or discursive reason, but he, himself, does not seem to be convinced by their arguments.[45] Reasoning is independent of the body and stands on a higher level than the affective processes. The soul comprehends extension but it is not extended; it participates in actions but it is actually eternal and unchanging.[46] We have already seen that in pure thought there are no genuine changes, no distinction of body and soul, no polarity of knower and known.[47] It is in his discussions of thinking, reasoning, and contemplation that Plotinus best exhibits his creativity, using words to free his Supreme Being, which is really everything, from all that he himself actually knows and interacts with. With this method he transcends all space, time, movement, quantity, and quality.

We have now summarized the main tenets, both those of general philosophy and those specifically concerned with psychology, of the system worked out by Plotinus. His Neoplatonism, born of the miseries extant in Roman life of the third century, a reflection of the malaise and despair which was in his time the common fate of all classes of society in the Roman Empire, attained an institutional existence of its own with a persistent durability. Plotinus is not the originator of the spiritistic doctrine, but the perfecter of a tradition, an architect who, by formal organization stabilized it as a comprehensive system of thought which could be thoroughly established as an abiding institution of intellectual life. The secret of the survival of Plotinian doctrines is that they fitted so completely the religious civilization nourished by the need for release, for escape from the burdens of the actual world, and salvation in the heaven beyond.

[44] *Ibid.*, iv, 4, 28.
[45] *Ibid.*, iv, 3, 23.
[46] *Ibid.*, iv, 7, 8; v, 1, 10, *et passim.*
[47] *Ibid.*, iii, 8, 8; v, 8, 11, *et passim.*

SECTION SEVEN

SPIRIT INSTITUTIONALIZED

CHAPTER 16

AUGUSTINIAN TRANSNATURISM

THE TRIUMPH OF SPIRIT

IN MANY WAYS the fifth century of the Christian era is a period of great significance in every phase of Western European culture, especially in that of intellectual life. This is the century of transition from the Greco-Roman civilization to that of the new Christian era. Thus, we have reached an age of culmination and commencement. For the historian of psychology this period marks the definitive triumph of spirit; henceforth reflective thinking operates entirely with transnatural categories.

The triumph of spirit is followed by a complete dissipation of scientific work in favor of an intense preoccupation with the affairs of the transnatural world. Science leaves the scene of Western Europe and but for the harbor to be afforded by the culture of the Arab Empire, it would face almost total extinction. This age, which we call Augustinian to permit convenient description and to salute an effective spokesman, is characterized above all by its tendency to depreciate the world in which people live and work. As the writings of St. Augustine clearly show, the people of this age not only insist upon setting over against nature a superior spiritual domain, but wish to transform nature itself into spirit. For them the supernatural absorbs the natural, and what was for their predecessors the domain of the ultimate good has become the complete universe. What had previously been created as the ideal and the goal of life has now become the essence of everything. As we shall see, the primary means for achieving this transformation is by concretizing the deity, who in earlier days was constructed as a very remote and detached entity.

So far as the science of psychology is concerned, the Augustinian period inaugurated a tremendous paradox which has had its repercussions throughout the psychological tradition. St. Augustine has been influential in separating psychology from the rest of the natural sciences and making it into a system of verbal institutions which still dominates the psychological tradition. The Bishop of Hippo labored mightily to build constructs that completely transform the behavior of human and other organisms into nebulous psychic processes that cannot even be considered analogies of behavioral adjustments.

As in previous periods, we will do well to consider the matrix underlying the cultural events in order to understand better the changes that are taking place in psychology and the other sciences. When we take account of the geographic and ethnic aspects of the history of the fifth century, we find a tremendous enlargement of European civilization. We are no longer confined principally to the countries bordering on the Mediterranean; the greater part of the European continent is now involved. It is now increasingly the turn of the numerous Germanic and Celtic tribes to exert as great an influence upon the civilization of the Greco-Roman world as the latter had first exerted upon them. An authentic universality influenced the development of the religion, law, and social organization of European cultures.

From the political standpoint the outstanding event is the complete collapse of the Roman Empire and its replacement by the Christian commonwealth. The universal and powerful "Republic" which the revered Augustus had hoped to restore for the ages, changed its character, endured innumerable vicissitudes, and in the fifth century became completely eclipsed. Concomitant with this inglorious liquidation of the political structure was the decay or destruction of the established institutions in the domains of economics, science, philosophy, and pagan religion. Civilization in all its phases appears to be tottering on the brink of annihilation, the grandeur of Rome to be extinguished. But all this, of course, means only change. Eternal Rome could only become permanent by metamorphosing into the more radiant Kingdom of God in which a poignant dichotomy separated actual human living from the presumed eternal life. This dichotomy signifies nothing less than a new intellectual order. In this period arises a new sophistication, a new way of looking at the world and the people in it. A full-fledged spiritual world is perfected, giving a new character to man and his earthly home, and, most important of all, establishing a revolutionary attitude toward his destiny.

On the intellectual level the great change taking place in European culture may be summed up as the complete domination of all branches of human behavior by the Christian religion. *Knowledge* of nature as exemplified by the sciences is replaced by the *wisdom* of intuitive revelation concerning God and spirit. In conjunction with the doctrine of salvation through Christ, the Christian religion exhorts men "to transfer their affections from earth to heaven, from sense to spirit, from time to eternity."[1] This religion, which contrasts so strikingly with the formal and ritualistic religion espoused by the Greeks and Romans, Augustine characterizes in his treatise, *On the True Religion* as follows:

> To turn away from earthly things towards the one true God . . . to despise this world of sense and to submit the soul to God to be cleansed by virtue . . . to run in response to the call from the desire of temporal and passing goods to the hope of eternal life and to the good things of the spiritual world.[2]

Yet these novelties of life, these transformations of society and its conditions, do not really shatter the continuity of European civilization, for they are only the culmination of developments that have been in process for centuries, ever since the circumstances of the Hellenistic period caused a break with the culture of classical or Hellenic antiquity. But there is an even deeper continuity connecting the Augustinian and Patristic periods. It is this. Not only does the Augustinian doctrine derive from Neoplatonism and, eventually, from Philo and the earliest Christian Fathers, but, like them, it looks forward to the future. And this future, according to its formulators, is not merely a temporal continuation of earthly affairs but a leap into eternity.

ST. AUGUSTINE: SPOKESMAN OF THE NEW AGE

In a most admirable way St. Augustine (354-430) speaks for the new age. In the first place, he is an eyewitness of and a participant in the great transition in which the vauntedly eternal Rome gives way to the new City of God. He is of African origin and residence, a man who participated in a number of philsophical movements and religious sects of the great empire before finally achieving what he believed to be the true and lasting illumination. As the son of a pagan father and a Christian mother, he was not completely immured in a single set of traditions. To the anguish of his mother, Monica, he allowed himself to go astray toward the pagan classics, then toward the Manichaeans, and only in his thirty-third year was he redeemed by baptism to her profound joy.

In a second way, in his attitude toward science, Augustine mirrors the circumstances of his day. He was not a learned man with a sense of responsibility to a stable and definite culture, such as, in fact, no longer existed. He belonged to that group of early Christians who

[1] See Burnaby, *Amor Dei,* p. 25.
[2] *De Vera Religione,* Ch. 6 (quoted from Burnaby, *loc cit.*).

were sure that the less they were debauched by worldly learning, the more capable they were of entering mystically into the inner sanctum of religious comprehension. Without interest in nature and science and working only as a teacher of rhetoric, Augustine sustained no commitments to the descriptive laws of nature as formulated by science and was thus free to create a new world in line with the character of the true God, and to formulate a new set of institutions to answer to the needs of men in their daily anxieties and struggles amid a turbulent world.

If Plotinus and his philosophy well represent the crumbling fabric of the society of his day, all the more does Augustine mirror the complete breakup of what was still left of imperial Roman society and culture. Whereas in Plotinus we still have recollections of what was once a flourishing science, in Augustine we have efforts to marshal good reasons for despising all that the pagans wrought and cherished in the scientific domain. Augustine harps interminably on the theme that in every respect there must be a renunciation of the older civilization—intellectual, practical, and personal. Away with all the old beliefs and occupations of the pagan world. Although there have been many attacks on pagan science, none has excelled Augustine's in exaggerating its unworthiness by comparison with the true light of internal illumination. Augustine asserts that nothing is of interest to a Christian except God, who is everything and who is the author and creator of everything.

All this is reflected in St. Augustine's classic work, *De Civitate Dei.* In this book he argues that it is not true that Christiantiy, with its emphasis upon the Kingdom of God, has been responsible for the destruction of secular Rome. No, the seeds of Rome's destruction lie in the worldly principles of its organization and qualities. No state, no community can long endure which is founded only upon the values arising in the activities of men and their contacts with each other. The true bases of human institutions, whether political, economic, religious, or moral, are faith in God and the achievement of sanctity and identification with the supernatural. It is a fundamental assumption of the *De Civitate Dei* that religion, with its roots in the eternal and spiritual, is not just one of the components of civilization but the basic support, perennial and indispensable, upon which all others must rest.

This extreme emphasis on religion is of high significance in the context of the new societal order represented by Augustine. Since the religion in question is a new type conflicting sharply with the official

Plate V. Saint Augustine, see p. XV.

religion of the Roman Empire, Augustine is espousing nothing short of the overturning of the pillars of Roman conventions and institutions. This audaciousness bespeaks a deep faith in personal experiences and autistically selected beliefs. The emphasis on personal experience corresponds exactly with Augustine's private life. Not only was he the child of a mixed marriage, but he had led a sinful life of idleness, willfulness, and debauchery on his way to the bishopric which he occupied in so saintly a manner during the latter half of his life in Hippo.

PERSONALISM AND INWARDNESS

It appears to be the consensus of scholarly opinion that St. Augustine formulated his basic attitudes closely after Neoplatonic doctrines. Plotinus doubtless has been an agent in the transmission of mystical and spiritual constructions to Augustine and his successors. It is, however, clearly evident that Augustine has completely inverted the Plotinian doctrines. Whereas Plotinus attempted to exteriorize the soul as a spiritual entity, Augustine tends to interiorize the great ocean of spirit. Obviously, he is humanizing the cosmos. Augustine is the great apostle of egoism, and thus interiorizes and personalizes the universe. The human soul or mind is so great in compass that it really contains the universe, and, though Augustine does not say so, it contains also the creator and the governor of that universe. All that he dares indicate is that his mind or memory, that vast storehouse which itself is nowhere, contains the image of God as of all things else.[3] How great is this power of mind or memory Augustine indicates when he implies that by the study of himself he can dispense with the study of things.

> Great is this force of memory, excessive great, O my God; a large and an infinite roominess: who can plummet the bottom of it? Yet is this a faculty of mine, and belongs unto my nature: nor can I myself comprehend all that I am. Therefore is the mind too strait to contain itself: so where could that be which cannot contain itself? Is it without itself and not within? How then doth it not contain itself? A wonderful admiration surprises me, and an astonishment seizes me upon this. And men go abroad to wonder at the heights of mountains, the lofty billows of the sea, the long courses of rivers, the vast compass of the ocean, and the circular motions of the stars, and yet pass themselves by, nor wonder that while I spake of all these things I did not then see them with mine eyes; yet could I not have spoken of them, unless those mountains, and billows, and rivers, and stars which I have seen, and that ocean which I believed to be, I saw inwardly in my memory, yea, with such vast spaces between, as if I verily saw them abroad.

[3] *Confessiones* x, Chs. 25 and 26.

Yet did I not absorb them into me by seeing, when as with mine eyes I beheld them. Nor are the things themselves now within me, but the images of them only. And I distinctly know by what sense of the body each of these took impression in me.[4]

Inasmuch as we are tracing out the evolution of psychological institutions, it is well to be reminded once more that what is happening here is the establishment of many of the basic doctrines of psychology. Chief among them, of course, is the postulate of the primacy of the person, the assumption that there is something unique about the human organism, that it is the thing which has in it a principle or a power that differentiates it from other things. The inner being knows other things, retains that knowledge of other things, including God, and directs the organism in every possible way.

As is evident, these ways of thinking, which have historically become crystallized as doctrines of soul, mind, consciousness, and thought, arose as constructions in answer to the needs of the time. The soul, the inner powers, and their properties extending even as far as immortality were certainly developed in the interest of personal salvation, for the purpose of easing the tensions and the terrors of earthly existence. It is these inner processes that have become explanatory principles for acts of knowing, feeling, and willing.

The scaffolding which Augustine uses for building his tower of inwardness is the Delphic injunction *Gnothi seaton.* He makes this injunction into a slogan which proclaims the reflection by the mind upon itself. Actually, for Augustine, this is an inevitable process which worldly needs enjoin, but the injunction encourages the appreciation of the invariable presence and ultimate essentiality of the soul. The inescapability and the omniscience of the soul are, of course, the basis for the certainty of faith and for the knowledge based on faith. These are merely processes of the soul revealing itself to itself.

THE HUMANISTIC THEOLOGY OF ST. AUGUSTINE

So thoroughly representative of our culture is Augustine that scholars interpret his writings as though they were completely in accord with modern conventions and immune to critical reading. This is especially clear in the case of Augustinian theology. Commentators upon St. Augustine accept the view of him as a humble and simple soul kneeling before the omniscient and omnipresent God. But a more critical reading of Augustine reveals a different attitude.

The intense intimacy with which Augustine reacts to God gives his

[4] *Ibid.,* x, Ch. 8.

theology a distinct humanistic cast. True enough, God is the creator of man as well as of heaven and earth. but God is in man as much as man is in God. This is well expressed in the second chapter of the *Confessiones.*

And how shall I call upon my God, my Lord and God? because that when I invoke him, I call him into myself: and what place is there in me fit for my God to come into me by, whither God may come into me; even that God which made heaven and earth? Is it so, my Lord God? Is there anything in me which can contain thee? Nay, can both heaven and earth which thou hast made, and in which thou hast made me, in any wise contain thee? Or else because whatsoever is, could not subsist without thee, must it follow thereupon, that whatsoever hath being, is endued with a capacity of thee? Since therefore I also am, how do I entreat thee to come into me, who could not be, unless thou were first in me? For I am not after all in hell, and yet thou art there: For if I go down into hell, thou art there also. I should therefore not be, O God, yea I should have no being at all, unless thou wert in me: or rather, I should not be, unless I had my being in thee; of whom and through whom, and to whom are all things. Even so it is, Lord, even so. Wherefore, then, do I invoke thee, seeing I am already in thee? Or whence canst thou come into me? For whither shall I go, beyond heaven and earth, that from thence my God may come into me? who hath said, The heaven and earth do I fill.[5]

The God of Augustine obviously is a definite person full of human traits though in exaggerated forms. Despite all of Augustine's professions of humility and self-abnegation in the presence of the Lord, it is clear that there is an extreme arrogance displayed in his knowledge and mastery of God and his ways. Augustine's God is a god of the people with whom all can easily intercommunicate and transact affairs. Indeed, Augustine makes God out to be so effective an agent in smoothing man's way through the mazes of petty circumstances that the argument is overdone and prevents God from executing the great service of saving people from the ravages and the chaos following the destruction of the state.

In the end, however, Augustinian theology with its informality and descriptions remote from the things described typifies the general intellectual characteristic of the time, that of creating the creator as well as the universe and all that it contains. The dwelling place of truth and all being is in the interior of man; they live in the placeless place of the soul. And if the words "God," "Lord," are invoked, there is no denying that they represent something willfuly and verbally created by the man who uses them.

[5] i, 2.

AUGUSTINIAN PHILOSOPHY

Concerning St. Augustine Labriolle asserts,

> He was the most philosophic of the Fathers of the Primitive Church. We will say more: among the Latin Fathers he is the only one who really possesses speculative genius and the gifts of a close thinker.[6]

Still, before considering the nature of Augustinian philosophy, we must face the question as to whether St. Augustine was a philosopher at all. It must be granted at once that whatever philosophy Augustine exhibits is entirely an informal affair. In other words, Augustine stands at the opposite pole from Plotinus or Plato, whom he mentions so often. Unlike these philosophers, he has no organized system of attitudes representing the results of his reflections. Nevertheless, one can collect from the Augustinian writings some vigorously-expressed general attitudes; these are, however, large-scale borrowings from Plotinus, other Neoplatonists, and converted Stoics. There is no original Augustinian *Weltanschauung*.

Augustine's philosophy is aptly characterized as basically mystic and escapist. His philosophical attitudes did not concern the actual processes of nature, of social and political happenings, or of the means for obtaining knowledge of authentic events. On the contrary, Augustinian philosophy represented a blind acceptance of mystic postulates fashioned to achieve personal salvation and a transcendental refuge from the obvious evils of the day. What can be the method of such a philosophy? Nothing other than verbal dialectic. Having accepted the popular assumption that there is a Christian truth and that there can be no other, Augustine knows the answers to all questions and problems in advance. Even his famous *doubt* method is spurious, as he is utterly committed to the doctrine of *Crede ut intellegam.* After all, there is an internal light which supplies not only all knowledge but the uttermost cognition, which he calls wisdom.

Whether we regard Augustinian thinking as religious or grant it philosophic status, it is in the extremest sense authoritarian and absolute. Everything is unrolled from inner consciousness, and since this and this only can be the final authority, it is easy to attain absolute truth and certainty. In the final analysis, the soul of man is a true image of God. This inerrant dialectic or form of argument is excellently exhibited in the following excerpt from the *Trinity*

> But apart from the mind's dependence on the senses how few things remain which we know as surely as we know that we are alive? There at least

[6] *History and Literature of Christianity from Tertullian to Boethius,* p. 421.

we need not fear to be deceived by the plausibility of appearance, since it is certain that he who is deceived is alive; and this assurance does not come to us in the way of impressions from the outer world: in it there can be no optical illusion, as when the oar in water appears as broken, towers on the land seem to men on shipboard to be in motion, and in so many other cases of difference between appearance and reality. Here it is not the eye of flesh whereby we see: we know that we are alive by an interior knowledge, which cannot be touched by the suggestion of the Academic that we may be asleep without knowing it, and dream that we see. We all know that things seen by the dreamer are much like those seen by the waking man. But certainty in the knowledge of living leads a man to say, not "I know that I am awake," but "I know that I am alive": whether asleep or awake, he is living. In that knowledge he cannot be deceived by dreams; for it takes a living man both to sleep and to dream. Nor can the Academic dispute that knowledge by saying, "You may perhaps be mad without knowing it, for there is little difference between the impressions of madness and those of sanity." The madman must be alive; and the reply to the Academic is not "I know that I am not mad," but "I know that I am alive." Thus the claim to know that one is alive can never be convicted of illusion or falsity. Any number of deceptive impressions of all kinds may be urged against it; but he who makes the claim will remain entirely unmoved, since no man can be deceived who is not alive.[7]

The informal and discursive nature of Augustine's philosophy is also well demonstrated by his discussion of time. Of course, time for him becomes of speculative interest in connection with God's actions in creating and regulating the world. Typical of Augustinian informality and superficiality is his concern with such a question as to what God's work was before he created the world and what indeterminately determined him to create it just when he did.[8] When he made the famous comment,

What, then is time? If no one asks me, I know what it is. If I wish to explain it to him who asks me, I do not know. Yet I say with confidence that I know that if nothing passed away, there would be no past time; and if nothing were still coming, there would be no future time; and if there were nothing at all, there would be no present time.[9]

he was referring precisely to his utter reliance upon intuitive procedures to treat complex problems, though he could not altogether conceal the intrusion of events when such problems are under consideration.

As the pace-setter for the entire succeeding line of Western philoso-

[7] *De Trinitate* xv, Ch. 12, 21 (Burnaby tr.).

[8] *Confessiones* xi, Ch. 12.

[9] *Ibid.*, xi, 14. (modified quotation from E. B. Pusey translation, "Everyman's Library," London, J. M. Dent, reprinted 1949, p. 262).

phers, Augustine may be said to have initiated the so-called empirical and phenomenological method of philosophizing. Not only the certainty of knowledge but also the essentiality of things are drawn out of the inexhaustible source of the inner mind or soul. Such is the crowning glory of a philosophical system which is designed to shield one from the distressing rigors of things and events with which one finds it difficult to cope.

When we return to the question of whether Augustine was a genuine member of the philosophical fraternity, we now have a convincing answer. Religious philosophy is indeed one method of creating a universal system. And one who fashions the reflective methods for ages to come cannot be excluded from the communion of the philosophical elect.

AUGUSTINIAN ANTHROPOLOGY

Augustine's views concerning man and his nature are completely determined by his mystical and theological interests. From man as an individual and as a member of a social community, Augustine retreats, even as he does from the mountains and the sea as features of nature. But man, after all, is not merely a natural being, since he possesses an immortal soul. Accordingly, anthropological problems take on a considerable interest for him.

Now since St. Augustine was exclusively and completely committed to the view that the soul, as the image of God, is the most important feature of man, he greatly reduced the body and the flesh in value and significance. Though he obviously could not allow his spiritualistic convictions to carry him to the extreme of ignoring the body, he did denigrate it as much as possible. From a practical standpoint the body is vile and temporary by contrast with the radiant and immortal soul. More theoretically viewed, the body is spatially located and inevitably subject to the spatial dimensions of height, breadth, and thickness. Movement and change too are essential attributes of body. By contrast, the soul, which is akin to the utter spirituality of God, is in no sense subject to change, movement, corruption, or dissolution. Among the singular arguments for the soul's immortality is that it harbors truth, which is immortal.

> If science exists anywhere, and if it can exist only in the realm of that which lives and always is, and if anything, in which something else dwells forever, must itself always be, then that must live forever in which science exists.
>
> If we who reason exist, that is, if our mind does, and if correct reasoning

without science is impossible—and only a mind in which science does not exist can be without science—then science exists in the mind of man.

Moreover, science is somewhere, for it exists, and whatever exists cannot be nowhere. Again, science can exist only in that which lives. For nothing that does not live learns anything, and science cannot possibly exist in something that does not learn.

Again, science exists always. For whatever exists and is immutable must necessarily exist always. On the other hand nobody denies that science exists. And whoever asserts that only the straight line drawn through the center of a circle is longer than any other line not drawn through the center, and that this statement belongs in the realm of science, as much as admits that there is an immutable science.

Also, nothing in which something else exists always, cannot be but always. Nothing, however, that always is ever suffers the loss from itself of that in which it always exists.

And, when we reason, it is an act of our mind; for only that reason which understands can reason. Neither the body understands, nor the mind, aided by the body, understands, because, when the mind wishes to understand, it is turned away from the body. That which is understood is so always; nothing, however, pertaining to the body is so always. Truly, the body is not able to be of aid to the soul in its striving toward understanding, since it cannot even be of hindrance.

Moreover, no one reasons correctly without science. Correct reasoning, of course, is the cogitation [the way of thinking] that advances, to the investigation of things not certain, from principles that are certain; nothing is certain in the mind of which it has no knowledge.

But, all that the mind knows it possesses within itself; knowledge does not encompass anything except those things that pertain to some branch of science. For, science is the knowledge of all things. The human mind, therefore, lives always.[10]

Despite Augustine's antipathy toward science and the objective study of nature, he scatters through his writings beliefs about man and his actions which he absorbed from his reading and from his general cultural atmosphere. Naturally, these beliefs do not always harmonize. For example, the soul he regards as not localized in any particular part of the body but located everywhere, though it is not extendable. Again, as Pagel[11] points out, St. Augustine holds two incompatible views about strict localization. On the one hand, he follows the suggestion laid down by Nemesius of Emesa in his book, *A Treatise on the Nature of Man,* that the faculties of the soul are localized in the ventricles, though he diverges from Nemesius in some details, as indicated in the following comparison.

[10] *The Immortality of the Soul,* Ch. 1.

[11] "Medieval and Renaissance Contributions to Knowledge of the Brain and its Functions," *The History and Philosophy of Knowledge of the Brain and its Functions* (Poynter, ed.), p. 100 *f.*

TABLE VI. COMPARISON OF THE VENTRICULAR BRAIN LOCALIZATIONS OF NEMESIUS AND AUGUSTINE

Brain Ventricle	*Nemesius*	*Augustine*
Anterior	Sensory Processes	Sensory Processes
Middle	Cogitation and Reason	Remembering
Posterior	Remembering	Motion

On the other hand, Augustine also localizes psychological functions in the substance of the brain and not in the ventricles. The front part of the brain he makes responsible for imagination and phantasy, the middle part he connects with rational functions, while the posterior part is made to subserve memory functions. Despite such vacillations, scholars who accept the brain doctrine must find it laudable of Augustine, who is so immured in his religious and mystical transnaturism, to adopt notions of brain action at all.

Although, as we shall see, Augustine stresses man's freedom of action, his ultimate destiny is predetermined in every detail. Moreover, the greater part of the human race is predestined to end in Hell. Only a few individuals selected to enjoy the free blessing of divine grace are to be spared. In general, man's environment, according to Augustine, is full of transnatural beings—angels, devils, good or bad spirits—carrying on their activities in the service of God or of lesser masters.

AUGUSTINE'S THEOLOGICAL PSYCHOLOGY

Two well-defined characteristics mark Augustine's writings on psychological topics as theological. In the first place, his copious works have no place for a technical consideration of psychological or indeed of any type of scientific event. In the second place, and in close relation with the first, all that Augustine has to say about psychological happenings is rooted in his religious thinking. Anything of a psychological nature belongs to the realm of mystic being and is interesting only from a theological standpoint. As a matter of fact, Augustinian "psychology" is developed as an illustration or an analogy of trinitarian unity in the purely theological domain. Obviously what we have just said derives its validity from an acceptance of scientific postulates. The case stands otherwise with those philosophers and psychologists who follow in the spiritualistic tradition which Augustine did so much to establish. Consider Windelband, who writes of Augustine:

The soul is for him—and by this he rises far above Aristotle, and also above the Neo-Platonists—the living whole of *personality,* whose life is a unity, and which, by its self-consciousness, is certain of its own reality as the surest truth.[12]

Again, Dessoir in his *History of Psychology* writes:

He viewed the relation of the soul to the body as of secondary importance, but compassed instead the entire field of the purely psychical, and thus indicated for the first time the possibility of psychology as an independent science.[13]

The same writer says,

The soul was now elevated to the principle of knowledge, not only for psychology, but for science in general. And with this a new period began.[14]

Similar applause for the spiritistic aspects of Augustine's thought appears in the following:

. . . he stands with the greatest, with Plato and with Aristotle, and in one respect is superior to them. Psychology reaches a second great climax when its expositor can say that the foundation of the soul is continuous self-consciousness and thought is simply life reflected into itself.[15]

Although Augustine can in no sense qualify as a psychologist, we can distinguish in his writings references to psychological events which contrast with his persistent arguments about the immortality, the origin, and the powers of the soul.[16] These references Augustine uses to establish his anti-Arian ideas concerning the trinity of persons in the godhead. By examining these points in Augustine's own words we learn precisely what are the bishop's qualifications to be the philosophical and theological instructor of the entire Middle Ages, and the arbiter of modern psychology as well.

THE NATURE OF SOUL OR MIND. As a Neoplatonic spiritualist, Augustine regards the Soul or Mind as a simple, self-contained, incorporeal substance. Unlike matter, which has length, breadth, height, and spatial position and which is known by revelation, soul is spaceless and known only by inner awareness or introspection. While soul is all-pervasive, it is indivisible. The activity of introspection is following out the precept of "Know thyself," "For what is so much in the mind as mind itself?"[17]

[12] *A History of Philosophy,* p. 278.
[13] *Outlines of the History of Psychology,* p. 46.
[14] *Ibid.,* p. 4.
[15] Brett, *A History of Psychology,* Vol. I, p. 348.
[16] *The Immortality of the Soul, The Magnitude of the Soul, A Treatise on the Soul and its Origin.*
[17] *De Trinitate* x, Ch. 8, 11.

MIND AN IMAGE OF THE TRINITY. For Augustine, as for other Church Fathers, the soul is the cosmos or God writ small, or a microcosm. In the case of the mind or soul, the triune phases are memory, intelligence or understanding, and will. In the following long excerpt from *On the Trinity,* we observe the inwardness and the unity of the triune soul:

13. Let it not then add anything to that which it knows itself to be, when it is bidden to know itself. For it knows, at any rate, that this is said to itself; namely, to itself, that is, and that lives, and that understands. But a dead body also is, and cattle live; but neither a dead body nor cattle understand. Therefore it so knows that it so is, and that it so lives, as an understanding is and lives. When, therefore, for example's sake, the mind thinks itself air, it thinks that air understands; it knows, however, that itself understands, but it does not know itself to be air, but only thinks so. Let it separate that which it thinks itself; let it discern that which it knows; let this remain to it, about which not even have they doubted who have thought the mind to be this corporeal thing or that. For certainly every mind does not consider itself to be air; but some think themselves fire, others the brain, and some one kind of corporeal thing, others another, as I have mentioned before; yet all know that they themselves understand and are, and live; but they refer understanding to that which they understand, but to be, and to live, to themselves. And no one doubts, either that no one understands who does not live, or that no one lives of whom it is not true that he is; and that therefore by consequence that which understands both is and lives; not as a dead body is which does not live, nor as a soul lives which does not understand, but in some proper and more excellent manner. Further, they know that they will, and they equally know that no one can will who is not and who does not live; and they also refer that will itself to something which they will with that will. They know also that they remember; and they know at the same time that nobody could remember, unless he both was and lived; but we refer memory itself also to something, in that we remember those things. Therefore, the knowledge and science of many things are contained in two of these three, memory and understanding; but will must be present, that we may enjoy or use them. For we enjoy things known, in which things themselves the will finds delight for their own sake, and so reposes; but we use those things, which we refer to some other thing which we are to enjoy. Neither is the life of man vicious and culpable in any other way, than as wrongly using and wrongly enjoying. But it is no place here to discuss this.

14. But since we treat of the nature of the mind, let us remove from our consideration all knowledge which is received from without, through the senses of the body; and attend more carefully to the position which we have laid down, that all minds know and are certain concerning themselves. For men certainly have doubted whether the power of living, of remembering, of understanding, of willing, of thinking, of knowing, of judging, be of air, or of fire, or of the brain, or of the blood, or of atoms, or besides the usual four elements of a fifth kind of body, I know not what; or whether the

combining or tempering together of this our flesh itself has power to accomplish these things. And one has attempted to establish this, and another to establish that. Yet who ever doubts that he himself lives, and remembers, and understands, and wills, and thinks, and knows, and judges? Seeing that even if he doubts, he lives; if he doubts, he remembers why he doubts; if he doubts, he understands that he doubts; if he doubts, he wishes to be certain; if he doubts, he thinks; if he doubts, he knows that he does not know; if he doubts, he judges that he ought not to assent rashly. Whosoever therefore doubts about anything else, ought not to doubt of all these things; which if they were not, he would not be able to doubt of anything.

15. They who think the mind to be either a body or the combination or tempering of the body, will have all these things to seem to be in a subject, so that the substance is air, or fire, or some other corporeal thing, which they think to be the mind; but that the understanding is in this corporeal thing as its quality, so that this corporeal thing is the subject, but the understanding is in the subject, viz., that the mind is the subject, which they rule to be a corporeal thing, but the understanding, or any of those things which we have mentioned as certain to us, is in that subject. They also hold nearly the same opinion who deny the mind itself to be body, but think it to be the combination or tempering together of the body; for there is this difference, that the former say that the mind itself is the substance, in which the understanding is, as in a subject; but the latter say that the mind itself is in a subject, viz., in the body, of which it is the combination or tempering together. And hence, by consequence, what else can they think, except that the understanding also is in the same body as in a subject?

16. And all these do not perceive that the mind knows itself, even when it seeks for itself, as we have already shown. But nothing is at all rightly said to be known while its substance is not known. And therefore, when the mind knows itself, it knows its own substance; and when it is certain about itself, it is certain about its own substance. But it is certain about itself, as those things which are said above prove convincingly; although it is not at all certain whether itself is air, or fire, or some body, or some function of body. Therefore it is not any of these. And that whole which is bidden to know itself, belongs to this, that it is certain that it is not any of those things of which it is uncertain, and is certain that it is that only, which only it is certain that it is. For it thinks in this way of fire, or air, and whatever else of the body it thinks of. Neither can it in any way be brought to pass that it should so think that which itself is, as it thinks that which itself is not. Since it thinks all these things through an imaginary phantasy, whether fire, or air, or this or that body, or that part or combination and tempering together of the body: nor assuredly is it said to be all those things, but some one of them. But if it were any one of them, it would think this one in a different manner from the rest, viz., not through an imaginary phantasy, as absent things are thought, which either themselves or some of like kind have been touched by the bodily sense; but by some inward, not feigned, but true presence (for nothing is more present to it than itself); just as it thinks that itself lives, and remembers, and understands, and wills. For it knows these things in itself, and does not imagine them as though it had touched them

by the sense outside itself, as corporeal things are touched. And if it attaches nothing to itself from the thought of these things, so as to think itself to be something of the kind, then whatsoever remains to it from itself, that alone is itself.[18]

Because of Augustine's tremendous emphasis on the singleness and individuality of spirit, he is not perturbed by the obvious multiplicity of the psychic manifestations of man's soul or mind. This unity in multiplicity, he insists, is clear not only in the division of the inner man, with his intelligence or understanding, from the outer man, with his bodily senses, but also in the variety of processes occurring in both parts. In the following excerpts Augustine presents his arguments for the unity in a trinity. First is one dealing with the trinity of the inner soul:

And now, setting aside for the moment the other activities which the mind is sure of its possessing, let us take for particular consideration these three: memory, understanding, will. On these three points we are accustomed to examine the capacities of children, to find what talents they display. The more tenacious and ready is a boy's memory, the more acute his understanding, the more eager his will to learn, so much the more praiseworthy do we count his disposition. When, however, it is a question of the learning of any individual, we enquire, not how much strength and readiness of memory or sharpness of understanding he possesses, but *what* he remembers and *what* he understands. And seeing that a person is judged praiseworthy not only according to his learning but also according to his goodness, we take note not only of what he remembers and understands but of what he wills: not simply of the eagerness of his will, but first of what he wills and then of how much he wills it. For a person who loves intensely only merits praise when he loves what ought to be loved intensely. In the three fields of disposition, learning, and practice or use, the test of the first depends upon the individual's capacity in respect of memory, understanding and will; the test of the second, upon the content of his memory and understanding, and the point to which an eager will has brought him. But the third, use, belongs entirely to the will as it deals with the content of memory and understanding, whether as means relative to a particular end, or as an end in which it may rest satisfied. To use, is to take a thing up into the disposal of the will; whereas to enjoy is to use with a satisfaction that is not anticipated but actual. Thus all enjoyment is a kind of use, since it takes up something into the disposal of the will for final delectation; but not all use is enjoyment, if what is taken up into the disposal of the will has been sought after not for its own sake but as a means to something else.

Now this triad of memory, understanding, and will are not three lives, but one; nor three minds, but one. It follows that they are not three substances, but one substance. Memory, regarded as life, mind, or substance, is an absolute term: regarded as memory, it is relative. The same may be said

[18] *Ibid.*, x, Ch. 10, 13-16 (Haddan and Shedd trs.).

of understanding and of will; for both terms can be used relatively. But life, mind, essence, are always things existing absolutely in themselves. Therefore the three activities named are one, inasmuch as they constitute one life, one mind, one essence, and whatever else can be predicated of each singly in itself, is predicated of them all together in the singular and not in the plural. But they are three inasmuch as they are related to one another; and if they were not equal, not only each to each but each to all, they could not cover or take in one another as they do. For in fact they are covered, not only each by each but all by each. I remember that I possess memory and understanding and will: I understand that I understand and will and remember: I will my own willing and remembering and understanding. And I remember at the same time the whole of my memory and understanding and will. Whatever I do not remember as part of my memory, is not in my memory; and nothing can be more fully in my memory than the memory itself. Therefore I remember the whole of it. Again, whatever I understand, I know that I understand, and I know that I will whatever I will; but whatever I know, I remember. Therefore I remember the whole of my understanding and the whole of my will. Similarly, when I understand these three, I understand all three in whole. For there is nothing open to understanding that I do not understand except that of which I am ignorant; and that of which I am ignorant I neither remember nor will. It follows that anything open to understanding that I do not understand, I neither remember nor will, whereas anything open to understanding that I remember and will, I understand. Finally, when I use the whole content of my understanding and memory, my will covers the whole of my understanding and the whole of my memory. Therefore, since all are covered by one another singly and as wholes, the whole of each is equal to the whole of each, and the whole of each to the whole of all together. And these three constitute one thing, one life, one mind, one essence.[19]

When Augustine turns to the outer man or outer soul, he plans his demonstration of the trinity by choosing sight from the fivefold bodily senses and showing its triune character of visible thing, vision, and attention. But we must allow Augustine to speak for himself.

When, then, we see any corporeal object, these three things, as is most easy to do, are to be considered and distinguished: First, the object itself which we see; whether a stone, or flame, or any other thing that can be seen by the eyes; and this certainly might exist also already before it was seen; next, vision or the act of seeing, which did not exist before we perceived the object itself which is presented to the sense; in the third place, that which keeps the sense of the eye in the object seen, so long as it is seen, *viz.*, the attention of the mind. In these three, then, not only is there an evident distinction, but also a diverse nature. For, first, that visible body is of a far different nature from the sense of the eyes, through the incidence of which sense upon it vision arises. And what plainly is vision itself other than perception informed by that thing which is perceived? Although there

[19] *Ibid.*, x, Ch. 11, 17-18 (Burnaby tr.).

is no vision if the visible object be withdrawn, nor could there be any vision of the kind at all if there were no body that could be seen; yet the body by which the sense of the eyes is informed, when that body is seen, and the form itself which is imprinted by it upon the sense, which is called vision, are by no means of the same substance. For the body that is seen is, in its own nature, separable; but the sense, which was already in the living subject, even before it saw what it was able to see, when it fell in with something visible, —or the vision which comes to be in the sense from the visible body when now brought into connection with it and seen,—the sense, then, I say, or the vision, that is, the sense informed from without, belongs to the nature of the living subject, which is altogether other than that body which we perceive by seeing, and by which the sense is not so formed as to be sense, but as to be vision. For unless the sense were also in us before the presentation to us of the sensible object, we should not differ from the blind, at times when we are seeing nothing, whether in darkness, or when our eyes are closed. But we differ from them in this, that there is in us, even when we are not seeing, that whereby we are able to see, which is called the sense; whereas this is not in them, nor are they called blind for any other reason than because they have it not. Further also, that attention of the mind which keeps the sense in that thing which we see, and connects both, not only differs from that visible thing in its nature; in that the one is mind, and the other body; but also from the sense and the vision itself: since this attention is the act of the mind alone; but the sense of the eyes is called a bodily sense, for no other reason than because the eyes themselves also are members of the body; and although an inanimate body does not perceive, yet the soul commingled with the body perceives through a corporeal instrument, and that instrument is called sense. And this sense, too, is cut off and extinguished by suffering on the part of the body, when any one is blinded; while the mind remains the same; and its attention, since the eyes are lost, has not, indeed, the sense of the body which it may join, by seeing, to the body without it, and so fix its look thereupon and see it, yet by the very effort shows that, although the bodily sense be taken away, itself can neither perish nor be diminished. For there remains unimpaired a desire [*appetitus*] of seeing, whether it can be carried into effect or not. These three, then, the body that is seen, and vision itself, and the attention of mind, which joins both together, are manifestly distinguishable, not only on account of the properties of each, but also on account of the difference of their natures.[20]

AUGUSTINIAN ELEMENTS IN MODERN PSYCHOLOGY

We have already made clear that not only is St. Augustine an excellent intellectual representative of his time but also a writer who has greatly influenced the thinking of later ages. What he constructed as the soul, self, and inner life became established as stable institutions

[20] *Ibid.*, xi, Ch. 2, 2 (Haddan and Shedd, trs.).

that were as powerful as they were long-enduring. Even though Augustine's formulations were direct consequences of the conditions of his day, they have been continuously maintained. The notions of inner life, of spirit, have become thoroughly ingrained in the cultural fabric of Western Europe. In the following paragraphs we indicate the particular forms in which the institutions established by Augustine and his immediate predecessors were transmitted to their successors in the psychological tradition.

Relation of Bodily Process and Sensation. While the general doctrine concerning the relation of body and mind was established long before Augustine's time, he refers to the problem of how specific bodily processes could be related to visual sensation. His belief so well expressed in the words,

> . . . sensation does not proceed from that body which is seen, but from the body of the living being that perceives, with which the soul is tempered together in some wonderful way of its own; yet vision is produced[21]

has passed down to our age with little modification of expression. To select only one sample from many others, here are the words of a modern biologist referring to pain sensations.

> Can we imagine how the passage of electrical impulses along certain nerve fibres to an end-station in the brain can result in a sensation of pain?[22]

The Doctrine of Immediate Experience. The establishment of spirit as a knowing process gave rise to the doctrine of immediate experience. This construct, though it is to a certain extent paralleled in some concrete activities of persons, came to represent happenings exclusively of or within the soul. What one discovered there was not only a deliverance or revelation but also a decided assurance of truthful testimony. In the moral sphere immediate experience crystallized as conscience —the inerrant source of the knowledge of right and wrong.

The Absolute Uniqueness of the Mental. Since the notions of soul and consciousness undoubtedly were derived from an interest in one's own person and its destiny, they became developed into the doctrine of absolute uniqueness and individuality. In modern times this doctrine has taken the form that one can only have knowledge of his own mind. The existence of minds in others and the nature of what goes on in those minds can only be matters of indirect inference. The famous and perennial argument that only the possessor of the aching tooth could

[21] *Ibid.*, xi, Ch. 2, 3 (Haddan and Shedd, trs.).
[22] Brain, *Mind, Perception and Science*, p. 66.

have direct experience or knowledge of the toothache is simply the product of the evolution of psychic doctrine. Those who accept the doctrine have always become influenced by the dogma of mind to overlook the fact that all events are unique. What *A* is digesting is not being digested by *B*. The fall of *A* is not the fall of *B*. Nor does the fact that neither *A* nor *B* can *see* what the other is digesting nor observe the fall of the other, unless both happen to be in a favorable situation, indicate that psychic stuff or principle is involved. Again, the subtlety of events lends no basis to their mentalization unless background institutions demand this. Privacy no more helps to establish transcendental mind than any of the other factors we have considered.

The Solipsistic Principle. A specialized doctrine derived from the belief in the utter privacy of the mental is the notion that in the final analysis knowledge is personal and private. In modern times the argument has been developed that because all knowledge is derived from personal mental experience, it is confined to a single mind and, in consequence, everything known is contained in the circle of a single consciousness or soul. In this manner, the world and all it contains are reduced to the mental states of particular persons.

Primacy and Uniqueness of Knowledge. From the time of Augustine, thinkers of the Western tradition have stressed and emphasized the uniqueness of the knowing process. Knowing has been taken out of the domain of adjustments or responses of individuals. Through the avenue of the psychic principle the act of knowing has become an attribute or process of soul. By establishing this primacy of spirit, which the great importance of will does not challenge, it was more or less inevitable for Augustine to anticipate Descartes and the modern philosophic tradition. Whatever one does psychically guarantees the existence of self, and this is an extension of the view that knowing is basic to existence altogether. Accordingly, certainty can arise from any psychic process, including doubting, erring, or other mental action. The doctrine that clear and distinct ideas are warrants of certainty and correctness springs from the same source.

The Introspective Principle. Following the establishment of the idea of the internal psychic there developed the introspective method or principle. How could one effectively enter into the inner domain of consciousness except by turning inward into one's own soul? Here is the authentic method of traditional mysticism. Instead of taking what account one can of one's own reactions or behavior with respect to things and persons, the flight is immediately made to the putative inward essence of oneself.

So persistent and weighty have the introspective ways of thinking remained throughout the history of psychology that even those wishing to combat spiritistic doctrines by developing materialism are still unable to dispense with the psychic. They merely increase the prominence and importance of the so-called material basis, but do not deny the presence or effectiveness of spirit.

In concluding our study of St. Augustine and his place in the history of psychology we should recall how closely the development of the powerful new psychological attitude of the fifth century fits in with the extinction of scientific psychology in the Alexandrian period. It is plain that the vigorous spiritistic psychology established to such a large extent by St. Augustine completes the destruction of all scientific approaches to the facts of human behavior. As we have often pointed out, this situation happens at the same time that science reaches a low estate in European culture. Science does not, however, become completely extinguished, but moves away towards the east, to return to Christian Europe only after a long absence.

SECTION EIGHT

ARAB TRANSFORMATION AND TRANSMISSION OF SCIENCE

CHAPTER 17

NEAR EASTERN CULTURE AND THE CAREER OF SCIENCE

SCIENCE MIGRATES EASTWARD

WITH THE DECLINE of Rome and the triumph of the Christian succession, the scientific aspects of Western culture became displaced toward a new, though more or less diffused, center in the East. When Rome fell victim to the Vandals of the North, the Eastern capital, Constantinople, assumed a greater prominence and the Byzantine Empire became the home of Greco-Roman civilization, including science. What the people of the Western Roman Empire accidentally lost or purposely rejected in favor of Christian doctrine was retained in Byzantium and its Egyptian and Syrian provinces, and in Persia.

The historical events that transpired in the Near East after the decline of Rome preserved that continuity without which modern science could not have been built upon the Greek heritage. Thus, they are of the utmost importance in our study of psychological history. Technical psychology, uncultivated since the Hellenistic period, resumed its course during and as a consequence of the rise of the Islamic state and culture. It is well, then to recount briefly the events which made it possible for Greek scientific institutions to be eventually reactivated in the West.

The importance of Arab culture lies in the fact that, unlike the Christians of the time, the Near Easterners conserved and then returned to the mainstream of European civilization the sciences, including psychology, developed in Hellenic and Hellenistic times. The reception and preservation of Greek science by Islamic culture is an enormously complicated affair. We may readily accept the conclusion that there were many specific routes by which science came to Arab culture. One, of course, must have been directly from Alexandria and another, again directly, from Byzantine and Syrian centers. Outstanding as receivers and preservers of Greek science, especially medicine, and the works of Aristotle, were the Nestorian Christians of southern Persia. At their primary center, the city of Gundi-Shapur, they labored mightily to translate Greek scientific writings into Syriac, which in the

East had become the great literary language in succession to Greek. More indirect routes by which science reached the Arabs passed through Bactria and India.[1]

Science is subject to and follows the fortunes of states. This is, of course, in no way surprising since science is one of the factors composing the culture complex of any sophisticated community. Wherever science is pursued there will always be interaction between it and other facets of the particular culture involved. To uncover these authentic, though often subtle interactions is usually a difficult task indeed. Often we have to content ourselves with broad and generalized mutual influences of science, technology, politics, and economics, as well as other phases of civilization. Questions are frequently easier to ask than to answer. Nevertheless, we find it profitable to speculate on the influence which the eastward migration of science has had upon the general course of scientific history. For example, to what extent did Islamic civilization assimilate Greek science? What transformations would the Arab conquerors have made in Greek science if Nestorian Christians had not previously composed their interpretations? Did the translation of Western scientific treatises into Arabic entail a special kind of interpretation, or did it simply reinforce the characteristics already imposed by Byzantine and Nestorian thinkers? These questions will appear very significant as we study the Arab influences on the development of science in general and psychology in particular.

From the standpoint of science, Arab culture may be characterized as primarily retentive and transmissive. What the Arabs acquired in the way of intellectual institutions from Hellenistic sources—science, Neoplatonic philosophy, Judaeo-Christian religion—they passed on to the peoples they conquered or traded with. The end result was the preservation of ancient science, albeit in a greatly modified form. Historians loudly and concertedly proclaim that Arab civilization lacked originality or creativity and was capable only of transmitting its borrowed intellectual goods to others. This is a short-sighted view when the intricacy and specificity of detail involved are considered. Into the Arab alembic were poured not only the science of the Greeks and their predecessors, but also the technologies of the Chinese, Persians, and Romans, while the religion of the Jews, Christians, and Persians provided the basis for a unique Islamic amalgam which later flowed into the stream of European science and speculation. It is not to be overlooked that cultural creation is a matter of combining and transform-

[1] For a comprehensive study of this problem see O'Leary, *How Greek Science Passed to the Arabs.*

ing available ingredients. So important are the transformations and transmissions of science effected by Arab culture that we must orient ourselves concerning the nature and scope of this civilization.

THE RISE AND EXPANSION OF ARAB CULTURE

Arab culture consists of that far-reaching system of activities and institutions which germinated on the periphery of the Byzantine and Sasanian states and grew to encompass Palestine, Syria, Mesopotamia, Persia, Turkestan, and the more easterly Punjab in Asia; Egypt and the rest of North Africa; Sicily, and most parts of Spain in Europe. What is customarily referred to as the Islamic or Arab civilization consists of a conglomerate of cultures made one by the relative unity of the Arab kingdoms and the dominance of the Islamic religion. It is the marvel of historians that the tribal society of the Arabian desert could more or less suddenly develop into a great world empire, which played its part in European history as the competitor and partial successor to the Christian Roman Empire. It may well be that the rapid expansion of the Islamic Caliphates testifies more to the weakness of the Byzantine, Roman, and Sasanian states than to the potency of the Caliphs. Nevertheless, conditions were ripe in the seventh century for the rise of an imperial system which ruled great territories and assimilated the economic and intellectual institutions of the conquered peoples. Arab culture was not only spread throughout a vast geographic area but was also thoroughly syncretistic. More than most cultures it was made up of innumerable nonhomogeneous traits and was common to a population with a wide variety of different ethnic backgrounds.

The accepted story concerning the origin of this great mixture of practical and doctrinal civilization centers around the activities of Mohammed and his family. Though Mohammed was reputed to be an ignorant and inexperienced person, he is credited with the ability to formulate comprehensive and bold ethical and religious ideas. Despite the polytheistic and idolatrous civilization from which he stemmed, he adopted the notion of a single, powerful, personal God. By reciting, since he could not write, stories of a future life, of the marvels and sensual delights of paradise where the faithful are rewarded, and of the concrete torments of hell where sinners would be punished on the impending day of retribution, he contributed to the composition and institution of the Koran. It became the nucleus of an extremely attractive religion, centering around the ideas of universal brotherhood, equality, and the utter submission to Allah, and a powerful instrument for far-flung military conquests and for the development of an enormous new Oriental civilization. Islamic religion was linked, too, with the Arabic language, which thereby became widespread and tremendously influential. But the Arabic language and the Islamic religion are only two outstanding marks of unity, only two nuclei around which the new Oriental culture rallies. Thus while the Arabic language was by far the dominant means by which the medieval culture of the Near East was held together and propagated, yet it must not be overlooked that the translation process is only carried on to satisfy the linguistic needs of a social group. We cannot forget the Syriac, the Hebrew, the Aramaic, the Greek, the Coptic, and the Latin originals. Similarly, while the dominant religion is Islamic, the minority religions never had lost their basic integrity. It is to be remembered that Oriental culture was universalistic and receptive.

From the standpoint of the sciences and learning, the Arabic language became the long-reigning successor of Greek and Latin. As history records, it was in translations from Arabic and other languages such as Syriac, Hebrew, and Persian, which existed in subordinate commensualism with Greek and Latin, that the science of Western Europe could succeed to and revive the learning of the classical world.

In effect, Arab culture is more assimilative than dominating. We question the usual interpretation of the slogan "either Islam or the sword" as implying only domination and subjection. Recall that the agglutinative attitude is already established by the preexisting pattern of the *Pax Romana.* Of course, the sword of conquest was an effective instrument and widely employed, but without a mollifying tolerance it could not have led to that free exchange of economic and cultural goods between diverse populations which actually occurred. In such an enormous system as the Islamic Empire, all things are included and allowed for. Medieval Islamic civilization is characteristically tribal and individualistic, with a sustained balance between the claims of power and influence on the one hand, and the toleration and hospitable reception of nonhomogeneous elements on the other. In the intellectual and scientific domains, it is impossible to exaggerate the intermixture of doctrines. Arab culture includes Hebraic, Greek, Persian, Indian, Egyptian, Syriac, Byzantine and Roman Christian elements.

With the Islamic conquests of Syria (636), Mesopotamia (637), and Egypt (639), there begins the great fermentation that brought into one vast complex the science and learning of the Greeks with their nucleus of Mesopotamian and Egyptian wisdom and lore, the knowledge of India and the technology of China, and the remains of Greek and Roman civilization as transmuted by pagan mystics and Christian theologians.

THE RANGE AND CHARACTER OF ARAB CULTURE

Despite the fact that Arab culture contains many different ethnic components, it still has its own unique characteristics. This applies to the arts and crafts as well as to general intellectual institutions and special scientific ones. An outstanding trait of Arab society is that, even more than the Hellenistic-Greek or Roman states, it is based on a commercial foundation. The original conquests are clearly enterprises of economic acquisition. There is an egress from a desert home to take over the wealth of securely-established urban centers.

Another outstanding characteristic to be expected in a trading and essentially acquisitive culture is ostentatious display. Even learning and science are cultivated as accomplishments, not as integral qualities of an investigative civilization. Scholars and their writings were collected as adornments and not as basic elements deeply rooted in a civilization complex.

Finally the Arab culture is relatively more intermixed than that of most societies dominated by a single ethnic unit. Trade and conquest favor accumulation of even the most heterogeneous elements. These intermixtures appear on various institutional levels. They may result in a synthesis or fusion of tribal organizations or administrative systems, or a mixture of science and superstition. This admixture of traits is also apparent in the fact that Arab culture is materialistic, on the one hand, but on the other loaded with spiritistic dogmas of all sorts. It could assiduously cultivate chemistry, but alongside it alchemy also. Astronomy could stand together with astrology. Arab medicine could tolerate all sorts of superstitious formulae alongside genuine knowledge. The syncretistic character of Arab culture is reflected in the great emphasis on systems. In the scholarly domain there is a great accumulation of encyclopedias and codices or commentaries. The Arab system of Galenic medicine affords an excellent example. Similar systems are available in the domains of mathematics, chemistry, philosophy, theology, and other disciplines.

Such intermixtures of cultural traits are both advantageous and disadvantageous. The disadvantages center around the modification and fixation of components to fit into systems. Often this mutilates and deforms the individual items. More serious, perhaps, is the development of the attitude that items once fitted into a system are completely known and require no further investigation. The advantages of the mixing of disparate elements lie in the possibility of modifications arising from the interaction of items. Cultural progress is frequently accelerated by foreign influences. What is properly called Arab or Islamic philosophy or science consists precisely of modified doctrines derived from other cultures. The Arabs, the Jews, the Syrians, and the Persians who developed Arab culture have made their contributions to such sciences as physics, especially optics, alchemy or chemistry, astronomy, mathematics, and medicine, primarily by juxtaposing materials derived from different traditions. It is not difficult to specify what greater or lesser transformation the Arabs made in Greek and Indian mathematics, in the medical doctrines of Hippocrates and Galen, and in the philosophy inherited from Greece, Syria, Byzantium, and Persia.

THE PHILOSOPHICAL BACKGROUND OF ARAB SCIENCE

Since the culture of the Arabs, spread far and wide through military and political adventures, is justly renowned for its influence upon European science, it is of the utmost importance to analyze the philosophical basis of Arab science. By philosophy we are to understand the intellectual institutions which provide the assumptions for unifying and directing scientific work. Such basic assumptions constitute the protopostulates underlying scientific procedures and doctrines.[2]

Despite the excellent development of arts and crafts throughout the Islamic Empire, as well as the preoccupation with various sciences, the basic Arab attitudes are transcendental. Through two channels, religious institutions on the concrete level and Neoplatonic ways of thinking on the more abstract one, there was poured into Arab philosophical assumptions a permanent ingredient of nonnaturalism. One of the basic Islamic protopostulates is that a spiritual reality underlies all observable events. Though it is possible for practical pursuits, including scientific procedures and investigations, to remain partially free from the basic spiritual assumptions, the interpretive products of science can hardly escape contamination from the fountainhead of philosophical doctrine. Philosophical literature is full of assertions that Arab philosophy is materialistic and so opposed to the spiritualistic assumptions of Christian philosophy that even the Schoolmen, who were influ-

[2] See Kantor, *Interbehavioral Psychology,* especially, Ch. 6.

enced by the Arabs, derived their spiritistic doctrines from elsewhere. However, these assertions really pertain only to local quarrels within the transcendental movement of the Moslems. It is only a question as to whether some Arab philosophers were pantheists or just theists. Wherever doctrine is concerned, the Moslem philosophers cultivated assumptions localized at the opposite pole from those of authentic natural science. When they performed their greatest service to science by conserving Hippocratean works or those of Aristotle and Galen, they incrusted them with interpretations derived from the monotheistic doctrines of Semitic religion and even from the Koran itself. No less a philosopher than the great Averroes advises a close adherence to the words and teachings of the prophet.[3]

The glory of the Arab appreciation and transmission of Aristotle is considerably dimmed by the modifications which Arab scholars introduced into his various treatises. Instead of treating Aristotle as a naturalistic scientist of the Hellenic culture, they transformed him into a partially mystical figure. Though we say this was done by the Arab scholars, it is clear that this mysticization of Aristotle is basically a fact of cultural change. Because of the spiritistic culture in which they lived, they could not understand Aristotle in any other way. The fact must be stressed, however, that despite the transcendental orientation of Islam, Greek science interested Arab scholars. This redounds to their credit even though this interest may be partly accounted for by the technological and commercial characteristics of Arab culture.

SCIENCE IN THE EASTERN AND WESTERN CALIPHATES

Historians of science agree that Arab science is not only essentially Greek in origin, but also derived from classical sources indirectly through Hellenistic and post-Hellenistic writers. Even if the Arabs had developed some elementary scientific knowledge of their own, their main body of institutionalized science was carried to them by way of Syrian and Persian intellectual establishments. It was the systematic scientific structures of the Greeks which the society of the Caliphs preserved and cultivated, while the mainstream of European culture which had given birth to them dried up. And it was this set of scientific institutions which the Arabs eventually carried back to Europe, where, transformed and desiccated, they became the basis for the institutions of medieval and modern science. Prominent among the scientific systems in question are those of medicine, chemistry including alchemy,

[3] Wallace and Thatcher, "Arabian Philosophy," p. 280.

astronomy, and mathematics. Because these are the outstanding sciences of Arab culture and because they form a convenient basis for discussion, we plan to treat them separately although they were intimately linked with each other.

Medicine

It has been aptly said that Arab medicine was really Greek medicine modified by the dictates of religion and rehabilitated in Arabic script.[4] In reviewing briefly the developments in the Eastern and Western Caliphates, we must take into account the modifications which the great representatives of Arab medicine made in the documents and doctrines of the famous Greek writers, Hippocrates and Galen, which they first knew through Syriac translations. Arab medicine was influenced also by Persian and Indian doctrines. In fact, when Arab medicine attained its mature and distinctive form in Baghdad from the ninth century on, its greatest personages were all Persians; for example, al Razi (Rhazes; 860-926), Ali ibn Abbas (Haly Abbas; d. 994), and Ibn Sina (Avicenna; 980-1037?).

If we attempt to sum up the significance of Arab medicine aside from the virtues of particular physicians and their specific achievements, we find the attachment to events painfully lacking. Even the famous Rhazes, who produced from his excellent clinical experience a noteworthy treatise on smallpox and measles, believed that a thousand books were better than a thousand years of observation. The Arab medical writers were mainly compilers and summators. Thus, the great work of Rhazes, the *Continens,* was a compilation in twenty-five books. Ali ibn Abbas in his *Book of Kings* (*Liber Regius*) produced a similar work in twenty books containing about four hundred thousand words. This could hardly have been a scientific production based on investigation and theoretical analysis of actual findings. The medical fame of Avicenna rests primarily on his *Canon of Medicine,* which contains a million words written to codify not only Greek but Arab medicine also. This work is not, naturally, without its metaphysical impositions, although it does reveal Avicenna's receptivity to certain objective aspects of Aristotle's work. This latter feature of the *Canon* must have been the one that earned it the opprobrium of medieval thinkers. For example, Arnold of Villanova (1235-1312?) thought it to be so much "waste-paper."

Although the writers of the Western Caliphate with their seat in

[4] See Campbell, *Arabian Medicine and Its Influence on the Middle Ages,* p. 3.

A

B

Plate VI. A. Solon and His Students, B. Aristotle and His Students, *see p. XV.*

Cordova were not blind followers of the Eastern scholars, they do belong to the same cultural tradition. Naturally there were modifications reflecting the different local situations in which they lived. To illustrate the views of the medical writers of the Western Caliphate, we consider four writers, Albucasis, Avenzoar, and the two commanding figures, Averroes and Maimonides.

The encyclopedia produced by Albucasis (1013-1106) is clearly based upon previous writers, especially Rhazes, Paul of Aegina, and others. As to his own ideas and practice, he is credited with improving the surgical technique of his time, though by cleaving to the anatomical doctrines of Galen, he helped to retard the general advancement of the subject. Still, he is reputed to be the only great surgeon of the Arab period.[5] He is also credited with the attempt to apply chemical knowledge to medical problems.[6]

The very fact that Avenzoar (1113-1162?) was critical of Avicenna's *Canon of Medicine* indicates a laudable inclination toward actual experience and a reaction against established abstractions. It was to Avenzoar's credit also that his principal work, the *Altersir* or *Theisir,* is a treatise on practical medicine and not a highflown encyclopedia. Although a staunch admirer of Galen, he did not bow to every tenet in Galen's treatises but rather reserved his critical judgment about specific details.

Averroes (1126-1198), the friend of Avenzoar and the extreme admirer of Aristotle as he understood him, stands far apart from the writers of the Eastern Caliphate. Also, despite his reputation among the Christian Scholastics and his influence upon them, he appears very different from them in his detailed beliefs. As a medical writer Averroes prepared a résumé of medical science under the title of *Kitab-al-Kullyyat,* which was called the *Colliget* by the Latin writers. The subjects he treated were anatomy, physiology, pathology, diagnosis, materia medica, hygiene, and therapeutics. Although Averroes is credited with some knowledge derived from personal observation, for example, that no one suffers twice from smallpox,[7] he was still primarily a commentator. Indeed, he was long occupied as a cadi before he became physician to the Caliph of Marrakesh. In Dante's *Inferno,* IV, 144, he is distinguished as "Averrois che il gran comento feo," "he who made the great commentary."

As our last example of a physician of the Western Caliphate we

[5] Ackerknecht, *A Short History of Medicine,* p. 78.
[6] Campbell, *op. cit.,* p. 90.
[7] Sarton, *Introduction to the History of Science,* Vol. II, p. 356.

name the Jew, Maimonides (1135-1204). On the whole, although he is said to have practiced medicine after losing his fortune in Cairo and was personal physician to Saladin, his medical fame stems from his writings and translations. He translated the *Canon* of Avicenna into Hebrew and some aphorisms of Hippocrates and Galen into Arabic. His original medical writings include works on hygiene, asthma, reptile poisons and their antidotes, and haemorrhoids.

In summing up the medical science of the Arab period, it must be stressed that its contact with Greek science, though attenuated, had given it a definitely naturalistic tinge. We have only to compare Arab medicine with the ideas expressed by some of the Church Fathers such as Tatian or Tertullian, who held it improper to employ medicines rather than prayer or exorcism. Tatian wrote,

> . . . medicine and everything included in it is an invention of the same kind [deceitful]. If anyone is healed by matter, through trusting to it, much more will he be healed by having recourse . . . to the power of God.[8]

But on the other hand, because Arab medicine was thoroughly contaminated by Christian and Neoplatonic metaphysics and by the consequent inclination toward sterile authority rather than anatomical and physiological investigation, it could become so far removed from natural situations as to include astrology, alchemy, and other insalubrious elements.

Astronomy and Astrology

> Though Europe owes a debt of gratitude to the Arabs for keeping alive the flame of science for many centuries and for taking observations, some of which are still of value, it cannot be denied that they left astronomy pretty much as they found it. They determined several constants anew, but they did not make a single improvement in the planetary theories.[9]

This summary parallels the conclusion of other historians of science concerning how much credit should be given to the Arab period for its conservation and investigation of science. Certainly the Arabs were intensely interested in astronomical events quite independently of the influence of scientific traditions. But according to the constant refrain of historians of science, Arab achievements were extremely limited. However, despite the specter of spiritistic tradition looming on the Arab scientific horizon, there was considerable astronomical activity. The Omayyad Caliphs established an observatory near Damascus,

[8] *Address to the Greeks,* Ch. 18.
[9] Dreyer, *A History of Astronomy from Thales to Kepler,* p. 249.

while the Abbasid one that al Maimun erected at Baghdad became an active center of astronomical work. There continuous observations were recorded, tables of planetary motions constructed, and an important attempt to determine the size of the earth made.[10] Important work was carried on also in the Western Caliphate where an astronomical tradition was established which eventually led to the preparation of the famous tables named after King Alfonso X of Castile (1252-1284).

At this point arises the question as to how far the technical observations can be separated from the larger astronomical complex which included astrology. Sarton asserts that in Islam, as compared with other cultures, astrology was checked by the vigorous development of astronomy.[11] In any case, the threat posed by astrology only emphasizes that a nonnaturalistic domain of interpretation constantly bordered on and influenced the astronomy of the Arab period.

Chemistry and Alchemy

So clearly is chemistry an outgrowth of simple and common procedures with respect to specific materials that we should expect a large development among people who are themselves craftsmen as well as cosmopolitan traders. We are reminded that the far-flung trade of the Arab period rests firmly on technological foundations, as is to be expected. To progress from domestic cookery to the mixing, shaping, and decoration of clay in pottery making, or to the preparation of vegetable and mineral solutions in medical practice requires many different procedures. Accordingly, practical chemistry should flourish among the Arabs even more than astronomy, physics, or other sciences.

Scholars differ in their estimates concerning how much chemistry the Arabs discovered as compared with what they borrowed. Perhaps because of its Arabic name, the discovery of alcohol as a substance is often attributed to them, even though it has been pointed out that as "spirits of wine" it was known to Pliny. The list of substances aside from alcohol distinguished in the Arab period is large. For example, Arab chemists are credited with discovering potassium, nitrate of silver, corrosive sublimate, nitric acid, and sulphuric acid.[12] As we should expect, the famous chemists would also be the great physicians of the period. Accordingly, it is pointed out that Rhazes, who was the first

[10] *Ibid.*, p. 245 *f.*
[11] Sarton, *op. cit.*, Vol. I, p. 19.
[12] Thatcher and Schwill, *A General History if Science*, p. 191.

to introduce chemical preparations into the practice of medicine,[13] wrote a treatise giving an elaborate classification of substances. For example, extending the work of the Egyptian alchemist, Zosimus of Panopolis (4th c.), he divided mineral bodies into classes as follows:

1. Bodies: the metals;
2. Spirits: sulphur, arsenic, mercury, and sal ammoniac;
3. Stones: marcasite, magnesia, *et cetera;*
4. Vitriols (known to Pliny);
5. Boraces: borax, natron (soda), plant ash;
6. Salts; common salt, kali (potash), "salt of eggs" (probably saltpetre, used in China for fireworks), *et cetera.*[14]

In consonance with the general intellectual character of Arab culture, chemistry is hardly distinguishable from alchemy. This is understandable if we consider that the interest in elixirs and the transformation of the baser into the nobler metals is only an extension of chemical technology. In the alchemical field the outstanding worker is usually taken to be Jabir ibn Hayyan, who flourished in the latter part of the eighth century. His alchemical doctrines were very anthropomorphic and animistic.[15] In this department of science, then, as in others, the keystone is a system of ideas far removed from observable events.

Mathematics

Historians of mathematics appear to espouse the view that the Arab period was probably more fertile in the mathematical domain than in any other branch of science. By their mastery of both Greek and Indian methods, the Arabs contributed new materials. While their good results show the sovereign influence of the interaction of procedures and theories, they also did excellent work by recovering and transmitting the mathematics of their predecessors. By their translation of Apollonius, Archimedes, Euclid, Ptolemy, and others they established an intimate continuity between ancient and modern mathematics that made for essential progress. Here al Khwarizmi in the ninth century stands out as a transmitter of the notion of decimal position. And, of course, it was chiefly through Arab mathematics that Europeans became acquainted with Hindu numerals.

The success of the mathematicians of the Islamic period in advancing their subject is well indicated by the fact that when Europeans

[13] Campbell, *op. cit.*, p. 66; see also Holmyard, *Alchemy,* Ch. 5.
[14] Partington, *A Short History of Chemistry,* p. 29.
[15] Sarton, *op. cit.*, Vol. I, p. 532.

Plate VII. Socrates and Two Students, see p. XV.

resumed scientific work, they found astronomy in practically the same state in which Ptolemy had left it, whereas in mathematics the Arabs had forged a powerful tool by altering Ptolemy's calculus of chords into the calculus of sines or trigonometry, a tool by which astronomy could be advanced in a most important manner.

In appraising the achievements of the present period, the extent to which Arab mathematics maintained and cultivated the transcendencies of the Neoplatonic philosophy may not be so evident, yet we need not question that it was considerable. The great shift of interest from the compactness and solidity of geometry to the axiomless airiness of flexible algebra serves to suggest such probable influences.

ARAB PSYCHOLOGY

As one of the most important links between Hellenic civilization and its later continuation, Arab culture has exerted a profound influence on the development of psychology. It is impossible to overestimate the importance of the Arab writers in the history of psychology.[16] Their influence is in no way lessened by the circumstance that Arab culture possesses a nucleus of theological doctrine similar to that of the Roman Christian tradition. How, then, did Arab culture influence psychology? In the first place, along with the medical lore of Hippocrates and Galen, the mathematics of Euclid and the Indians, and the astronomy and physics of Alexandria, the *De Anima* of Aristotle was brought back into intellectual circulation. By preserving the Aristotelian *De Anima,* the Arabs not only established a continuity between the psychology of ancient and modern times, as was the case with astronomy, chemistry, mathematics, and physics, but, beyond this, they conserved the status of psychology as an independent discipline. It is clear enough that the other sciences would have kept their identities by virtue of their several subject matters. Not so with psychology. In its case, the events would have become hopelessly and permanently submerged in the depths of theology and philosophy. This, indeed, did become the fate of psychology during much of its history. But the possibility of the recovery of its identity was certainly greatly aided by the work of the Arab writers. By transmitting the *De Anima* to the not-so-tender mercies of the Scholastics, especially of St. Thomas, they made it possible for psychology to maintain an uninterrupted existence from its first formulation by Aristotle to the present day.

As in the case of all other doctrines and documents, the Arab writers

[16] See Afnan, *Avicenna,* Ch. 5.

left their own individual stamp upon the *De Anima* and upon psychological doctrine. Especially through the agency of Averroes the complexion of Greek psychology was changed to conform to the cultural characteristics of post-Greek times. With his Neoplatonic protopostulates, Averroes imposed upon the *De Anima* characteristics entirely unrelated to the biological and cultural doctrines of Aristotle. There is good warrant for analyzing this situation on the basis of the Arab interpretation of Aristotle's doctrine of *nous*. As we have seen in Chapter 9, Aristotle arrives at the point where abstract thought is not discernible as the activity of any part of the organism or even the whole organism; but, inasmuch as such thinking is identical with things, he regarded it as autonomous and immortal. In other words, an organism may reach the stage of thinking that a ship will either sink or not sink, but that is because Aristotle accepts as a fact of nature that there is no alternative. The Arab thinkers, dominated by the mystical doctrine of soul, have turned this naturalistic theory into theological paths and made Aristotle's *nous* into a generalized and immortal psyche. Thus they traduce Aristotle's doctrine of active intellect by making it psychic and formulating its immortality as the continuing existence of a psychic entity. This goes counter to the Hellenic notion of immortality as simply the perfect or the imperishable, as circularity is immortal.

Hence we see clearly the role of the Arab writers in the history of psychology. We must credit them with transmitting to the awakening intellectual and scientific European culture an organized psychological institution, but one that is vastly different from the one which the Hellenic Greeks formulated. Through the injection of later cultural factors, Neoplatonic mysticism and the other-worldly traits of soteric Christian dogma, the naturalistic psychology of the Greeks became transformed to meet the circumstances and requirements of a new course of history. Henceforth Aristotelian psychology will be the base and center of a developing psychological science, but it will not be Hellenic psychology, but rather a psychology adversely influenced by the spiritistic and mystic attitudes of the Greco-Roman and Arab civilizations.

What may be characterized as Arabic artistic transformation of Greek subjects are represented by Plates VI A and B, VII, and VIII. The rendering of Solon, Socrates, Aristotle and their students is clearly orientalizing.

CHAPTER 18

SCIENCE REENTERS EUROPEAN CULTURE

PROBLEMS OF SCIENTIFIC HISTORY

IT IS CERTAINLY a paradox that science, which had been highly developed in Western European civilization, had to be borrowed again from another culture which had modified but not improved it. What changes occurred in Western European culture to make its own science acceptable only after it had been radically transformed in the Near East? These are only samples of problems that have to be faced by the historian of science.

The solution of at least some of the problems of scientific development certainly lies in the nature of scientific institutions themselves. First and foremost is the fact that scientific work consists of the activities of persons who are motivated to satisfy themselves about the nature of things. Accordingly, scientific work begins when permitted or demanded by the life conditions of such persons. Here is at least one key to the varying fortunes of scientific activities. In this chapter, then, we plan to consider some of the political, military, economic, and intellectual conditions of both the Near Eastern and the Western European communities which led to the reentrance of science into European culture.

THE GROUND PREPARED FOR SCIENCE: EUROPEAN INTELLECTUAL CULTURE, 400-1100

Although we cannot accept the popular view that science is an autonomous cultural entity which shapes civilization and its history, there is no denying that it is a potent feature of the cultural complexes in which it occurs. But science is only one of the factors in a culture and is as much influenced by the others as they, in turn, are influenced by it. Science is, nevertheless, a unique cultural element since it cultivates knowledge and aids in the formulation of attitudes based on objective criteria. Thus it helps to establish the character and stability of a culture in which it flourishes.

To prepare the ground for scientific work is naturally a gradual process and the actual resumption of such work required a many-staged evolution. When we glance briefly at some of these stages, we find that one of the earliest centered around a developing interest in Aristotle and other classical writers. Important here is the service rendered by Boethius (470-526) in the sixth century by his translation of Aristotle's *De Categorii,* and the commentary (*Isagoge*) of Porphyry. These works provided a firm basis for the formalistic and verbalistic studies of the succeeding centuries. Though Boethius was the gateway for logical and mathematical interests and prepared the way for the battles concerning universals, he at the same time encouraged the tradition of abstaining from close investigation of actual things and events. In other words, his achievements did not induce authentic scientific attitudes. The knowledge and the wisdom which he cultivated were more verbal and attitudinal than investigative.

No matter how dark historians regard the centuries following the sack of Rome in 410 to have been, some intellectual light was perforce still present. Though life was paralleled by little lore, a fairly complex civilization continued. Despite the extinction of Greek learning by the sixth century, the influence of Martianus Capella, the institutor of the notion of the seven liberal arts, continued for centuries. We must recall, too, that some vestige of classical learning was kept alive through Capella's commentary on Plato's *Timaeus* and through the one made by Macrobius (*fl.* 395-423), which was based on the translation of Chalcidius. Great honor, too, was accorded Priscian's *Institutes of Grammar,* while the *Ancient History* of Orosius (*fl.* 5th c.), the pupil of Augustine, was appreciated as the depiction of the calamities of the pagan world which ameliorated the distresses of contemporary times. So much for the preservation of book learning.

No complex community could be altogether insensitive to the facts of life. Even though to a great extent learning became the province of monastic personalities, especially after St. Bernard set the monastic fashion in Western Europe by founding Monte Cassino in 529, men could not live better by words alone than by bread alone. There were problems of food production, the care of animals, and, of course, the health of persons. Here is a striking injunction of Cassiodorus (*ca.* 490-580) to the monks of his monastery for the cultivation of knowledge about medicinal plants needed for the monastic infirmary:

> Learn, therefore, the nature of herbs, and study diligently the way to combine various species . . . and if you are not able to read Greek, read above all translations of the *Herbarium* of Dioscorides, who described and drew the herbs of the field with wonderful exactness. After this, read translations of Hippocrates and Galen, especially the *Therapeutics* . . . and

Aurelius Celsus' *De Medicina* and Hippocrates' *De Herbis et Curis,* and divers other books written on the art of medicine, which by God's help I have been able to provide for you in our library.[1]

Influenced by Cassiodorus and others, Isidore of Seville (560-636) also helped to keep Greek learning alive, though with an admixture of worthless verbiage. Isidore was far from being an observer; he kept strictly to the process of copying older writers. Accordingly, he sometimes did seize upon good material, though for the most part he did not. Still by his interest in learning and by composing his peculiar work, the *Etymologiarum,* he helped to prepare the ground for the reception of the Aristotelian scientific writings when they finally came.

Notable as an early scholar who prepared the ground for science was Bede, the Venerable (673-735), who cultivated the sciences in a simple, schoolmasterly way. In addition to the humanistic subjects of grammar and orthography, he wrote on the nature of the universe and on chronology, through which he earned the credit of popularizing the dating of events as either before or after Christ. He also made good observations on the tides.

By the eighth and ninth centuries even that learning which carried memories of the theologically diluted Greco-Roman science had become thoroughly attenuated. This is the period when the sheer ability to read Latin and to become familiar with the grammatical traditions of Donatus (4th c.) and Priscian (6th c.) was to disappear. At this time there stand out the efforts of Alcuin (*ca.* 735-804) and his pupil Hrabanus Maurus (776-856) to keep alight the torch of learning. Both these writers have earned the titles of mediocre and uninteresting scholars. For all that, they illustrate admirably the recognition of the need for learning and also the lack of it. Somewhat earlier, John of Damascus (8th c.) attempted to make use of ancient school logic to systemize the doctrines of the church.[2] He, too, is an excellent indicator of the low state of free investigation and the domineering influence of the religious thought of his time.

The intellectual status of the ninth century can be well gauged by the fact that the mystical writer from Ireland, John Scotus Erigena (*ca.* 810-880), is reputed to be the highlight of the period. Probably the greatest significance that can be attributed to him is that he kept alive a feeble interest in Platonic writings, though these were now thoroughly saturated with mystic ingredients which are not Greek, but Christian.

[1] From Cassiodorus *Institutio Divinarum Litterarum* i, 31 quoted by Crombie, *Augustine to Galileo: The History of Science A.D. 400-1650,* p. 10.

[2] Windelband, *History of Philosophy,* p. 273.

No matter how unfavorable social and economic conditions had been throughout the Dark Ages and the early feudal period for the development of effective scientific work, the intellectual ground has still not been completely forbidding and barren. Changes were taking place unceasingly which gradually facilitated the development of an active scientific tradition.

SCIENCE REESTABLISHED: HISTORICAL FACTORS: 700-1100

We have now summarized briefly the intellectual developments in Europe up to the tenth century. It has been primarily a story of internal and isolated European development. Now we have reached the point when the great acceleration in scientific interest and endeavour begins in Europe. We have already mentioned that there were many specific factors that initiated and facilitated the reawakening of scientific institutions in the West and we will now describe some of these conditions. From the historical standpoint the momentous and complex events surrounding the transmission of organized scientific institutions to the West can be summed up under two main headings, first that of foreign relations and stimulation and, second, that of the expansion of European society itself, signalized, for example, by the growth of towns, the multiplication of trade and technology, and the evolution of secular states.

The Role of Islam and Byzantium

The foreign relations which played such a major role in the stimulation of European science were complex and long continued. Two great eastern powers were involved, Christian Byzantium and Arab Islam. Both of these states had developed civilizations which supplied Westerners with highly prized items of science and art. Byzantine and Arab relations with the West can for our purposes be divided into two stages. The first, the earlier one covering approximately the eighth to tenth centuries, is that in which the various Arab states and the Byzantine Empire were at the apex of political power, which enabled them to exert particularly imposing direct influence on the less cultured West. The second stage is that of the late tenth to fourteenth centuries and is marked by a decline in the political fortunes of the eastern powers and the rise of new invaders from Central Asia in the East and of powerful states in the West.

THE APOGEE OF ISLAM AND BYZANTIUM. Great as was the first service rendered to science by the Arabs, the conservation of Greek scientific works, it was certainly matched in value by their second service, the transmission of Greek science back to the mainstream of European culture. This process of returning to European civilization factors once borrowed from it was to a great extent facilitated by the Islamic conquests, which gained for Arab culture strongholds in Europe itself, strongholds that provided direct and immediate points of contact with Western culture. The culture of the Abbasid Caliphate developed into a rich intellectual treasury. From whatever sources the items were taken, the collection in its entirety was great enough and valuable enough to enrich the civilization of Western Europe. It is probable that the treasures laid up in Baghdad were carried primarily to Spain, where they became widely distributed, both in the Islamic and Christian parts of the country. Centers of learning were located in Toledo, Cordova, Seville, Malaga, Granada, and other cities.

The Islamic conquests of North Africa and the Iberian peninsula proved to be only the beginning of the contacts between Eastern and Western populations. Throughout the eighth, ninth, and tenth centuries, interrelations were vigorous through the agencies of war and trade, and laid the foundations for the intellectual connections, which became of paramount importance in the eleventh and twelfth centuries, when the impact of Islamic culture upon Western thinking was exceedingly striking. This is the period when Arab scholars would pass on to the West the translations they had made of classical writings.

Like the Arab civilization, that of Byzantium played a very significant role in our story. At times in its long career, in the ninth and tenth centuries, for example, the Byzantine Empire was the acknowledged queen of European culture. Even of eleventh century Byzantium Fisher says that

> . . . it could show a society easily superior to that of any western city in art, learning, and civilized habits.[3]

It is easy to see, then, how it was possible for the Byzantine Empire to influence its neighbors, such as the Bulgarian and Serbian nations, and even more distant cultures. We may date the prominence of Russia in the European scene from the time when Vladimir (980-1015) drew so heavily upon the Byzantines for such cultural elements as the Greek orthodox religion, the modified Greek alphabet, and other phases of Greco-Roman culture; effects from these borrowings are still felt in world affairs today. On the direct scientific side, probably the most

[3] *A History of Europe*, p. 219.

pronounced influences of Byzantine culture on European civilization were felt in Italian cities, particularly in Venice and Genoa.

THE DECLINE OF THE NEAR EASTERN STATES AND THE CRUSADES. The tenth and eleventh centuries brought to the Near East a large number of profound political and social changes which favored the growth of Western civilization, including the cultivation of science. For the history of science great importance centers around the decay of the two great political units that had formerly held sway in the East—the Byzantine Empire and the Caliphate of Bagdad. Many, of course, were the factors that made for the disintegration of both the Abbasid Caliphate and the Byzantine Empire, but probably of the greatest importance was the movement of Central Asiatics toward the west. Especially to be mentioned is the influence of the Seljuk Turks, who entered the lands bordering on the eastern Mediterranean and wrought tremendous changes in all the cultures occupying that area. Turkish emirs came to power at Jerusalem, Damascus, Aleppo, and Antioch, strongholds from which they opposed the Crusaders. Outstanding here is the great campaign in which the Byzantine Romanus IV and the Turk Alp Arslan fought each other and which ended with the annihilation of Romanus' army in 1071 at Manzikert, north of Lake Van in Armenia.

The decline of the Eastern states contributed to the political and social matrix of science, not so much by the direct transmission of classical treatises and tradition, as in the preceding stage of East-West connections, but by opening the way for the development of western nations and for the intense confrontation of East and West during the wars and intrigues of the Crusades. Thus, by means of war and trade the Pisan, Genoan, and Venetian republics established their power in many strategic areas of the eastern Mediterranean at the expense of Byzantium and Islam. Even today in such spots Venetian fortifications and castles, many still displaying the lion of St. Mark, testify to the expansion of the Adriatic republic.

Although the First Crusade (1095-1099) was organized under the slogan *Dieu le veut,* everyone knows that, like all complex human events, it was compounded of many factors. Aside from religious interest, the Crusaders were influenced also by military, political, and commercial considerations. It has been repeatedly shown how the complex drama of the Crusades served as an important agency for the intermingling of the cultures of East and West. Now, whether or not the Crusades contributed directly to the advancement of Greek learning in the West, they surely served as indirect facilitators of such learning.[4] The Aristotelian writings may already have reached Europe by way of Spain and Sicily; still, this does not detract from the importance of the Crusades in transferring Greek science to the West.

It must not be overlooked that the Crusades constitute a set of events intricately related with innumerable happenings in both the East and the West. Historians speak of the awakening of the West. Changes in military, political, demographical, and industrial circumstances sharpened the appetites for lands and political domination in the East and for control of trade routes. Such stirrings are leavened by the need for various branches of science, in order to command principles for establishing stability in social organization and also the technology for improving agriculture, metallurgy, navigation, and other crafts. Through all these conditions, scientific ideas became more and more appreciated and welcomed in the West. The Crusades contributed a great deal to the evolution of the complex European culture of today.

The Expansion of Medieval Society

The renewed establishment of science in European history clearly corresponds to a number of changes in the conditions of European countries. These changes are of such a nature as to justify the hypothesis that the rebirth of Western science, including psychology, became possible because social, economic, and political conditions in Europe began to approximate those that had existed in Greece and the Near East when science first began to flourish. We will briefly survey some of the outstanding new cultural conditions characteristic for the expansion of medieval society.

THE SECULARIZATION OF SOCIETY. Although Western civilization is characterized by the dominance of transcendentalism, it is still true that interest in scientific work evolved collaterally in correspondence with the increasingly worldly attitude of the European populations after the tenth century. Typifying this relative secularization of Europe is the struggle of various monarchs to free themselves from the control and domination of the Popes and the Church. Even the popes were never completely sacerdotal, but they did attempt to base their power and sway upon religious principles. The monarchs, on the other hand, stressed the commercial and economic sources of their claim to rule. An excellent example of the secularization of medieval society is

[4] Gibbon, *The Decline and Fall of the Roman Empire*, Ch. 58. Runciman, *A History of the Crusades*, Vols. II, pp. 316-321; III, p. 470 *f.*

offered us by the career of Frederick the Second of Naples and Sicily in the thirteenth century. It might well be argued that Frederick was the *stupor mundi* not because of his learning, which was considerable, or his success as a ruler, but precisely because he was an effective destroyer of hallowed traditions. Among the institutions he flouted were religious as well as political and economic ones.

Rulers were increasingly successful in establishing and maintaining their power in centralized, non-feudal secular states. Such states promoted the development of individual national institutions and provided circumstances in which their citizens could prosecute their professions and intellectual interests. Certainly the especial importance of the rise of secular states for science is clear.

THE INTENSIFICATION OF SOCIETY AND THE GROWTH OF TOWNS. From the eleventh century on there developed in Europe an increasingly settled and orderly way of living, a social organization that has to a great extent continued to modern times. The population increased and became concentrated into towns and cities possessing particular societal advantages and cultural possibilities. With the multiplication of towns, the basis was laid for a great variety of associations for carrying on elaborate economic and political functions. Self-protection and the maintenance of independence from feudal lords are signified by the construction of town walls and fortifications. The growth of cities and towns bespeaks an intensification of manufacturing and trading pursuits. The cities developed as centers where craftsmen could carry on their work with all its division of labor and specialization of operations. Guildhouses served all the purposes of organization, control, and protection of craft members as the crafts expanded and grew into clearly distinguishable units within the large town systems. Naturally, too, the necessary processes of interchange of raw materials and finished products made the towns links in longer or shorter chains of mercantile centers. Water and land routes were evolved or reestablished as the means of carrying on the complicated processes of economic interchange and international communication.

Without committing oneself to the theory that science is a function of industry and commerce, one may still stress the need for a proper economic setting in order that science can flourish. Certainly we may expect that a suitable state of technological evolution is prerequisite for the development of the interest in and contact with things and events, as we shall point out in some detail below. Then there must be opportunities for specialized occupations. There is hardly a doubt that the social conditions that gave rise to guilds with their regulatory functions also favored the cultivation of scientific work. All of these factors became effective in connection with population growth.[5]

In addition to being centers of industrial activity with the consequent evolution of skills and tools of various sorts, the new population centers served the purpose of science in other ways. The cities and towns provided a basis for an interest in social autonomy and competition, which could only result in an interest in knowledge for both peaceful and warlike purposes. Not to be overlooked here are the intensifications of personal and organizational competitiveness into orthodox and heterodox systems of law, artistic styles, religious sacraments, and religious, moral, or scientific theories. In summation, we may say that the appearance and growth of cities and towns coincided with a greatly increased interest in concrete things and the problems concerning them.

CASTLES, CHURCHES, AND CATHEDRALS. While castles with their complex walls for defense may appear to be the most elaborate secular buildings, they do not represent the growth and development of the new forms of secular society as well as the great churches and cathedrals which sprang up in Europe during the Middle Ages. True enough, they appear to be sacerdotal structures. They were controlled and in many cases built by ecclesiastical authorities and directed the thoughts of their visitors toward the ethereal. Still, they are best looked upon as centers for intercommunication and interpersonal relations of various sorts. They were the homes of rituals and communal practices that bound individuals and families into varying types of social organization. They were civic centers, not only the meeting places of city dwellers for religious purposes, but also for social and economic ones. They harbored the schools which culturalized the young to owe allegiance to a particular community and its mores. In their physical fabric the churches and cathedrals represent the feeling for art, the wealth, and the competitive powers of individual cities. Thus the number and variety of churches demonstrate the differences between communities and the ways of living of the groups who build and maintain them.

UNIVERSITIES AND LEARNING. Among the most interesting and important factors both for stabilizing populations and for preparing the ground for the development of science, is the establishment of universities in Central and Western Europe. They must be looked upon

[5] For a study of population problems, see J. C. Russell, "Late Ancient and Medieval Population."

as the apparatus for the institutionalization of learning. Although the earliest universities grew for the most part out of schools fostered by religious institutions, they still served as a basis for encouraging secular learning. This was inevitable since one cannot look for a sharp specialization and separation of sacred from secular studies in medieval times. Furthermore, in some cases universities were actually founded to further a particular branch of secular learning. This was true especially in Italy, where the University of Bologna was founded before the eleventh century to foster law studies. Other universities emphasized various secular studies. Salerno was famed in the tenth century for its medical interests, which passed on to Naples and Padua, both founded by Frederick II, the former in 1224 and the latter in 1238. As we know, Padua became particularly famous as the seat of scientific studies, and it would have been truly remarkable if an institution founded by Frederick II had been especially devoted to sacred studies.

Although the university at Paris appeared to be strongly inclined toward theology, the French nation could boast of a strong seat of medical and scientific studies at Montpellier and a law school at Orleans. In the fourteenth century German universities were founded at Prague (1347), Vienna (1365), Erfurt (1379), Heidelberg (1386), and Cologne (1388). These came later, of course, than Oxford (1167) and Cambridge (1209). Other university foundations in various countries are exemplified by Angers (1229) and Toulouse (1280) in France; Pavia (1361) and Florence (1349) in Italy; Lisbon (1290) in Portugal; Cracow (1362) in Poland; Buda (1589) in Hungary, and many, many others.

It is to be emphasized that nowhere were the universities more than moderate strongholds of science in a proper sense. But as organized centers of study, they were instrumental in stimulating intellectual activity. They were primarily teaching institutions and, even more, centers for the dissemination of conventional and favored doctrines, rather than centers to encourage unfettered research. Nevertheless, they are more important for what they did in the way of scientific work than for what they may have been designed to accomplish. Such is the power of events.

TECHNOLOGICAL INVENTION. Scientific research grew up in close connection with astrology, alchemy, and the practical arts. Because to see is to believe, and to touch is to be convinced of the actuality of what appears, some of the most impressive factors for the development of science are the things and processes employed in industry and manufacturing. There is, of course, a sound basis for this circumstance in the fact that science is essentially a process of interacting with things, a process which involves manipulation and transformation. It is only in the description and formulation of the results of dissection, experimentation, and analysis that the scientist can adopt an attitude of remoteness from the things or events studied. To a great extent, then, it is true that science is deeply rooted in the technological development of agriculture, mining, metallurgy, dyeing, brewing, medicine, architecture, and even warfare. Such developments are the inevitable counterparts of population growth, trade, travel, and conquest. It is impossible to underrate the impact of such elementary procedures as distillation, sublimation, solution, condensation, and the like upon the development of theoretical and practical chemical science, for example. Such processes and the cultural conditions promoting their use are of great importance for the expansion of science.

It is suggestive and useful to mention a few of the technological inventions which played a part in the revival of science in the scholastic period. One striking example is the development of lenses which was accomplished by a study of the anatomy of the eye and in turn led to the invention of many optical instruments, the series culminating in microscopes and telescopes. This technological series made possible an elaborate evolution of the astronomical and biological sciences. Other examples are the many valuable technological products imported from the east, especially from China and India. Here it is a commonplace to mention the use of water and wind power for various operations, cog-wheel gearing as the basic feature of clocks and watches, the mariner's compass, gunpowder, and paper.

When we reach the twelfth and thirteenth centuries we have not only considerable advances in protoscientific operations but also expressions of the necessity of contacts with nature for the development of science and social life. Here may be cited such writers as Robert Grosseteste (1175-1253), John of Peckham (1220-1292), Peter Peregrine (13th c.), Roger Bacon (1214-1294), and many others. An interesting example of the admonition to manipulate things and to experiment is found in the following passage from Peter Peregrine, who says that an investigator,

> . . . must himself be very diligent in handicraft also, in order that through the operation of this stone [magnet] he may know wonderful effects. For by his carefulness he will be able in a short time to correct an error which in an age he could not possibly do by means of his knowledge of nature and mathematics, if he lacked carefulness in use of hands. For in occult [i.e.

scientific] operations we search out much by manual industry; and for the most part, without it we can make nothing perfect or complete.[6]

Similar reminders of the proper way to progress in knowledge can be found even in scholastic writers, for example Adelard of Bath (*ca.* 1090-1150).[7] Holmyard quotes Jabir Ibn Hayyan (*ca.* 720-813) to the same effect.

The first essential in chemistry is that thou shouldst perform practical work and conduct experiments, for he who performs not practical work nor makes experiments will never attain to the least degree of mastery. But thou, O my son, do thou experiment so that thou mayst acquire knowledge.[8]

The operational method was beginning to be an accepted institution in the new dawn of scientific work.

The evidence just surveyed shows how the mainstream of science is definitely based upon technological arts and medical traditions. These are central to scientific development in every culture in which science plays a part for three reasons. We have just seen how technology and medicine provide, on the one hand, substantive material for science, namely a great body of information about natural things and processes, and, on the other, indicate the need for direct observation. In the third place, technology and medicine fulfil universally urgent needs. Hence their tremendous importance for the continuity of science. Actually, it is not yet fully recognized that the continuity of intellectual and scientific thought is even more marked than the continuity in the social and political fields. Historians have long since given up the notion of a complete break between the Dark, Middle, and Modern ages in so far as ordinary history is concerned. The analogous situation of science and the role of technology and medicine in providing the continuity are shown in Fig. 20, which stresses the confluence of Hellenistic intellectual institutions with the Hellenic science brought to Western Europe by the agency of Arab culture.

BASIC PROTOPOSTULATES OF MEDIEVAL SCIENCE

We have already had many occasions to point out that any sort of scientific work is deeply involved with the cultural institutions of its time. This relationship even goes so far as the lack of organized scientific components in some societies. As shown in the first part of this chapter, during the European Dark Ages there was hardly anything

[6] *Epistle* (Thompson, trans.), quoted from Taylor, *Physics: The Pioneer Science,* Vol. II, p. 585.

[7] Crombie, *From Augustine to Galileo,* pp. 13, 16.

[8] *Makers of Chemistry,* p. 60.

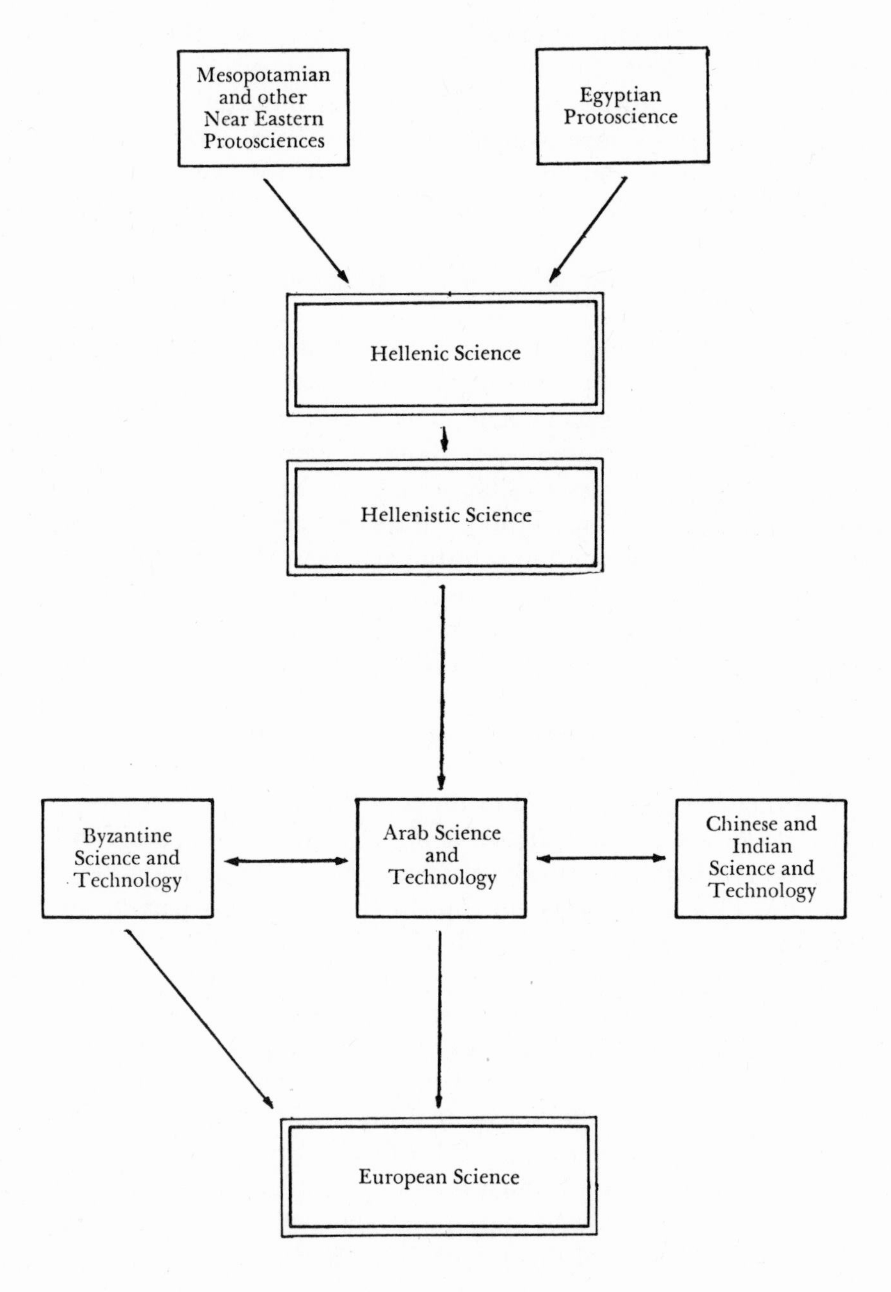

Medical and technological arts, represented by arrows, provide the basis and continuity of scientific development

FIG. 20. THE CULTURAL SOURCES OF EUROPEAN SCIENCE

more than soil growing gradually more receptive for the planting of scientific institutions. But now that we are approaching the twelfth and thirteenth centuries, there is an obvious burgeoning of scientific institutions. As we have sampled the socio-historical factors which favored the effective development of science in the West, it is time to examine the philosophical basis upon which the new scientific edifices are to be erected.

Scholastic science like all science is deeply set in a matrix of presuppositions. The wide range of presuppositions includes both vague judgments and such explicit formulations of assumptions as are called postulates. Because fully formed postulates testify to a relatively high peak of scientific endeavour and achievement, it is advisable to consider the presuppositions of the scholastic period as protopostulates. Although it is not always possible to differentiate sharply between the different stages of presupposition, we seldom are at a loss to describe the relations of presuppositions to the actual work done or the effects of presuppositions on investigations.

Obviously, there is a great difference between the medieval and the naturalistic postulates of the Greeks. Medieval presuppositions are decidedly transcendental. There is a considerable penetration of theological assumption into what becomes the stream of scientific thinking and investigation. In the following paragraphs we give some of the outstanding protopostulates of medieval science.

Protopostulate 1. The Spiritual Is the Real. The presupposition here is that everything that is good, permanent, basic, and worthy belongs to the realm of the transcendent. Spirituality does not partake of the qualities and dimensions of visible and tangible things. We have observed the rise of these notions, and now we observe their establishment and transmission as parts of the scientific heritage.

Protopostulate 2. Things and Events Are Symbols of Moral Reality. The medieval scientists of our tradition, even when they studied things that they encountered, did not value them for their qualities and conditions, but were interested in them for the evidence that they provided of more significant things which they represented or symbolized. Thus is established the notion of appearance and reality. The extreme and perhaps original form of this notion is the Psalmist's statement:

> The Heavens declare the glory of God;
> And the firmament showeth His handiwork.[9]

On a simpler level, this protopostulate is exemplified by the doctrine

[9] *Psalms* 19, 1.

Plate VIII. Aristotle and His Assistant, see p. XV.

of signatures, according to which each object, whether animal, plant, or mineral, displays a mark symbolizing its hidden qualities or powers.

Protopostulate 3. There Are Two Sorts of Existence. The evolution of the notion that there are two sorts of existence, the natural and the nonnatural or supernatural, had become highly institutionalized during the Dark Ages. It is a fixed postulate by the time that science reappears. This metaphysical or ontological presupposition had already taken on different forms—spirit and flesh, intellect and matter, moral and natural, and many others depending upon the particular context in question. Of especial interest to the historian is the viability of this postulate, which is just as potent a factor in twentieth-century thinking as it is in the thinking of the second and third centuries of the Christian Era.

The modern dichotomy of the naturalistic and humanistic realms, or the division between the external world of physical or mechanical things indifferent to men and the interior world of human spirit, the realm of beauty, conscience, and the intuition of God, are simple variants of the dualistic ontological postulate. Schrödinger, the physicist declares:

Science cannot tell us a word about why music delights us, of why and how an old song can move us to tears.[10]

Probably one of the best indicators of the continuity of the dualistic postulate is the current problem concerning the dichotomy between the realms of science and non-science. Crombie offers an excellent statement of this dichotomy.

It can be seen clearly now in the 20th century, though it did not altogether escape notice in earlier times, that a scientific theory of itself never provides grounds for denying a belief held in a context outside the range of the scientific method; and further, that, although scientific theories are themselves conceptual and hypothetical, there is nothing in the scientific method that either denies or affirms the validity of other methods of making sense of experience, or the attainability of objective truth. Science can provide no capital for either theologians or atheists, moralists or libertines. It has nothing to say about aesthetics or ethics, about the existence of God or miracles. And whatever other philosophical disciplines may have to say about these subjects, they may speak independently of natural science, as it speaks, in its own language, independently of them.[11]

Protopostulate 4. Some Knowledge Is Certain and Absolute. As long as men continue to investigate and analyze the things they encounter,

[10] *Nature and the Greeks,* p. 95.
[11] *Augustine to Galileo,* p. 402 *f.*

they need never resort to problems of absolute knowledge. For it is obvious that the work they do is incomplete and contingent. A somewhat different situation exists when scientists concern themselves with abstracted relations, as in mathematics. There, it seems that closed systems of relations may give a semblance of simple finality and certainty. The notion of absolute certainty and determinism arises only when one deals with arbitrary beliefs. Throughout the prescientific era we find innummerable arguments for the existence of God, angels, demons, and other verbally-constructed entities all based on intuitive certainty. In the present period the protopostulate of absolute cognitive certainty has become a thoroughly accepted institution.

If we go no further back than St. Augustine, we find an excellent argument for mathematical certainty.

Even if I did perceive numbers with the bodily senses I could not in the same way perceive their divisions and relations. . . . Moreover, all that I contact with a bodily sense, such as this sky and this earth and whatever I perceive to be in them, I do not know how long it will last. But seven and three make ten not only now but always. In no circumstances have seven and three ever made anything else than ten, and they never will. So I maintain that the unchanging science of numbers is common to me and to every reasoning being.[12]

By the time of St. Thomas, in the thirteenth century, we find a full elaboration of the notion of absolute knowledge and the contrast of such knowledge with that derived from the study of concrete objects.

Reasoning may be brought forward for anything in a twofold way: firstly, for the purpose of furnishing sufficient proof of some principle, as in natural science, where sufficient proof can be brought to show that the movement of the heavens is always of a uniform velocity. Reasoning is employed in another way, not as furnishing a sufficient proof of a principle, but as showing how the remaining effects are in harmony with an already posited principle; as in astronomy the theory of eccentrics and epicycles is considered as established, because thereby the sensible appearances of heavenly movements can be explained; not, however, as if this proof were sufficient, since some other theory might explain them. In the first way we can prove that God is one, and the like. In the second way, arguments may be said to manifest the Trinity; that is to say, given the doctrine of the Trinity, we find arguments in harmony with it.[13]

[12] *De Libero Arbitrio* ii, Ch. 8, 21.

[13] *Summa Theologica,* Part I, Question 32, Article 1, Reply Objection 2.

SECTION NINE

THE SCHOLASTIC TRANSFORMATION OF ARISTOTLE'S PSYCHOLOGY

CHAPTER 19

NATURE BEGINS TO PARALLEL GRACE

PSYCHOLOGY REEMERGES IN WESTERN EUROPE

In many ways the thirteenth century looms as a great transition point in the history of psychology. This age of Bacon, Dante, Albertus Magnus, and St. Thomas is especially important since in it systematic psychology reappears among the cultural institutions of Europe. Through the agency of Arab scholars the formalized doctrines of Aristotelian psychology arrive and from this point on psychology is cultivated by modification and transformation which adapt it to changing cultural conditions until, finally, in our own day it has become increasingly co-ordinated with current scientific traditions. With the thirteenth century we have reached the stage when, in accordance with the historical factors discussed in the preceding chapter, scholars were no longer overwhelmingly preoccupied by theological problems alone. Theology's monopoly of the realm of thought is broken to the extent, at least, that nature was accepted as a parallel to grace. Once again in Europe aspects of the natural world are thought to be worthy of serious attention, even though often only as secondary to otherworldly matters. From a philosophical and scientific standpoint Scholasticism is deeply rooted in religious and theological soil. No matter how rapidly technology and the social system are advancing, the overshadowing atmosphere is otherworldly and supernatural. For all the Scholastics the highest and the noblest science is sacred doctrine, as is clearly stated by St. Thomas:

> . . . sacred doctrine is a science because it proceeds from principles made known by the light of a higher science, namely the science of God and the blessed.[1]

In this period St. Thomas, who was strongly influenced by Averroes, the Neoplatonic Aristotelian—whose works dominated the University of Naples, where St. Thomas studied during his Dominican education, is a key figure in the development of thought as a whole and of psychology in particular. In fact, though in other fields he is overshadowed

[1] *Summa Theologica,* Part I, Q. 1, Art. 2.

by St. Albert and others, among all the Scholastics it is St. Thomas who plays the outstanding role in the psychological tradition. Accordingly, we will center our study of psychological development in the Middle Ages on this great scholar.[2] By the fortunes of history, he became the effective stabilizer of the basic protopostulates of modern psychology.

For students of psychological history, the primary event of the thirteenth century is the advent of Aristotle's *De Anima* and St. Thomas' interest in promoting it. We must, however, emphasize that all knowledge and understanding of the biopsychology of Aristotle has passed away.[3] Nonetheless, the fact that St. Thomas and the other Scholastics, who are the active agents in the renewed development of systematic psychology, transformed Aristotle's *De Anima* is of lesser importance than the return of the treatise, for this ensured the inclusion of psychology among the galaxy of sciences to be cultivated in one form or another down to our own day. It is impossible to overestimate the value of the *De Anima,* for it served as a palpable institution bridging the great gap between the classical intellectual heritage and the psychistic tradition of psychology.

The reintroduction of the *De Anima* into the psychological tradition was no simple matter. We know that the study of Aristotelian works, even in their Neoplatonic modification, was resisted by the church authorities. For example, the provincial Council of Paris expressly forbade the study of Aristotle's natural philosophy and commentaries in 1209, while in 1212 it also struck at the *Metaphysics* and *Physics,* along with Averroes' commentaries. This was a clash of vested intellectual interests. Whereas the Arab transformation of Aristotle stressed the cosmic aspect of Soul, the churchmen clung to the more personal and humanistic features of Spirit. Averroes transformed Aristotle's theory that active reason is identical with the thing reasoned about into one according to which active reason is the fusion of man's spiritual intellect with the cosmic soul, which he completely separated from the individual; in consequence he denied personal immortality. This was, of course, anathema to Christian Scholastics. Not until this matter could be cleared up was Aristotle able to gain entrance into the charmed circle of thirteenth-century scholars.[4]

[2] Siebeck declares that St. Thomas represents the high point of the elaborated systematic psychology of Scholasticism: *Geschichte der Psychologie,* Vol. II, pp. 488 *ff*. See also Hessen, *Thomas von Aquin und Wir*.

[3] Graphic indication of the dissipation of Aristotle's naturalistic views concerning psychological action by the time of St. Thomas and of the beginning upward curve of naturalistic psychology at that time is given in Fig. 16 on p. 161 above.

[4] Meyer, *Thomas von Aquin,* p. 4 *f*.

Both St. Albert (1193-1280) and his pupil, St. Thomas (*ca.* 1224-1274), accused Averroes of traducing Aristotle. They interpreted Aristotle as allowing personal immortality because the rational soul was not separated from the sensory soul or even from the vegetative soul. So far did St. Thomas go in allowing nature to parallel grace that he agreed that bodily processes were contributory to psychic action.[5] In contrast to the traduction of Aristotle by Averroes, that of Albert and St. Thomas is the orthodox one.

THE DOCTRINES OF SCHOLASTIC PSYCHOLOGY

The transformation of Aristotelian psychology at the hands of St. Thomas and his peers can be most easily visualized by tabulating some of the principal contrasts between the original Greek work and the scholastic interpretation of it.

TABLE VII. THE CONTRAST BETWEEN THE *De Anima* OF ARISTOTLE AND THE COMMENTARY OF ST. THOMAS

Topic	*Aristotle*	*St. Thomas*
Subject Matter of Psychology	Actions = Behavior of Organisms	Human Soul
Nature of Psyche or Nous	Organic Functions or Acts in interaction with Things	Immortal psychic Substance
Nature of Man	Man an animal Organism	Man partly animal, partly theistic Spirit
Method of Study	Observation and Dissection	Reasoning, Revelation, Acceptance of Authority
Orientation of Psychological Events	Psychology a Branch of Physics; the Science of Motion of natural Things	Psychology a Branch of Theology
Relation of Psyche to Soma	Structure—Function = Biological Relation; no Mind-Body Dualism	Immortal Soul indissolubly connected with the Body
Nature of Reason	A Type of Function or Act	Unique theistically endowed Property of human Soul

Thomistic psychology is of striking significance not for its transformation of the biological psychology of Aristotle, but rather for its attempt to assimilate Aristotle's pagan and naturalistic doctrines. However, this remains on a purely verbal level. Except for the inescapable

[5] *Commentary on Aristotle's De Anima,* Book i, Lectio 2 (403^a 2-403^b 23). See also St. Thomas' own *De Anima,* Articles II, VIII, and X.

circumstance that the culture called for some acknowledgment of the natural scene—for example, that psychology is concerned with organisms and their behavior—Thomistic psychology appears to make use only of the words of Aristotle and not at all of the referents of those descriptive terms.

We must keep constantly before us that St. Thomas is a theologian and not really a scientist. The end of all study is God, and if actual things are discussed, it is only to show how they are related to God, Who is the sole creator of them all. As compared even with his teacher, Albert, there is in Thomas no great striving to deal with events, even if only to bring them into harmony with Christian dogma and belief. Thomas is the great controversialist, the great codifier who brings everything together into a system. Though it is true that Thomas does his best to spiritualize or Christianize the pagan *De Anima,* actually he succeeds only in emphasizing his heritage derived from Plotinus, Tertullian, Augustine, and others in the direct line of spiritistic thought. God and Spirit are, above all, his themes. Perhaps even more than earlier writers he features the verbally-created Spirit as if to prevent church doctrine from being outweighed by the naturalism still remaining in Aristotle's works, despite their contamination by Neoplatonism.

The psychology of St. Thomas covers not only the knowing and doing of man, but also that of God and, of course, the angels, who are intermediate between the two. In this fact we have an excellent index to the thinking of St. Thomas as well as into the nature of the Spirit concerning which he speculates. God knows Himself through Himself since for Him knowing and the known are identical. What He knows consists of all reality, that which exists, has been, or will be. For in the rarefied domain of ultimate and detached Spirit, knowing embraces all time and all power. God's knowing coupled with will is the cause of all things.

> The knowledge of God is the cause of things. For the knowledge of God is to all creatures what the knowledge of the artificer is to things made by his art. Now the knowledge of the artificer is the cause of the things made by his art from the fact that the artificer works through his intellect. Hence the form in the intellect must be the principle of action. . . . Now it is manifest that God causes things by His intellect, since His being is His act of understanding; and hence His knowledge must be the cause of things, in so far as His will is joined to it. Hence the knowledge of God as the cause of things is usually called the *knowledge of approbation.*[6]

[6] *Summa Theologica,* Part I, Q. 14, Art. 8 (this and the following references are to the Pegis edition).

Inasmuch as angels are incorporeal creatures, pure spirits though capable of assuming bodies, they can know and act in a very different way from humans, who are as composite creatures limited in knowledge and partially mortal in existence. Angels may appear as living men, but are so far unlike humans that they may pass from one place to another without traversing the intervening space, and they have no memory as they know all things without intervening periods, though not without the aspects of before and after. Angelic knowledge, too, proceeds without argument or proof.

Thomistic psychology is completely dominated by the doctrine of man's partial spirituality. Here is the Thomistic transformation of the Aristotelian doctrine of man as a highly specialized animal which reasons as well as remembers, senses, and moves. But though the human being is only in part spirit, it is that part which is of the greatest importance. So great an intellectual distance separates Thomas from Aristotle that his interest in the body arises only from its temporary connection with the soul or spirit. Here is evidence of the primacy of Thomas' theological interests and his difference from scientists or naturalists. For St. Thomas, basically, it is the bodily part of man which limits him with respect to knowledge, will, and general perfectibility of being.

St. Thomas is by far not the first to make psychological actions or functions into psychic processes. That is the culmination of centuries of development. But it is he who grafted psychic processes onto Aristotle's *De Anima,* and this is a distinctive event in the history of psychology, one that will be fertile in evil consequences from the thirteenth century until our own day. What Thomas achieved is the construction of a new psychological institution. For the Christianized *De Anima* has never ceased to exert its influence even in the twentieth century, the era of objective psychology.

It is most instructive to examine some samples of the Thomistic procedure. Consider Thomas' dualism of soul and body. He argues that because Aristotle says that the *intellectual principle* can operate separately from the organism, the psyche is not a form of the body.[7] Further, if the soul is the form of the body and the body cannot exist without a form, then, since the body exists, it has its unique form. In consequence of this, the composite that is man consists of a body plus a soul and hence is a definitely double being. Accordingly, for St. Thomas the spiritual nonspatial soul is an inevitable feature of man's constitution.

[7] *Ibid.,* Q. 76, Art. 1.

The cultural and specifically theological background of St. Thomas imposes on him as basic assumptions the absence of any specific bodily processes in abstruse reasoning and the idea that complex reasoning is practically identical with the existence of the problem worked on and the processes of solving it. As we should say today, the operations of specifying and organizing a set of relations are not distinguishable from the system of relations. Furthermore, Thomas' theological assumptions prevent him from seeing that nothing in Chapters Four and Five of Book III of the *De Anima* leaves any base for a spiritual interpretation. It is clear that Thomas simply assimilates the *De Anima* by injecting into it interpretations in no wise possible for Aristotle himself or his culture. In a similar way, Aristotle's notion of man as a natural being—a type of animal—is perverted so as to change man into a partially godlike creature charged with numerous theological properties. For the soul is the spirit or breath which is derived directly from God and which, being incorruptible, returns to its Giver when the corruptible body perishes.

So far we have been considering St. Thomas' views for the most part in their relationship to and contrast with those of Aristotle. Now we turn to the fundamental aspects of the psychological system of St. Thomas. After this task has been completed, we will be in a position to characterize with some definitiveness the relationship of scholastic psychology to the tradition of modern mentalistic psychology.

What St. Thomas and the other Scholastics wrought in the psychological domain and in the other sciences may be best delineated by constructing a brief system of the spiritistic psychology which became the heritage of modern scientists. Such a system must include as a minimum the definitional and postulational propositions of the system and its underlying metasystem.[8] Because of the great revolution which Thomistic psychology effected in the psychological tradition, we indicate also the protopostulates which embody the basic Thomistic assumptions. These three sets of propositions constitute the scientific logic upon which the system is erected. Since the Thomistic system constitutes a transformation of the Aristotelian psychology, we will stress the differences between the two.

THE PROTOPOSTULATES OF THOMISTIC PSYCHOLOGY

Before we present the Thomistic protopostulates we must remind ourselves that any scholastic scientific discussion is dissected out of a

[8] See Kantor, *Interbehavioral Psychology*, Ch. 5.

deep matrix of theology. A tremendous amount of the *Summa Theologica* is devoted to such questions as the existence of God and the manner of His existence. How does God operate? What does He know and how? What is the nature of His will? What kind of powers does He possess? The source of all this theological material is the Scriptures and the innumerable commentaries upon them. Even the pagan Aristotle, of course, was not treated otherwise than as one who provided a gateway from the commonplace world of nature to the glories of the medieval God. From the type of cultural background out of which Thomistic psychology emerged there could arise only notions of psychological science widely divergent from those of Aristotle and the Hellenic Greeks. The relation between the protopostulates of Thomistic psychology and those of general medieval science given on pages 322-326 above is obvious.

Protopostulate 1. Psychological Science Transcends Observed Events. The activities of persons are not the intrinsic data of psychology. They merely point to underlying principles which are manifested in such surface happenings. Though nature is allowed to stand beside grace, the former is of little importance in the realm of being. So far as cognition goes faith counts for more than knowledge.

Protopostulate 2. The Source of Knowledge and Wisdom Is Mainly Authority and Tradition, and not the Welter of Natural Happenings. The interpretation of events is based upon the opinions of authoritative persons and not upon activities observed in things and events. Science proceeds by argument, analogy, and the attachment to self-evident first principles called the light of reason.

Protopostulate 3. Things are Transformed in the Act of Observation. This proposition introduces an epistemological note into science, and implies that the knower in whole or part absorbs the known. Science thus loses its original events, which become overlaid with endowed properties. Instead of dealing with autonomous events brought under observation, science is determinative and prescriptive. This protopostulate was to have the most far-reaching influence, as we shall see.[9]

Protopostulate 4. Knowledge Is Creative. The assumption that knowledge is a creative process is an inference emanating from a theological matrix. Existence depends upon a creator. Scientific work includes a large number of intuitive processes which even result in the creation of primary being.

[9] See below pp. 355 *ff*.

THE METAPOSTULATES OF THOMISTIC PSYCHOLOGY

Since the Thomistic commentary on the *De Anima* is part of a theological system and not a scientific treatise as in the case of Aristotle's *De Anima,* it possesses, strictly speaking, no metasystemic propositions. But the circumstance that traditional psychology includes materials which St. Thomas helped to institutionalize makes it easier to recognize such propositions in the Thomistic writings. St. Thomas' metapropositions are only modified theological assertions.

Metaproposition 1. The Study of Soul Is a Unique Discipline. Instead of specifying the particular kinds of events handled by psychology, this metaproposition ascribes ultimacy and nobility to soul substance.

Metaproposition 2. The Study of Soul Articulates with Theology and Ethics. By contrast with Aristotle, whose motive in the *De Anima* is the description of the way organisms act, St. Thomas is interested in the soul for theological and ethical purposes. The ultimate aim is the understanding of God and man's relation to Him. This involves the discovery of the way of salvation, the knowledge of the destiny of man, and the securing of his happiness now and forever.

Metaproposition 3. Soul Is Studied by Intuition and Reason. The method of studying the soul is purely subjective. In terms of modern appraisal, this amounts to verbal argument based on accepted authorities. Everything depends upon dictates of the transformed Aristotle, of St. Augustine, Avicenna, Diogenes, the pseudo-Areopagite, St. Albert, and similar custodians of truth. Where observations are concerned, the sources are the introspective inner life of the soul itself.

THE POSTULATES OF THOMISTIC PSYCHOLOGY

Since Thomistic psychology, when assessed by the criteria of investigative science, is so limited in scope, there is little point in attempting to elaborate its system. The postulates, metapostulates, and protopostulates all merge, so that an exposition of them becomes repetitive and redundant. To exhibit the basic characteristics of Thomism and its divergence from the Aristotelian prototype, it will suffice to indicate here some of the Thomistic postulates and in the following section St. Thomas' treatment of some salient types of action.

Postulate 1. Dualistic Composition of Man: Soul Is Part of Man. Man is a composite being consisting of a soul and a body. These are two absolutely different sorts of components. The soul is not man, but only the incorruptible part of him which remains after the flesh and bones of the body fall away.[10] The soul is the form of the body, which is the matter or material part of man.

Postulate 2. Unity of Soul. Soul Absolutely One Essence Though with Different Powers. The soul is a single form and there can be no parts. It is impossible to separate the soul into form and matter. The three powers of the soul are nutritive, sensitive, and intellectual or rational.[11]

Postulate 3. The Human Soul's Absolute Uniqueness and Difference from Animal Souls. The animal soul has the sensitive power of knowing external objects in so far as concerns their qualities and the *vis estimativa,* the power to transcend sensory qualities, as when birds select straws to build nests or sheep flee from wolves.[12] Both of these powers operate in conjunction with the body and are perishable. In the human soul sensory processes are interrelated with rational or intellectual principles which are separable from the body and incorruptible. Furthermore, the human soul is endowed with the power of intuiting first principles without going through the processes of demonstration.

Postulate 4. The Human Soul Operates with or without Instrumentation of Body. Many acts of the soul are carried on by means of the body or a bodily part; for example, seeing by means of the eye or hearing by means of the ear. This is the case with all the sensitive and nutritive operations. The powers which are the principles of these operations are localized in the composites of soul and body. Understanding and willing are performed without the action of a corporeal organ or of the body as a whole. The power to carry out these operations is inherent exclusively in the soul.[13]

ACTS OF THE SOUL: THE TREATMENT OF SPECIAL TOPICS IN THOMISTIC PSYCHOLOGY

The study of St. Thomas' treatment of special psychological topics reveals at once the crucial difficulties arising from the interpretation of Aristotle's naturalistic views in terms of the transcendentalism of Christian theology. The changing civilization of the thirteenth century calls for an increasing emphasis on natural things and processes, even though man's ultimate happiness consists in the knowledge of God, which is possible only when he is freed from his mortal encumbrances

[10] *Summa Theologica,* Part I, Q. 75, Art. 6.
[11] *Ibid.,* Q. 76, Art. 3.
[12] *Ibid.,* Q. 78, Art. 4.
[13] *Ibid.,* Q. 77, Art. 5.

in the life after death.[14] Each of the following topics will show the transformations made in the descriptions of action in Aristotle's *De Anima.* In each case the primacy of the transcendent factors will appear evident.

PERCEIVING AND SENSING. Of these two activities, sensing is the one which is more definitely an action of the soul determined by external or material things. Sensing begins when the object known acts upon the composite of body and soul. The reception of the object or its qualities, which is a type of knowledge, consists of the existence of the objects or its qualities in the soul in an immaterial fashion. Organisms that cannot receive immaterial forms in this way, such as plants, have no powers of knowledge whatever.[15]

However, sensing is only the most primitive form of knowledge. Perceiving or internal sensing involves the common sense, that is the activity of soul which synthesizes the isolated immaterial qualities of things possessing sweetness, sourness, hardness, softness, and the like so as to produce in the soul knowledge of the objects which possess the qualities. Following upon this receptive and synthetic knowledge, the soul can perform the more complex actions like interpreting, judging, and evaluating things. Intellectual action, as we shall see, reaches a high degree of aloofness from both the material object and the bodily participants in the sensing and perceptual actions.

INTELLECTUAL ACTIONS. The intellect or intellectual actions are intrinsic faculties of the soul unconnected with sensory actions. It is the cultural matrix and the protopostulates of St. Thomas' commentary on the *De Anima* which preclude the derivation of intellect from sensory and perceptual situations. Despite his acceptance of transformed Aristotelian psychology, St. Thomas cannot tolerate any essential relationship between the rational soul and the sensitive soul, which is so intimately connected with the body. The intellect is absolutely individual, separable in action from any cosmic soul, and absolutely immortal.

The intellect is a storehouse of concepts, that is forms of apprehension derived from experience. From such experiential derivations arises the power to judge and reason. But the mind or soul also is fitted with innate principles which provide intuitive apprehensions. Among such principles is the immediate recognition that the same thing cannot at the same time be affirmed and denied or that one must

[14] *Summa contra Gentiles,* Ch. 48 (Pegis edition).
[15] *Summa Theologica,* Part I, Q. 84, Art. 2.

do good and avoid evil.[16] To the extent that the soul is furnished with principles, it approximates to the divine intellect, which requires no demonstration of truth since all truth is immediately evident to it.

IMAGINATION. Knowledge, which is the essence of soul, requires not only the immediate apprehension of things but also their retention. Otherwise, animals could not with their sensitive souls be moved to seek absent things. Motion and action must follow apprehension. Thus, there are two types of retention; first, the imagination or phantasy for conserving the data of sense and, second, the memory for conserving in the mind or soul dated phantasms, that is sense data carrying the marks of time.

Imagination is a storehouse of forms received through the senses.[17] The soul has the power of being imprinted, as wax takes on the form of the seal. It can thus be the storehouse of innumerable representations (phantasms) of things that had at some time been presented to the senses. Once these images or phantasms are stored in the soul, they may be psychically manipulated and elaborated; the human soul possesses the power of making new phantasms, which is the basis for artistic and literary creation.

MEMORY. By comparison with imagination, memory is the power to store up in the soul the data or impressions that transcend the purely sensory reproductions or representations. The reception of intentions is the work of the estimative power. Now, one of the most fundamental intentions is the temporality of a thing, so that a reproduction carries the stamp of past time.[18]

The memorative power, like the imagination, is both passive and active. The soul can simply apprehend the intentions stored within it, or it can actively manipulate the intentions. This provides a power of control over and utilization of the stored intentions. Active memorial power is called reminiscence.

HABITS. The topic of habits provides an excellent example of the way St. Thomas transforms Aristotelian doctrine. For Aristotle habits are dispositional activities or characteristics inclining the possessor or performer to act in a certain way. They differ from other dispositions by their resistance to change. On the whole, such activities are practical, and the treatment Aristotle gives them is found in his ethical writings. St. Thomas, by contrast, regards habits as qualities of the immaterial soul, which as powers are developed to a certain extent by reason and

[16] Moore, *Cognitive Psychology*, p. 128.
[17] *Summa Theologica*, Part I, Q. 78, Art. 4.
[18] *Ibid.*, Q. 78, Art. 4.

also infused into the soul by God.[19] Although St. Thomas follows Aristotelian discussion in the ramifications of the ethical domain, he completely shifts the subject matter from naturalistic acts of organisms to qualities of soul.

INSTINCT. With a soul-centered psychology, St. Thomas has vast room for innate powers. Again, with his belief that psychology is anthropology, the science of man, his system allows great scope for treating the traditional determiners or springs of action. Moreover, as a presumed respecter and follower of the biologically-motivated philosopher Aristotle, St. Thomas might have become interested in adjustments of organisms. Nevertheless, for obvious reasons, the topic of instinct plays a minor role in the Thomistic system. Although he refers to animal behavior, he sets up an impassible barrier between animals and men. His psychological constructions pertain only to soul and emphasize the cognitive processes, whose existence in animals he denies. In general, despite all Thomistic protestations that man is an ensouled body, his descriptions of actions are primarily spiritual. For St. Thomas the body is merely a remote instrument of intellectual knowledge.[20]

The closest approach of St. Thomas to the behavior of animals is his consideration of the *vis estimativa.* As we have already seen, this power is the moving force behind such acts of animals as nest building, web spinning, and the like. The motives of the animals are also shaped by their innate appreciation of conditions and circumstances beyond the presentations of sense. Thomistic psychologists of today regard the estimative power as the cognitive part of an instinct which is correlated with sensitive appetite and the faculty of locomotion.[21]

THE APPETITIVE POWERS. St. Thomas' argument for including appetites among the powers of the soul is one of the clearest indicators of the great distance that separates his verbal and spiritistic doctrine from Aristotle's psychology of organismic behavior. The very references which St. Thomas makes to actual events show how remote his interests are from the actual behavior of animals, whether human or nonhuman.

It is necessary to assign an appetitive power to the soul. To make this evident, we must observe that some inclination follows every form: for example, fire, by its form, is inclined to rise, and to generate its like. Now, the form is found to have a more perfect existence in those things which participate in knowledge than in those which lack knowledge. For in those which lack knowledge, the form is found to determine each thing only to

[19] *Ibid.,* Q. 52, Art. 4.
[20] *Ibid.,* Q. 89, Art. 1.
[21] See Brennan, *Thomistic Psychology,* p. 134.

Plate IX. Saint Thomas, see p. XV.

its own being—that is, to the being which is natural to each. Now this natural form is followed by a natural inclination, which is called the natural appetite. But in those things which have knowledge, each one is determined to its own natural being by its natural form, but in such a manner that it is nevertheless receptive of the species of other things. For example, sense receives the species of all sensible things, and the intellect, of all intelligible things; so that the soul of man is, in a way, all things by sense and intellect. In this way, those beings that have knowledge approach, in a way, to a likeness to God, *in Whom all things pre-exist,* as Dionysius says [the Pseudo-Areopagite, *De Divinus Nominibus* v, 5].

Therefore, just as in those beings that have knowledge forms exist in a higher manner and above the manner of natural forms, so there must be in them an inclination surpassing the natural inclination, which is called the natural appetite. And this superior inclination belongs to the appetitive power of the soul, through which the animal is able to desire what it apprehends, and not only that to which it is inclined by its natural form.[22]

Though St. Thomas regards it as necessary to assign various appetitive powers to the soul, he still does not escape the pangs of an intellectual struggle. After all, the soul is a cognitive entity, and, accordingly, to be forced to introduce appetites as movements of the soul is exceedingly uncomfortable. But, undaunted, St. Thomas proceeds to distinguish between actions and passions. While, strictly speaking, only the sensitive appetites are passions, all the appetites, both the sensitive ones and the intellectual ones, are activities of the soul in comparison with the passive intellectual powers.[23]

There is another way out of the difficulty, and that is to reduce appetites, in the final analysis, to cognitive processes of the soul. For the central feature of an appetite is desire, and desire involves some intention or apprehension with respect to some things or condition. In general, the appetite is a mover, but a moved mover.[24] The basic cognitive component of appetites makes it desirable to differentiate between the appetites proper and the will. By contrast with the former, the will is a superior power of the soul and belongs to the intellectual phase of orectic powers.

The passions, or sensitive appetites, St. Thomas divides into two types, the concupiscible and the irascible. These are distinguished on the following grounds:

. . . since the sensitive appetite is an inclination following sensitive apprehension (just as natural appetite is an inclination following the natural form), there must needs be in the sensitive part two appetitive powers:—

[22] *Summa Theologica,* Q. 80, Art. 1.
[23] *Ibid.,* Q. 81, Art. 1.
[24] *Ibid.,* Q. 80, Art. 2.

one, through which the soul is inclined absolutely to seek what is suitable, according to the senses, and to fly from what is hurtful, and this is called the *concupiscible;* and another, whereby an animal resists the attacks that hinder what is suitable, and inflict harm, and this is called the *irascible.* Whence we say that its object is something arduous, because its tendency is to overcome and rise above obstacles.[25]

Brennan has prepared a table which effectively illustrates the passions of man.[26]

TABLE VIII. THE PASSIONS OF MAN ACCORDING TO ST. THOMAS

CONCUPISCIBLE	*good*	love	affective complacency
		desire	affective approach
		joy	affective possession
	evil	hatred	affective repugnance
		aversion	affective retreat
		sorrow	affective possession
IRASCIBLE	*arduous good*	hope	affective approach to the attainable
		despair	affective approach to the unattainable
	arduous evil	courage	affective retreat from the vincible
		fear	affective retreat from the invincible
		anger	affective possession

THE WILL. We have already made clear the basis on which St. Thomas separates the will from the sensitive appetites. In general, the will is an agent that moves all the powers of the soul to perform their respective acts. This applies, of course, to all situations where judgment or knowledge provides a choice as to whether certain acts will or will not occur. St. Thomas asumes that it is this power of the soul that operates in all the complex situations of human life. In the quaint terms of the Middle Ages, by the powers of the will the soul governs and directs the actions of man, leads him to adjust himself to all sorts of practical situations, and makes it possible for him to achieve morality and, in general, demonstrate his likeness to the angels and to God. But despite

[25] *Ibid.,* Q. 81, Art. 2.
[26] *Thomistic Psychology,* p. 158. Courtesy of Macmillan Co., Publishers.

the exalted nature of the will, St. Thomas values the intellect higher than the will. He makes the position clear in the following passage.

> The superiority of one thing over another can be considered in two ways: *absolutely* and *relatively*. Now a thing is considered to be such absolutely when it is considered such in itself; but relatively, when it is such in relation to something else. If therefore the intellect and will be considered with regard to themselves, then the intellect is the higher power. And this is clear if we compare their respective objects to one another. For the object of the intellect is more simple and more absolute than the object of the will. For the object of the intellect is the very notion of the appetible good; and the appetible good, the notion of which is in the intellect, is the object of the will. Now the more simple and the more abstract a thing is, the nobler and higher it is in itself; and therefore the object of the intellect is higher than the object of the will. Therefore, since the proper nature of a power is according to its order to its object, it follows that the intellect, in itself and absolutely, is higher and nobler than the will.
>
> But relatively, and by comparison with something else, we find that the will is sometimes higher than the intellect; and this happens when the object of the will occurs in something higher than that in which occurs the object of the intellect. Thus, for instance, I might say that hearing is relatively nobler than something in which there is color, though color is nobler and simpler than sound. For, as we have said above, the act of the intellect consists in this—that the likeness of the thing understood is in the one who understands [*Summa Theologica,* Q. 16, Art. 1]; while the act of the will consists in this—that the will is inclined to the thing itself as existing in itself. And therefore the Philosopher says in *Metaph.* vi. that *good* and *evil,* which are objects of the will, are *in things,* but *truth* and *error,* which are objects of the intellect are *in the mind* [Aristotle, *Metaphysica,* VI, 4]. When, therefore, the thing in which there is good is nobler than the soul itself, in which is the understood likeness, then, by comparison with such a thing, the will is higher than the intellect. But when the thing which is good is less noble than the soul, then, in comparison with that thing, the intellect is higher than the will. Hence, the love of God is better than the knowledge of God; but, on the contrary, the knowledge of corporeal things is better than the love of them. Absolutely, however, the intellect is nobler than the will.[27]

THOMISTIC CONTRIBUTIONS TO MENTALISTIC PSYCHOLOGY

Our exposition of Thomistic psychology has demonstrated the thorough inversion of the biopsychology of Aristotle and also the manner by which this transformation was brought about. Obviously, when dealing with the history of psychology, we must distinguish sharply between true Aristotelian doctrines and Aristotelianism, the attributed doctrines. It appears evident that St. Thomas and doubtless other

[27] *Summa Theologica,* Q. 82, Art. 3.

Scholastics were aware of the improvements they were making on the pagan writings. Klubertanz believes that it was quite clear that St. Thomas appreciated the fact that there was no doctrine of distinct internal powers in the work of Aristotle.[28] It is impossible to believe, however, that St. Thomas could have realized that Aristotle was a biopsychologist. The medieval European culture in which he was immersed precluded that. Jaffa asserts that although St. Thomas never appeals to any non-Aristotelian principles in order to interpret Aristotle's words, he nonetheless imputes non-Aristotelian principles to Aristotle while apparently believing them to be Aristotelian.[29] Six such imputed principles are listed by Jaffa as follows.

1. Belief in divine particular providence.
2. Belief that perfect happiness is impossible in this life.
3. Belief in the necessity of personal immortality to complete the happiness intended, evidently, by nature.
4. Belief in personal immortality.
5. Belief in the special creation of individual souls.
6. Belief in a divinely implanted "natural" habit of the moral principles.

What is of overwhelming significance to the historian of psychology are the consequences that St. Thomas' transformation of the *De Anima* had in the development of the mentalistic tradition of psychology.

Any summary of Thomistic psychology more detailed than that just given would have to elaborate the theme of spiritistic transformation to cover every topic treated. Such a summary would also have to take cognizance of the linguistic tools and techniques employed to make this transformation. We have already indicated that St. Thomas uses the terms *vis estimativa* and *vis cogitativa* to distinguish similar behavior in human and nonhuman organisms. Other terms like power, principle, and intention are likewise employed to implement spiritistic views at the expense of describing directly the adjustments of organisms to environing things and conditions.

Now it remains to stand beside St. Thomas and the other churchmen and to look forward to the much later mentalistic tradition of psychology. We will illustrate the institution of mentalistic traditions by discussing some of the most significant scholastic doctrines which verbally transformed psychological events.

INTERNALITY VERSUS ADJUSTMENTS. The most characteristic heritage that psychology has received from the Middle Ages is the construction

[28] *The Discursive Power: Sources and Doctrines of the Vis Cogitativa according to St. Thomas Aquinas,* pp. 191, 193.
[29] *Thomism and Aristotelianism,* p. 186 *f.*

of internality. The scientific psychology of the Aristotelian period was limited to the description of events taken as objective occurrences more or less directly observable by the investigator. Medieval psychology, on the contrary, deals primarily with occult processes not observable, but passively intuited through sympathetic psychic relationship. This is the manner of knowledge of God and the angels. This aspect of internality is based on the principle of spiritual creativity as over against a causal correlation of factors. Linked with this internality is the tradition that psychology concerns itself with consciousness, that cognition is primary, that the movements and actions of organisms are secondary and determined by cognition.

The domination of psychology by the notion that psychological events are organism-centered may be traced back to the internality constructed and established by St. Augustine and medieval thinkers. Even if modern and contemporary psychologists have shifted to the brain as the surrogate of the soul, instead of keeping to the soul itself as the source and basis of action, the underlying view is a cultural inheritance from Thomism. The internality has simply been modified. Instead of a direct determiner in the soul, the brain is interpolated as a mediator by the changing institutions of the psychological tradition.

Traditional notions of innateness, instinct, drives, and other internal powers are undoubtedly derivatives from the doctrine of soul with its creativity and inwardness. It is clear that what St. Thomas understands by nature or the necessity of nature is certainly a matter of theistic dictation and prescription. The instinctive activity of animals reflects the care that God takes of his creatures.

EXPERIENCE AND PRIVACY. It is a thoroughly established institution of our culture that each individual carries within himself a world of experience and that each such world is private and unique to the individual. Philosophical and psychological literature is replete with demonstrations and arguments about this private world. Even experimental scientists in all branches adopt this institution as an inevitable cultural assumption. The most blatant instances of adherence to this assumption are expressed in the solipsistic doctrine that the universe is contained in the mind of the observer. While modern writers think that they base their faith on the unimpeachable evidence or revelation that no one can share their toothache, actually, they overlook the fact that they are merely victims of the institutions of psychic privacy.

THE ISODYNAMISM OF INNER AND OUTER. Once the ship of internality became launched in the intellectual sea, a whole host of problems followed in its wake. Internality is polar to externality. Hence there has arisen the problem of the external world. How can the internal be matched with outside things? The psychological tradition yields a fine example in the perceptual field. The naive Aristotle simply treated the problem in terms of the organism and the object with which it was in interaction. But the Thomist had to add his spiritual factors. Perception is a complex process, the objective thing makes a change in the end organ of the body; then in the soul there is a change, a series of sensations, which must be synthesized by an internal sense to form an immaterial internal object isodynamic with the external object. The apprehension or apperception of the object is another change in the soul and provides the basis for concepts or ideas.

All the changes in the basic scholastic doctrines developed by the succession of mentalistic psychologists, for example, the making of the external object into a stimulus or the addition and interpretation of neural conduction and brain termination, have simply kept viable the inner-outer tradition. What the Scholastics wrought even the behaviorists have been unable to eradicate, but, indeed, have merely carried on in their own fashion.

We conclude our discussion of Thomistic psychology by emphasizing that it did not merely contribute significant individual concepts to later psychology, but shaped its very fabric. Any comparison of medieval and modern psychology demonstrates the unbroken continuity of the psychological tradition. This is true because psychological events are so near and so readily open to investigation. Accordingly, the psychology of the Scholastics is not only a definite nodal point in the history of psychology, but, far more important, the psychological views formulated by the Scholastics provide the basic substance for the conventional psychology of today. Thus, the entrenched mind-body presupposition continues with unabated strength to influence psychological theories even in the face of some opposing and negative attitudes. A more striking example could not be found than the reaffirmation of spirit even among the psychologists of presumably materialistic Soviet Russia. The following abstract of an article entitled "On the reflective Activity of the Brain" speaks for itself.

> Psychic processes reflect the outer world in the brain and regulate human behavior. Psychic processes must be viewed as a "special form of motion of cerebral matter." "Vulgar materialism," which identifies consciousness with matter, must be rejected, as must also "vulgar mechanism," which reduces the psychic to the lowest forms of "motion of matter," particularly to the physiological form. Problems in psychics must be looked at from "two

mutually connected, but not identical" points of view—the gnoseological and the natural-scientific. "Gnoseologically, consciousness is the ideal reflection of being, since the images of things in the brain do not contain the matter of the objects reflected." From the point of view of natural science, however, these images are to be seen as the result of a special reflective function, mirroring an objective world and involving a form of "cerebral motion.[30]

Can anyone doubt that the Greek naturalistic psychology as completely transformed by the Neoplatonists, the Near Eastern mystical philosophers, and above all, the Scholastics still maintains itself as a component of contemporary psychological institutions.

[30] N. V. Medvedev in *Voprosy Filosofii i Psikhologii,* 1961, **14**, pp. 109-119 summarized by I. D. London, *Psychological Abstracts,* 1962, **36**, p. 199.

CHAPTER 20

SOUL IN A MATRIX OF SCIENTIFIC INSTITUTIONS

WE HAVE NOW ARRIVED at the threshold of the Renaissance, at the beginning of the modern period of psychology. With the conclusion of our survey of the ancient and medieval periods of psychological thought, we have reached a great transition point in psychological history. The details of modern developments will be discussed in a second volume, but in order to underline the continuity of the psychological tradition we must round out the present volume with a brief preview indicating the extent to which modern developments in psychology were shaped by their antecedents.

REVOLUTIONS AND EVOLUTIONS IN PSYCHOLOGY

Psychology naturally shares with other special sciences an integral participation in the scientific revolution so clearly manifest in the fifteenth and sixteenth centuries. This does not mean, of course, that the terms "psychology" or "psychologist" were in evidence at the time. The days of high specialization were yet to come. Physicists were still physicians, natural philosophers, or mathematicians—that is, geometers. Biologists were medical practitioners or dispensers of physick. Yet who can overlook the fact that Kepler, Galileo, and Newton, as students of psychological interactions, were not only psychologists, but also definite links in the historical chain of psychological theorists. Moreover, they were pacesetters in instituting psychological doctrine, which in fulsome detail they transmitted to our own age.[1]

Revolutions, when a sufficient number of relevant minutiae are taken into account, can be recognized as evolution, albeit greatly accelerated. Certainly it is possible for the student of scientific history to follow through the development of various confrontations of persons with events, from the everyday contacts with things to the stirring, major operations on them which mark the revolutions in particular courses of study because of concentrated and explosive cultural happenings.

[1] For Newton's description of the visual process see p. 355 *f* below.

What is properly called the scientific revolution of the fifteenth and sixteenth centuries is basically the increased sensitivity of the scientists of that time to the great changes taking place in the social life of the Western European populations. Various social, political, and economic conditions whose tentative beginnings can be traced as early as the seventh century, have become so intensified and varied as to challenge successfully the monastic and Augustinian attitudes of introspection and withdrawal from the affairs of the world. In the fifteenth and sixteenth centuries there exist stable nations, with improved technologies and trade. This is a time of geographic discoveries, introducing new sources of wealth and new products. The civilizations of Europe are developing new scope for old cultural values and room for entirely new ones. The living conditions are taking on new interest for men, and, in fact, are forcing new ways of thinking and a greater adaptation to things as they are. Certainly the intense overconcern with a future life and with problems of redemption and salvation characteristic of medieval thought is slackening. It is clear that with these changes in human conditions, the sciences must become more active. Astronomy is deeply involved with voyaging and discovery, chemistry or alchemy with technological procedures and manufacturing, physics with types and strengths of materials, as well as with the behavior of things. Accordingly, medieval science and practice must perforce take on an extreme urgency and undergo rapid expansion.

Now, although psychology could not yet be properly treated as a study of interbehavior of organisms and objects, it, too, has become solidly established. A great peak of development is visible though the content of psychology is still considered to be transcendental. From our present vantage point we know the steps by which the discipline moved forward and how it exerted itself to keep abreast of the other sciences. No matter how great the lag between them and psychology, it never left the race and never relinquished the ambition to win for itself a place among those who attained the scientific goal.

THE TRANSPARENT PARADOX OF MIND AND NATURE

Aside from the fact that psychology was not applicable to concrete problems as was physics or astronomy, there was another flaw in it. After all there was something unique about psychology. The soul or mind is not localized in nature; indeed it stands opposed to it. The mind or soul transcends nature. As that by which natural things are known, it cannot itself be known. No kind of confrontation with mind or soul is possible.

However, the difficulties of this paradoxical science were smoothly passed over. So strong was the tradition of soul and its invisible source that this gap between the sciences just had to be accepted. The scientific domain was forced to make room for different orders of subject matter. There grew up a tradition of the dichotomization of nature. The argument was developed that science must become large enough to absorb even what appeared to be the extremest improbability. A long-lived variation of this argument is represented by the principle of complementarity current today. Things confrontable are set beside things not confrontable, the natural is matched by the super- and subnatural. Probably an outstanding factor that made this paradoxical dichotomy intellectually palatable was the belief that all sciences had to accept it, or could at least adapt it to their needs. Basically, of course, the existence of thoroughly established transcendental institutions endowed the dualistic way of thinking with an aura of inevitability.

THE POLARIZATION OF CONSTRUCTS AND EVENTS

In scientific or any other intellectual activity, assumptions or postulates and events are invariably aspects of specific situations. Assumptions are definite constructs formulated for dealing with events. The nature of the constructs depends upon many factors. They may be built as simple indications that certain events have been confronted, as means for identifying or describing events, as proposals for manipulating or controlling them, or as means of evaluating events as well as the potentialities for interacting with them. Any other relation of constructs and events would be improper, vain, or inept.

Numerous illicit relations have been presumed to exist between constructs and events. Outstanding among them is the relation of identity. Events are confused with descriptive or prescriptive constructs. Usually events are presumed to be swallowed by descriptions. In such cases, things and events are identified with words and sentences originally created to describe them. Psychological actions are taken to be sensation, psychic willing, or reason. Events which actually involve an organism confronting another organism or object are made into subjective states of the confronting organism. Another hardly less unfavorable treatment of the relations between constructs and events is to assume a license to impose all sorts of constructs upon events. The reacting organism is presumed to be operating under the influence of occult powers or forces. For the history of science, probably the most lasting as well as the most detrimental imposition upon nature is the proposition that it has a dual nature and that the two phases sustain various sorts of important relations one to the other. Of importance to the psychological historian is the age-old assumption that the soul and occult things could be naturalized by dichotomizing nature. So important is this dichotomization procedure that we must examine it carefully.

THE DICHOTOMIZATION OF NATURE

The division of nature in the history of science is a definite outcome of the fact that while the early modern scientists concerned themselves with particular things and events, they were all at the same time dominated by transcendent traditions. Thus, they invented the dichotomic doctrines of spirit and matter, of the objective and subjective, of primary and secondary qualities, and of noumena and phenomena. It is an established fact that the great heroes of modern science were mystics and theologians. Call off the list: Copernicus, Kepler, Descartes, Galileo, Boyle, Newton. It is true enough that not all of these have overtly declared their theological interests, but that is only incidental. All subscribed to various forms of psychic dualism stemming from the institutions established in the post-Greek period of our cultural history.

Throughout the history of psychology the dichotomization procedure determines that psychology's primary subject matter continues to be some alleged non-spatiotemporal things or processes, despite the performance of experiments and the application of mathematical techniques. The only novelty in the procedure is supplied by the many individual attempts to naturalize the soul. This continuation of commerce with transcendent principles will for centuries prevent the emergence of the view that psychology is actually concerned with the behavior of organisms under specified conditions. Obviously, then, this dichotomizing of nature requires our meticulous consideration.

The cultural acceleration which occurs at this period of scientific expansion, that is from the fifteenth century on, drew attention to the importance of concrete events. But the philosophy of the time dictates an assimilation of those events to established transcendental traditions with the result that there arises actually a double dichotomy, one in the theological field and the other in metaphysics.

The theological dichotomy brings to the front the polarity of a creator and everything he has created and continues to create. So well established is the spiritistic tradition that theology need no longer occupy the center of the stage. Accordingly, learning is growing specialized; it becomes possible to occupy oneself with the great world of created things while leaving to one side the special problems of the creator and his work of creation. Thus arises a tradition of lay learning, of specialized science. The ample and virulent attacks upon the "Aristotelian," that is, the scholastic, way of thinking attest this specialization.

The metaphysical dichotomy separates the created world into extension or the manipulable and measurable on the one hand, and the ideological or rational on the other. The extensionable covers very well all the objects studied in the realms of physics and chemistry, but it excludes parts of biological events and all psychological happenings. Thought as the inextensible is frankly the domain of spirit—the world of the intangible and the invisible. Let us examine now some of the doctrinal products of dichotomization.

PRIMARY AND SECONDARY QUALITIES. Kepler is on record for not only separating sharply the mathematical and the sensory qualities but also for deprecating the latter as less real and important. It is the quantitative qualities that are stable and reliable. Boyle (1627-1691), who insisted just as much on the distinction, was willing to allow secondary, sensory qualities an importance comparable with that of the primary qualities.

For illustrations of the elaborate and weighted argument for the distinction of qualities we turn to the writings of Galileo and Newton. Galileo set forth the doctrine in especially clear terms in his *Il Saggiatore,* written in 1623:

> . . . I want to propose some examination of that which we call heat, whose generally accepted notion comes very far from the truth if my serious doubts be correct, inasmuch as it is supposed to be a true accident, affection and quality really residing in the thing which we perceive to be heated. Nevertheless I say, that indeed I feel myself impelled by the necessity, as soon as I conceive a piece of matter or corporeal substance, of conceiving that in its own nature it is bounded and figured in such and such a figure, that in relation to others it is large or small, that it is in this or that place, in this or that time. that it is in motion or remains at rest, that it touches or does not touch another body, that it is single, few, or many; in short by no imagination can a body be separated from such conditions: but that it must be white or red, bitter or sweet, sounding or mute, of a pleasant or unpleasant odour, I do not perceive my mind forced to acknowledge it necessarily accompanied by such conditions; so if the senses were not the escorts, perhaps the reason or the imagination by itself would never have arrived at them. Hence I think that these tastes, odours, colours, etc., on the side of the object in which they seem to exist, are nothing else than mere names, but hold their residence solely in the sensitive body; so that if the animal were removed, every such quality would be abolished and annihilated.

Nevertheless, as soon as we have imposed names on them, particular and different from those of the other primary and real accidents, we induce ourselves to believe that they also exist just as truly and really as the latter.

I think that by an illustration I can explain my meaning more clearly. I pass a hand, first over a marble statue, then over a living man. Concerning all the effects which come from the hand, as regards the hand itself, they are the same whether on the one or on the other object—that is, these primary accidents, namely motion and touch (for we call them by no other names)—but the animate body which suffers that operation feels various affections according to the different parts touched, and if the sole of the foot, the kneecap, or the armpit be touched, it perceives besides the common sense of touch, another affection, to which we have given a particular name, calling it tickling. Now this affection is all ours, and does not belong to the hand at all. And it seems to me that they would greatly err who should say that the hand, besides motion and touch, possessed in itself another faculty different from those, namely the tickling faculty; so that tickling would be an accident that exists in it. A piece of paper, or a feather, lightly rubbed on whatever part of our body you wish, performs, as regards itself, everywhere the same operation, that is, movement and touch; but in us, if touched between the eyes, on the nose, and under the nostrils, it excites an almost intolerable tickling, though elsewhere it can hardly be felt at all. Now this tickling is all in us, and not in the feather, and if the animate and sensitive body be removed, it is nothing more than a mere name. Of precisely a similar and not greater existence do I believe these various qualities to be possessed, which are attributed to natural bodies, such as tastes, odours, colours, and others.

But that external bodies, to excite in us these tastes, these odours, and these sounds, demand other than size, figure, number, and slow or rapid motion, I do not believe; and I judge that, if the ears, the tongue, and the nostrils were taken away, the figure, the numbers, and the motions would indeed remain, but not the odours nor the tastes nor the sounds, which, without the living animal, I do not believe are anything else than names, just as tickling is pricisely nothing but a name if the armpit and the nasal membrane be removed; . . . and turning to my first proposition in this place, having now seen that many affections which are reputed to be qualities residing in the external object, have truly no other existence than in us, and without us are nothing else than names; I say that I am inclined sufficiently to believe that heat is of this kind, and that the thing that produces heat in us and makes us perceive it, which we call by the general name fire, is a multitude of minute corpuscles thus and thus figured, moved with such and such a velocity; . . . But that besides their figure, number, motion, penetration, and touch, there is in fire another quality, that is heat—that I do not believe otherwise than I have indicated, and I judge that it is so much due to us that, if the animate and sensitive body were removed, heat would remain nothing more than a simple word.[2]

[2] Quoted from Burtt, *Metaphysical Foundations of Modern Physical Science,* pp. 75-76, 78.

Galileo, as the great founder of dynamics, must be credited with the meritorious intention to abandon the medieval idea of innumerable ultimate properties independently existing in nature and to cleave instead to such properties of things as can be manipulated and measured. From the historical standpoint Galileo's position testifies to an impatience with the status of science in his day. Another lesson of history is that he is unfortunately influenced by the continued prevalence of transcendental ideas, especially that of the existence of soul. From our superior angle of observation, it is clear that in his discussion of heat Galileo is unaware of the distinction between heat as a nonhuman event and the event in which an organism reacts to these heat events. In the latter type of event, of course, a fundamental component is the presence and behavior of the organism. When Galileo asserts that tickling is not in the feather but in the organism tickled, he naively assumes that tickling is a quality or property which has a location or place in the organism. It was absolutely impossible for Galileo to understand the difference between (a) the differentiating reactions of organisms to things and their qualities, that is the interaction of organisms with things, and (b) a soul receptacle for secondary properties different from those of shape, size, and contact. That such a keen thinker and observer could overlook all this is a fact of scientific evolution. Because he clung so tightly to motion and figure, which were the only available properties of things in his day, he could not anticipate the development of chemistry and the other sciences which allow colors, tastes, and odors to be regarded as properties or qualities of things which can be reacted to, evaluated, manipulated, and measured. In the meantime, it was Galileo's great scientific power and achievement which provided a dominating and effective authority to maintain irrational and transcendent assumptions from his day to this.

The events of scientific history always constitute a continuous system. Given certain cultural conditions productive of particular kinds of basic assumptions and ideological institutions, the work and the results of scientists are closely integrated with those basic assumptions. Thus, the history of psychology shows that as knowledge of the details of perception develops, it takes a form in which transcendent factors are combined with knowledge of the anatomy and physiology of the organism. This knowledge itself is, of course, influenced by long-established transcendent institutions. An excellent example of this combination is the way Hobbes focalizes and institutes for psychology beliefs like those expressed by Galileo. The following quotation makes this plain:

That the subject wherein colour and image are inherent is *not* the *object* or thing seen.

That there is nothing *without us* (really) which we call an *image* or colour.

That the said image or colour is but an apparition unto us of the *motion,* agitation, or alteration, which the *object* worketh in the *brain,* or spirits, or some internal substance of the head.

That as in conception by *vision,* so also in the conceptions that arise from the other senses, the subject of their *inherence* is not the object but the sentient.[3]

Historians of psychology fail to tell us of the great role Newton plays in the development of the perceptual model. And yet he has been one of the primary pacesetters in the construction of the doctrinal institutions which continue to play an important part in psychological science today. Through his optical work in 1666 he developed and brought into line with the dualistic way of thinking a nucleus of facts which is still the basis for the physical, physiological, and psychological sciences of light and color.[4] Newton's contributions may be summed up as the discovery of the diffraction of the supposedly homogeneous white light and the correlation of the individual components of white light with various colors. However, going beyond this discovery, he set up, in consonance with the assumptions of the time, a theory of how the rays of light, each according to its own refrangibility, produces in the mind a particular color. It is to be noted how he stresses the nonexistence of colors in the world of nature and how the light rays appear as colors in the sensorium.

If at any time I speak of light and rays as coloured or endued with Colours, I would be understood to speak not philosophically and properly, but grossly, and according to such conceptions as vulgar people in seeing all these Experiments would be apt to frame. For the rays to speak properly are not coloured. In them there is nothing else than a certain power and disposition to stir up a sensation of this or that Colour. For as sound in a Bell or musical String, or other sounding Body, is nothing but a trembling Motion, propagated by the Object, and in the Sensorium 'tis a sense of that Motion under the form of sound; so Colours in the Object are nothing but a disposition to reflect this or that sort of rays more copiously than the rest; in rays they are nothing but their dispositions to propagate this or that Motion into a Sensorium, and in the Sensorium they are sensations of those Motions under the forms of Colours.[5]

As the history of psychology and the other sciences makes clear, this basic model, though modified from time to time in order to assimilate

[3] Hobbes, *The Elements of Law, Natural and Politic,* p. 3.

[4] See the paper on "New Theory about Light and Colors," in I. B. Cohen, ed., *Isaac Newton's Papers and Letters on Natural Philosophy and Related Documents,* p. 47 *f.*

[5] Quoted from S. Horsley, ed., *Isaaci Newtoni Quae Exstant Omnia,* Tome IV, p. 80.

new findings in anatomy and physiology, has remained the dominant optical theory. Among the most important accretions have been some details of knowledge of the brain and nervous system, which, however, have not liquidated the mystery of how the brain could be connected with color sensations. The acommpanying diagram sums up the situation (Fig. 21).

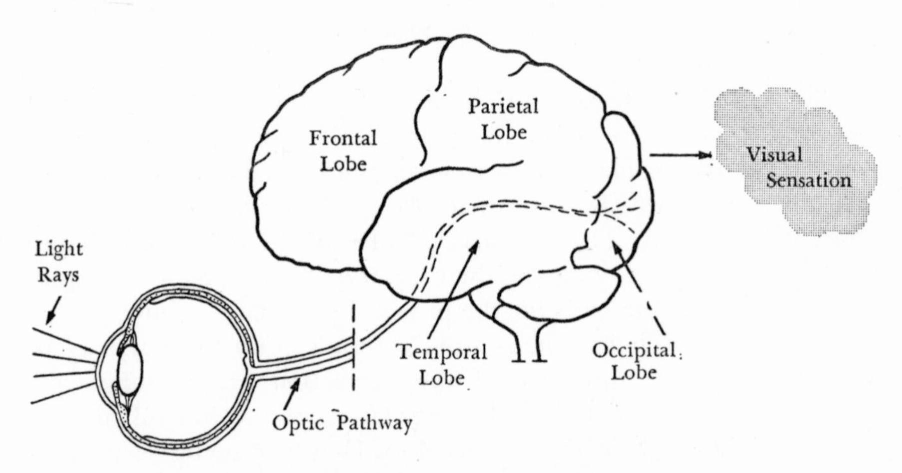

FIG. 21. CONVENTIONAL THEORY OF THE FUNCTION OF THE BRAIN IN MEDIATING BETWEEN PHYSICAL LIGHT AND MENTAL QUALITIES

THE SUBJECTIVE AND THE OBJECTIVE. The absolute separation of the subject from the object follows closely on the dichotomization of things. A place is made for objects as things within the domain of nature, but, in addition, there is a something that stands over against them. Once more transcendental traditions stimulate the construction of an absolute difference between actual things and the putative things which are hidden, ineluctable, and inexorably private. Clearly, here some features of an interaction of things are confounded with a kind of entity which transcends the spatiotemporal boundaries of all other events. Once more, reactions to things are confused with things, but this time with things that exist only as verbal creations of medieval thinkers.

THE KNOWER AND THE KNOWN. Another historical duality separates absolutely the knower and the known. The central feature of the knower is regarded as a unique internal psychic process belonging to a completely different world than that of the object known. Obviously the astronomer who is observing the motions of the moon is not the moon. But the difference is one of specific traits in a single continuum and not a difference in orders separating psychic from natural things and events. As a matter of course all the activities deservedly called knowing are usually different sorts of events from the things and events known; this is true even when the individual zealously studies his own structural and functional characteristics and actions. But all the differences between knowing events and other kinds of events are differences in natural details. Once the construction is made of the existence of absolute differences between the knower and his knowing, on one side, and other things and events, on the other, the path is opened for such improper distinctions as (a) the psychic knower and knowing and (b) the psychic known and the non-psychic known.

THE DIREMPTION OF NATURE AIDS AND HINDERS SCIENCE

We have often had to note the opposition in the history of science between basic assumptions established as institutions and the things and events about which the assumptions are made, as well as the influence of the former on the latter. The most striking illustration of this influence is that even when concrete events are assiduously studied, they are described in accord with cultural assumptions rather than on the basis of their actual traits or the observer's contacts with them. An opposition then arises between constructs on one side and events on the other. The scientist studies reactions of organisms to other organisms or non-organic things and the interpreter declares that what is operating are internal psychic powers.

Historically the diremption of nature has played a paradoxical role in the scientific domain. Modern scientists have endeavored to remove from their base of operations the traditional psychic entities, but have actually maintained them by shifting them into the domain of biology and psychology. Thus has arisen the great diremption which puts the behavior of astronomical and physical objects on one side and the behavior of organisms on the other. This procedure has been variously described. It is said, for example, that the modern scientist has taken away from the domain of mechanics the final and material causes and left only the formal and efficient causes of the classical four. It might be added that in the chemical domain the material cause is prominent. But in the organic domain and especially the psychological area, all the transcendent processes presumed to be involved, for example, with intention, subjectivity, and ineluctable spirit are left intact.

It is a common view that in the period of scientific advancement the search for ends has been abandoned in favor of the search for laws concerning the actions and interactions of things. In addition, a potent factor in the success of the astronomer and physicist is thought to be the adoption of the principle of limited objectives; that is, the isolation of some particular concrete situation for analysis and experiment, leaving to one side such universal and cosmic questions as were involved in the theological period of the Middle Ages. It was this employment of the specificity principle, with its implication that science is the work of man in his endeavor to understand and control the concrete and particular things and processes in his environment, that marks the success of science. It is such concentration upon limited and specific problems that make possible the construction of scientific laws as descriptions of events.

How well the dichotomy of the world served the scientist of the fifteenth, sixteenth, and seventeenth centuries is recorded in the great advancement of science in that period. How ill this dichotomy served the organic sciences is equally well recorded in the perennial backwardness of psychology, in the appalling development of the contrast between the physical and psychic, between the natural sciences (*Naturwissenschaften*) and the humanistic sciences (*Geisteswissenschaften*), between human and animal behavior and between human and nonorganic behavior, as well as by the perennial attempts to bring psychological events into some semblance of order, regularity, and lawfulness.

How in detail, then, has the diremption principle benefited the Renaissance scientists? The answer is clear; by differentiating between the material and the spiritual and by then choosing to work on the so-called material things, they were able to manipulate and measure. The paradox is that because they could not free themselves from the transcendental, they clung closely to the spatial and extensional aspects of events. How wise and valuable this procedure was may be symbolized by Kepler's achievement of his famous laws, which may be summed up and represented as follows:

$$A_1^3 : A_2^3 :: P_1^2 : P_2^2$$

Similarly Galileo's law of falling bodies,

$$S = \tfrac{1}{2}gt^2$$

and Newton's gravitation formula,

$$F = k\frac{M_1M}{r^2}$$

testify to the success of the sciences in suppressing transcendental constructions in favor of the observed interactional fields of component things.

By the same token, the acceptance by psychology of the transcendental psychic or inextensible principles perpetuated the notion of the unreality of colors, tastes, odors, and other qualities of the same objects dealt with by the nonpsychological scientists. This put psychology beyond the pale of the scientists who were achieving objective results and initiated a struggle to rectify the situation which continues to the present.

What happened in scientific history can be summed up by indicating that the students of astronomy and physics followed the authentic rules of scientific work which demand that the observer should keep in strict contact with events. The accompanying diagram illustrates this procedure in astronomy and physics (Fig. 22, A). This procedure, however, was not followed in the treatment of biological and psychological events. Instead of accepting the fact that the organism in biology and psychology is a natural thing interacting with environmental things, that is, with objects having original physiochemical and organic properties as well as various attributed ones based on prior contacts, it was assumed that the observed things comprised as one of their components thought or inextensible substance. The scientist in this case is presumed to be studying actions of an organism which were interpreted as manifestations of some internal directing and recording psychic processes (Fig. 22, B).

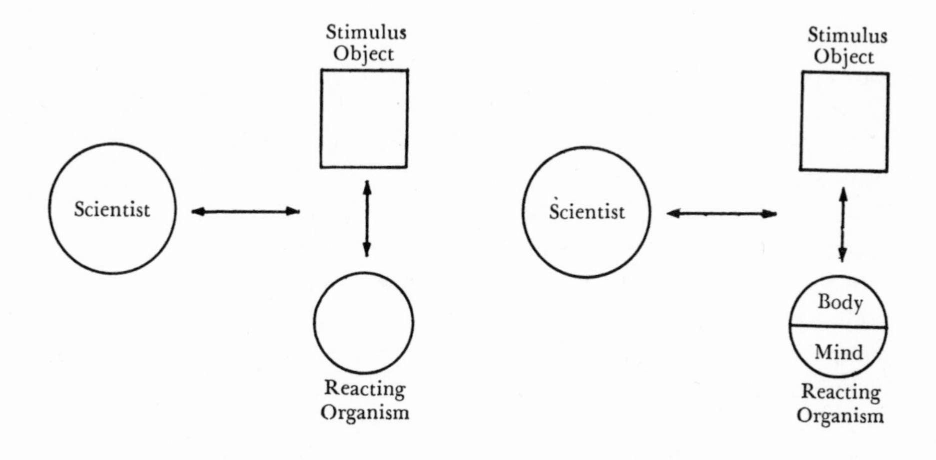

FIG. 22. THE CONTRASTING PROCEDURES OF PHYSICAL (A) AND BIOLOGICAL AND PSYCHOLOGICAL SCIENTISTS (B)

(↔ = Interbehavior with observed objects)

The establishment of the dichotomy of nature saddled psychology with special assumptional institutions. These may be collectively referred to as the mind-body dualism. The interacting organism becomes a dual or split object. The mental becomes a set of powers, faculties, or, in general, internal principles. Throughout the entire history of psychology this dualism persists with numerous variations. We shall find it in psychosomatics, psychophysiology, psychoneurology, psychopharmacology, and in numerous other guises. With its establishment in the psychological field there began the centuries-long struggle to make psychology conform to the rules of science already adopted by the nonpsychological scientists.

VARIOUS TRADITIONAL MEANS OF NATURALIZING THE SOUL

The history of psychology furnishes an unimpeachable demonstration of the corrigibility of science. Although the transcendental traditions have set a low limit of achievement for the psychologist's efforts, the work of all the centuries since the seventeenth may be interpreted as concerned with the solution of the dualistic problem. Although, unfortunately, the central core of cultural tradition still remains powerful today, perennial efforts to diminish its baneful interference with the basic project of science, namely the confrontation of the observer with events, were made throughout the history of psychology. We propose, then, to round out this chapter and this volume by examining five outstanding means by which scholars have tried to naturalize the soul and thus escape the pitfall of arbitrary intervention with ongoing events.

PSYCHOBIOLOGY. There is probably a direct continuity between the emphasis upon the soul-body relation in the Renaissance period of soul-naturalization and the emphasis upon salvation with its stress on besouled man as the object of intellectual concern in the medieval soteric period. We may regard the emphasis on the unity of soul and body by St. Thomas as a middle point in this continuity. As we have seen, this motive of unity is simply the inversion of Aristotelian biopsychology.[6]

In the seventeenth century the psychobiological principle displays two definite scientific trends. In the first place, there is an intensification of the sensitivity to events on the part of the thinkers of the period; in the second, these thinkers take definite account of the me-

[6] An interesting reference to this unity theme from the medical standpoint is furnished by Entralgo, *Mind and Body*.

chanical and other technological advancements evolved at the time. The body is definitely envisaged as a mechanical apparatus capable of carrying on certain movements and actions and effecting certain results. This is the period when innumerable manikins operating by trains of wheels or by hydraulic pressures were made. Such imitation human figures could march, strike bells to mark the passing hours, and perform many other interesting acts. As we know, the anatomists of the time made copious use of the analogy with mechanics by considering the human frame to be a series of interrelated members capable of mechanized actions. Howsoever successful these contrivances appeared and however much genuine knowledge they inspired, they had no influence at all on the development of genuinely scientific attitudes concerning the biological and psychological character of organisms. In plain words, the elaborate development of ideas concerning bodily mechanics and reflexes did not disturb the tradition of soul. Transcendentalism, in fact, received great support from the mechanization of the body. The existence of the mechanisms of the body, crude as they were, being granted, the demand was made for a psychic control and motivating power for the apparatus. The detailed evolution of psychobiology may be represented by a series of symbols showing changes in the views concerning the body-soul relations. In the period of psychobiology which lasted up to the nineteenth century the importance of the soul is inordinately out of proportion to that of the body, as symbolized in Fig. 23, left. Throughout the nineteenth century, and especially when materialism reared its head, the body and the soul were regarded as almost or quite equal in importance (Fig. 23, middle). With the advancement of exact scientific knowledge in biology, especially in physiology and neurology, the original relations of body and soul were reversed (Fig. 23, right). But even in the twentieth century the relationship is maintained despite the reversal of the relative importance of the two components. In our second volume we shall discuss a minor exception to this statement.

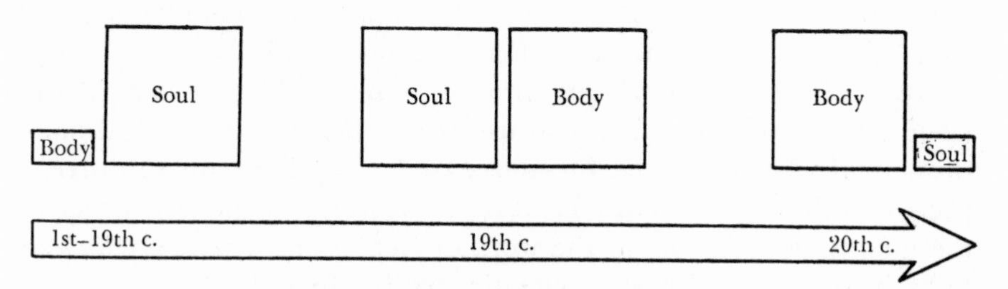

FIG. 23. THE VARYING IMPORTANCE OF BODY AND SOUL IN PSYCHOBIOLOGY

To illustrate and evaluate the psychobiological principle in psychological history we mention briefly the views of some of its outstanding proponents. If we begin with the seventeenth century we must mention Hobbes, Descartes, Spinoza, and Leibniz. In each case we have variant views concerning the actual relationships between the two factors in the dualism. In the case of Hobbes and Spinoza, we have specific attempts to identify the spiritual side of man with the unknown but presumably intricate workings of the body. Descartes, as is well known, enlarged upon the mechanical character of the body and assumed an intimate interaction between it and the soul. Leibniz, on the other hand, not only would not identify the soul with the body but would not allow any interaction between them. Accordingly, he proposed a strict parallelism of existence and action based upon a mystical transcendent harmony between the two.

As biologists learned more details about the nervous system, the crude mechanics of Descartes and others gave way to a more adequate notion of organic motion and operation. There ensued elaborate constructions concerning the localization of psychic functions in the nervous system, especially the brain. Individual parts of the brain were made into the seat of the mental powers. The brain became more and more, and in an increasingly refined manner, a kind of surrogate for the mental processes which had now replaced the unified soul as the psychic counterpart of the mind-body system. At the very peak of this dualistic development in the twentieth century the doctrine developed that the psychic was simply the "integration" of subtle processes in the cortical parts of the brain. The elaboration of psychobiological doctrine not only perpetuated transcendental constructions, but likewise subjected the nervous system and its functions to the debilitating impositions of nonbiological and even nonnatural constructions.

QUANTIZATION. No cultural institution has had so great an appeal to every advanced cultural group as that of numbers and measure. As examples we may note the scriptural assertion that the universe is organized according to numbers and measure or the Platonic saying that "god ever geometrizes." There are many cultural bases for the strong inclination toward quantization. One of the first that suggests itself is obviously the functional use of numbers and numerical operations in dealing with the inevitable and ubiquitous quantitative aspects of things and events. Historical examples in modern times are the quantization factors in the work of Kepler and Galileo, which are links in a long chain of pragmatic mathematics that begins mainly with geometric work and goes on to algebraic, analytical, and other branches. Another chain of numerical tradition is the long development of mystic interest in mathematics. Striking in this connection are the assertions of St. Augustine, Cardinal Cusanus, and St. Thomas concerning the mystical absoluteness of numbers. Such mystical attitudes probably should be referred to the domain of numerology instead of to mathematics. An important historical phase of this numerology was the Pythagoreanism of the Renaissance as represented by Pico della Mirandola.

In the development of psychology a mixture of the mystical and the mathematical was utilized to naturalize the soul. When we consider Fechner's psychophysics, we see how this scientist argued that sensations, which represent the nineteenth-century diffraction of the soul, can be measured to produce numbers. The result is shown in the famous formula $S = \log r$. Obviously, despite Fechner's domination by the transcendental, a characteristic which he shared with all others interested in psychological matters, his actual work consisted of the study of interactions of individuals, called subjects, with objects of particular sorts—lines of different lengths, drawn figures of different shapes, and cards of various proportions. Fechner and the psychologists of his time and later hailed this psychic measurement as a great triumph of mensuration and quantization. Lacking was the slightest glimmer of realization that Fechner and his contemporaries, instead of making psychology scientific, were clinging to the paradox of operating upon processes that transcended all space and time. At the same time the quantizing psychologists of the nineteenth century blinded themselves completely to the actual behavioral facts with which they were concerning themselves.

It was only around the middle of the twentieth century that mathematical methods became applied to problems of authentic psychological behavior. Even during the great vogue of "mental testing" in the early part of the twentieth century, psychologists overlooked the facts that they were actually dealing with, and assumed that they were measuring the intelligence phase of mind, which was a recent successor to the traditional soul.

EXPERIMENTATION. The advancement of any science is a function of the intensity with which its adherents pursue their confrontation with events. And naturally the variations in the methods of confrontation attain their peak in experimental procedures. For the greater part, then, the history of modern science is the record of an increasingly accelerated development of experimental investigations in all fields where such procedures are possible.

Experimentation was naturally developed first in the manipulative domains of chemistry or alchemy and physics, and, as was inevitable, it eventually found its place in the biological field. In general, of course, since all events are interrelated, chemical substances and processes must come to be involved with medical materials, physical problems, and biological events of various sorts. Accordingly, in the nineteenth century, biologists, and especially physiologists, began to use experimental methods. Here Helmholtz can serve as an outstanding example. By formulating the assumption that science consists of aligning all events with the laws of matter and motion, he, among others, drew psychology away from vitalistic commerce with transcendent processes to deal instead with events capable of direct and experimental confrontation. Although Helmholtz no more than the eminent Johannes Müller actually escaped involvement with transcendentals, they both did much to lead psychology, as well as physiology, toward experimentation.

The question now arises as to how the trend toward experimentation could fit together with psychologists' attempts to naturalize the soul. Since the great cultural institution of soul and body was so firmly established, it was very simple for physiologists, who were the forerunners of the future experimental psychologists, to assume that palpable observations on so-called bodily processes would correspond to absolutely parallel psychic processes. It is common knowledge that Fechner, Helmholtz, Wundt, and many, many other workers made use of this dualistic theory to naturalize the soul. They utilized also the subsidiary assumption that changes in the optic, auditory, or other sensorimotor systems correspond to the creation of psychic states, whether or not contained in the soul. In this situation, as in the many others we have noted, there was very little connection between what the workers thought they were doing and what they actually did. We must make clear that the naturalization of the soul was not the focus of their efforts. They thought of themselves as doing what other scientists did as a matter of normal practice, namely accumulating scientific data. But in the meantime the scientific public assumed that psychic experimentation was possible; thus the noose of science had helped to ensnare the transcendent.

EVOLUTION. Psychological events, as the behavior of organisms in interaction with other organisms or other objects and events, are intimately interrelated with biological events, so that psychology inevitably felt the impact of evolutionary doctrine even more than most other sciences. In fact, it has long been thought that the doctrine of evolution solved many problems for the psychologist. Among these are the origin and perpetuation of mental qualities, the resemblance of behavior in men and animals, and the superiority of man over non-human organisms despite his presumed descent from them. In general, the scientific improvement that evolution was presumed to bring into biological and also psychological science was the naturalistic view concerning the origin and variation of animal species, by contrast with the doctrine of special creation.

So far as psychology was concerned, evolutionists valued very highly the support the doctrine provided for the existence and variation of psychic characteristics. This is indicated by Darwin's own attempts to create a comparative and genetic form of psychology. In his *The Expression of the Emotions in Man and Animals,* Darwin proposed to trace the descent of corresponding mental states with the linear descent of bodily forms and actions. Then, Galton established the distinction between nature and nurture in the psychological domain. He proposed to differentiate between psychic qualities and actions that were hereditarily and evolutionally derived from the characteristics and activities acquired by habit and practice. Implied, of course, was that psychic variations of species were facilitated or inhibited on the basis of evolutionary processes. Evolutionary doctrine tremendously stimulated interest in the habits and learning of animals, an influence which gave rise to the whole science of animal behavior. This development was rooted in the notion that evolution supported the yearning of psychology to become scientific. Underlying the preoccupation with animal behavior lay the belief that in this fashion transcendent entities could be scientifically dealt with. Actually, the prevailing dualistic tradition was maintained by the new developmental views. Darwin's great authority was an undoubted agency in this direction. It is indisputable, however, that in reality evolutionary events as well as evolution doctrine served to make delusory the enterprise of naturalizing the soul.

THE PSYCHOLOGICAL REVOLUTION IN THE TWENTIETH CENTURY

BEHAVIORISM. A viewpoint which appeared to be a major revolution in psychology arose in the early decades of the twentieth century. It can be briefly described as a realization that psychology could not be a science as long as it concerned itself with transcendent materials. The new attitude, which implied that the naturalistic character of events must be respected, may be traced back specifically to the dissemination of evolutionary theory and the interest in animal studies which followed. The question was raised as to why psychologists should concern themselves with sensations, consciousness, and other transcendent matters when the behavior of organisms is actually all that is being investigated. An increasingly large place in this revolution was taken by the Pavlovian principle of conditioning.

In its early stages, behaviorism was negativistic or, more euphemistically speaking, methodological. Psychologists proposed simply to ignore the transcendent processes. Then came a reductionistic phase according to which psychology was presumed to be the science of the behavior of organic structures. It was easy to find plenty of materials for investigation among the reactions of organisms to stimulus objects. For the most part, these reactions were of the sort called learning, and for a time the problems of sensing, perceiving, and affective conduct were held in abeyance. For a number of decades psychologists worked out many kinds of behavioral problems involving animals, especially the white rat. As a consequence, the basic issues concerning the nature of psychological subject matter were set aside. It is proper to say that psychology changed its entire character in America, at least. Nonetheless, the scientific problems neglected by the behaviorists did not lose their urgency and relevance merely because there were many other kinds of questions available for study.

INTERBEHAVIORISM. Following closely on the development of behaviorism, there grew up in psychology an attempt to achieve a really basic revolution in science. The interbehavioral psychologist proposes a radical departure from traditional doctrine and practice. He proposes for science in general and psychology in particular a new set of postulates which will be totally dissociated from every form of historical dualism. Interbehavioral psychology concerns itself exclusively with events made up of many factors and, accordingly, needs neither to avoid nor to adapt itself to the mind-body dualism. Every psychological event is taken to be a field containing many factors. A sample enumeration would include at least: (a) the action of an organism; (b) the action of an interbehaving object or event, whether organic or nonorganic; (c) a medium of contact, such as air in hearing situations or light in visual interbehavior; (d) an assortment of specific setting factors; and (e) the interbehavioral history of organisms with objects. Upon this basis there is no need to concern oneself with any of the historical problems which have arisen from nonscientific sources.

Though it goes unnoticed, practically all scientific work is projected and performed on an interbehavioral basis. This was obviously the case when Kepler, Galileo, and Newton formulated their laws on a crude mechanical model. It is even more the case in modern atomic physics when particles with their various life spans are observed to operate in specific situations on the basis of particular factors and conditions.

IN RETROSPECT

Whether we regard the career of psychology as having covered a long history or just a long past, it is certain that that most interesting career has been extremely tortuous. Now that we have familiarized ourselves with many details of the development of psychology, both as a science and as a tradition, we have a perspectival view of the dramatic transformations that marked the scientific psychological evolution.

Of necessity we began our study with what must seem a miraculous occurrence—that the Greeks of the fourth century B.C. could set up an objective and naturalistic system of psychology, however simple and incomplete it was. As we have seen, Aristotle's *De Anima* and *Parva Naturalia* admirably sum up basic psychological principles and the descriptions of events without a trace of a transcendental hypothesis. Whatever mystery appeared to surround this achievement was quickly dissipated by examination of the social and political circumstances amid which the first systematic development of psychology took place at the hands of Socrates, Plato, and Aristotle. The materials out of which the latter constructed his system were precipitated from the observations of his Greek and Oriental predecessors as well as from his own observations.

Scientific achievements are integral features of cultural periods and areas, and we found that the changes in civilization from Hellenic to Hellenistic times were unfavorable for the continuation of such a scientific psychological edifice as that developed in Athens. Accordingly, the career of scientific psychology was cut short. The decline of Greece, including Hellenistic Alexandria, and later of Rome coincided with cultural conditions which culminated in the most unfavorable circumstances for the cultivation of scientific work altogether. After the brilliant scientific period of Alexandria came the Late Roman, Dark, and Middle Ages. The torch of learning was kept feebly alight with the study of man, his nature and destiny, while physics, astronomy, mathematics, and biology languished. Throughout the Roman period men like Tertullian, Plotinus, and St. Augustine intensified the tradition that man was mostly a part of a transcendental domain and that his vocation lay in his search for salvation.

For the largest portion of its career, therefore, psychology has been concerned with the cultivation of spirit. In the third century of our era the great transition in the psychological tradition occurred. The study of the behavior of organisms became changed into an interest in man's transcendental nature. We have discussed in detail the efforts of Plotinus, dominated by the urge to escape the rigors of society, to create a mystical world out of Plato's cognitive abstractions. What the Jewish-Christians and the early Church Fathers had initiated, Plotinus developed more or less systematically.

The spiritual realm which Plotinus so effectively established as a cosmic system was transformed by Saint Augustine into a more personal and individual form. In the fifth century Augustine made excellent use of the cosmic spiritism of Plotinus to bring spirit down to the intimate confines of the human being. Man was made into a spiritual being as a pale reflection of the cosmic spirit which Saint Augustine personalized as the creator of all things. Man was endowed by Augustine with a soul which was the basis of all knowledge, willing, and desiring. Thus, Augustinian Personalism became the means of saddling psychology with a load of transcendental elements which still are the most prominent components of psychological systems.

With the reestablishment of safe and solid social and political conditions in Europe, scientific institutions streamed in from the East and psychology took on a more naturalistic cast. Although in the thirteenth century the psychological tradition was fostered by churchmen, the much transformed psychology of the Greeks was gradually brought into Western Europe. Doubtless an important influence at work here was the prominence of physicians as the students of psychological processes. At any rate, a new phase of the psychological tradition set in and the spirit of man was yoked to a body. From that time on, the dualism of mind and body became firmly established. By contrast with the Greek period, when psychology was an integral part of natural science, a branch of physics—the science of motion, in the thirteenth century and later psychology only developed a tenuous aspiration toward scientific status.

From the thirteenth century on psychological history is thoroughly dualistic. With the renewed cultivation of the sciences in the sixteenth and seventeenth centuries, scientists attempted to articulate the transcendent mentality of man with the events observed in the natural sciences. From the time of Descartes a large portion of psychological history is devoted to aligning the heritage of soul doctrine with the methods of the physical and biological sciences. We have discussed this movement briefly under the theme of the naturalization of the soul, in order to indicate the significance of the scholastic systematization of psychological thought for the later phases of the psychological tradition.

As the records of psychological history clearly show, the coordination of the mental and the bodily attains enormous proportions in the nineteenth century, when the thoroughly established institution of science displays striking achievements in physics, chemistry, and biology. On the basis of borrowings from physiology and anatomy, psychology aspires to exploit the complementarity principle in order to claim that the transcendent mental can be quantized and experimentally manipulated.

When we reach our own stage of psychological history, the cultural background is so complex that we must look to specialized aspects of social life to account for detailed factors of theory and practice. Social life in the twentieth century is so conglomerate that there are numerous schools of thought based upon specializations of interest and occupation. Many variations of the dualistic theme are propagated, some looking back to the springtime of Thomistic thought, while others so constrict the psychic factor as to reduce psychology to the study of biological activities. Anyone who is sympathetic to the view that scientific theory is correlated with cultural circumstances can discover detailed occurrences which have given rise to the complete rejection of all dualistic postulation. This development will be elaborated as one of the themes of our next volume.

BIBLIOGRAPHY

Abetti, G. *The History of Astronomy*. N.Y., Abelard-Schuman, 1962.

Ackerknecht, E. H. *A Short History of Medicine*. N.Y., Ronald Press, 1955.

Afnan, F. M. *Avicenna*. London, Allen and Unwin, 1956.

Apollonius of Perga. *Treatise on Conic Sections* (T. L. Heath, ed.). Cambridge, Cambridge U. Press, 1896.

Archimedes. *The Works of Archimedes* (T. L. Heath, ed.). N.Y., Dover Publications, n.d.

Aristotle. A. J. Smith and W. D. Ross, eds., *The Works of Aristotle,* 12 vols. Oxford, Clarendon Press, 1908-1952.

Armstrong, A. H. *Plotinus*. London, Allen and Unwin, 1953.

Augustine, Saint. *The City of God against the Pagans = De Civitate Dei contra Paganos* (G. E. McCracken, tr., Loeb Classical Library), 7 vols. London, Heinemann, 1957.

——— *Confessions = Confessiones* (W. Watts, tr.; Loeb Classical Library). London, Heinemann, 1912.

——— *On Free Will = De Libero Arbitrio* in J. Baillie, J. T. McNeill, and H. P. van Dusen, gen. eds., *The Library of Christian Classics,* Vol. VI: *Augustine: Earlier Writings* (J. H. S. Burleigh, tr.), pp. 113-217. London, SCM Press, 1953.

——— *On the Immortality of the Soul = De Immortalitate Animae* in L. Schopp, tr., *Writings of Saint Augustine,* Vol. II (The Fathers of the Church: A new Translation; L. Schopp, founder), pp. 15-47. N.Y., Cima Publishing Co., 1947.

——— *On the Magnitude of the Soul = De Quantitate Animae* (J. J. McMahon, tr.) in Schopp, *op. cit.,* pp. 59-149.

——— *The Manual on Faith, Hope and Love = Enchiridion de Fide, Spes et Caritas* in Baillie, McNeill, and van Dusen, gen. eds., *The Library of Christian Classics,* Vol. VII: *Augustine: Confessions and Enchiridion* (A. C. Outler, tr.), pp. 337-412. London, SCM Press, 1955.

——— *On the Soul and its Origin = De Anima et ejus Origine* (P. Holmes and R. E. Wallis, trs.; B. B. Warfield, reviser) in P. Schaff, ed., *A Select Library of the Nicene and Post-Nicene Fathers,* First Series, Vol. V: *St. Augustine: Anti-Pelagian Writings,* pp. 315-371. N.Y., Christian Literature Co., 1887.

——— *On the Trinity = De Trinitate.* Complete in Schaff, ed., *op. cit.,* Vol. III: *St. Augustine: Doctrinal and Moral Treatises,* pp. 17-228 (A. W. Haddan and W. G. T. Shedd, trs.); Buffalo, Christian Literature Co., 1887. Books viii, ix, xiv, and xv in Baillie, McNeill, and van Dusen, gen. eds., *The Library of Christian Classics,* Vol. VIII: *Augustine: Later Works* (J. Burnaby, tr.), pp. 38-181; London, SCM Press, 1955.

——— *Of True Religion = De Vera Religione* in Baillie, McNeill, and van Dusen, gen. eds., *op. cit.,* Vol. VI: *Augustine: Earlier Writings* (J. H. S. Burleigh, tr.), pp. 225-283. London, SCM Press, 1953.

Aurelius, Marcus. *The Communings with Himself of Marcus Aurelius*

Antoninus, Emperor of Rome (C. R. Haines, tr.; Loeb Classical Library). London, Heinemann, 1924.

Bacon, F. T. "Fuel Cells: Will They soon become a Major Source of Electrical Energy," *Nature,* 1960, **186,** 589-592.

Bell, E. T. *The Development of Mathematics,* N.Y., McGraw-Hill, 1940.

Bernal, J. D. *Science in History*. London, Watts, 1954.

Bevan, E. R. "Hellenistic Popular Philosophy," Ch. 3 in J. B. Bury *et al., The Hellenistic Age,* 2nd ed. Cambridge, Cambridge U. Press, 1925.

Bohr, N. H. D. *Atomic Theory and the Description of Nature*. Cambridge, Cambridge U. Press, 1934.

Bowle, J. *Hobbes and His Critics*. London, Jonathan Cape, 1951.

Bowra, C. M. *The Greek Experience*. London, Weidenfeld and Nicholson, 1957.

Boyle, R. *The Sceptical Chymist* (Everyman's Library). London, Dent, 1911.

Brain, W. R. *Mind, Perception and Science*. Oxford, Blackwell, 1951.

Bréhier, É. *The Philosophy of Plotinus* (J. Thomas, tr.). Chicago, U. of Chicago Press, 1958.

Brennan, R. E. *General Psychology,* N.Y., Macmillan, 1937.

——— *Thomistic Psychology: A Philosophical Analysis of the Nature of Man*. N.Y., Macmillan, 1941.

Brett, G. S. *A History of Psychology,* Vol. I: *Ancient and Patristic*. London, George Allen, 1912.

Burnaby, J. *Amor Dei: A Study of the Religion of St. Augustine* (The Hulsean Lectures for 1938). London, Hodder and Stoughton, 1938.

Burnet, J. *Essays and Addresses*. N.Y., Macmillan, 1930.

Burtt, E. A. *The Metaphysical Foundations of Modern Physical Science*. N.Y., Harcourt Brace, 1925.

Bury, J. B. "The Hellenistic Age and the History of Civilization," Ch. in Bury *et al., The Hellenistic Age,* 2nd ed. Cambridge, Cambridge U. Press, 1925.

Butterfield, H. *The Origin of Modern Science, 1300-1800*. London, Bell, 1950.

Caird, E. *The Evolution of Theology in the Greek Philosophers,* 2 vols. Glasgow, MacLehose, 1904.

Campbell, D. *Arabian Medicine and Its Influence on the Middle Ages,* 2 vols. London, Kegan Paul, 1926.

von Campenhausen, H. F. *Die griechischen Kirchenväter*. Stuttgart, Kohlhammer, 1955.

Carr, E. H. *What is History?* London, Macmillan, 1961.

Case, S. J. *The Origins of Christian Supernaturalism*. Chicago, U. of Chicago Press, 1946.

Celsus, *De Medicina* (W. G. Spencer, tr.; Loeb Classical Library), 3 vols. London, Heinemann, 1935-1938.

Clement of Alexandria. *Miscellanies = Stromata* in A. Roberts and J. Donaldson, eds., A. E. Coxe, reviser, *The Ante-Nicene Fathers,* Vol. II: *Fathers of the Second Century,* pp. 299-567. Grand Rapids, Eerdmans, 1951.

Cochrane, C. N. *Christianity and Classical Culture*. N.Y., Oxford, 1944.

——— *Thucydides and the Science of History*. London and Oxford, Oxford U. Press, 1929.

Cohen, M. R. *The Meaning of Human History*. LaSalle, Ill., Open Court, 1947.

Coolidge, J. L. *A History of Geometrical Methods. Oxford,* Clarendon Press, 1940.

Cornford, F. M. *Greek Religious Thought from Homer to the Age of Alexander*. Boston, Beacon Press, 1950.

Crawley, A. E. *The Idea of the Soul*. London, Black, 1909.

Crombie, A. C. *Augustine to Galileo: The History of Science A.D. 400-1650*. London, Falcon Press, 1952.

Darwin, C. *The Expression of the Emotions in Man and Animals*. N.Y., Appleton, 1873.

Descartes, R. E. S. Haldane and G. R. T. Ross, eds., *The Philosophical Works of Descartes,* Vol. II. Cambridge, U. Press, 1912.

Dessoir, M. *Outlines of the History of Psychology* (D. Fisher, tr.). N.Y., Macmillan, 1912.

Dewey, J. and Bentley, A. F. *Knowing and the Known*. Boston, Beacon Press, 1949.

Diels, H., ed. *Die Fragmente der Vorsokratiker,* 6th ed. (W. Kranz, ed.), 3 vols. Berlin, Weidmann, 1951-1952.

Dingle, H. "Science and modern Cosmology," *Science,* 1954, **120**, 513-521.

Diogenes Laertius. *Lives of Eminent Philosophers* (R. D. Hicks, tr.; Loeb Classical Library), rev. ed., 2 vols. London, Heinemann, 1950.

Dodds, E. R. *The Greeks and the Irrational*. Berkeley, U. of California Press, 1951.

Dreyer, J. L. E. *A History of Astronomy from Thales to Kepler,* 2nd ed. N.Y., Dover Publications, 1953.

Dunbabin, T. J. *The Greeks and their Eastern Neighbours: Studies in the Relations between Greece and the Countries of the Near East in the Eighth and Seventh Centuries B.C.* London, Society for the Promotion of Hellenic Studies, 1957.

Dunlap, K. "The Historical Method in Psychology," *Journal of General Psychology,* 1941, **24**, 49-62.

Ebbinghaus, H. "Psychologie," in P. Hinneberg, ed., *Die Kultur der Gegenwart: Ihre Entwicklung und ihre Ziele,* Part I, Section 6: *Systematische Philosophie,* 3rd ed., pp. 135-205. Leipzig, Teubner, 1921.

Entralgo, P. L. *Mind and Body*. London, Harvill, 1955.

Erdmann, J. E. *A History of Philosophy,* (W. S. Hough, tr.), 3 vols. London, Sonnenschein, 1890.

Farrington, B. *Greek Science,* 2 vols. Harmondsworth, Penguin Books, 1944, 1949.

Fisher, G. P. *History of Christian Doctrine* (The International Theological Library, C. A. Briggs and S. D. P. Salmonds, eds., Vol. IV). N.Y., Scribners, 1923.

Fisher, H. A. L. *A History of Europe*. London, Eyre and Spottiswoode, 1938.

Frazer, J. G. *The Golden Bough,* 3rd ed., 12 vols. London, Macmillan, 1935.

Galileo, G. *Discoveries and Opinions of Galileo* (S. Drake, tr.). Garden City, N.Y., Doubleday Anchor Books, 1957.
Gibbon, E. *The History of the Decline and Fall of the Roman Empire* (J. B. Bury, ed.). N.Y. Heritage, 1946.
Gilbert, W. *De Magnete* (D. S. Price, ed.). N.Y. Basic Books, 1958.
Glover, T. R. *The Ancient World: A Beginning*. Cambridge, Cambridge U. Press, 1935.
Goldenweiser, A. *History, Psychology and Culture*. N.Y., Knopf, 1933.
Goodenough, E. R. *The Church in the Roman Empire*. N.Y., Holt, 1931.
Gregory of Nyssa. *On the Making of Man = De Opificio Hominis* (H. A. Wilson, tr.). in P. Schaff and H. Wace, eds. *A Select Library of Nicene and Post-Nicene Fathers of the Christian Church,* Second Series, Vol. V: *Gregory of Nyssa,* pp. 387-427. Grand Rapids, Mich., Eerdmans, 1956.
—— *On the Soul and the Resurrection = De Anima et Resurrectione* (W. Moore, tr.) in Schaff and Wace, eds. *op. cit.,* pp. 430-468.
Gregory Thaumaturgus. *On the Subject of the Soul = De Anima* (S. D. F. Salmond, tr.) in A. Roberts and J. Donaldson, eds., *The Ante-Nicene Fathers,* Vol. VI: *Fathers of the Third Century,* pp. 54-56. Grand Rapids, Eerdmans, 1951.
Gressmann, H. *Die orientalischen Religionen im hellenistisch-römischen Zeitalter*. Berlin and Leipzig, Walter de Gruyter, 1930.
Guthrie, W. K. C. *The Greeks and their Gods*. Boston, Beacon Press, 1954.
Haldane, E. S. and Ross, G. R. T., see Descartes
Hall, A. R. *The Scientific Revolution*. N.Y., Longmans, 1954.
Harnack, A. *History of Dogma* (N. Buchanan, tr.), 3rd ed., 6 vols. Boston, Little, Brown, 1898-1905.
—— "Origen," *Encyclopaedia Britannica,* 13th ed., Vol. XVI. N.Y., Encyclopaedia Britannica, Inc., 1926.
Heath, T. L. See Archimedes.
Henning, W. B. *Zoroaster: Politician or Witch-Doctor?* (Ratanbai Katrak Lectures, 1949). London, Geoffrey Cumberledge, 1951.
Henry, P. "Plotinus' Place in the History of Thought," Introduction to *Plotinus: The Enneads* (S. MacKenna, tr.), 2nd ed., pp. xxxiii-li. London, Faber, 1956.
Herodotus. *Herodotus* (A. D. Godley, tr.; Loeb Classical Library), 4 vols. London, Heinemann, 1928-1931.
Hessen, J. *Thomas von Aquin und Wir*. Munich, Reinhardt, 1955.
Hippocrates. *Hippocrates* (W. H. S. Jones, tr.; Loeb Classical Library), 4 vols. London, Heinemann, 1923.
Hippolytus of Rome. *The Refutation of All Heresies = Philosophumena* (J. H. McMahon, tr.) in A. Roberts and J. Donaldsen, eds., *The Ante-Nicene Fathers,* Vol. V: *Hippolytus et al.,* pp. 9-153. Grand Rapids, Eerdmans, 1951.
Hobbes, T. *The Elements of Law, Natural and Politic* (F. Tönnies, ed.). Cambridge, Cambridge U. Press, 1928.
—— *Leviathan* (Everyman's Library). London, Dent, 1934.
Holmyard, E. J. *Makers of Chemistry*. Oxford, Clarendon Press, 1931.

——— *Alchemy*. Harmondsworth, Penguin Books, 1957.

Hume, D. *A Treatise on Human Nature* (L. A. Selby-Begge, ed.). Oxford, Clarendon Press, 1896.

Inge, W. R. *The Philosophy of Plotinus*, 2 vols. London, Longmans Green, 1918.

Isocrates. *Isocrates* (G. Norlin, tr.; Loeb Classical Library), 3 vols. London, Heinemann, 1929-1961.

Jaeger, W. *The Theology of the Early Greek Philosophers* (ms. trans. by E. S. Robinson; Gifford Lectures, 1936). Oxford, Clarendon Press, 1947.

Jaffa, H. V. *Thomism and Aristotelianism*. Chicago, U. of Chicago Press, 1952.

Jourdain, P. E. B. *The Nature of Mathematics*. London, Jack, [1913].

Kant, I. *Critique of Pure Reason* (F. M. Müller, tr.), 2nd ed. London, Macmillan, 1881.

Kantor, J. R. *Interbehavioral Psychology*, 2nd ed. Bloomington, Ind., Principia Press, 1959.

——— *The Logic of Modern Science*. Bloomington, Ind., Principia Press, 1953.

——— *An Objective Psychology of Grammar*. Bloomington, Ind., Principia Press, 1936.

——— *Principles of Psychology*, 2 vols. Bloomington, Ind., Principia Press, 1949.

Kitto, H. D. *The Greeks*. Harmondsworth, Penguin Books, 1952.

Klemm, O. *History of Psychology*. N.Y., Scribners, 1914.

Klubertanz, G. P. *The Discursive Power: Sources and Doctrines of the Vis Cogitativa according to St. Thomas Aquinas*. St. Louis, The Modern Schoolman, 1952.

Labriolle, P. C. *History and Literature of Christianity from Tertullian to Boethius* (H. Wilson, tr.). N.Y., Knopf, 1925.

Lactantius. *A Treatise on the Anger of God = De Ira Dei* (W. Fletcher, tr.) in A. Roberts and J. Donaldson, eds. *The Ante-Nicene Fathers*, vol. VII: *Fathers of the Third and Fourth Centuries*, pp. 259-280. Grand Rapids, Eerdmans, 1951.

——— *On the Workmanship of God or the Formation of Man = De Opificio Dei* (W. Fletcher, tr.) in Roberts and Donaldson, *op cit.*, pp. 281-300.

Latourette, K. S. *A History of the Expansion of Christianity*, Vol. I. N.Y., Harpers, 1937.

Leibniz, G. W. *Philosophical Works of Leibnitz* (G. M. Duncan, ed.), 2nd ed. New Haven, Tuttle, Morehouse, and Taylor, 1908.

Lévy-Brühl, L. *How Natives Think* (L. A. Clare, tr.). London, Allen and Unwin, 1926.

——— *Primitive Mentality* (L. A. Clare, tr.). London, Allen and Unwin, 1923.

Liddel, H. G. and Scott, R. *A Greek-English Lexicon*, rev. ed., 10 parts. Oxford, Clarendon Press, 1925-1940.

Linton, R. *The Tree of Culture*, 1st ed. N.Y., Knopf, 1955.

Lones, T. E. *Aristotle's Researches in Natural Science.* London, West, Newman, 1912.

Lucas, F. L. *Tragedy in Relation to Aristotle's "Poetics."* N.Y., Harcourt, Brace, 1928.

Lucretius. *On the Nature of the Universe = De Rerum Natura* (R. E. Latham, tr.). Harmondsworth, Penguin Books, 1951.

McKenzie, D. *The Infancy of Medicine.* London, Macmillan, 1927.

Mach, E. *Science of Mechanics.* Chicago, Open Court, 1903.

Mandelbaum, M. H. *The Problem of Historical Knowledge: An Answer to Relativism.* N.Y., Liveright, 1938.

Medvedev, N. V. "On the reflective Activity of the Brain," *Voprosy Filsofii i Psikhologii,* 1961, **14,** 109-119 summarized by I. D. London, *Psychological Abstracts,* 1962, **36,** 199.

Meyer, A. *The Collected Papers of Adolf Meyer* (E E. Winters, gen. ed.), 4 vols. Baltimore, Johns Hopkins Press, 1950-1952.

Meyer, H. *Thomas von Aquin: Sein System und seine geistesgeschichtliche Stellung,* 2nd ed. Paderborn, Ferdinand Schöningh, 1961.

Miller, H. *History and Science.* Berkeley, U. of California Press, 1939.

Minucius Felix. *Octavius* (G. H. Rendall, tr.) in *Tertullian-Minucius Felix* (Loeb Classical Library), rev. ed., pp. 314-437. London, Heinemann, 1953.

Moore, T. V. *Cognitive Psychology.* Philadelphia, Lippincott, 1939.

Mossé-Bastide, R-M. *Bergson et Plotin* (Bibliothèque de philosophie contemporaine). Paris, Presses Universitaires de France, 1959.

Murchison, C., ed. *Handbook of Experimental Psychology.* Worcester, Clark U. Press, 1934.

Murray, G. *Five Stages of Greek Religion.* N.Y., Doubleday, Doran, 1955.

Needham, J. *A History of Embryology.* Cambridge, Cambridge U. Press, 1934.

Nemesius of Emesa. *A Treatise on the Nature of Man = De Natura hominis* (W. Telfer, ed.) in J. Baillie, J. T. McNeill, and H. P. van Dusen, gen. eds., *The Library of Christian Classics,* Vol. IV: *Cyril of Jerusalem and Nemesius of Emesa* (M. Telfer, ed.), pp. 224-453. London, SCM Press, 1955.

Neugebauer, O. *The Exact Sciences in Antiquity.* Princeton, Princeton U. Press, 1952.

Newton, I. *Isaac Newton's Papers and Letters on Natural Philosophy and related Documents* (I. B. Cohen, ed.). Cambridge, Harvard U. Press, 1950.

——— *Isaaci Newtoni Quae Exstant Omnia,* (S. Horsley, ed.), Vol. IV. London, Nichols, 1782.

Nordenskiöld. E. *The History of Biology.* N.Y., Tudor, 1936.

O'Leary, D. L. E. *How Greek Science passed to the Arabs.* London, Routledge, 1949.

Onians, R. B. *The Origins of European Thought.* London, Cambridge U. Press, 1951.

Partington, J. R. *A Short History of Chemistry,* 3rd ed. London, Macmillan, 1957.

Payne, E. J. *History of the New World called America,* 2 vols. Oxford, Clarendon Press, 1892 and 1899.

Pegis, A. C. *Introduction to St. Thomas Aquinas* (The Modern Library). N.Y., Random House, 1948.

Philo. *Philo: Philosophical Writings* (H. Lewy, ed.). Oxford, East and West Library, 1946.

Plato. *The Dialogues of Plato* (B. Jowett, tr.), 4th ed., 4 vols. Oxford, Clarendon Press, 1953.

Plotinus. *The Enneads* (S. MacKenna, tr.), 2nd ed. (B. S. Page, reviser). London, Faber, 1956.

Porphyry. "On the Life of Plotinus and the Arrangement of his Work," in Plotinus, *The Enneads,* pp. 1-20.

Poynter, F. N. L., ed. *The History and Philosophy of Knowledge of the Brain and its Functions.* (An Anglo-American Symposium, London, July 15th-17th, 1957). Oxford, Blackwell Scientific Publications, 1958.

Pratt, C. C. *The Logic of Modern Psychology.* N.Y., Macmillan, 1939.

Quasten, J. *Patrology,* 3 vols. Utrecht and Antwerp, Spectrum Publishers, 1959-1960.

Radin, P. *Primitive Man as Philosopher.* N.Y., Appleton, 1927.

——— *The World of Primitive Man.* N.Y., Schuman, 1953.

Randall, J. H., Jr. *Aristotle.* N.Y., Columbia, 1960.

Reymond, A. *History of the Sciences in Greco-Roman Antiquity* (R. G. de Bray, tr.). London, Methuen, 1927.

Ribot, T. *German Psychology of Today: The Empirical School* (J. M. Baldwin, tr. and preface by J. McCosh). N.Y., Scribners, 1886.

Roberts, A. and Donaldson, J., eds.; Coxe, A. E., reviser. *The Ante-Nicene Fathers,* Vols. I-X. Grand Rapids, Eerdmans, 1951.

Ross, W. D. *Aristotle.* London, Methuen, 1923.

Rostovtseff, M. I. *The Mentality of the Hellenistic World and the After-Life* (The Ingersoll Lecturer for the Academic Year 1937-1938), Harvard University, *Divinity School Bulletin,* 1938-39, 5-25

——— *The Social and Economic History of the Roman Empire* (P. M. Frazer, ed.), 2nd rev. ed., 2 vols. Oxford, Clarendon Press, 1957.

Runciman, S. *A History of the Crusades,* 3 vols. Cambridge, Cambridge U. Press, 1951-1954.

Russell, J. C. "Late Ancient and Medieval Population," *Transactions of the American Philosophical Society,* 1958, New Series **48**, Part 1, 1-152.

Sambursky, S. *The Physical World of the Greeks.* London, Kegan Paul, 1956.

Sarton, G. *Introduction to the History of Science,* 3 vols. in 5. Cambridge, Harvard U. Press, 1927-1948.

——— *A History of Science,* 2 vols. Cambridge, Mass., Harvard U. Press, 1952-1959.

Schrödinger, E. *Nature and the Greeks.* Cambridge, Cambridge U. Press, 1954.

Sextus Empiricus. *Sextus Empiricus,* Vol. I: *Outlines of Pyrrhonism* (R. G. Bury, tr.; Loeb Classical Library), revised ed. London, Heinemann, 1955.

Shotwell, J. T. *The History of History,* Vol. I. N.Y., Columbia U. Press, 1939.

Shute, C. *The Psychology of Aristotle: An Analysis of the Living Being.* N.Y., Columbia U. Press, 1941.

Siebeck, H. *Geschichte der Psychologie,* 2 vols. Gotha, Perthes, 1880 and 1884.

Sigerist, H. E. *History of Medicine,* Vol. I. N.Y., Oxford U. Press, 1951.

Singer, C. J. *A Short History of Medicine.* Oxford, Clarendon Press, 1928.

——— *A Short History of Science to the Nineteenth Century.* Oxford, Clarendon Press, 1943.

Spencer, H. *Principles of Psychology,* 2 vols. N.Y., Appleton, 1883.

Strabo. *The Geography of Strabo* (H. L. Jones, tr.; Loeb Classical Library), 8 vols. London, Heinemann, 1917-1932.

Struik, D. J. *A Concise History of Mathematics,* 2 vols. N.Y., Dover Publications, 1948.

Tatian of Assyria. *Address of Tatian to the Greeks = Oratio ad Graecos* (J. E. Ryland, tr.) in A. Roberts and J. Donaldson, eds., *The Ante-Nicene Fathers,* Vol. II: *Fathers of the Second Century,* pp. 65-82. Grand Rapids, Eerdmans, 1951.

Taylor, L. W. *Physics: The Pioneer Science.* Boston, Houghton-Mifflin, 1941.

Teggart, F. J. *The Theory and Processes of History.* Berkeley, U. of California Press, 1941.

Telfer, E., ed. *The Library of Christian Classics* (J. Baillie, J. T. McNeill, and H. P. van Dusen, gen. eds.), Vol. IV: *Cyril of Jerusalem and Nemesius of Emesa.* London, SCM Press, 1955.

Tertullian. *Apology = Apologeticum* (E. J. Daly, tr.) in R. Arbesmann *et al.,* trs., *Tertullian's Apologetical Works and Minucius Felix: Octavius* (The Fathers of the Church: A new Translation, L. Schopp, founder), pp. 7-126. N.Y., Fathers of the Church, Inc., 1950.

——— *On the Flesh of Christ = De Carne Christi.* E. Evans, *Tertullian's Treatise on the Incarnation.* London, S.P.C.K., 1956.

——— *On Idolatry = De Idololatria* (S. Thelwall, tr.) in A. Roberts and J. Donaldson, eds., A. E. Coxe, reviser, *The Ante-Nicene Fathers,* Vol. III: *The Works of Tertullian,* pp. 61-76. Grand Rapids, Eerdmans, 1951.

——— *On the Pallium = De Pallio* (S. Thelwall tr.) in Roberts, Donaldson, and Coxe, *op. cit.,* Vol. IV: *Third Century Fathers,* pp. 5-12.

——— *On the Soul = De Anima* (E. A. Quain, tr.) in Arbesmann *et al., op. cit.,* pp. 179-309.

Thatcher, O. J. and Schwill, F. *A General History of Europe (350-1900).* N.Y., Scribner, 1900.

Thomas, Saint. *Commentary on Aristotle's De Anima.* K. Foster and S. Humphries, trs. *Aristotle's De Anima in the Version of William of Moerbeke and the Commentary of St. Thomas Aquinas* (W. Stark, ed., Rare Masterpieces of Philosophy and Science). New Haven, Yale U. Press, 1951.

——— *Disputed Questions on the Soul = De Anima.* J. P. Rowan, *The*

Soul: A Translation of St. Thomas Aquinas' De Anima. St. Louis, Herder, 1949.

——— *Compendium against the Nations = Summa contra Gentiles* (in part). A. C. Pegis, ed., *Basic Writings of Saint Thomas Aquinas,* Vol. II. N.Y., Random House, 1945.

——— *Compendium of Theology = Summa Theologica*. Pegis, *op. cit.,* Vols. I-II. 1944-1945.

Thomas, W. I. *Primitive Behavior: An Introduction to the Social Sciences*. N.Y., McGraw-Hill, 1937.

Thucydides. *History of the Peloponnesian War* (R. Crawley, tr.; Everyman's Library). London, Dent, 1910.

Toynbee, A. J. "The ancient Mediterranean View of Man," in J. B. Brebner, ed., *Man's Right to Knowledge,* First Series: *Tradition and Change* (An International Symposium in Honor of the Two-hundredth Anniversary of Columbia University, 1754-1954), pp. 1-8. N.Y., Columbia U. Press, 1954.

Uhlhorn, G. *The Conflict of Christianity with Heathenism* (E. C. Smyth and C. J. Ropes, eds. and trs.). N.Y., Scribner, 1879.

Vitruvius. *De Architectura* (F. Granger, tr.; Loeb Classical Library). London, Heinemann, 1931.

Wallace, W. and Thatcher, G. W. "Arabian Philosophy," *Encyclopaedia Britannica,* 13th ed., Vol. II, pp. 276-283. London, Encyclopaedia Britannica, Inc., 1926.

Watson, W. H. *On Understanding Physics*. Cambridge, Cambridge U. Press, 1938.

Weindl, Th. *Monotheismus und Dualismus in Indien, Iran und Palästina* (Sonderheft 3 zur *Zeitschrift für Religionspychologie*). Vienna, Verlag der Internationalen Religionspsychologischen Gesellschaft, n.d.

Wesendonk, O. G. *Urmensch und Seele in der iranischen Überlieferung: Ein Beitrag zur Religionsgeschichte des Hellenismus*. Hannover, Orient-Buchhandlung Heinz Lafaire, 1924.

——— *Das Weltbild der Iranier*. Munich, Ernst Reinhardt, 1933.

Whitehead, A. N. *Introduction to Mathematics,* N.Y. Holt, 1911.

Whittaker, T. *The Neo-Platonists: A Study in the History of Platonism*. Cambridge, Cambridge U. Press, 1918.

Windelband, W. *A History of Philosophy* (J. H. Tufts, tr.), 2nd ed. N.Y., Macmillan, 1910.

Wolfson, H. A. *Philo: Foundations of Religious Philosophy in Judaism, Christianity, and Islam,* 2 vols. Cambridge, Mass., Harvard U. Press, 1947.

Woodger, J. H. *Physics, Psychology, and Medicine: A Methodological Essay*. Cambridge, Cambridge U. Press, 1956.

Xenophon. *Memorabilia* (E. C. Marchant, tr.; Loeb Classical Library). London, Heinemann, 1923.

Zeuner, G. "Domestication of Animals," in C. J. Singer, E. J. Holmyard, and A. R. Hale, eds., *A History of Technology,* Vol. I. pp. 327-352. Oxford, Clarendon Press, 1954.

NAME INDEX

SUBJECT INDEX